C0-GKI-369

WITHDRAWN

LIBRARY
North Dakota State University
Fargo, North Dakota
58105

GIFT OF

Thomas Gates
Kent State University
1994

PAUL GAUGUIN

PAUL GAUGUIN

A Bio-Bibliography

RUSSELL T. CLEMENT

Bio-Bibliographies in Art and Architecture,
Number 1

GREENWOOD PRESS
New York • Westport, Connecticut • London

Library of Congress Cataloging-in-Publication Data

Clement, Russell T.
Paul Gauguin : a bio-bibliography / Russell T. Clement.
p. cm.—(Bio-bibliographies in art and architecture, ISSN 1055-6826; no. 1)
Includes bibliographical references and indexes.
ISBN 0-313-27394-4 (alk. paper)
1. Gauguin, Paul, 1848-1903—Bibliography. I. Title. II. Series.
Z8328.3.C54 1991
[N6853.G34]
016.7'092—dc20 91-13903

British Library Cataloguing in Publication Data is available.

Copyright © 1991 by Russell T. Clement

All rights reserved. No portion of this book may be reproduced, by any process or technique, without the express written consent of the publisher.

Library of Congress Catalog Card Number: 91-13903
ISBN: 0-313-27394-4
ISSN: 1055-6826

First published in 1991

Greenwood Press, 88 Post Road West, Westport, CT 06881
An imprint of Greenwood Publishing Group, Inc.

Printed in the United States of America

The paper used in this book complies with the Permanent Paper Standard issued by the National Information Standards Organization (Z39.48-1984).

10 9 8 7 6 5 4 3 2 1

Contents

Preface vii
Acknowledgments xi
Biographical Sketch xiii
Chronology 1
Primary Bibliography: Writings by Paul Gauguin 43
I. Articles by Gauguin Published During His Lifetime (entries 1-13) 43
II. Articles by Gauguin Published After His Death (entries 14-16) 45
III. Letters 45
A. Published Editions (entries 17-26) 45
B. Letters in Periodicals and Books (entries 27-60) 48
C. Unpublished Manuscript Letters and Writings (entries 61-68) 51
IV. Published Sketchbooks (entries 69-72) 52
V. Unpublished Sketchbooks (entries 73-76) 52
VI. Manuscripts (entries 77-92) 53
VII. Graphics Published During Gauguin's Lifetime (entries 93-100) 55
VIII. Photographs (entry 101) 56
Contemporary Accounts and Critiques of Gauguin's Life and Work Published Through 1906 (entries 102-220) 57
Works (Oeuvre) 65
I. Catalogues Raisonnés (entries 221-232) 65
II. Gauguin's Paintings 68
A. Gauguin's Paintings By Year 70
B. Gauguin's Paintings Throughout the World 70
III. Gauguin's Ceramics 78
IV. Gauguin's Prints 79
Secondary Bibliography 81
I. Biography and Career 82
A. Monographs (entries 233-367) 82
B. Articles (entries 368-482) 102
II. Gauguin and Contemporaries in France (Paris, Pont-Aven, Le Pouldu) 110
A. Monographs (entries 483-550) 110
B. Articles (entries 551-662) 123
III. Paul Gauguin and Vincent van Gogh 138
A. Monographs (entries 663-680) 138
B. Articles (entries 681-717) 141
IV. Gauguin in Panama and Martinique, April to October, 1887 147
A. Monographs (entries 718-719) 147
B. Articles (entries 720-723) 147
V. Gauguin in Tahiti and the Marquesas Islands 148
A. Monographs (entries 724-767) 148
B. Articles (entries 768-829) 157
VI. Oeuvre in General 163
A. Monographs (entries 830-842) 163
B. Articles (entries 843-864) 166

VII. Oeuvre-Paintings 168
A. Monographs (entries 865-878) 168
B. Articles (entries 879-886) 170
VIII. Individual Works-Paintings 171
A. Monographs (entries 887-897) 171
B. Articles (entries 898-999) 172
IX. Self-Portraits 184
A. Monographs (entries 1000-1002) 184
B. Articles (entries 1003-1018) 185
X. Oeuvre-Drawings 187
A. Monographs (entries 1019-1023) 187
B. Articles (entries 1024-1034) 188
XI. Oeuvre-Prints and Graphic Art 190
A. Monographs (entries 1035-1047) 190
B. Articles (entries 1048-1079) 192
XII. Oeuvre-Ceramics and Sculpture 195
A. Monographs (entries 1080-1082) 195
B. Articles (entries 1083-1113) 196
XIII. Oeuvre-Miscellaneous Media 199
A. Monographs (entries 1114-1115) 199
B. Articles (entries 1116-1125) 199
XIV. Museums and Collections (entries 1126-1209) 200
XV. Technique 209
A. Monographs (entries 1210-1211) 209
B. Articles (entries 1212-1222) 210
XVI. Iconography 211
A. Monographs (entries 1223-1240) 211
B. Articles (entries 1241-1283) 215
XVII. Japonisme 223
A. Monographs (entries 1284-1294) 223
B. Articles (entries 1295-1305) 226
XVIII. Mentions of Paul Gauguin in Monographs and Articles 229
A. Monographs (entries 1306-1407) 229
B. Articles (entries 1408-1502) 244
XIX. Films, Videos, Recordings and Other Media (entries 1503-1507) 254
Exhibitions 257
I. Individual Exhibitions During Gauguin's Lifetime (1884-1903) 257
II. Group Exhibitions Before His Death in Which Gauguin Participated (1876-1903) 259
III. Retrospective and Individual Exhibitions After Gauguin's Death (May 8, 1903) 262
IV. Group Exhibitions After Gauguin's Death (1903) 271
Index of Art Works 293
Index of Personal Names 297

Preface

Those who survey the literature on Paul Gauguin will surely be struck not only by its quantity but also by the diversity of opinions expressed on every aspect of the artist's life and work. Since his acceptance in the Impressionist salons in the early 1880s, Gauguin's life and art have appealed to the popular, critical, and scholarly communities on many levels. As an *artiste maudit* who fled civilization in quest of the primitive, Gauguin may forever be romanticized in the popular imagination, with his once roommate Vincent van Gogh, as a misunderstood and rebellious artist who sacrificed everything for art. A substantial mythology, amply represented here, surrounds the Gauguin mystique.

Paul Gauguin has also been appreciated on a critical and scholarly level for nearly as long. A tireless self-promoter (as evident in the Primary Bibliography), Gauguin's artistic career began as a Sunday painter in the 1870s. He first associated with the Impressionists. By 1886, Gauguin was at Pont-Aven in Brittany, where, during the next four years, he became a leading proponent of Symbolism. Gauguin's taste for the exotic led him to Martinique in 1887 and finally to Tahiti and the Marquesas, where his mature style developed during two periods, 1891-93 and 1895-1903. Although never a financial success, his art did sell during his lifetime. Beginning in the late 1870s, and particularly from 1889 on, Gauguin's works have received considerable critical attention. Gauguin's lasting reputation is based on his bold use of color, subjects, symbolism, and primitivism. On the strength of his followers and influence alone, Gauguin's place is secure among the greatest of the late nineteenth-century artists.

Gauguin's reputation grew in the last years of his life. In 1902, his faithful friend Monfreid warned him against returning to France: "You must not return. Now you are as the great dead. You have passed into the history of art." Appreciation increased following two important retrospective exhibitions in Paris, at Vollard's gallery in November, 1903, and at the Salon d'Automne in 1906, where 227 works were shown.

Louis Brouillon, under the pseudonym Jean de Rotonchamp, wrote the first book-length biography of Gauguin in 1906. As entries in the Secondary Bibliography attest, popular and scholarly interest in Gauguin has continued unabated. Attention intensified during centennial exhibitions in 1948-50, and following another round of major exhibitions in the United States and in Europe in 1959-60. Since 1959, critical interest in Gauguin's drawings, prints, sculptures, and art works in other media has dramatically increased. During the last several decades Gauguin's writings and manuscripts have also been studied intensely. The most important recent exhibition, *The Art of Paul Gauguin*, was shown at three venues in 1988-89 and featured 280 works.

Scope and Methodology

This bibliography and research guide concentrates on printed materials on the life, art, and legacy of Paul Gauguin. Selected manuscripts are also included.

The first section, the Primary Bibliography, lists articles, essays, letters, manuscripts, and sketchbooks by Gauguin. The Primary Bibliography is followed by Contemporary Accounts and Critiques of Gauguin's Life and Work Published Through 1906, the year of one of Gauguin's most important retrospective exhibitions and the publication of his first biography. A section on Gauguin's works or *oeuvre* (paintings, ceramics, and prints), including catalogues raisonnés, follows.

The main part of the bibliography and research guide, the Secondary Bibliography, comes next. It lists monographs (including first, later editions, and translations), catalogues, dissertations, theses, periodical literature, films, sound recordings and musical scores, and selected newspaper articles. Book reviews are included in the monograph sections when judged to be of sufficient substance to constitute review articles. Review articles are valuable in assessing the significance of particular publications and in clarifying the main lines of development. Similarly, for exhibitions only the more substantial reviews are provided.

From 1989 to 1991, relevant literature was gleaned from computer and card catalogues, and from other printed indexes and guides to the library and archival collections of major art museums, universities, and scholarly and artistic institutes in the United States, Western Europe, and the Pacific. Standard art indexes and abstracting services, such as *Art Index; ARTbibliographies MODERN; International Repertory of the Literature of Art; Répertoire d'art et d'archéologie*; Chicago Art Institute, Ryerson Library's *Index to Art Periodicals; Frick Art Reference Library Original Index to Art Periodicals; Arts and Humanities Citation Index; Humanities Index; MLA Bibliography; Worldwide Art Catalogue Bulletin;* and *Répertoire des catalogues de ventes* were consulted, along with pertinent bibliographic databases such as RLIN, SCIPIO, and OCLC. The work attempts to be as comprehensive as possible, within time, travel, budget, and length constraints. It should not, however, be considered exhaustive.

This guide is intended as a briefly annotated bibliography, and not as a critical one. Annotations are provided for entries where titles give incomplete or unclear information about works and their content. Monographs and dissertations are annotated with more regularity than periodical articles. Annotations are of necessity brief and are intended only to note the subject matter discussed, the general orientation, or the conclusion of the study. Obviously, a few sentences can hardly hope to represent fairly and adequately even a short article, to say nothing of a major book.

My apologies to authors who may feel that the annotations have misrepresented, misconstrued, misunderstood, or even distorted their work in this process of radical condensation. My own opinion and critical judgment have in no case been conscious criteria for inclusion or exclusion. Foreign language titles, particularly in French, abound. Since a reading knowledge of French is essential for serious Gauguin research, only titles in other foreign languages are occasionally translated.

How to Use the Secondary Bibliography

The Secondary Bibliography is divided into sections, accessible by the Table of Contents. Entries are numbered consecutively throughout. In every section, monographs are listed first, followed by periodical articles. Within each section, citations are listed alphabetically by author. Anonymous works are alphabetized by title. When several entries are credited to the same author, they are arranged chronologically. Authors whose surnames have changed and those who have rearranged their given names or initials are generally listed as they appear in print. They may, therefore, be found in the Personal Name Index in more than one location.

To some degree any system of classification is arbitrary, and this one is no exception. I have attempted to organize a great variety of material under headings most useful for art historical study rather than placing them in what at first may have seemed the most appropriate place. This arrangement is not always satisfactory. Hopefully, users perplexed by omissions in certain sections will be compensated by finding titles that they were unaware of in other sections.

Ideally, some titles should be listed in more than one section. In most instances, however, this was not practical. The division of the Secondary Bibliography into many categories is intended to serve as a simple subject index. Citations in the "Mentions of Paul Gauguin" section concentrate on major sources deemed historically significant prior to about 1960. These entries are historically interesting as a reflection of the critical evaluation of Gauguin at the time of publication. The Exhibitions section contains information and publications about Gauguin exhibitions, including a few sales catalogues, arranged by categories in chronological order.

The most effective use of the Secondary Bibliography is by means of the Table of Contents and the Personal Names Index and Art Works Index. Entries are indexed with reference to their citation numbers. Particular publications may be located in the Personal Names Index under the author or any other persons associated with the work.

Common Abbreviations

col.	color
diss.	dissertation
ed(s).	edition(s)
illus.	illustrations
min.	minutes
p. or pp.	page(s)
pl.	plates
ser.	series
supp.	supplement
vol.	volume

Acknowledgments

The idea of a research guide and bibliography of Paul Gauguin germinated with a library reference question about a dozen years ago, although serious work did not begin until nearly a decade later. Numerous library colleagues, art historians, and Gauguin specialists--my giants--provided encouragement and invaluable assistance in ferreting out sources. Brigham Young University and the Harold B. Lee Library in particular gave exceptional institutional support. Special thanks are extended to A. Dean Larsen, Madison U. Sowell, and Martha M. Peacock, BYU colleagues who critiqued the expository section and provided helpful suggestions about organization. Also at BYU, Annick Houzé proofread and edited the French citations; Richard D. Hacken edited the German, Italian, and Scandinavian; and Rafael Ulloa the Spanish and Portuguese. Kathleen Hansen and her able Interlibrary Loan staff procured important books and journals essential to the project. Aleisha Ann Cheney, Audrey Stephens, Julie Roueché and Jennifer P. Duffin performed the laborious tasks of data entry, word processing, and formatting. Each commands a compelling mastery of word processing; collectively, they represent a force to be reckoned with. On a personal note, appreciation is expressed to my parents, Ted and Jean Clement, for enduring two trying trips to Europe and the vicissitudes of nocturnal Eurail journeys. My wife, Jo, gave her unflagging support and confidence as well. The work is dedicated to our children--Esther, Jon, Sam and Ben--who didn't go anywhere and never really understood what was being done or why.

Biographical Sketch

Paul Gauguin, in his rambling *Intimate Journals*, jotted down a brief dialogue with himself:

How much does society owe me?
A great deal too much.
Will it ever pay?
Never![1]

Never in Gauguin's lifetime did society pay him the honor, fame, or fortune due a great artist. But in the years since he died in poverty on Hivaoa, a South Pacific island in the Marquesas, the world has paid his memory handsomely in the hard coin of lasting esteem. It has also paid handsomely in hard currency for his paintings. On May 9, 1989, for example, Gauguin's *Mata Mua* (*In Olden Times*, 1892) was auctioned at Sotheby's for $24.2 million. More important than auction records, though, is his widely recognized influence on early twentieth-century art.

"Perhaps I loved paintings too much,"[2] Gauguin said shortly before he died. He had given up everything to pursue his vision--career, family, and homeland. Since 1903, Gauguin's legend (abetted by such works as Somerset Maugham's *The Moon and Sixpence*, 1919) has held up well: Parisian stockbroker, seized by impulse to create, leaves respectable but stifling bourgeois family; escapes to Tahiti, and instantly becomes an immortal artist admired by the Polynesian ladies.

An aura of romance has long surrounded Gauguin's life, veiling the truth behind the self-promoted image of the noble savage. In his paintings, Gauguin is chiefly remembered for his tropical settings, exotic women, and brilliant colors. He is equally known for his pursuit of primitive life in Brittany, Panama, Martinique, and Polynesia. Gauguin's arrogance, conceit, and inclination to self-pity were eclipsed by the boldness of these adventures. Although his quest for the primitive was typical of a general contemporary interest in returning to the origins of art, and his fugitive retreat to Polynesia symptomatic of a widely felt despair with European civilization, Gauguin's exploits hastened the appreciation of primitive art. Further, his unconventional use of media and his symbolism and *synthetism* expanded the range of art beyond the confines of the *beaux-arts* tradition.

Irreconcilable conflicts contend within this rebel painter. In his life he aspired to acclaim and renown, but at the same time he defiantly pretended to despise the public and refused to conform--the savage at once rejected but superior. In his art, too, his professed contempt for rules concealed an interest in aesthetic theory on the expressive effects of line, form, and color. Thus, without making any consistent formulation, he strove to achieve emotive effect through simplification of form and the arbitrary use of color.

Another feature of Gauguin's style is "visual quotation," or borrowing from the works of several painters, including Degas, Puvis de Chavannes, Cézanne, Manet, and Bernard, as well as from a number of photographs. "He is always poaching on someone's ground," Pissarro once groused; "now he is pillaging the savages of Oceania."[3] Gauguin intended, it seems, to produce a confluence of associations within the same picture. Figures and poses in Gauguin's paintings become images impregnated with special significance. Many reappear in later works. Frequently, Gauguin used motifs to suggest an idea rather than an explicit allegory or event. As he once told his friend Georges-Daniel de Monfreid, "In painting one must search rather for suggestion than description, as is done in music. Sometimes people accuse me of being incomprehensible only because they look for an explicative side to my pictures that is not there."[4]

Early Years

Born in Paris on June 7, 1848, Eugène Henri Paul Gauguin was taken to Peru in 1849 because his journalist father feared political events in France. When his father died en route, his French-Peruvian mother was forced to continue the arduous journey alone with Paul and his sister Marie. After five years in Peru, they returned to Paris and settled in Orléans. Gauguin's penchant for the exotic can be partly explained by his early association with foreign cultures, although his claims to savage Peruvian ancestry are tenuous. Little is known of his years spent in the French naval service from 1865-1871, but these sea voyages set a pattern for the roving adventures of the rest of his life.

Gauguin's early artistic tastes were guided and shaped by Gustave Arosa, a wealthy financier, contemporary art collector, photographer, and owner of a large collection of Peruvian and Oriental artifacts. Some of Arosa's objects later appeared in Gauguin's paintings. On the death of Gauguin's mother, Aline, in 1867, Arosa became his guardian. In the two years before his marriage in 1873, Gauguin lived with Arosa and was infected by Arosa's passionate attitude toward painting. Gauguin had begun to sketch at sea and, under Arosa's tutelage, was encouraged to pursue art as a hobby. Through Arosa, Gauguin obtained a position as a stockbroker and began to work in 1872 for Paul Bertin in Paris. Here he met Emile Schuffenecker, a fellow stockbroker and also an amateur painter, who remained a loyal friend for many years. By 1873, his success on the Bourse qualified him as an approved match for a young Danish girl, Mette Gad, whom he married in November of that year.

It is not precisely known at what point Gauguin first ventured into painting. Clearly, he began oil painting in the early 1870s. Gustave Arosa's younger daughter aspired to become a painter, and Gauguin sometimes painted with her. In 1874, the year of the birth of Gauguin's first child, Emil, Gauguin became a regular Sunday painter and occasionally went to the Atelier Colarossi with Schuffenecker to draw models. His early painting style reveals the strong influence of the Barbizon School tradition, particularly Corot and Daubigny.

Sometime in 1875 Gauguin's style came under the influence of Camille Pissarro, who taught him the Impressionist technique. Through Pissarro, Gauguin made the acquaintance of other Impressionists in Paris. Gauguin's leisure hours continued to be occupied with painting. By 1876, Gauguin felt ready to exhibit at the Salon. That the conservative jury accepted Gauguin's somber landscape, while it refused works by Manet and Cézanne, helps to explain why the Impressionists had initiated a series of independent exhibitions two years earlier.

As the years passed Gauguin spent more and more time in the company of the radical painters. For the Fifth Impressionist Exhibit in 1880, Gauguin submitted several landscapes in Pissarro's style. The next year he entered a wooden statuette, a painted plaster medallion, and seven pictures, including *Nude Study, or Suzanne Sewing* (1880). Thus he firmly allied himself with the Impressionists. By 1882, with profits from his speculation on the Bourse, Gauguin had amassed a private collection of works by Manet, Pissarro, Renoir, Degas, Cézanne, Sisley, Guillaumin, Jongkind, and Daumier.

Gauguin's presence was not well received by everyone. He aroused distrust and dislike even in those who shared his passions. Other artists sensed a hardness in him that clashed with their own vulnerabilities. Open dissension within the Impressionist ranks became increasingly apparent in the 1880s. Gauguin gradually pulled away from the *plein-air* Impressionism of Pissarro and Monet and edged toward Manet and Degas, whose attention was focused more on pictorial interest than on the recording of transient visual phenomena. Gauguin played an integral role in the reaction against Impressionism in the 1880s by utilizing the color experiments of Impressionism for the description of a personal, inner vision in new pictorial terms.

Painting Full Time

By 1883 Gauguin felt the attraction to a full-time career as a painter too strongly to continue with his job at the stock market. In November, Gauguin and his family left Paris for Rouen, in the mistaken hope of finding cheaper lodgings and a better market for his paintings. Their departure marked the tenth year of marriage, and Mette was pregnant with their fifth child. Gauguin's financial troubles began at this point and soon multiplied. His economic failure as an artist reduced the family capital considerably and embittered relations with Mette, who viewed his metamorphosis with utter dismay. She eventually left for Copenhagen in August 1884 but returned in October when Gauguin agreed to go and live with her in Denmark.

Poor lodgings and Mette's hostile family made Gauguin's tenure in Copenhagen a time of darkness. He attempted to sell tarpaulin for a French company, but this proved as futile as his first one-man exhibition at the Society of the Friends of Art, which was ignored by the press and public. His inefficiency made him an object of ridicule and contempt in the eyes of Mette and her respectable bourgeois family. Finding this intolerable, he left with his son Clovis for Paris in the summer of 1885. In the bitter winter that followed, he was forced to work as a bill-poster while Mette, perhaps vindictively, resorted to selling pictures from his prized collection.

Gauguin's personal relationships with fellow painters suffered as well during this miserable period. During a stay in Dieppe in 1885, he quarreled with Degas, and in the following year he fell out with Seurat. The latter quarrel was aggravated by Gauguin's jealousy of Seurat's rising reputation. Seurat had conspicuously broken with Impressionist tradition and Gauguin felt that Seurat had stolen his role as the new Messiah. He also attacked the divisionism of the Neo-Impressionists, including his master Pissarro.

Searching for the Primitive

Under these desperate conditions, Gauguin decided to go to Brittany in late June of 1886. There, new subjects could be found, steeped in folklore. Further, he had learned of an inexpensive inn, the Pension Gloanec in Pont-Aven, where credit was extended to painters. At Pont-Aven Gauguin met Charles Laval, who accompanied him to Panama and Martinique in the following year. Emile Bernard, another young painter, was instrumental in transforming Gauguin's style toward *synthetism*--the reduction of forms to essentials and the application of colors as flat, nonshaded fields bounded by strong contour lines. Contrary to Gauguin's opinion, the majority of painters who frequented this increasingly popular artist's retreat was not much influenced by him, although his impact on the colony was considerable.

On his return to Paris in November, he tried his hand at ceramics, but as a commercial venture this too failed. Physical illness forced him to spend most of December in a hospital. Weary of misfortune, he announced to Mette in early April 1887 his intention of going to live "like a savage" in Panama. He and Laval set sail the same month. His sister, on whose hospitality he had counted, gave them a poor reception. He rapidly became disillusioned and caught malaria and dysentery. The adventure would have ended ingloriously if Gauguin had not decided to disembark at Martinique on the return journey.

In Martinique Gauguin completed twenty paintings in four months. The breakthrough in his Martinique canvases is not in color, which is still somber. Rather, the real breakthrough is the size and surface of his canvases, and the care with which some of figures are drawn. Gauguin used larger canvases and increased the size of the figures he painted, particularly the island women. Where Martinique inspired him to break most strongly with Impressionism, though, was in the way he painted shapes. By outlining the figures in deep blue, and then painting them in large, flat strokes, Gauguin created works that are deliberately two-dimensional. The ensuing exhibition by Theo van Gogh, Vincent's brother, at Goupil's gallery in Paris in January resulted in only three sales.

Dispirited by yet another failure, Gauguin set off again for Brittany. Emile Bernard was among the painters at Pont-Aven. Bernard was intellectually curious and well versed in the literary and aesthetic ideas then current in Paris. He acted as a foil to the older man, stimulating and clarifying some of Gauguin's ill-formed theories. Bernard brought with him some Gauguin canvases done in St. Briac that had been admired by the art critic Albert Aurier. Bernard later insisted that his own pictures inspired Gauguin's *Vision after the Sermon* (1888) and the style of *synthetism*, which aimed at gaining more forceful expression through simplification of forms, flat planes, and bold non-naturalistic colors in conjunction with symbolic subjects. Bernard's dispute eventually provoked bitter animosity between the two. Actually, Gauguin's new style owed much to *synthetism*, the flat simplicity of Japanese prints, and to a technique devised by Bernard's friend Louis Anquétin, known as *cloisonnism*, which had been inspired by stained glass. In his ceramics Gauguin had already reduced designs to simple shapes and outlines. Regarding the new theory itself, in a letter to Schuffenecker two years earlier (in January 1885), Gauguin outlined a *synthetist* program by suggesting that simplicity of form could transmit immediacy of sensation.

In October 1888 Gauguin accepted a frequently expressed invitation from Vincent van Gogh to join him in Arles. They had first met in November 1886 and had formed a friendship on the strength of their enthusiasm for painting. In Arles wide differences in temperament underlined those in their art. Gauguin continued to paint Breton themes in Arles (such as *Vintage at Arles*, *The Alyscamps*, *Old Woman at Arles*, and *Farm at Arles*), but a noticeable lightening of his palette occurred and his touch became livelier. While he later made unjustified claims to having radically influenced van Gogh's style, which admittedly showed a temporary change, it is clear that Gauguin benefitted from the two months with Vincent. After van Gogh's well-known tragedy of the last days of 1888, Gauguin returned to Paris.

In Paris he set about organizing an exhibition of painters of his choice, designed to enter the Exposition Universelle of 1889 by the back door. It was entitled "Groupe Impressionniste et Synthétiste" and covered the walls of a café at the exposition run by a proprietor named Volpini. A failure as far as the public was concerned, the Volpini exhibition nonetheless served Gauguin's purposes in furthering his leadership of a small following and in bringing to the notice of the Symbolists, especially Félix Fénéon, Gustave Kahn, and Albert Aurier, a style that they found conveniently illustrative of their own ideas. Gauguin was fascinated by parts of the Exposition Universelle itself. He was particularly delighted with the Far Eastern displays, which included a Javanese village complete with dancing girls. The whole exposition whetted his appetite for the primitive, and he made several drawings.

In the early summer of 1889 Gauguin drifted back discontentedly to Brittany. He first stayed at the Pension Gloanec in Pont-Aven but later moved to the inn run by Marie Henry at Le Pouldu, the dining room of which he and his disciple-friends decorated with paintings and carvings. The religious themes of several of his pictures at this time (such as *The Yellow Christ*) were suggested by some of Aurier's writings and also by Bernard's devout Catholicism. Gauguin's self-portrait as Christ symbolized not only a sense of martyrdom but also a Messianic hope fostered by the attentions of his disciples at the inn, and later by the Symbolists in Paris.

During his stay at Arles, Gauguin had enjoyed a successful one-man show at Theo van Gogh's gallery in Paris. Later in 1889, however, Theo's enthusiasm waned noticeably and with it Gauguin's chances of selling. Gauguin's style in 1889-90 lacked consistency and a firm ideological foundation. The outlines softened and the stark simplicity of *cloisonnism* was modified by a reversion to Cézannesque modeling. Gauguin wavered between pictures inspired by Breton subjects and others less conventional whose unusual themes invited acclaim by the Symbolists, particularly Aurier. However, the latter demurred despite pressure from Bernard. Apart from an article in *La Cravache* by Fénéon, not entirely favorable, Gauguin remained without recognition. At an exhibition with "Les Vingt" in Brussels, he was mocked openly, and both Theo and Degas increasingly expressed dislike for his latest pictures.

It comes as little surprise, then, to discover that he applied for a colonial post in Tonkin (now northern Vietnam) with the vain hope of tapping the art and philosophy of the Orient. In Paris early the next year, conversations with Mme. Odilon Redon, who had visited Madagascar, suggested this locale as an alternative. Emile Bernard, one of the group Gauguin planned to take, had meanwhile unearthed the romantic novel on Tahiti by Pierre Loti, as well as an official handbook on Tahiti. Gauguin soon resolved what course to take.

Tahiti's special attraction for him was the promise of a cheap and carefree life, unfettered by the chains of progressive materialism and as free from constraint in art as in sexual morality. But another consideration, the promise of new subject matter, further expanded the opportunities Tahiti offered. Vincent van Gogh had first pointed out the commercial success of hitherto unpainted regions, but the Symbolists alerted Gauguin's attention to other aspects. He was introduced to this admiring literary circle by Aurier. Contemporary accounts, however, indicate that Gauguin's rough and ready theories fell so ill on their refined ears that he prudently decided to profit from exploiting their ideas rather than attempting to preach his own. A number of themes were current in their discussions: the *rêve*, mystery, decadence and pessimism, all with a common source in Baudelaire. They sighed over Europe and dreamed of faraway isles. Gauguin needed no introduction to Baudelaire, whose admiration for Delacroix he shared, but the preoccupations of the literary Symbolists enlivened his own ideas, and the mysterious enchantment of Tahiti promised to be fertile in the essential material of Symbolist art.

In order to obtain funds for a ticket, Gauguin organized a sale of his paintings and applied for an official commission to the Minister of Education. In both he succeeded. The sale at the Hôtel Drouot in late February 1891 received tremendous publicity from the Symbolists, especially from Octave Mirbeau, whose lengthy article in *L'Art moderne* had already begun to spin myths about the artist. Gauguin fondly made amends with Mette during a brief trip to Copenhagen in March, with the agreement to resume married life upon his return in three years. The Symbolists celebrated his departure with a farewell dinner at the Café Voltaire on March 23, presided over by Stéphane Mallarmé. A week later, on April 1, 1891, Gauguin set sail from Marseilles.

Tahiti

Gauguin's first impression of Tahiti was bound to be disappointing. European influence had spread to every part of the capital, Pape'ete, and although he enjoyed high social status on account of his commission, he failed to discover the fabled glamour of his dreams. He gravitated to the less respectable levels of Tahitian society, and the portrait commissions ceased when the strange style of his first portrait became known. After three months he wearied of the capital and withdrew to the country, still hoping to find the ancient culture of Tahiti unspoiled. His departure was delayed by an internal hemorrhage, symptomatic of an advanced syphilitic condition. To his disappointment, even in the country the marvels of civilization had replaced ancient Tahitian society, just as Christianity had effaced the ancient religion. Through a lucky acquaintance with an amateur painter, he gained access to the remoter region of Paea, where his *Man with an Axe* was painted. After his return to Pape'ete he set out for the district of Mataiea, which provided sufficient new subjects for him to complete about twenty pictures in which a happy mood predominates.

Gauguin had come to Tahiti with naive preconceived ideas about native life in the tropics. Consequently, he tended to idealize his surroundings to the extent of believing in the magical world he created on canvas. His ideal savages splashed in the lagoons, wandered on lovely beaches, hacked down fruit from trees, and hunted game in the forests. Unfortunately, without the necessary skills to obtain native foods, he had to buy what he could at a local store. His sophisticated tastes in drink meant that in spite of his cheap bamboo hut, life was not cheap. Out of economic necessity he eventually sought a post as a magistrate in the Marquesas Islands. Upon refusal, he wrote to France for repatriation in 1892. It was granted a year later.

His early pictures, such as *Matamoe*, *Ia Orana Maria*, and *Fatata te mouà*, idealize Tahiti. With masterful simplicity and colors more glowing than ever, he depicted an idyllic environment. He interpreted Christian themes in Tahitian terms, but the discovery in 1892 of J. A. Moerenhout's account of ancient Tahitian mythology released a new stream of ideas. From this work he extracted certain sections and compiled them with illustrations in a volume entitled *L'Ancien culte Mahoire*. This work also supplied the basic material for a book he later called *Noa Noa*. Moerenhout's writings also inspired several paintings, woodcuts, and woodcarvings.

During this first Tahitian period he met a young girl named Teha'amana, who was offered and wedded to him in Tahitian style. In Tahitian women generally he found not beauty, but "a sort of fascination, something infinitely mysterious."[5] Teha'amana, with a countenance as innocent as Eve's, helped him make believe in his garden of Eden. She steadied him and gave him strength.

Back in France

Both the painter and his pictures found a mixed reception in Europe when he returned to Paris in August 1893. In Copenhagen the Free Exhibition of Modern Art was well attended but realized few sales. Theo's old gallery, now under new management, refused to handle his pictures, forcing him to seek exhibition at the Galerie Durand-Ruel. Some of his most celebrated Tahitian paintings, including *Ia Orana Maria* (1891) and *Nafea faaipoipo* (1892), were greeted with derision and abuse. Only eleven of the 44 exhibits were sold. A heavy heart and light purse persuaded him to leave Europe for good. With hope still for success Gauguin began to collaborate with the poet Charles Morice on *Noa Noa*, a book designed to help the public understand his Tahitian works. For this enterprise he executed ten superb woodcuts. Gauguin's imaginative knife work, irregular shapes, and heavy gouges balanced by smaller engraver's gouges produced powerfully crude yet delicately refined blocks. Gauguin was as original a printmaker as any other in nineteenth-century France, and surely his most sustained graphic achievement is the *Noa Noa* series.

Gauguin's fortunes took a brief turn for the better in September 1893 when he succeeded in obtaining a legacy of 13,000 francs from an uncle in Orléans. Of this he spitefully sent Mette very little. His new wealth enabled him to decorate a fabulous studio in a large room in the rue Vercingétorix. The unsold paintings from the Durand-Ruel exhibition as well as his sculpture, his current works, and his ethnographic collection were placed in this extraordinary space painted olive green and brilliant chrome yellow and lit with numerous windows, one of which he painted with *Te Faruru*. Gauguin also kept a new mistress, a mulatto model called Annah la Javanaise, who resembled the Javanese girls he had admired at the 1889 Exposition Universelle.

In late April 1894 he returned with Annah for his last and ill-fated trip to Brittany. On an excursion to Concarneau he and his companions became involved in a brawl with some sailors, during which his right ankle was broken. While Gauguin was recovering, Annah deserted to Paris and rifled his studio of all but the paintings. To add to his misery, his case against Marie Henry for the illegal retention of some his paintings failed. He resolved to escape again to the South Seas, this time for good. Gauguin again arranged a sale of his works to raise money. Despite his ingenious tactic of obtaining publicity by the publication of a letter from August Strindberg in the preface of the catalogue, only nine of 47 paintings sold. His departure in July 1895 was further delayed by a syphilitic attack that impaired his health for several months.

Return to Polynesia

En route Gauguin touched at Sydney and then Auckland before arrival at Pape'ete, now so civilized he immediately proposed to travel on to the remoter Marquesas Islands. He remained, however, because his poor health required proximity to Tahiti's hospital. He built a hut in Punauia with carved wooden panels and posts. At first he spent his time recklessly, and as funds ran out another syphilitic attack and the recurrence of pain in his ankle increased his misfortune. These ailments restricted painting and required at first pain-killing drugs and then hospital treatment. He resumed work at the end of October and modelled some clay statues for his garden. Financial support from Paris gave him a brief period of relief. Then, in April 1897, news came of the death of his favorite daughter, Aline.

Not long after, the owner of the land on which his hut was built died suddenly and Gauguin was obliged to move. He lavished a bank loan of 1,000 francs on a large home, well beyond his means. In a period of acute unhappiness, when money troubles again coincided with severe illness, he wrote *The Modern Spirit and Catholicism*, a confused metaphysical discussion that attacks the Catholic Church. His increasing unhappiness reached its climax in December 1897. After painting a monumental canvas, *Where do we come from? What are we? Where are we going?*, Gauguin attempted suicide with arsenic. This thirteen-foot mural, described as a "spiritual testament," was left for the world to puzzle over after he was gone. The suicide attempt failed.

The remainder of his stay in Polynesia was marked by the recurrence of illness and debts. The latter forced him to take a job in the Public Works Department in Pape'ete until a large sum of money arrive in January 1899 from the faithful Monfreid. Eventually, he was able to live in moderate comfort when the Parisian dealer Ambroise Vollard agreed in March 1900 to pay a regular monthly allowance in exchange for paintings.

Gauguin's financial agreement with Ambroise Vollard imposed a certain level of productivity, and he finished his last paintings relatively quickly. The rapidity with which he worked had a liberating effect. His compositions, such as *Riders on the Beach* and *Primitive Tales* (both 1902), became more varied as he experimented even more dramatically with color relationships. He also completed several "transfer drawings," 27 of which dominated Vollard's last major Gauguin exhibition in November 1903. The sheer power and originality of these drawings had an enormous impact on Matisse, Picasso, and others.

From 1898 on, Gauguin indulged in a spate of political activities against the French authorities. After publishing vitriolic articles in *Les Guêpes* (The Wasps), a monthly newspaper of the Catholic party, he founded his own magazine, *Le Sourire* (The Smile), in August 1899 as the mouthpiece of attacks against the administration.

In September 1901, Gauguin carried out his original intention of moving to the Marquesas. There, beyond the range of colonial officials and in a more primitive environment, he hoped to immerse himself in ancient culture. He built his "House of Pleasure" in Atuona on the island of Hivaoa and increased his output of paintings. The erotic activities that took place there caused friction between Gauguin and the local authorities. In particular he antagonized the local bishop with a satirical wooden sculpture. Some of his renewed attacks on the administration, in his role as defiant champion of the natives, are recorded in a collection of memoirs and anecdotes entitled *Avant et après*. These attacks recoiled on him. On March 31, 1903, the local magistrate fined him 500 francs and sentenced him to three months imprisonment for libel against a gendarme. The strain of trying to fight this sentence, together with his deteriorating health, brought about his death at age 54 on May 8, 1903.

Toward the end of his life Gauguin felt a desire to return to Europe. In a letter to Monfreid he mentioned Spain as a possible source of new subject matter. Monfreid warned him against this: "You must not return. Now you are as the great dead. You have passed into the history of art."[6] To Monfreid he personally confided his estimation of his own achievement: "You have known for a long time what it has been my aim to vindicate: the right to dare anything . . . The public owes me nothing since my pictorial oeuvre is only relatively good, but the painters of today who are benefitting from this new-won freedom do owe me something."[7] This statement, made in a moment of rare modesty, is confirmed by the bold experiments in technique and use of materials made throughout Gauguin's work. Conversely, it is equally contradicted by the testimony of countless canvases in which subtle design is combined with unparalleled coloristic splendor.

In his last years Gauguin created the majority of his art works and literary texts for posterity. His residence in the Marquesas, far from those who bought and sold his paintings, meant that he could only imagine the response his work produced in France. After many years of rejection, Gauguin came to assume that the response was negative. The distance allowed him, however, to posture as a genius and make pronouncements on his art and on the state of the world without fear of contradiction. The innocence and naiveté of his Tahitian audience made his ideas bolder than they might have been in the more critical and competitive atmosphere of Paris.

Richard Brettell summarizes Gauguin's lasting reputation:

> . . . first in 1903 and then in larger numbers in 1906 and subsequently, artists have flocked to see the works of Gauguin. Picasso was clearly devastated by the power and raw, crude strength of the printed drawings. Matisse was overcome by the color and the apparently casual draftsmanship of the late paintings. Indeed, if one can measure the strength of an artist by that of his most brilliant followers, Gauguin would be among the very greatest from the late nineteenth century. Perhaps only Cézanne could rival him. Fortunately for Gauguin's reputation, his works entered the collections of major museums shortly after his death and have been part of the staple diet of modern artists since the 1920s. He still lies buried in Atuona, with the small bronze

cast of *Oviri* now on his tomb, but his art can be found on every continent, in socialist and capitalist countries, in public and private collections, and, in reproduction, on the walls of hundreds of thousands, perhaps millions of rooms across the world.[8]

Notes

[1]Paul Gauguin, *The Intimate Journals of Paul Gauguin* (London: KPI, 1985), 16.

[2]Quoted in "A Noble Rogue," *Art & Antiques* (May 1988): 118.

[3]Quoted in Paul C. Nicholls, *Gauguin* (New York: Tudor Publishing Co., 1967), 5.

[4]Quoted in Nicholls, 6.

[5]Paul Gauguin, *Lettres de Gauguin à sa femme et ses amis*, ed. Maurice Malingue (Paris: B. Grasset, 1949), CXIX.

[6]Quoted in Beril Becker, *Paul Gauguin, the Calm Madman* (New York: Albert & Charles Boni, 1931, 311.

[7]Quoted in Becker, 309-10.

[8]Richard Brettell, *The Art of Paul Gauguin* (exhibition catalogue; Boston: New York Graphic Society Books; Little, Brown and Company, 1988), 396.

Additional sources consulted for the Biographical Sketch include:

Wayne Andersen and Barbara Klein, *Gauguin's Paradise Lost* (New York: Viking, 1971).

Pierre Daix, *Paul Gauguin* (Paris: Lattes, 1989).

Bengt Danielsson, *Gauguin à Tahiti et aux îles Marquises* (Pape'ete: Editions du Pacifique, 1975).

Michel Hoog, *Paul Gauguin, vie et oeuvre* (Paris: Nathan, 1987).

Belinda Thompson, *Gauguin* (London: Thames and Hudson, 1987).

PAUL GAUGUIN

Chronology

This chronology is based on chronologies by Isabelle Cahn and Gloria Groom in Richard Brettell, et al., *The Art of Paul Gauguin* (exhibition catalogue; Boston: New York Graphic Society Books; Little, Brown and Company, 1988. See pages 2-9, 44-50, 205-08, 291-95, and 379-87 for entries and documentation). Additional sources include *Correspondance de Paul Gauguin*, Victor Merlhès, ed. (Paris: Fondation Singer-Polignac, 1984) and Bengt Danielsson, *Gauguin à Tahiti et aux îles Marquises* (Pape'ete: Editions du Pacifique, 1975), among others.

1848

June 7

Eugène Henri Paul Gauguin is born at 52 (today 56) rue Notre-Dame-de-Lorette in Paris, son of Pierre Guillaume Clovis Gauguin, an editor at the *National*, and Aline Marie Chazal. His maternal grandmother was the socialist writer Flora Tristan (1803-1844).

1849

July 19

Baptized at Notre-Dame-de-Lorette. His father, absent from the ceremony, is listed as "unemployed." His godfather is his paternal grandfather, Guillaume Gauguin.

August 8

The Gauguin family leaves Le Havre for Peru aboard the *Albert*.

October 20

Gauguin's father dies of a ruptured aneurism in the Gulf of Port-Famine (Puñta Areñas) in the Strait of Magellan, Chile, where he is buried. Aline Gauguin and her children, Paul and Marie (b. April 29, 1847), move in with their great-uncle, Don Pio de Tristan Moscoso in Lima.

1853
September 19
In Orléans, France, Guillaume Gauguin agrees to a trust fund divided between his two grandchildren.

Late 1854-Early 1855
Aline Gauguin returns to France with her children. Her passport is issued in Lima on August 9, 1854. They move into the family's residence in Orléans where Paul is registered as a day student at the local école.

1855
April 9
Guillaume Gauguin dies at 25, quai Tudelle, in Orléans.

April 20
Isadore Gauguin (a paternal uncle) is named guardian for Paul and Marie.

1856
Don Pio de Tristan Moscoso, Paul's great-uncle, dies in Lima.

1859
Paul continues his education at the Junior Seminary of the Saint-Mesmin Chapel in Orléans.

1861
Aline moves to 33 rue de la Chaussée d'Antin in Paris and works as a seamstress. She befriends the Arosa family.

1862
Paul joins his mother in Paris to prepare for the entrance exam at the Naval Academy. He is a student at the Loriol Institute, 49 rue d'Enfer.

1864
For his final year at school he boards at the lycée in Orléans.

1865
November 13
Aline draws up a will and names Gustave Arosa as legal guardian of her children. She leaves her portraits and paintings to her son and suggests that he "get on with his career, since he has made himself so unliked by all my friends that he will one day find himself alone." She lives in the village de l'Avenir, at 3 rue de la Paix, on the route to Romainville.

December 6
Too old to take the Naval Academy entrance exam, Paul enlists as an officer's candidate in the merchant marines aboard a three-masted ship, the *Luzitano*, bound for Rio de Janeiro. The voyage lasts three months, 21 days.

1866
May 2
Departs on second voyage to Rio on the *Luzitano*, lasting three months, 29 days.

October 1
Aline Gauguin moves to 2 rue de l'Hospice in Saint-Cloud.

October 27
Paul leaves Le Havre as a second lieutenant aboard the *Chili*, which travels around the world (Cardiff, Valparaiso, Iquique [Peru]), for 13 1/2 months.

1867
July 7
His mother dies in Saint-Cloud. Gauguin learns of her death during a stopover in India.

December 14
The *Chili* is laid up in Le Havre.

1868
January 22
Gauguin officially enlists in the military.

February 26
He is registered in the Cherbourg Division as a third-class sailor, based in Le Havre. He is listed as a professional seaman, 1.603 meters tall, with brown hair and eyes.

March 3
He is assigned to the *Jérôme-Napoléon*.

June-July
The *Jérôme-Napoléon* cruises the eastern Mediterranean and the Black Sea.

September
The ship arrives in London.

1869
April-May
The *Jérôme-Napoléon* again cruises the Mediterranean, stopping at Bastia, Naples, Corfu, the Dalmation Coast, Trieste, and Venice.

June
Gauguin, now legally an adult, and his sister Marie inherit 32,707.87 francs from their mother and 6,215.84 francs from their paternal grandfather. Sums represent houses and property in Orléans, stocks and other assets.

September 25-October 29
Gauguin is hospitalized.

1870
July 1
Promoted to second-class sailor.

July 3
The *Jérôme-Napoléon* proceeds toward the North Pole and arrives in Bergen, Norway, five days later.

July 13
The ship crosses the Arctic Circle.

July 19
France declares war on Prussia.

July 21
Gauguin's ship returns to Calais via Edinburgh and London and leaves for the North Sea four days later.

August 26-30
Stopover in Copenhagen.

October 11-November 1
The *Jérôme-Napoléon*, renamed the *Desaix* after September 19, captures four German boats including the *Franziska*, to which Gauguin is transferred until November 1.

1871
January 25
His mother's house at 2 rue de l'Hospice in Saint-Cloud is burned by the Prussians.

April 23
Released from military service on six months of renewable leave.

1872
Lives at 15 rue La Bruyère in Paris. No profession listed. Recommended by Gustave Arosa, he is hired as a broker by Paul Bertin, a stockbroker at 11 rue Laffitte. Meets Emile Schuffenecker at the Bertin office.

Autumn
Mette Gad (b. September 7, 1850) and her friend Marie Heegaard travel from Denmark to Paris on vacation. They stay at the pension, avenue d'Eylau, of Pauline Fouignet, a friend of the Arosa family.

1873
January
Gauguin proposes marriage to Mette Gad.

Summer
He paints while on vacation.

November 22
Marries Mette Gad at the municipal building of the ninth district. Paul Bertin, Gustave Arosa and Oscar Fahle (Secretary of the Danish Consulate) are witnesses. A church ceremony takes place the same day at the Evangelical Lutheran Church of the Redemption, rue Chauchat. The couple's address is 28 Place St. Georges.

1874
August 31
Their first son, Emil Gauguin, is born at 28 Place St. Georges.

October 14
Mette's sister, Ingborg Gad, marries the painter Fritz Thaulow.

1875
January
Gauguin moves to 54 rue de Chaillot.

May 8
Emil is baptized at the Evangelical Lutheran Church of the Redemption. His godfather is Fritz Thaulow; his godmothers Elisabeth Möller and Marie Gauguin, Gauguin's sister.

1876
May-June
Exhibits a work for the first time at a salon, *Sous-bois à Viroflay* [Seine et Oise]. See Yriarte, "Le Salon de 1876," *Gazette des Beaux-Arts* (July 1876):36.

End 1876-Beginning 1877
Stops working as a stockbroker for Paul Bertin.

1877
Moves to 74 rue des Fourneaux (Vaugiard). His landlord is the sculptor Bouillot who introduces him to sculpture techniques. Meets Danish art critic Karl Madsen and the sculptor Jean-Paul Aubé.

December 24
Birth of their first daughter, Aline Gauguin.

Chronology

1878
February 25
Gustave Arosa's art collection sold at the Hôtel Drouot.

1879
Gauguin is employed by the banker André Bourdon at 21 rue Le Peletier.

April 10-May 11
Gauguin is invited at the last minute by Degas and Pissarro to participate in the fourth impressionist exhibition. His marble portrait of the head of his eldest son Emil is entered too late to be included in the catalogue. Three Pissarros are lent to the exhibition by Gauguin. Becomes a regular at the Café de la Nouvelle-Athènes, where he associates with Manet, Degas, Renoir, Pissaro, and the art critic Louis Edmond Duranty.

May 10
Birth of Clovis Henri Gauguin.

July
Buys a painting by Pissarro.

Summer
Visits Pissarro in Pontoise for the first time.

1880
April 1-30
Participates in the fifth Impressionist exhibition with eight works.

Summer
Moves to 8 rue Carcel, house sublet from the painter Félix Jobbé-Duval. One of the doors opened onto the rue Blomet where Haviland later began operating a pottery factory in April, 1882 at number 153. Ernest Chaplet became the director of the factory in 1883. Works for the Thomereau Agency, 93 rue Richelieu, which is involved in the sale and purchase of insurance company stocks. Emil is sent to live in Denmark with Mette's friend, Karen Lehmann.

1881
March 16
Paul Durand-Ruel makes his first purchase from Gauguin, three paintings totaling 1,500 francs.

March 25
Gauguin buys a seascape by Manet from Durand-Ruel.

April 2-May 1
Participates in the sixth Impressionist exhibition with eight paintings and two sculptures.

April 12
Birth of Jean-René, Gauguin's fourth child.

April 27
Durand-Ruel sells *The Church at Vaugirard* to Baroux and gives Gauguin two Renoirs as payment.

October 12
Buys a painting by N. Harris Brown from Durand-Ruel.

October 19
Durand-Ruel buys *Effet de nuit* for 200 francs.

December 16 and 19
Buys two paintings by Johan Jongkind from Durand-Ruel.

1882
January
L'Union Générale declares bankruptcy, causing the stock market to collapse.

March
Despite rivalries among the artists, participates in the seventh impressionist exhibition with 11 paintings, one pastel, and one sculpture. Gauguin's stock investments are in a state of collapse and he hesitates between financial and artistic careers. He often visits Pissarro on Sundays, first in Pontoise, then in Osny.

1883
April 14
Gustave Arosa dies. Gauguin is not present at the burial two days later.

May 3
Gauguin is not present at Manet's burial.

June 15-July 5
Spends three weeks with Pissarro in Osny. Expresses desire to make designs for impressionist tapestries.

August
Goes to Cerbère on the Spanish border, on a mission for radical Spanish republicans.

September
Looks for employment and has someone recommend him to the art dealer Georges Petit.

November 1
Arrives at Pissarro's in Rouen where he plans on settling.

December 6
Paul (Pola) Rollon is born. On his son's birth certificate, Gauguin lists himself as an artist-painter.

1884
January
Moves with his family to an apartment at 5 impasse Malherbe in Rouen.

April
Travels in the south of France for 15 days with Emile Armand Bertaux, a brokerage cashier, on behalf of the Spanish republicans. Visits the Fabre Museum in Montpellier where he makes a quick copy of Delacroix's *Aline, the Mulatto Woman.*

April 9
He leaves Durand-Ruel seven pictures on consignment.

Summer
Eugène Murer holds an exhibition at the Hôtel du Dauphin et d'Espagne in Rouen. He includes a Gauguin painting from his collection.

July
Mette leaves for two months in Denmark with Aline and Paul Rollon. In need of money, Gauguin sells his life insurance policy at a 50% loss.

August 12
Opening of the *Exposition municipale des Beaux-Arts* in Rouen where Gauguin, who exhibits one pastel and one sculpture, is listed as a student of Jobbé-Duval.

Autumn
Exhibits two still lifes and a portrait at the *Kunstudstillingen* in Kristiana [Oslo], Norway.

October
Works as a salesman for a canvas manufacturer in Roubaix, A. Dillies and Company, representing Denmark. Also studies graphology. At the end of the month, Mette returns to Copenhagen with her children.

November
Joins his family in Denmark, bringing with him his art collection, which will ultimately remain in Copenhagen. Stays temporarily with Madame Gad, Mette's mother, "Lille Rosenborg," 29 Frederiksbergallé.

December
The family moves to 105 Gammel Kongevej. Mette gives French lessons. Gauguin is listed as a traveling salesman.

1885
Writes *Notes synthétiques* in a notebook he had bought in Rouen. He receives 1300 francs from the sale by Portier of his Manet, *View of Holland*, to Alexander Causatt.

April 23
Moves to 51 Norregade.

May 1-6
Exhibits at the Society of the Friends of Art in Copenhagen.

June
Returns to Paris with his son Clovis. Nearly broke, asks Durand-Ruel to buy back a Renoir and a Monet from him. He lives with the Schuffeneckers, 29 rue Boulard.

July
Visits a friend in Dieppe where he resides until early October.

End August-Mid September
Goes to London on "Spanish business." When he returns to Dieppe, he encounters Degas, with whom he apparently quarrels.

Early October
Returns to Paris where his son Clovis, who has spent several months with Gauguin's sister, comes to live with him at M. Favre's, 19 rue Perdonnet. Rents an apartment at 10 rue Cail. Mette sells several of his paintings left in Copenhagen.

December
His paintings are rejected at a Danish exhibition. Clovis contracts smallpox. Gauguin takes a job first as a poster hanger, then as an inspector, and finally as an administrative secretary for the train stations.

Winter 1885-1886
Copies a text purportedly by a Turkish poet Vehbi Mohamed Zunbul-Zadé, which he will later include in *Avant et après*. Lends the text to Georges Seurat.

1886
May 6
Attends a dinner organized by Pissarro, in honor of the eighth Impressionist exhibition at the Lae St. Fargeau, a music hall at 296 rue de Belleville.

May 15-June 13
Participates in the eighth Impressionist exhibition with 19 paintings and one wood relief. Clovis is a boarder at Lennuier's in Antony. Sells a painting for 250 francs to Félix Bracquemond who puts him in contact with the ceramist Ernest Chaplet.

June
Gauguin frequents Chaplet's rue Blomet studio.

July
Goes to Pont-Aven in Brittany with a loan from one of his relatives, Eugène Mirtil, and moves into the Gloanec Inn for three months. During his stay he probably visits Le Pouldu. Meets the painter Charles Laval. Schuffenecker visits Gauguin and prepares shipment of his paintings for the Nantes exhibition.

August 15
Meets Emile Bernard but does not work with him until 1888.
August 21
Refuses to exhibit in the Independents' exhibition.

October 10-November 30
Participates in the Nantes *Exposition des Beaux-Arts* with two paintings, *Church in Rouen* and *Park--Denmark.*

Mid-October
Returns to Paris and moves to 257 rue Lecourbe. Makes pottery in Chaplet's studio.

November
First meets Vincent van Gogh. Refuses to shake hands with Pissarro and Paul Signac at the Café de la Nouvelle-Athènes. By so doing he breaks with the Neo-Impressionists. Sells one of his Jongkinds for 350 francs. He is hospitalized for 27 days due to tonsilitis.

1887
January 6
Gauguin, Degas, and Federico Zandomeneghi are witnesses at Armand Guillaumin's wedding. Bracquemond attempts to help Gauguin by trying to sell his paintings and pottery. Gauguin may have visited Saint-Quentin this year to see La Tour's works.

April
Mette goes to Paris to get Clovis. She takes several of her husband's works with her when she leaves.

April 10
Leaves from Saint-Nazaire for Panama with Charles Laval.

April 30
Arrives in Colón and spend several days in Panama where his brother-in-law, Juan Uribe, lives. Works for the Society of Public Works on the construction of the Panama Canal. Following a reduction in staff, he is laid off after 15 days. He leaves for Martinique with Laval.

July
Lives in a hut on a plantation two kilometers from Saint-Pierre in Martinique. Shortly after his arrival, Gauguin becomes seriously ill with dysentery and malaria. Albert Dauprat buys some of Gauguin's pottery at Chaplet's factory.

October
He leaves for France on a schooner and arrives about November 13.

November
Stays with Schuffenecker at 29 rue Boulard. Meets Daniel de Monfreid at Schuffenecker's. Exchanges a painting with Vincent van Gogh.

December
Theo van Gogh presents four of Gauguin's paintings and five ceramics on consignment at Boussod and Valadon, and at 19 Boulevard Montmartre in Paris. On December 26, he sells *The Bathers* to Mr. Dupuis for 450 francs.

1888
January
For several months Gauguin still suffers from the effects of malaria and dysentery. Theo van Gogh (probably accompanied by his brother) visits Gauguin at Schuffenecker's and buys three paintings for 900 francs, including a large work done in Martinique, *Aux Mangos*. Theo exhibits a recent Gauguin, *Two Bathers*, at Boussod and Valadon. Gauguin teaches in the open studio of Mr. Rawlins, a London businessman.

End January-Early February
Leaves for Pont-Aven where he moves into the Gloanec Inn.

March
Van Gogh writes to Gauguin of his plans to form an association of painters to facilitate the sale of their works.

May
Van Gogh asks Gauguin to come live and work with him in Arles.

June
Theo offers Gauguin monthly payments of 150 francs in exchange for one painting a month if he goes to Arles. Out of financial necessity, Gauguin agrees to the arrangement.

End July
Stays in Plestin-les-Grèves (Côtes-du-Nord) for several days at the home of Yves-Marie Jacob, head of customs in Pont-Aven.

Early August
Emile Bernard joins Gauguin and Laval, who has just returned from Martinique, in Pont-Aven. Gauguin meets Emile's sister, Madeleine, who is vacationing with her brother and mother.

September
Van Gogh suggests to Bernard and Gauguin that they exchange portraits of one another.

October
Paul Sérusier paints *The Talisman* (Musée d'Orsay, Paris), a landscape of the Bois d'Amour near Pont-Aven, under Gauguin's instructions. Vincent receives Gauguin's self-portrait *Les Misérables* and Bernard's self-portrait. He sends in exchange his own portrait. Theo sends Gauguin 300 francs from the sale of some ceramics.

October 21
Gauguin settles his debts and leaves Pont-Aven for Arles, arriving two days later.

October 22
Theo sells Dupuis another painting, *Bretonnes*, for 600 francs and sends Gauguin 500. Gauguin asks Schuffenecker to send some of his pots to Arles, including the "horned one". He sends his Pont-Aven paintings to Theo where they are widely admired. The banker Mirtil selects Gauguin's *Le Champ Derout* at the Boussod and Valadon gallery as repayment of the 300 franc loan to Gauguin in July, 1886.

November
Plans to return to Martinique to found a studio. Theo van Gogh exhibits some of Gauguin's recent paintings and ceramics in two small rooms on the mezzanine in the Boussod and Valadon gallery.

November 10, 12-13
Theo sells three paintings for a total of 1,200 francs. Gauguin sends Theo five more paintings. He is invited to exhibit with the Belgian group, Les XX, in Brussels. The shipment of paintings will be handled by Theo.

December 4
Theo sells *Fishermen in Brittany* to Mr. Clapisson for 400 francs. He also sells some ceramics. Gauguin sends Mette 200 francs.

December 17 or 18
Goes with Vincent to Montpellier to see once again the Bruyas Collection at the Fabre Museum.

December 23
In Arles, van Gogh threatens Gauguin during a sudden outburst and cuts off part of his own ear. Gauguin is arrested by the police and then released. Gauguin asks Theo to come and stay with his brother.

December 26
Gauguin returns to Paris with Theo van Gogh and stays with Schuffenecker.

December 28
Attends the execution of a criminal, Prado, in front of the Petite Roquette prison.

1889

January 5
Rents a studio at 16 rue du Saint-Gothard, Paris. He begins a series of prints intended for publication.

February
He exhibits 12 works with Les XX in Brussels.

Mid-February
Leaves Paris for Pont-Aven.

March 21
Theo sells *Shepherd and Shepherdess* to Anna Boch for 400 francs. Octave Maus, leader of Les XX, sends Gauguin 400 francs from the sale of the painting during the exhibition.

Mid-April
Returns to Paris to make arrangements for a group exhibition he and Schuffenecker, with whom he is staying, are organizing and to fire a statue.

June-October
Exhibition of Paintings by the Impressionist and Synthetist Group is held during the Exposition Universelle at the Café des Arts. Schuffenecker had convinced the proprietor, Mr. Volpini, to exhibit paintings in lieu of the costly mirror decorations he had originally intended. Gauguin exhibits 17 works. An album of ten lithographs by Gauguin is available on request (called *The Volpini Suite*).

Early June
Returns to Pont-Aven and rents a studio in Lezaven.

June 18
Theo sells *Negresses in Martinique* to Henri Lerolle.

End June
Moves into the Destais Auberge in Le Pouldu, then into Marie Henry's inn with Sérusier.

July 4 and 13
Gauguin's article on the Exposition Universelle appears in two parts in *Le Moderniste illustré* (4 and 13 July 1889):84-86, 90-91.

July and August
He works in Le Pouldu for a month with Jacob Meyer de Haan, then returns to Pont-Aven and moves into the Gloanec Inn where he lives on credit. Rents a room on the first floor of the Furnic farmhouse for use as a studio.

September
Sends a new shipment of paintings to Boussod and Valadon. With the exception of *La Belle Angèle*, Theo is disappointed in the new pictures.

September 16
Theo sells *Little Breton Girls Dancing* to Montandon for 500 francs.

September 21
Gauguin's article, "Qui trompe-t-on ici?" which attacks art criticism and government policies for purchasing works of art is published in *Le Moderniste illustré* (21 September 1889):170-71.

October 2
Returns to Le Pouldu with Meyer de Haan, who helps support him. They rent the attic of the Mauduit Villa in Les Grandes Sables for a studio. It is probably during this period that Gauguin recopies excerpts from Richard Wagner's writings (*Texte Wagner*). Sends more pictures to Theo in Paris. André Gide spends several days in Le Pouldu at the inn of Marie Henry. He writes about the visit in *Si le grain ne meurt* (Paris: Gallimard, 1924) II:193-96.

October 31-November 11
The Friends of Art Association in Copenhagen [Kunstforeningen] puts on an exhibition of French and Scandinavian impressionists. A major part consists of Gauguin's early works and paintings from his art collection which had been left in Denmark.

Early November
Sends Theo the wood relief *Be in Love and You Will be Happy*. Has himself recommended for a position in Tonkin.

Mid-November to Mid-December
Gauguin and Meyer de Haan decorate the dining room of Marie Henry's inn.

1890
January
Still planning on traveling to Tonkin, Gauguin suggests to Vincent that he open a studio (in Gauguin's name) in Antwerp with Meyer de Haan and later Theo van Gogh.

February 7
Returns to Paris with money sent to him by Schuffenecker and moves in with him at 12 (now 14) rue Durand-Claye. Teaches at the Vitti Academy, a studio in the Montparnasse district. Gives van Gogh one of his paintings in exchange for two pictures of sunflowers, replicas of those that had decorated Gauguin's room in Arles, and a replica of *La Verceuse*.

February
Boussod and Valadon exhibits a sculpture and several ceramics by Gauguin along with a selection of Pissarro's recent paintings.

March 20-April 27
The Salon des Indépendants includes works by van Gogh which are admired by Gauguin. He wants to exchange on of his own paintings for one depicting "Alpines" [sic].

April 30
Theo van Gogh buys Gauguin's still life *Oranges in a Vase* for Boussod and Valadon for 225 francs.

May
Gauguin hopes to sell 38 paintings, including 14 from Boussod and Valadon to the inventor Dr. Charlopin for 5,000 francs. Dreams of using the money to found a "studio of the tropics" in Madagascar with Bernard and Meyer de Haan.

Early June
Leaves for Le Pouldu with Meyer de Haan.

Around June 20
Spends five days in Pont-Aven with Meyer de Haan.

July
Theo van Gogh sells two paintings by Gauguin. Back in Le Pouldu, Gauguin, de Haan, and Charles Filiger are joined by Paul Emile Colin at the Hôtel de la Plage.

July 29
Vincent van Gogh dies at Auvers-sur-Oise.

Summer
Gauguin paints the ceiling of Marie Henry's inn. Sérusier and Filiger help decorate the rest of room.

August 19
Theo van Gogh sells *Oranges in a Vase* to Chausson for 300 francs.

September
Gauguin wants to return to Paris but remains in Le Pouldu because of his debts.

October 14
Theo van Gogh is committed to the clinic of Dr. Blanche because of mental illness.

October
Gauguin's projected sale to Dr. Charlopin falls through. Eugène Boch pays Gauguin 500 francs from the sale of five of his paintings to five collectors, including Octave Maus. Boch and Bernard had chosen the works from those at Boussod and Valadon. The remaining canvases and ceramics in the gallery are sent to Schuffenecker.

November 8
Returns to Paris and stays with Schuffenecker. Eventually quarrels with his host and moves to a furnished hotel at 35 rue Delambre. He uses Monfreid's studio at 55, rue du Château. Meets the writer Charles Morice for the first time at La Côte d'Or restaurant. Gauguin is a regular at the Gangloff brasserie, 6 rue de la Gaité, and at the gatherings of symbolist writers at the Café Voltaire.

Autumn
Monfreid introduces him to Juliette Huet, a young seamstress living at 15, rue Bourgeois, who becomes his model and mistress.
December 31
Gauguin's friend Julien Leclercq engages in a duel with Rodolphe Darzens. Gauguin and Jules Renard are the seconds.

Late December-Early January
Morice introduces Gauguin to Stéphane Mallarmé.

1891
Often visits the studio shared by Bonnard, Denis, Vuillard, and Legné-Poe at 28 rue Pigalle.

January
Jean Dolent suggests to the novelist and playwright Rachilde (Marguerite Eymery) that Gauguin do a drawing for her new drama, *Madame la mort*.

January 5
At the request of Morice, Mallarmé asks Octave Mirbeau to write an article publicizing Gauguin who intends to sell his works in order to finance his trip to Tahiti.

January 18 or 25
Gauguin and Morice visit Mirbeau at his Les Damps property.

January 25
Theo van Gogh dies in Utrecht, Holland.

February
Gauguin receives authorization to copy Manet's *Olympia* in the Musée du Luxembourg. Exhibits two wood reliefs, three ceramics, and an enameled statute in the exhibition of "Les XX" in Brussels.

February 2
Attends the symbolist banquet in honor of Jean Moréas. Mallarmé presides over the event. See "Echos divers et communications," *Mercure de France* (March 1891):189-91.

February 5
Attends dinner of the "Têtes de bois" with Jean Dolent as the master of ceremonies, at the Auberge des Adrets. See "Dîners artistiques," *Le Journal des Artistes* (11 February, 1891):191. Sends two drawings to Rachilde to illustrate her dramatic work *Madame la mort*.

February 16
Mirbeau publishes an article on Gauguin in *L'Echo de Paris* (16 February 1891):1. Published later as the preface to *Catalogue d'une vente de 30 tableaux de Paul Gauguin* (Paris: Grande Imprimerie, 1891):3-12. Reprinted in *Des artistes* (Paris: Flammarion, 1922):119-29.

February 20
Claude Roger-Marx's article on Gauguin appears in *Le Voltaire* (20 February 1891):1-2.

February 22
Exhibition of paintings to be sold at the Hôtel Drouot.

February 23
Sale of Gauguin's paintings at the Hôtel Drouot. The article by Mirbeau in *L'Echo de Paris* (16 February 1891):1 serves as the catalogue preface. Revenues from the sale total 9,635 francs for 30 paintings, one of which was bought back by Gauguin himself. (For a record of the sale see Paris, Orangerie 1949, exh. cat., pp. 95-96.) Jules Huret publishes "Paul Gauguin devant ses tableaux" in *L'Echo de Paris* (23 February 1891):2.

February 24
Announcement in *L'Echo de Paris* of special presentation at the Théâtre d'art to benefit Paul Verlaine and "the admirable symbolist painter, Paul Gauguin."

March
"Le symbolisme en peinture: Paul Gauguin" is published by Albert Aurier in *Mercure de France* 2:5 (March 1891):155-65.

March 7
Gauguin arrives in Copenhagen where he sees Mette and his children for the last time. Stays at the Dagmar Hotel, Halmtorvet 12.

March 14
Mirbeau purchases *The Red Christ* for 500 francs.

March 15
Gauguin writes to the Minister of Public Education and Fine Arts to request a government-sponsored artistic mission to Tahiti.

March 18
Gauguin's request is endorsed by Georges Clémenceau.

March 23
A banquet honoring Gauguin's departure is held at the Café Voltaire. Mallarmé presides over the 40-odd guests. See "Dîners artistiques," in *Le Journal des artistes* (29 March and 5 April, 1891):94.

March 26
Receives notice that the Ministry of Public Education and Fine Arts has agreed to grant funding of his mission to "study and ultimately paint the customs and landscapes of [Tahiti]."

March 28
At the request of the Director of Fine Arts, the Compagnie des Messageries Maritimes issues Gauguin a second-class ticket at a 30% discount from Marseilles to Nouméa, New Caledonia.

April 1
The Director of Fine Arts recommends Gauguin to the Under-Secretary of State for the Colonies. Leaves Marseilles on the *Océanian.*

April 7-11
Crosses the Suez Canal and docks in Aden.

April 16-17
Disembarks at Mahé in the Seychelles Islands.

April 17-May 12
Stops in the Australian cities of Adelaide, Melbourne, and Sydney.

May 6
Sale, Achille Arosa Collection, Hôtel Drouot, Paris.

May 12
Arrives in Nouméa, New Caledonia. Waits nine days before departing for Tahiti aboard the war transport *La Vire.*

May 15
Opening in Paris of the Salon of the Société Nationale des Beaux-Arts, which includes four objects by Gauguin. Mette visits Paris. She discusses with Schuffenecker her plans to sell Gauguin's paintings in Copenhagen.

May 21
At the Vaudeville Theater's benefit matinée for Gauguin and Paul Verlaine, several ceramics and paintings by Gauguin are exhibited in the foyer. The benefit raises only 100 francs.

June 9
Arrives in Pape'ete (see *Messager de Tahiti* 361, 12 June 1891). The islanders surprised by his long hair, nickname him *taata-vahine* (man-woman). Gauguin is greeted by Lieutenant P. Jénot, who helps find him a room.

Around June 11
Writes to Mette of his hopes for "some well-paid [portrait] commissions." Receives only known portrait commission in Tahiti for 200 francs.

June 16
Makes sketches at the funeral of King Pomare V, who had died in Pape'ete four days earlier.

June-July
Cuts hair and buys a white colonial suit. Mingles with colonists and at the officer's club where Jénot had introduced him. Carves stylized decorations into native wooden bowls. Paints portraits of neighbor's children.

August 13
Birth of a daughter, Germaine, to his former mistress Juliette Huet in Paris.

August-September
Tries unsuccessfully to learn Tahitian while staying with Gaston Pia, a drawing instructor, at Paea, 13 miles south of Pape'ete. Photographs of works by Gauguin shown at the Champ de Mars exhibition in Paris are published.

September-October
Accompanied by Titi, an Anglo-Tahitian woman from Pape'ete, he visits Mataiea, a small village 40 miles south of Pape'ete, and decides to rent a native house. Returns to Pape'ete for supplies and leaves Titi. Fined for public indecency when caught bathing in the nude in Mataiea.

November
Writes to Monfreid that he has yet to do a major work, but that he is accumulating "documents" (drawings) for paintings he will do when he returns to Paris. Sends for Titi, who leaves Mataiea after a short time. Probably meets Tehamana, who becomes his vahine and model.

December
Without Gauguin's consent, one of his Arles landscapes is included in the first exhibition of modern art at Le Barc de Bouteville gallery. By Christmas, Gauguin has painted 20 scenes of life in Tahiti.

1892

Early 1892
Gauguin begins hemorrhaging and is hospitalized in Pape'ete. Leaves against doctor's orders because of the expense. Recovered by March, writes to Monfreid that he was coughing blood, "a quarter liter per day."

January
Gallery owner and art publisher Maurice Joyant accepts five ceramics and ten paintings by Gauguin on consignment from Monfreid.

February
Gauguin's application for a vacant civil service post in the Marquesas Islands is refused by Governor Lacascade.

March 5
Death of 18-month-old son of Gauguin's friend, the pharmacist Suhas. Gauguin paints a deathbed portrait which the mother immediately rejects.

March 11
Writes to Monfreid that he is working more and more, primarily on studies or "documents" to be used later, if not by him then by others.

Mid-March
Instructs Monfreid to take *Vahine no te tiare*, his first Tahitian work sent to Paris, to the Goupil gallery. Hopes it will sell because it is "new and different."

March 22
In Copenhagen, Mette receives a group of pre-Tahitian paintings sent by Schuffenecker.

March 25
Gauguin announces to Paul Sérusier that he is penniless and needs to return to France. Has evidently read J.A. Moerenhout's *Voyage aux îles du Grand Océan* (1837), an account of the islander's beliefs, customs, language, and politics, lent to him by a lawyer and coconut magnate, Auguste Goupil. It will be the basis for Gauguin's own illustrated manuscript, *Ancien Culte Mahorie.*

April 1
Important article published in Paris designates Gauguin the "prime minister of the [symbolist] movement." See Albert Aurier, "Les symbolistes," *Revue encyclopédique* 2:32 (April 1892):474-86.

April
Emile Bernard organizes a van Gogh retrospective of 16 paintings at Le Barc de Boutteville gallery in Paris. Gauguin seeks local patronage for money to return to France. Writes to Mette of the possibility of painting a portrait of Captain Arnaud's wife for 2,000 francs and that he has finished a total of 32 canvases. Compiles an inventory of Tahitian paintings in his *Carnet de Tahiti* notebook.

June 1?
Desperate to obtain the funds necessary to return to France, Gauguin goes to Pape'ete to appeal to Governor Lacascade.

June 12
Still anxious about his financial situation, Gauguin writes to Henry Roujon, Director of Fine Arts in Paris, for permission to repatriate.

July
A painted fan by Gauguin is included in the second exhibition of modern art at Le Barc de Boutteville gallery.

August
Gauguin boasts in a letter to Mette that after 11 months, he has completed 44 "fairly important" paintings, worth 15,000 francs, and that he will go to the Marquesas if he can afford the 1,000 franc ticket. His vahine, Tehamana, is pregnant.

September
Gauguin's first Tahitian painting, *Vahine no te tiare* is exhibited at the Boussod and Valadon gallery in Paris.

October
Complains in a letter to Monfreid that he has run out of canvases and that he has not painted for a month. Instead, he is carving wood statuettes and cylinders, two of which he has managed to sell.

October 5
Death of the critic Albert Aurier, at 27, of typhoid fever. Gauguin does not learn of this until the following year.

Early November
Learns that his request for repatriation has been granted by the French government. Abandons plan to go to the Marquesas so he may return to France in January.

November-December
Third exhibition of modern art at Le Barc de Boutteville gallery includes an *Etude* by Gauguin.

Early December
Gauguin sends eight canvases back to Europe with Audoye, a friend of Jénot, for an exhibition to be held in Copenhagen in 1893.

December
Portier returns to Monfreid the seven unsold Gauguin canvases remaining in his gallery. Governor Lacascade refuses to provide passage for Gauguin to return to France, forcing him to reapply for repatriation. Begins to write *Cahier pour Aline*, a notebook

dedicated to his daughter. Finishes three canvases which he considers to be his best work.

1893
January 21
Mette receives 700 francs in Copenhagen for the sale of her husband's paintings.

February
Gauguin is furious to learn that Charles Morice sold several of his paintings in May to Joyant in Paris, without sending him the proceeds. Asks Mette to help obtain recommendations for a drawings inspector position in Paris.

March 13
Mette receives ten of her husband's paintings from Monfreid for the *Free Exhibition of Modern Art* [Frie Udstilling] in Copenhagen.

March 24
Joyant returns 26 works of art to Monfreid's studio in Paris.

March 26
Opening of the *Free Exhibition of Modern Art* in Copenhagen, with a room devoted to the art of Gauguin and van Gogh. Gauguin exhibits 50 paintings, ceramics, and sculptures from his impressionist, Brittany, and early Tahitian periods. The same day, the Kleis Gallery in Copenhagen opens its March exhibition of Nabi and Symbolist art with seven paintings and six ceramics by Gauguin.

Late March
Gauguin writes to Monfreid that he will have finished several sculptures and 60 canvases by the end of his stay in Tahiti. Returns to Pape'ete with Tehamana and rents a room in the suburb of Paofai near his friends Jénot, Drollet, and Suhas.

Early May?
Paints the four glass window panes above his doorway to prevent his landlady, Mme. Charbonnier, from spying on his work with native models.

May 25
Receives letter from the Minister of the Interior authorizing him to return "last class" to France.

June
Several works on exhibit at Le Barc de Boutteville gallery in Paris.

June 4
Leaves Tahiti for Nouméa on board the cruiser *Duchauffault* with 66 paintings and several sculptures.

June 21
The *Duchauffault* docks at Nouméa where Gauguin is forced to stay at a hotel for 25 days, spending almost all of the 650 francs he had brought with him.

July 16
Leaves on the *Armand Béhic* for Marseilles, paying a surcharge for second-class passage.

August 30
Arrives in Marseilles with four francs in his pocket.

August 31
Receives 250 francs from Paul Sérusier, wired to him by Monfreid. Takes a train to Paris.

September
Rents a room, 8 rue de la Grande Chaumière, from Mme. Caron, owner of a small restaurant and crémerie known as "Chez Charlotte." Alphonse Mucha offers Gauguin use of his studio in the same building.

September 3-4
Goes to Orléans for the funeral of his Uncle Isadore (Zizi).

September 19
Entreats Mette to come to Paris with their son Pola.

September 12-15
Returns to Orléans to attend the reading of his uncle's will. Inherits half the money from the estate; the other half goes to his sister.

Mid-September?
Convinces the dealer Paul Durand-Ruel to hold a one-man show of his work. Asks Mette to send the Tahitian paintings in her possession as soon as possible.

September-October
Stretches, retouches, and places in simple white frames 40 to 50 canvases for the Durand-Ruel exhibition. A Gauguin self-portrait and his portrait of Louis Roy are included in the *Portraits du prochain siècle* exhibition at Le Barc de Boutteville gallery in Paris.

Mid-October?
Begins *Noa Noa*, a book intended to "facilitate the understanding" of his Tahitian works.

October-November
The fifth exhibition of modern art at Le Barc de Boutteville gallery includes Gauguin's *Copy of Manet's Olympia*. Gauguin gives Morice two manuscripts, *Ancien Culte*

Mahorie and the first draft of *Noa Noa*. Gauguin agrees to pay for the invitations, posters, and catalogue for his upcoming exhibition, totaling 237.25 francs.

November 8?
Offers to donate his painting *Ia Orana Maria* to the Musée du Luxembourg but it is refused.

November 10
Public opening at Durand-Ruel's following a private viewing the previous day. The exhibition consists of 41 paintings from Tahiti, three from Brittany, one ceramic, and "tiis," or wood sculptures. Prices range from 1,000 to 4,000 francs (see priced catalogue, *Vente de tableaux de Paul Gauguin*, Metropolitan Museum of Art Library).

November 11
"Têtes de bois," a group of symbolist painters and writers, hold a dinner in Gauguin's honor. See *Journal des arts* (19 November 1893):370.

November 25
Gauguin's exhibition closes with only 11 paintings sold. Degas, who had been instrumental in the exhibition's organization, purchases *Hina Tefatou* and *Te Faaturma*. In appreciation, Gauguin gives him a carved cane from the exhibition. Press coverage during and after the show ranges from the enthusiastic remarks of Thadée Natanson in *La Revue blanche* 5:26 (December 1893):418-22, to the caustic criticism of Olivier Merson in *Le Monde illustré* (16 December 1893):395. Although the exhibition was a financial disappointment, Gauguin considers the publicity a positive sign: "The most important thing is that my exhibition has had a very great artistic success, has even provoked passion and jealousy. The press has treated me as it has never treated anybody, that is to say, rationally, with words of praise." Gauguin pasted several critical reviews into his *Cahier pour Aline*.

December
Ambroise Vollard opens a new gallery at 6 rue Laffitte with impressionist paintings, including early paintings by Gauguin. Gauguin writes to Mette that he cannot take time out from working on his book *Noa Noa* to go to Denmark.

December 14
Premiere of Ibsen's *An Enemy of the People* at the Théâtre de l'Oeuvre. Charles Morice proclaims Ibsen's drama and Gauguin's November exhibition as two of the most significant cultural events of the year (*Mercure de France* 5:48 (December 1893):289-300).

Late December
Gauguin receives first letter from his children in Denmark. Responds immediately.

1894

Early January?
Rents two large rooms on the top floor of 6 rue Vercingétorix and paints the walls chrome yellow. Covers the walls from floor to ceiling with his own paintings and others in his collection by Cézanne and van Gogh. Meets his neighbors, William Molard, a composer, and his wife, Ida Ericson, a sculptress, as well as their daughter Judith Molard. Takes in Annah la Javanaise, a 13-year-old native of Ceylon, whom he met through Vollard.

January
A flattering article on Gauguin, one much admired by the artist, is published by Achille Delaroche in the symbolist journal, *L'Ermitage* 5 (January 1894):36-39. Gauguin's article on van Gogh, "Natures mortes," is published in *Essais d'art libre* 4 (January 1894)273-75; reprinted in *Essais d'art libre* (Geneva: Slatkine, 1971).

January 11
Hosts his first in a series of Thursday receptions, for a coterie of painters, writers, and musicians, where he occasionally reads from *Noa Noa*. Occasionally attends Mallarmé's Tuesday night gatherings throughout the next year.

February 5
Asks Mette to convince her brother-in-law, Edvard Brandès, to retrieve the Cézanne painting formerly in his collection, *Zola's House at Médan*, by offering him several of his own paintings. During this month, Jénot visits from Tahiti.

February 15
Roger-Marx's illustrated review of the Durand-Ruel exhibition appears in *Revue encyclopédique* 4:7 (1 February 1894):33-34.

February 17
Attends the opening of the first exhibition of *La Libre esthétique* in Brussels which contains five of his own paintings. Writes to Brandès in the hopes of buying back all the Pissarros and Cézannes which had been sold to him by Mette. Brandès refuses.

February 18-22
Visits museums in Brussels, Antwerp, and Bruges with Julien Leclercq. Gauguin's review of the Brussels exhibition appears in *Essais d'art Libre* 5 (February-April 1894):30-32; reprinted in *Essais d'art libre* (Geneva: Slatkine, 1971).

February-March
Carves ten woodcuts from boxwood to illustrate *Noa Noa*. Prints them in his bedroom with some assistance from Flouquet, an engraver living on the same block.

March 2
Opening of the sixth exhibition of modern art at Le Barc de Boutteville gallery. Gauguin contributes *Nave Nave Moe* and an unidentified "nude study" entitled *Taurna*.

March 29
Writes to Theo van Gogh's widow, asking that she send him the paintings by Vincent that belong to him.

March-April?
Juliette Huret, Gauguin's former model and mistress, insults Annah and leaves Gauguin for the last time. Works with the artist-engraver Louis Roy on the printing of 25 to 30 impressions of the *Noa Noa* woodcuts.

April 7
Attends artist's dinner of the "Têtes de bois". See *Journal des artistes* (15 April 1894):543.

April 26
Attends opening of the Salon for the Société des Beaux-Arts with, among others, Morice, Leclercq, Annah, and Judith.

April 27
Death of Charles Laval, Gauguin's painting companion who had accompanied him to Panama and Martinique in 1887.

End April?
Gauguin leaves Paris for Brittany with Annah and her monkey. Julien Leclercq moves into Gauguin's apartment.

Early May
Lodges briefly with the painter Wladyslaw Slewinski and his wife in their villa at Le Pouldu. Goes to Pont-Aven where he stays at the Hôtel Ajoncs d'Or, now run by Marie Jeanne Gloanec. Learns that Marie Henry, the innkeeper at Le Pouldu and Meyer de Haan's mistress, refuses to return the paintings and sculptures that he left in her keeping during his trip to Tahiti. Gauguin's article, "Sous deux latitudes," is published in *Essais d'art libre* 5 (May 1894):75-80; reprinted in *Essais d'art libre* (Geneva: Slatkine, 1971).

May 25
A visit to Concarneau (near Le Pouldu) with the painters Armand Séguin, Emile Jourdan, and Roderick O'Conor and their girlfriends, ends disastrously when the group is assaulted by local sailors. Gauguin, whose leg is fractured above the ankle, is hospitalized briefly and incapacitated for the next two months. Throughout the summer, he takes morphine and alcohol for the pain and is unable to paint. Works on watercolor transfers and woodcuts.

June 2
Auction at the Hôtel Drouot of "Père" Tanguy's collection of paintings, organized by Octave Mirbeau to benefit Tanguy's widow. The six works included by Gauguin sell for very small sums (see priced catalogue, *Catalogue des tableaux...au profit de Mme. Vve. Tanguy*. Bibliothèque d'art et d'archéologie, Paris).

June 11
Publication of the first volume of *Portraits du prochain siècle* (see reprinted ed., Paris: L'Arche du livre, 1970). Gauguin's name is listed as "portraiteur" (author) for van Gogh. Gauguin's own "portrait" was to be undertaken by the writer Jean Dolent for the second volume, which never appeared (see *Essais d'art libre*, 5, 1894:71-72; reprinted in *Essai d'art libre* (Geneva: Slatkine, 1971).

End June
The writer Alfred Jarry stays with Gauguin at the Gloanec Inn in Pont-Aven. Jarry writes three poems dedicated to Gauguin and inspired by three of his Tahitian paintings from the November Durand-Ruel exhibition. Writes to Charles Morice's wife urging her to see that her husband finishes his section of the *Noa Noa* manuscript.

August-September
Annah leaves Brittany for Paris. Eventually pillages Gauguin's apartment, leaving only his paintings.

August 23
Travels 25 miles to Quimper to attend the trial of his assailants at Concarneau. They are fined only 600 francs.

September
Writes to Molard and Monfreid about his plans to return to the South Seas.

November 14
Loses his suit against Marie Henry and returns to Paris immediately.

November 18
Gauguin's letter to the editor of *Journal des artistes* about a fictitious visit to an artist's studio, presumably his own, is published. See "Lettre de Paul Gauguin," *Journal des artistes* 46 (18 November 1894):818.

November 22
Morice, Roger-Marx, Gustave Geffroy, and Arsène Alexandre organize a banquet in Gauguin's honor at the Café des Variétés.

December 2
First day of a week-long exhibition in Gauguin's studio of his woodcuts, watercolor transfers, wood sculptures, and Tahitian paintings.

December 7
At a "Têtes de bois" dinner at the Café Escoffier, announces his intention to return to Tahiti: "Paul Gauguin had to choose between the savages here and the ones over there: without a moment's hesitation, he will leave for Tahiti." See *Journal des artistes* (16 December 1894):862.

December 13
Dressed in his astrakhan hat and a long robe, Gauguin attends the premiere performance of August Strindberg's play *Father* at the Nouveau Théâtre.

Mid-Late December?
Works on the large stoneware sculpture *Oviri* in Ernest Chaplet's studio and the clay *Masque de Sauvage*.

1895
January 16
Offers Paul Durand-Ruel 35 canvases at 600 francs each.

January 31
Invites Strindberg to his Thursday evening gatherings and asks him to write a preface for the catalogue of his upcoming sale.

February
Strindberg, who has moved across the street from Mme. Caron's crémerie, joins the circle of writers, painters, and musicians that frequent Gauguin's studio at 6 rue Vercingétorix. Opening of Armand Séguin's exhibition at Le Barc de Boutteville gallery, with a catalogue preface by Gauguin, which is also published in the *Mercure de France*. His drawing of *Ia Orana Maria* is reproduced, together with prints by other artists in *L'Epreuve-Album d'art* (March 4 1895):62.

February 15
Gauguin sends Strindberg's letter of refusal and his open letter in response, to the publisher in *L'Eclair* as publicity for his upcoming sale. See "L'Actualité: Le misogyne Streinberg [sic] contre Monet," *L'Eclair* (15 February 1895):1.

February 16
Private showing at the Hôtel Drouot for Gauguin's auction.

February 17
Public opening for the February 18 sale.

February 18
The afternoon public auction at Drouot is poorly attended. Only nine paintings sell out of 47 works of art. Degas purchases two paintings, *Vahine no te vi*, *Copie de l'Olympia*, and six drawings. The sale realized 2,200 francs (*Journal des artistes*, 24 February 1895:940), but 830 francs of that represented works bought back by Gauguin under various names, leaving only 464.80 francs for Gauguin after expenses. He decides to postpone his trip to Tahiti and writes to Monfreid that he has caught "an unfortunate disease," probably syphillis.

March
Exhibition at Vollard's gallery of several landscapes and a ceramic from Gauguin's Brittany period.

April 23
Gauguin's open letter protesting the inauguration of a new kiln at Sèvres is published in *Le Soir* (23 April 1895):1.

April 25
Opening of the salon of the Société Nationale des Beaux-Arts. Gauguin submits his stoneware statute *Oviri*, allegedly rejected from the show at first but put back in when ceramist Chaplet threatened to withdraw his works in protest.

May 1
Gauguin's editorial protesting the selection of artists for the invitational *Exhibition of French Art* in Berlin is published in *Le Soir* (1 May 1895):2.

May 13
An interview with Gauguin by Eugène Tardieu is published in *L'Echo de Paris* (13 May 1895):2. It is satirized by Camille Mauclair, art critic for *Mercure de France* in 14:66 (June 1895):357-59.

Late June
Gauguin gives Morice his manuscript for *Ancien Culte Mahorie* and gives William Molard special power of attorney for the publication of *Noa Noa*. Leaves unsold paintings with the young artist Georges Chaudet and the dealer Lévy, who agree to act as his agents while he is away. (See *Les Arts*, 28 March 1947:1).

June 26
A final reception for Gauguin is held in his apartment by the Molards and the sculptor Francisco (Paco) Durrio.

June 28
Le Soir publishes Morice's article championing Gauguin's decision to return to Tahiti (see *Le Soir* 28 June 1895:2). The Molards and Paco Durrio accompany Gauguin to the station where he boards the train for Marseilles.

July 3
Leaves Marseilles aboard the steamer *L'Australien*.

August 9-29
Stops at Sydney, then Auckland, New Zealand, where he remains until the 29th. Studies and sketches the collections of Maori art in the newly opened wing of the Auckland Ethnological Museum.

September 9
Arrives in Pape'ete aboard the *Richmond*. Complains in a letter to Molard of the many changes that have occurred since his departure and announces his intention to leave for the Marquesas. Lodges in one of Mme. Charbonnier's unfurnished bungalows.

September 26
Sails to Huahine, a neighboring island, with several government officials. Meets two amateur photographers, Jules Agostini and Henry Lemasson.

September 28-29
Group sails to neighboring village of Bora Bora.

Early October
Returns to Pape'ete.

November
Having decided against going to the Marquesas, moves to Punaauia, three miles from Pape'ete on the west coast. Rents a small plot of land and enlists native help to build a traditional Tahitian hut of bamboo canes and palm leaves. Paints windows of his studio.

Early December
Sends for Tehamana, who, although now married, comes to Punaauia. She is frightened at the sight of Gauguin's diseased skin (eczema) and soon returns to her husband, Ma'ari.

1896
Early January?
Takes in Pahura, a 14-year-old girl from the district, as his *vahine* (woman).

March 23
Opening of an exhibition at the librarire de l'art indépendente, 11 rue de la Chaussé d'Antin, Paris, which includes several unidentified works by Gauguin. (See *La Chronique des arts et de la curiosité* March 1896:124).

Early April
Penniless, depressed, and suffering from severe leg pain for which he takes morphine, Gauguin writes to Morice that he is on "the verge of suicide."

April 10
Asks Schuffenecker to sell his two van Gogh paintings "of sunshine" to Vollard and send him the money. Is upset with Schuffenecker for having sent paintings to Mette but suspects that it is Mette who cajoled him. Sends Monfreid a drawing and description of *Te arii vahine* which he says is his best painting to date.

June
An issue of *Les Hommes d'aujourd'hui*, entitled "Paul Gauguin," is written by Morice and published with a cover illustration by Schuffenecker (see no. 9; published in abridged form in *Journal des artistes* 19 April 1896). Desperately poor and in need of hospitalization, Gauguin writes to Monfreid and the painter Maxime Maufra to propose that they start a subscription society of 15 art collectors to purchase his paintings.

July 6
Enters hospital at Pape'ete. The register of patients lists Paul Gauguin as "indigent." Sends several paintings with an officer to Monfreid in Paris.

July 14
Leaves hospital, weak but not in pain, without paying the 118.80 franc bill.

August
Gauguin is furious to learn that Schuffenecker has asked the Minister of Fine Arts to help him financially. In need of funds, he asks the lawyer Auguste Goupil to commission a painting. Paints portrait of Goupil's nine-year-old daughter, Vaïté. Gives drawing lessons to Vaïté and her sisters. Gauguin's health gradually improves.

October 11
Failed petition submitted to the Ministry of Fine Arts, Paris, by Judith Molard's future husband, to buy Gauguin's *Manao tupapau* for 1,050 francs, as well as paintings by van Gogh.

End October
Gauguin's contract at Goupil's is terminated. Shortly thereafter, he sculpts a deliberately crude statue of a woman to mock the antique copies that Goupil kept in his garden.

November 2
Monfreid receives the Paris shipment of paintings sent by Gauguin in July.

November 12
Schuffenecker lends Gauguin's painting *The Yellow Christ* to the exhibition of *L'Art mystique* at the Petit Théâtre Français in Paris, 10 Faubourg Poissonnière.

Late November
Gauguin exhibition opens at Galerie Vollard.

Early December?
Pahura, Gauguin's vahine, has a daughter who dies shortly after birth. Receives 200 francs from the Ministry of Fine Arts (requested by Schuffenecker) but disdains such "charity" and returns the money.

December 27
Arrival of Christmas boat in Pape'ete with a check for 1,200 francs from Chaudet who promises another 1,600 francs.

1897
January 7
Julien Leclerq asks Molard to send him some Tahitian paintings, in particular *Olympia noire*, for an exhibition of French modern art he is organizing in Stockholm. Gauguin

receives 1,200 francs from Georges Chaudet and tells Monfreid that he will enter the hospital since his poor health still prevents him from working.

Around Mid-January
The hospital classes him as indigent and he refuses to be admitted with soldiers and servants. Receives 1,035 francs from Chaudet. Writes in an optimistic letter to Paul Sérusier, "I want no other life, only this."

January 19
Aline, Gauguin's 20-year-old daughter, dies in Copenhagen of complications from pneumonia.

February 23
Opening of the fourth exhibition of *La Libre esthétique* in Brussels. Gauguin is represented by six paintings.

March 12
Sends eight paintings, including a self-portrait dedicated to Monfreid, to Vollard in Paris.

April
Learns of his daughter Aline's death in what he terms a short and brutal letter from his wife. Writes to Vollard that he cannot make drawings for commercial purposes and that he will not make more woodcuts or sculptures until those left in Paris have sold. Instead, sends the dealer "several poor attempts at making woodcuts."

End April
The French colonial who owns Gauguin's land dies and the heirs sell the property. Forced to move, Gauguin obtains a loan of 1,000 francs from the Caisse Agricole.

May 11
Purchases two parcels of land in Punaauia for 700 francs and begins to add a studio to a large wooden house.

May-June
Works on the house, adding more sculpted panels to those he has already made. His eczema flares up and he is unable to paint.

July 14
Writes to Monfreid that he is bedridden from his illness and has "lost all hope."

July-August
His health deteriorates. He suffers from an eye infection, complications from his ankle, eczema, and syphilis. His skin eruptions from the latter affliction are mistaken for a kind of leprosy by the natives and colonials. Financially destitute, he awaits word from Chaudet or Vollard. Begins writing long tract, *L'Eglise Catholique et les temps*

modernes, which becomes part of *Diverses choses* (see *Noa Noa*, Louvre mss. 273-310.)

Mid-August?
Writes bitter, reproachful letter to his wife that so upsets her that she ceases to correspond with him.

September 10
Morice finishes definitive version of *Noa Noa*, which he sends to Félix Fénéon, editor of *La Revue blanche*.

Around October 10-12
Suffers a series of heart attacks and writes Morice that he will probably not live to see *Noa Noa* published.

October 15
First part of *Noa Noa* is published in *La Revue blanche*. Receives 126 francs from Monfreid's mistress, Annette. Foregoes his intention to commit suicide.

November 1
Second part of *Noa Noa* is published in *La Revue blanche*.

November 10
Chaudet plans with Monfreid and Schuffenecker an exhibition of Gauguin's recent Tahitian works at the Galerie Vollard. Sends 700 francs to Gauguin.

December 1
Opening of the 15th exhibition of modern art at Le Barc de Boutteville gallery in Paris which includes a still life, *Fleurs* by Gauguin.

Early December
Gauguin suffers a heart attack and plans to enter the hospital. Begins work on the large "testament" painting *Where do we come from? What are we? Where are we going?*

December 30
The mail boat brings Morice's first installment of *Noa Noa*, but no money. Gauguin goes into the mountains and tries to commit suicide with arsenic. Returns to town the next morning exhausted, but alive. Describes the failed attempt in a letter to Monfreid with a drawing and description of *Where do we come from?*

1898
February 9
Leclercq organizes an exhibition of French modern art at the Swedish Academy of the Arts in Stockholm. In addition to two early paintings by Gauguin from Brittany and Martinique, Molard has sent *Manao tupapau*, *Arearea*, and *Te arii vahine*. *Manao tupapau* is considered indecent and is removed from the exhibition by the academy director.

End March
Feeling healthier, Gauguin applies for the post of Secretary Treasurer of the Caisse Agricole in Pape'ete. He is not hired and is forced to accept a job at six francs a day as a draftsman in the Public Works Department. Loses membership in the officers' prestigious military club.

March-April
In order to be nearer his job and a hospital, Gauguin moves with Pahura to Paofai, a western suburb of Pape'ete. Rents a small house from a friend of Tehamana. Gives up painting for the next five months. Receives a request from Julius Meier-Graefe, the German art historian and editor of the avant-garde journal *Pan*, for information for a serious study of his life and work.

May 15
Receives 300 francs from Monfreid for the sale of *No te aha oe riri* and the remaining 150 francs owed him by Maufra.

June 7
Degas and his friends, Henri and Ernest Rougart, each purchase paintings by Gauguin from Monfreid in Paris. Monfreid sends the proceeds, 650 francs, to Gauguin.

June 18
Sends Monfreid Lemasson's photograph of his enormous painting, *Where do we come from?*

Mid-July
Sends *Where do we come from?* and eight related paintings with an officer returning to France.

August
Pahura leaves him but returns occasionally to pilfer his belongings. When her friends break in and steal a ring, Gauguin unsuccessfully presses charges. The verdict is appealed to a higher court and dropped. Ambroise Millaud commissions a "comprehensible and recognizable" painting from Gauguin. The result, *The White Horse*, is refused and shipped by Millaud to Monfreid.

September
Gauguin's foot troubles him again and he enters the hospital for 23 days.

October 1
Gustave Kahn's article on art criticism is published in *Mercure de France* 28:196(October 1898):43-52. Gauguin excerpts passages and copies them into the notebook of essays and opinions that he compiles over the next four years and calls *Racontars de Rapin*.

November 11
Gauguin's July shipment of paintings arrives in Paris. Monfreid gives them to Chaudet to stretch and frame for the exhibition.

November 17-December 10
Exhibition at Galerie Vollard of *Where do we come from?* and eight other paintings related to one another in size and subject matter [reviews include Gustave Geffroy, *Le Journal* (20 November 1898):1-2; Thadée Natanson, *La Revue blanche* 17 (December 1898):544-46; and André Fontainas, *Mercure de France* 29 (January 1899):238]. Vollard buys all the paintings (through Monfreid) from the exhibition for 1,000 francs, a price which angers Gauguin when he learns of it in February.

December 12
Unable to paint or walk, Gauguin confesses to Monfreid that he has lost all his "moral reasons for living."

1899
January 12
Receives 1,000 francs from Monfreid. The amount includes 500 francs for the sale of *Nevermore*.

Late January
Quits his job at the Public Works Department and returns to Punaauia where he discovers Pahura is five months pregnant. Rats have destroyed the roof of his house. Besides rain damage, cockroaches have eaten several drawings and an unfinished painting.

Early March
Sends his etching of Stéphane Mallarmé to André Fontainas, art critic for the *Mercure de France*, with a long letter on color and music.

Early April
Writes to Monfreid that he is still unable to paint but is growing vegetables and flowers so that when he resumes paintings, he will have paradise at hand.

April 19
Pahura gives birth to a baby boy whom Gauguin names Emile.

May
Writes Monfreid that he has only 100 francs to live on.

June 10 or 11
Refuses Maurice Denis' invitation to participate in a reunion exhibition at the Café Volpini.

June 12
The first of Gauguin's numerous essays and editorials appears in the monthly satirical journal *Les Guêpes* ("The Wasps") in Pape'ete.

July
Complains to Monfreid that he has only a few colors and three meters of canvas with which to paint.

August
Begins his own four-page broadsheet *Le Sourire* ("The Smile"), which he writes, illustrates, edits and prints.

September
Having received a shipment of primed canvases from Monfreid, writes him that he wants to complete a dozen paintings in time for the 1900 *Exposition Universelle* in Paris in January.

September 19
Georges Chaudet dies. Gauguin learns of the young artist's death the next year when he attempts to recover his paintings and the money owed to him.

December
Writes to Monfreid that he has completed 15 woodcuts, which he will send to Paris.

1900
January
Exposition Universelle opens but Gauguin's paintings have not arrived in time. He is represented only by a *Brittany Landscape*. Outlines his terms for a contract with Vollard in a letter to the dealer.

Mid-January
Sends shipment of 475 prints, ten drawings, and ten paintings to Paris with instructions for their distribution, but uses the wrong address for Monfreid's studio, causing a nine-month delay.

Early February
Becomes editor-in-chief for *Les Guêpes* ("The Wasps"), increasingly devoted to attacking the Protestant party and Governor Gallet. Writes six of the seven articles in the February issue.

March
Agrees to contract with Ambroise Vollard (naming Monfreid as his private dealer and intermediary), whereby he sends the dealer 20 to 24 paintings a year at 200-250 francs each in return for a monthly salary of 300 francs.

March
Emmanuel Bibesco, a Rumanian prince who had purchased six paintings by Gauguin in January, writes Monfreid with an offer to replace Vollard as Gauguin's dealer. Gauguin eventually declines the offer.

April
Gauguin discontinues his own monthly, *Le Sourire*, to concentrate his energies on *Les Guêpes*. Enjoys period of relative security and begins to hold dinner parties for the friends he has made through his journalistic endeavors. Occasionally makes illustrated menus.

April-May?
At least one drawing (*Ia Orana Maria*) is exhibited with the "Esoteric Group" at the home of Paul Valéry on the rue de Londres in Paris.

Early May
Writes Monfreid that he is sick and that he has not been able to paint for six months.

May 16
Gauguin's son Clovis dies at the age of 21. Gauguin seems never to have learned of his death.

June or July
Receives shipment of canvas and tubes of color from Vollard.

September 23
Deliver speech in Pape'ete to the Catholic Party against Chinese emigration (excerpted in *Les Guêpes* no 21., 12 October 1900).

October
Complains constantly about money owed to him by Vollard, in spite of occasional payments from him, and the brother of Chaudet. Fears that his sculptures will be dispersed to those who "don't appreciate them" and wills them to Monfreid. Asks that *Oviri* be sent to Tahiti to be placed on his tomb.

December 18 or 19
Receives a check for 1,200 francs from Dr. Gustave Fayet, a director of the museum of Béziers. Enters the hospital.

December 27
At Gauguin's request, Monfreid, who has already retrieved several paintings from Vollard, informs the dealer that Gauguin wants all of his sculptures returned, and that none is for sale.

1901

January
Fragments of *Noa Noa* are published by Morice in the Belgian magazine, *L'Action humaine*.

February 2-March 23
In and out of the hospital three times. Receives payment of 600 francs, the full amount owed to him by Vollard. Begins making plans to move to the Marquesas where "life is simple and cheap."

April 12
Publishes excerpts from *Noa Noa* in *Les Guêpes*.

April-May
Four paintings and one ceramic, *Oviri* are included in Société des Beaux-Arts exhibition in Béziers, organized by Gustave Fayet.

May 1
First chapter of *Noa Noa* published in *La Plume* as an advertisement for the "Original Edition of the First Version" to be published in Louvain the same month. Makes final preparations for his move to the Marquesas.

July
Morice informs him that he has sent 100 copies of *Noa Noa*, which Gauguin never receives, and that there is a plan underway to purchase *Where do we come from?* by subscription for the Luxembourg Museum. The plan falls through and Vollard sells the painting to a doctor in Bordeaux for only 1,500 francs, much to Gauguin's displeasure.

August 7
Sells his land in Tahiti for 4,500 francs. Edits his last issue of *Les Guêpes*.

September 10
Leaves Tahiti for the Marquesas on the steamship *Croix du Sud*.

September 16
Arrives in Atuona on the island of Hivaoa in the Marquesas. Receives an enthusiastic welcome from the islanders who know his name from articles in *Les Guêpes*. One welcomer, Nyuyen Van Cam (called Ky Dong) becomes Gauguin's closest friend. Learns that the land he wants to buy is owned by Bishop Martin. Attends mass to demonstrate his piety.

September 27
The bishop sells Gauguin two plots of land for 650 francs in the center of the village, between the Catholic mission and the Protestant church. With the help of his neighbors, begins to construct his "House of Pleasure."

October
Van Gogh's letters are published in *Mercure de France*, where Gauguin's name is often mentioned.

October
Julien Leclercq dies, poor and forgotten. Gauguin learns of it in March, 1902.

November
Settles into his new home in Atuona with a cook (Kahui), two other servants, his dog, Pegau, and a cat. Sends Monfreid a sketch of his new residence.

November 18
Persuades a Marquesan chief to remove his 14-year-old daughter, Vaeoho Marie Rose, from the Catholic school to become his vahine.

1902
January-March
Works on his house and on completing the manuscript *L'Esprit moderne et le catholicisme*. Enters productive period of painting. Announces shipments for April of 12 paintings to Monfreid and 20 to Vollard.

Early March
Receives first shipment of mail in the Marquesas, with payments from Fayet and Vollard.

Early April
Incurs wrath of colonial authorities by refusing to pay taxes and encouraging the natives to do likewise.

June-July
Unable to walk without difficulty, Gauguin buys a horse and wagon.

Mid-August
Vaeoho, pregnant, returns to her parents to have her baby. She never returns to live with Gauguin. His attempts to dissuade native parents from sending their daughters to school are thwarted by the bishop's intervention. Gauguin retaliates by placing sculptures in caricature of the bishop and his nude chambermaid outside of his [Gauguin's] home.

August 25
Discouraged, Gauguin writes to Monfreid that he is seriously considering leaving the islands and settling in Spain.

September 14
Birth of daughter, Tahiatikaomata, to Vaeoho. Sends manuscript for *Racontars de Rapin* to Fontainas in the hopes of having it published in the *Mercure de France*, but the magazine's editor refuses the piece.

End October-November
His attack on Governor Petit is published in *L'Indépendant*, the monthly successor to *Les Guêpes*.

December
Gauguin's eczema flares up and he is unable to paint. Works almost exclusively on his diary-like book of recollections and observations, *Avant et après*.

1903
January 7-13
A cyclone hits the islands, striking Hivaoa but sparing Gauguin's house. Gives a section of his property to Tioka, his friend and neighbor whose house was destroyed by the storm.

February
Writes to Fontainas of his desire to have *Avant et après* published and asks Monfreid to sell paintings to ensure its publication. Unsuccessfully defends 29 natives accused of drunkenness. He is sent home on the first day of the trial for appearing in court wearing nothing but a dirty pareu.

March-May
Armand Séguin writes a series of three articles on Gauguin in *L'Occident* (see March 1903:158-67; April 1903:230-39; May 1903:298-305).

March 27
Charged with libel against the governor and given three days to prepare his defense.

March 31
Fined 500 francs and sentenced to three months in prison.

April 2
Appeals for a new trial in Pape'ete. Very sick, Gauguin writes to the Reverend Paul Vernier, "I am ill, I can no longer walk." Vernier finds the artist suffering from severely ulcerated sores on his legs.

Mid-April
Sends 14 canvases to Vollard, most from 1899, as well as a group of transfer drawings. Asks the dealer to send money owed him as he is desperately in need of funds for his upcoming trial.

End April
In Pape'ete, Gauguin is fined 500 francs and sentenced to one month in prison for slandering a M. Guicheray. Writes a scathing letter to the chief of police, M. Claverie.

May 8
Gauguin's health deteriorates. Tioka sends for the Reverend Vernier. Gauguin dies at 11:00 am after a large dose of morphine and possibly a heart attack.

May 9
Gauguin is buried at 2:00 pm in a Catholic cemetery above Atuona.

July 20
Public auction of Gauguin's miscellaneous household goods in Atuona.

August 23
Monfreid learns of Gauguin's death and circulates the news among friends and clients of the artist, claiming the death took place on May 9. Announcements appear in *l'Art moderne* (20 September: 324) and *Revue universelle* (15 October: 535).

September 2-3
Public auction of Gauguin's belongings, works of art, and other items from his home, in Pape'ete.

Primary Bibliography: Writings by Paul Gauguin

In addition to artistic works, Gauguin left writings which merit consideration as an expression of his creative personality. There is no complete edition of Gauguin's writings. The most important have been reproduced in facsimile editions noted below. His complete correspondence is in the process of being edited. Gauguin's writings are arranged chronologically in categories below.

I. Articles by Gauguin Published During His Lifetime (entries 1-13)
II. Articles by Gauguin Published After His Death (entries 14-16)
III. Letters
  A. Published Editors (entries 17-26)
  B. Letters in Periodicals and Books (entries 27-60)
  C. Unpublished Manuscript Letters and Writings (entries 61-68)
IV. Published Sketchbooks (entries 69-72)
V. Unpublished Sketchbooks (entries 73-76)
VI. Manuscripts (entries 77-92)
VII. Graphics Published During Gauguin's Lifetime (entries 93-100)
VIII. Photographs (entry 101)

I. Articles by Gauguin Published During His Lifetime

1. "Notes sur l'art à l'Exposition Universelle." Parts 1-2, *Le Moderniste illustré* (4 and 13 July 1889):84-86, 90-91.

2. "Qui trompe-t-on-ici?" *Le Moderniste illustré* (21 Sept. 1889):170-71.

3. "Natures mortes." *Essais d'art libre* 4 (Jan. 1894):273-275. Reprinted in *Essais d'art libre* (Geneva: Droz, 1971).

4. "Exposition de la Libre Esthétique." *Essais d'art libre* 5 (Feb.-April 1894):30-32. Reprinted in *Essais d'art libre* (Geneva: Droz, 1971).

5. "Sous deux latitudes." *Essais d'art libre* 5 (May 1894):75-80. Reprinted in *Essais d'art libre* (Geneva: Droz, 1971).

6. "Lettre de Paul Gauguin." *Journal des artistes* 46 (18 Nov. 1894):818.

7. "Armand Séguin." *Mercure de France* 13:62 (Feb. 1895):222-24. Preface to an exhibition of new works by Armand Séguin at the Galerie le Barc de Boutteville, Paris.

8. "Strindberg contre Monet." *L'Eclair* (16 Feb. 1895):2. See also "To breve" [Two letters], *Louisiana Revy* 23:1 (Oct. 1982):34-36. Text of two letters exchanged between August Strindberg and Gauguin, used as a foreword in the catalogue to an auction of Gauguin's works in 1895. Strindberg was asked to write the foreword but in his letter he states his lack of understanding and dislike for Gauguin's art. In his reply, Gauguin explains his artistic views and his relationship with Tahitian society.

9. "Une lettre de Paul Gauguin à propos de Sèvres et du dernier four." *Le Soir* (23 April 1895):1.

10. "Les peintres français à Berlin." *Le Soir* (1 May 1895):2.

11. *Les Guêpes*, 1899-1901. Gauguin's 24 articles from this newspaper (dated 12 June 1899 to 18 Aug. 1901) are reprinted in Bengt Danielsson and Patrick O'Reilly, *Gauguin journaliste à Tahiti et ses articles des 'Guêpes'* (Paris: Société des Océanistes, 1966).

12. *Le Sourire*, 1899-1900. Gauguin's newspaper which circulated in Pape'ete, Tahiti. *Le Sourire de Paul Gauguin*, Paris: G.-P. Maisonneuve et Cie et Max Besson Libraire, 1952, facsimile ed., 39p. Introduction and notes by L.J. Bouge. Does not include the issue of *Le Sourire* dated, probably incorrectly, "August 1891," in the Musée du Louvre, Département des Arts Graphiques, RF 28:844.
Review: *Burlington Magazine* 95 (March 1953):107.

13. *Oviri, Ecrits d'un sauvage*. Paris: Gallimard, 1974. Selections from Gauguin's letters, articles, and manuscripts, 1885-1903, expressing his opinions on life and art. English eds.: *The Writings of a Savage: Paul Gauguin*, trans. by Eleanore Levieux, introduction by Wayne Andersen (New York: Viking, 1978. Reprinted, New York: Paragon House, 1990). Spanish ed.: *Escritos de un salvaje: Paul Gauguin*, trans. by Margarita Latorre. Madrid: Editorial Debate, 1989.
Reviews: J. Hobhouse, *Art News* 77:6(Summer 1978):191; L. Dietrich, *Art Bulletin* 62:1(March 1980):172-74; V. Jirat-Waisutynski, *RACAR* 6(1979-10):142-45.

II. Articles by Gauguin Published After His Death

14. "Quatre pages inédites de Gauguin." Essay in *L'Art* (July-Sept. 1949).

15. "Huysmans et Redon." Essay in Jean Loize, "Un inédit de Gauguin." *Les Nouvelles littéraires* (7 May 1953):1.

16. "Notes sur Bernard." Essay in Henri Dorra, "Emile Bernard and Paul Gauguin." *Gazette des Beaux-Arts* 6th ser., 45 (April 1955):227-60.

III. Letters

A. Published Editions

Included here are published volumes that contain letters from Gauguin. One volume of the complete letters of Gauguin was published by Victor Merlhès in 1984; two additional volumes are forthcoming. Major sources for unpublished letters are the Danielsson Archives, Pape'ete, Tahiti; the Loize Archives, Papeari, Tahiti; the Archives of the Getty Center for the History of Art and the Humanities, Los Angeles; Musée du Louvre, Département des Arts Graphiques; and the National Archives, Paris.

17. Anne Joly-Segalen, ed. *Lettres de Paul Gauguin à Georges-Daniel de Monfreid* (Paris: 1918; rev. ed., Paris, 1950). Introductory essay by Victor Segalen. Revised edition includes the names and passages deleted from the original edition with new appendix and annotations.

18. *Lettres de Gauguin à Daniel de Monfreid.* With a tribute, "Hommage à Gauguin," by Victor Segalen. Paris: Crès, 1919; Plon, 1930. New ed. by Annie Joly-Segalen, Paris: Georges Falaize, 1950. German eds.: *Die Briefe an Georges-Daniel de Monfreid.* Trans. by Hans Jacob. Potsdam: G. Kiepenheuer, 1920; *Die Briefe Gauguins an Georges-Daniel de Monfreid.* Kuno Mittelstädt, ed. Berlin: Henschelverlag, 1961. 237 p. English eds.: *Letters to Daniel de Monfreid.* Trans. by Ruth Pielkovo, with a foreword by Frederick O'Brien. New York: Dodd, Mead & Co., 1922; London: William Heineman, 1923. See also André Lhôte, "Lettres de Paul Gauguin à Georges de Monfreid," *La Nouvelle revue française* 6 (1919):464-69; "The Wisdom of Paul Gauguin-Artist; From his Letters to Georges Daniel de Monfreid," *International Studio* 73 (1921):118-20; Henri Perruchot, "Les Archives Gauguin du Fonds Monfreid," *Jardin des arts* (Oct. 1961):14-17; and "Paul Gauguin i Citator fra Vreve og Boger," *Louisiana Revy* 23 (Oct. 1982):39-45.
Review: *International Studio* 73 (June 1921):118-22.

Names of contemporaries unfavorably referred to by Gauguin were disguised by false initials in the 1919 edition. In a new edition, established by A. Joly-Segalen, (Paris, 1950); the names are given in full. Extensive notes and new documents appear in the appendix, including letters by Georges-Daniel de Monfreid and Charles Morice to Gauguin, by Sérusier and Mette Gauguin to D. de Monfreid, etc. Condensed and inadequate English translation (New York: Dodd, Mead & Co., 1922).

19. *Lettres de Gauguin à André Fontainas*. Paris: Librairie de France, 1921. Introduction by André Fontainas.

20. Bernard, Emile. *Lettres de Vincent van Gogh, Paul Gauguin, Odilon Redon, Paul Cézanne, Elémir Bourges, Léon Bloy, Guillaume Apollinaire, Joris-Karl Huysmans, Henri de Groux à Emile Bernard*, Tonnerre, Paris: Edition de la Rénovation Esthétique, 1926. With short explanatory notes by Bernard; dates are not always correct. Revised edition: Brussels: Nouvelle Revue, 1942. M. A. Bernard-Fort, ed. New edition: *Lettres de Paul Gauguin à Emile Bernard, 1888-91*, Geneva: P. Cailler, 1954. Includes a long unpublished text by Bernard, "L'Aventure de ma vie." Dates are not always correct. For an additional letter to Bernard, see Vincent van Gogh, *Letters to Emile Bernard* (London-New York, 1938), no. 23, pp. 106-107.

21. *Paul Gauguin: Letters to Ambroise Vollard and André Fontainas*. John Rewald, ed. (San Francisco: Grabhorn Press, 1943; Engl. trans. by G. Mack). 88 p., 10 pl. Reprinted in Rewald, *Studies in Post-Impressionism* (New York: 1986; with one additional letter):168-213. Edition limited to 250 copies. Unpublished letters to art dealer Ambroise Vollard are translated and published here for the first time. Four letters to Fontainas appear for the first time in English. Also contains letters to Georges-Daniel de Monfreid. Woodcuts were selected from those executed during Gauguin's last sojourn in Tahiti. *Changement de résidence* is reproduced from an original Gauguin woodcut.
Reviews: *Gazette des Beaux-Arts* 6th ser., 25 (Feb. 1944):127-28; *College Art Journal* 5 (Nov. 1945):64-67.

22. *Lettres de Gauguin à sa femme et à ses amis*. Maurice Malingue, ed. (Paris: B. Grasset, 1946; rev. ed., Paris, 1949). Malingue's annotated working copy and a publication proposal for a new edition of Gauguin's letters (ca. 1973) are located at The Getty Center for the History of Art and the Humanities, Santa Monica, California. Revised edition includes expanded appendix; some incorrect datings remain. English trans. by Henry J. Stenning, *Paul Gauguin: Letters to His Wife and Friends* (London: Saturn Press, 1948; Cleveland: World Publishing Co., 1949). 255p. Contains 182 letters to the artist's wife, Schuffenecker, Bernard, Aurier, Mallarmé, Strindberg, Alexandre, Denis, Morice, Fontainas, and others. Also letters by Mette Gauguin to Schuffenecker. Unfortunately, these letters are carelessly transcribed and not always correctly dated. Very inaccurate English translation.

23. *Lettres de Gauguin, Gide, Huysmans, Jammes, Mallarmé, Verhaeren...à Odilon Redon*. Roseline Bacoue and Ari Redon, eds. (Paris: José Corti, 1960).

24. *Pisma, Noa Noa, Iz Knigi 'Prezhde i Potom'* [Selected Correspondance and Writings]. Leningrad: Izdvo 'Iskusstvo,' 1972. In Russian.

25. *Paul Gauguin: 45 Letters à Vincent, Théo, et Jo van Gogh*. Cooper, Douglas, ed. (Gravenhage and Lausanne: La Bibliothèque des Arts, 1983). 352 p. Facsimiles of 45 previously unpublished letters (1888-1894) by Gauguin, preserved in the Rijksmuseum Vincent van Gogh, Amsterdam. The annotated transcription of the text is preceded by a reproduction of the pertinent page of the letter. Redates letters from Malingue, 1946. The Getty Center for the History of Art and the Humanities in Santa Monica, California owns Cooper's research and working drafts.
Review: R. Dorn, *Oud Holland* 99:4(1985):324-28.

26. *Correspondance de Paul Gauguin: documents, témoignages. Tome Premier, 1873-1888*. Victor Merlhès, ed. (Paris: Fondation Singer-Polignac, 1984). 562 p., 80 illus., 15 col. Definitive edition of 194 letters from 1873 through 1888. 139 are fully transcribed from original documents. Includes more than 50 previously unpublished letters from Gauguin to Camille Pissarro, 1879-86, and important letters written to Gauguin. Other correspondents include his wife Mette, Paul Signac, van Gogh, and various business contracts. Two additional volumes are forthcoming.
Review: R. Pickvance, *Burlington Magazine* 127:987(June 1985):394-95.

B. Letters in Periodicals and Books

27. Letters to Camille Pissarro (1870s to early 1880s). Excerpts quoted in John Rewald, *History of Impressionism*. (New York: Museum of Modern Art, 1961).

28. Letters to Emile Schuffenecker (1880-1890s). Excerpts quoted in Arsène Alexandre, *Paul Gauguin, sa vie et le sens de son oeuvre* (Paris: Bernheim-Jeune, 1930). See also Claude Roger-Marx, "Lettres inédites de Vincent van Gogh et de Paul Gauguin." *Europe* 49 (15 Feb. 1939):163-74.

29. Letters to and from Emile Schuffenecker (April-May 1895). *Mercure de France* 13 (Jan. 1895):121-22.

30. Letters to Emile Schuffenecker (1896), "Deux lettres inédites de Gauguin à Schuffenecker aux Enchèves." *Arts* (19 November 1958):14.

31. Letter to Mette Gauguin (15 August 1886). Haavard Rostrup, "Gauguin et le Danemark." *Gazette des Beaux-Arts* 6 ser. 47 (Jan.-Apr. 1956):63-82.

32. Letters to Mette Gauguin (1888, etc.). Ursula F. Marks-Vandenbroucke, *Paul Gauguin* (Ph.D. thesis). Paris: Sorbonne, 1956.

33. Letters to Emile Bernard (1888). Facsimiles in Vincent van Gogh's *Letters to Emile Bernard* (London: Cresset, 1938). Edited and translated by D. Lord.

34. Letter to J. F. Willumsen (written at Pont-Aven, Autumn 1890). "Une lettre inédite de Gauguin." *Les Marges* 14 (May 1918):165-70. See also "Un inédit de Gauguin." *Bulletin de la Société des Etudes Océaniennes* (March 1919):43-45; S. Lövgren, *The Genesis of Modernism* (Stockholm: Almquist and Wiksell, 1959):163-65; and "Brev" [Letter], *Louisiana Revy* 23 (Oct. 1982):37-38.

In this letter to Willumsen in 1890, Gauguin expresses his attitude toward Denmark and its inhabitants. He comments on the materialistic struggle of Europe as opposed to life in the South Seas and dreams about the life he hopes to establish on Tahiti. He comments on his view of art in particular and specifically on Rembrandt and Velàsquez.

35. Letter to O. Maus (Autumn-Winter 1890-91). Madeleine-Octave Maus, *Trente années de lutte pour l'art (1884-1914)*. (Brussels: Oiseau Bleu, 1926):119.

36. Two letters to Rouvier (written in Paris, 15 March 1891 and in Tahiti, 12 June 1892), Minister of Fine Arts. Robert Rey, ed. *Onze menus de Gauguin* (Geneva: Cramer, 1950).

37. Two letters to Paul Sérusier (November 1891 and 25 March 1892 in Tahiti). Paul Sérusier, *ABC de la peinture: correspondance* (Paris: Henri Floury, 1950):52-55, 58-60.

38. Letter to the editor of *Le Journal des artistes* (Paris, 14 November 1894) in reply to: "Enquête sur l'évolution des industries d'art." *Journal des artistes*, (18 Nov. 1894). See also *Prisme des arts* 1 (14 March 1956).

39. Letters to a journalist, to Dr. M. Marx, and to Maxime Maufra (1894-96), reproduced in appendix of *Exposition du centenaire* (Paris: Orangerie des Tuilleries, 1949). Introduction by R. Huyghe, catalogue by J. Leymarie. Reprinted in *Gauguin et le groupe de Pont-Aven* (exh. cat. Quimper: Musée des Beaux-Arts, 1950). Introduction by R. Huyghe, catalogue by G. Martin-Méry.

40. Two letters to the editor of the newspaper *Le Soir*. Brussels (23 April and 1 May 1895).

41. Interview of Gauguin by Eugène Tardieu. *Echo de Paris* (13 May 1895):2.

42. Letter to Maurice Denis (1895) in Maurice Denis, *Journal* (Paris: La Colombe, 1957) I:113.

43. Letters to William Molard (1895-96) in Judith Gérard, "Présence de Gauguin." *L'Age nouveau* (Sept. 1949):49-52.

44. Letters to Alfred Valette (1895-96) in "Lettres à Alfred Valette." *Mercure de France* 298: 9, 999-1000, (1 July 1940-1 Dec. 1946):220-22.

45. Letters to officials in Tahiti and the Marquesas (1895-1903). Bengt Danielsson, *Gauguin in the South Seas* (London: Allen & Unwin, 1965).

46. Letter to Edgar Degas (1896). Marc Chadourne, "Toute la terre--Iles--Derniers paradis." *Conferencia* (15 March 1935):376-78.

47. Letter to Charles Morice, (ca. 1896-1897). Jean J. Ribault-Menetière, "Une lettre inédite de Paul Gauguin à Charles Morice." *L'Arts* (27 Sept. 1946):1. See also *L'Arts* (11 Jan. 1947).

48. Letter to Auguste Bauchy (1897). Jean J. Ribault-Menetière, "Une lettre inédite de Paul Gauguin." *L'Arts* (28 March 1947):8.

49. Letter to Ambroise Vollard (1897). John Rewald, "The Genius and the Dealer." *Art News* 58(May 1959):30-31, 62-65.

50. Letter to G. Fayet (Atuona, March 1902). *Arts décoratifs* (Nov. 1925):64; reprinted with Fayet's letter to Gauguin in *Lettres de Gauguin à Daniel de Monfreid*. 2nd ed. (Paris: Falaize, 1950):201-03.

51. Letter to Goupil (November 1902). "Lettre à Goupil." *Bulletin de la Société des Etudes Océaniennes* 9(Dec. 1955):498-99.

52. Letters to Carl Siger and to E. Petit, Governor of Tahiti, (Ivava, November 1902). "Paul Gauguin: *Mercure de France* (Aug. 1894):569-73.

53. "Une lettre inédite de Gauguin." *Bulletin de la Société des Etudes Océaniennes*. 113(1955):497-99.

54. Letter to a Judge in Pape'ete (Atuana, January 1903). Recopied by Gauguin in *Avant et après* (Paris, 1923):141-45.

55. Letter to M. Porlier, Captaine au cabotage (Atuana, 5 April 1903). Pierre Borel, "Les derniers jours et la mort mystérieuse de Gauguin." *Pro Arte Nova et Antiqua* (Sept. 1942):13-16.

56. Hewlett, Maurice. "Biography and Memoirs: Letters of Paul Gauguin," trans. by Ruth Pielkovo. *The London Mercury* 8 (1923):219-221.

57. Ribault-Menetière, Jean. "Sur deux lettres de Gauguin." *L'Arts* 11 (Jan. 1946).

58. Cooper, Douglas. "Letter: Paul Gauguin." *Burlington Magazine* 98 (Aug. 1956):283-84.

59. Letters to Léonce Brault. "Une correspondance inédite de Paul Gauguin." *Bulletin de la Société des Etudes Océaniennes* (Dec. 1960-March 1961):213-37.

60. Letter to Carey in Paris, Hôtel Drouot. *Sept lettres autographes* (2 April 1963).

See *Oeuvres écrites de Gauguin et van Gogh* (exh. cat., Institut Néerlandais, Paris, 1975) for additional letters and writings.

C. Unpublished Manuscript Letters and Writings

61. Letters and Writings, 1879-1903. 24 items. Collection consists of letters to Camille Pissarro, Emile Schuffenecker, Emile Bernard and to several other correspondents; letters of Mette Gauguin to Pissarro and André Level; and essays and notes written by Gauguin on social, religious and aesthetic issues. Located at The Getty Center for the History of Art and the Humanities, Santa Monica, California. Organization: I. Letters (folders 1-3); II. Essays and notes (folders 4-5). *Letters*: This group of 16 letters written over a 20-year period treats a wide variety of topics ranging from practicial and legal matters to issues in contemporary art. Of special interest are letters to Camille Pissarro concerning potential exhibitions and the promotion of Pissarro's work (1879-85); to Emile Schuffenecker discussing the sale of paintings and financial concerns (1885-90); to Emile Bernard describing in detail his plans for an "atelier du Tropique" and commenting on "primitive" life; to Henri Bataille, director of the *Journal des Artistes*, musing on the "style nouveau" in painting and the decorative arts (1894); and to the French lawyer and newspaper editor Léonce Brault protesting racial injustice in Tahiti. Other correspondents include Ambroise Vollard, George Daniel de Monfreid and William Molard. Collection also includes letters by Gauguin's wife Mette to Camille Pissarro recommending the painter Mogens Ballin and to the art dealer André Level (1914). Also includes a brief letter from Gustave Geffroy to Gauguin.

62. *Essays and Notes*: Consists of several sheets of an essay on social issues including the education of children, marriage and prostitution; a draft of a letter proposing a book on art and commenting on the "madness" of van Gogh; and a fragment of a letter describing technical aspects of his work and characterizing contemporary painting in Paris. Also includes 7 pages of notes containing musings on spiritual matters--the saints, the writings of Paul, the Bible and the parables of Jesus. With two pencil sketches and a note from Louis Vauxcelles verifying the authenticity of the manuscript (1932). Includes a previously unpublished letter from Gauguin to the Danish painter, J. F. Willumsen, as printed in *Les Marges* (*L'Année littéraire*).

63. Letters to Mette Gad Gauguin, Murer, etc. Paris: Bibliothèque d'Art et d'Archéologie, Fondation Jacques Doucet.

64. Carbon copies of letters to MM. Dillies et Cie. (Copenhagen, 1884-1885), Paris: Bibliothèque Nationale, National Archives of France, 14276.

65. Letters to Theo and Vincent van Gogh (1888-90), Collection of Laren Vincent W. van Gogh; now in Vincent van Gogh Museum,

Amsterdam. Quoted in Ziva Amishai-Maisels' *Gauguin's Religious Themes* (New York: Garland, 1985).

66. Letters to Emile Schuffenecker (1889-91). Paris: Louvre, Cabinet des Dessins. Album Schuffenecker (ca. 1889-90).

67. Letters to Octave Mirbeau (1891), Paris: Bibliothèque Nationale, National Archives of France, 14687, folios 76-83.

68. Letter to Armand Séguin. 1897. Paris: Bibliothèque Nationale, National Archives of France, 14827, folios 8-9.

IV. Published Sketchbooks

69. *Le Carnet de Paul Gauguin*. Paris: Quatre Chemins, 1952, René Huyghe, ed. 2 vol. Facsimile of a sketchbook from Brittany and Arles 1888, The Israel Museum, Jerusalem.

70. *Carnet de Tahiti*. Paris: Quatre Chemins, 1954, Bernard Dorival, ed. Facsimile of a sketchbook from Gauguin's first trip to Tahiti, 1891-93, now disassembled and dispersed.

71. *Paul Gauguin, A Sketchbook Carnet de Croquis*. Paris and New York: Hammer Galleries, 1962, Raymond Cogniat, John Rewald, eds. 2 vol: 1, English ed.; vol. 2, French ed. Sketchbook, c. 1884-1888, Armand Hammer Collection. Includes Gauguin's essay from 1885, "Notes synthétiques," first published as "Notes synthétiques de Paul Gauguin," *Vers prose* 22 (July 1910):51-55, with an introduction by Henri Mahaut. Reprinted in John Rewald, *Gauguin* (Paris, London, New York: Hyperion Press, 1938).

72. *French Drawings: Nineteenth Century*, ed. Per Bjurström, ed. (Stockholm: 1986). Includes reproductions of each page from a Gauguin sketchbook dating from 1877-1887, National Museum, Stockholm.

V. Unpublished Sketchbooks

73. *Album Briant*. Undated sketchbook (ca. 1885-1887), with one Tahitian sketch. Musée du Louvre, Paris, Département des Arts Graphiques, RF30273.

74. *Album Walter*. Undated sketchbook (ca. 1888-1889). Musée du Louvre, Paris, Département des Arts Graphiques, RF30569.

75. *Album RF 29877*. Undated sketchbook with drawings from 1882 to the Tahitian period. Musée du Louvre, Paris, Département des Arts Graphiques.

76. *Schuffenecker Album*. Undated sketchbook with photographs, drawings, etc. collected by Emile Schuffenecker. Musée du Louvre, Paris, Cabinet des Dessins.

VI. Manuscripts

77. *Le Texte Wagner* manuscript, 1889. Bibliothèque Nationale Département des Manuscrits, National Archives of France 14903, folios 43-46. Later recopied into *Diverses choses* manuscript (1896-97). See Henri Dorra, "Le 'Texte Wagner' de Gauguin," *Bulletin de la Société de l'historie de l'art français* (1984):281-88.

78. *Manuscrit tiré du livre des métiers de Vehbi-Zumbul Zadi*. Winter 1885-1886. 4 pages of notes. Bibliothèque Nationale, Département des Manuscrits, National Archives of France, 14903, folios 43-46. Later recopied into Gauguin's *Diverses choses* manuscript (1896-97) and *Avant et après* manuscript (1903).

79. *Cahier pour Aline* manuscript, begun ca. December 1892. Bibliothèque d'art et d'archéologie, Paris, Fondation Jacques Doucet. Includes Gauguin's essay, "Genèse d'un tableau." *Cahier pour Aline*, Suzanne Damiron, ed., facsimile edition with commentary by the editor (Paris: Société des amis de la Bibliothèque d'art et d'archéologie de l'Université de Paris, 1963). 2 vol. *A ma fille Aline, ce cahier est dédié: notes éparses, sans suite comme les Rêves, comme la vie toute fait de morceaux: journal de jeune fille*. Victor Merlhès, ed. Preface by Denise Gazier. Bordeaux: William Blake and Co., Société des amis de la Bibliothèque d'art et d'archéologie, 1984. Facsimile ed., illus.

80. *Ancien Culte Mahorie* manuscript, probably begun late 1893. Musée du Louvre, Département des Arts Graphiques, Cabinet de dessins, RF 10755. *Ancien Culte Mahorie*, René Huyghe, ed., facsimile edition. (Paris: La Palme, 1951). 98 p., 37 col. illus. Includes an essay by the editor, "Présentation de l'ancien culte mahorie - la clef de Noa Noa."

"Noa Noa" - Three Versions

81. *Noa Noa* Getty manuscript. Probably begun in October 1893, in Paris. The Getty Center for the History of Art and the Humanities, Santa Monica, California. 38 p. First draft of "Noa Noa." Unillustrated manuscript in Gauguin's hand (holograph in ink), before the collaboration of Charles Morice.

82. *Noa Noa*. Berthe Sagot-Le Garrec, ed. Paris: Sagot-le-Garrec, 1954. First facsimile ed. of the Getty manuscript. Contains the first printing of a

letter from Charles Morice, Gauguin's friend and collaborator, to Edmund Sagot, the print dealer and publisher who owned the original manuscript. *Paul Gauguin: Noa Noa, Voyage to Tahiti*, Jean Loize, ed. (Oxford: B. Cassirer, 1961). First English trans. (by Jonathan Griffin) of the Getty manuscript; includes an essay by Jean Loize, "The Real Noa Noa and the Illustrated Copy."

83. *Noa Noa par Gauguin*. Jean Loize, ed. (Paris: Andre Balland, 1966). Transcription of Getty manuscript. Includes extensive notes and essay by the editor.

84. *Noa Noa, Gauguin's Tahiti*. Nicholas Wadley, ed. (London: Phaidon; Salem, N.H.: Salem House, 1985). 160 p., 130 illus., 40 col. English trans. of the Getty manuscript (by Jonathan Griffin), with substantial annotations by the editor.

85. *Noa Noa*. Gilles Artur, Jean-Pierre Fourcade, Jean-Pierre Zingg, eds. (Papeari, Tahiti and New York: Editions de l'Association des Amis du Musée Gauguin à Tahiti et la Gauguin and Oceania Foundation à New York, 1987). Enlarged facsimile ed. of the Getty manuscript, with illustrations from the Louvre manuscript.

86. *Noa Noa*. Pierre Petit, ed. (Paris, 1988). Transcription of the Getty manuscript.

87. "Noa Noa," *Louvre manuscript* in collaboration with Charles Morice, 1893-1897. Musée du Louvre, Département des Arts Graphiques. In Gauguin's hand with abundant illustrations. "Noa Noa," excerpts in *Les Marges*, no. 21 (May 1910), 169-174. Other eds: *Noa Noa, Voyage de Tahiti* (Paris: Crès, 1924), transcription of Louvre manuscript. *Noa Noa* (Berlin: Marees, 1926). *Noa Noa, Voyage à Tahiti* (Stockholm: 1947). *Noa Noa e il primo viaggio a Tahiti di Gauguin* (Milan: Rizzoli, 1974).

88. *Noa Noa*. La Plume edition, 1901, in collaboration with Charles Morice. The unillustrated manuscript, in Charles Morice's hand and dated 1897, is in the Morice Archives, Paley Library, Temple University, Philadelphia. "Noa Noa," excerpts published in *La Revue blanche* 14:105 (15 October 1897):81-103; 106 (1 November 1897):166-190 (first publication of "Noa Noa" in any form). "Noa Noa" excerpts also published in *L'Action humaine* (January 1901);and in *La Plume* (1 May 1901):294-300. *Noa Noa* (Paris, 1901), definitive "La Plume" edition published as a book. "Noa Noa" excerpts published in *Kunst and Künstler* 6 (1907):78-81, 125-27, 160-64. *Noa Noa* (New York: N. L. Brown, 1919). Engl. trans. by O. F. Theis.

89. *Diverses choses*. 1896-1897; manuscript that follows *Noa Noa* in the Musée du Louvre, Paris. Département des Arts Graphiques. Unpublished

except for excerpts in Marcel Guérin, *L'Oeuvre gravé de Gauguin*. (Paris: Henri Floury, 1927). 2 vol.

90. *Racontars de Rapin*. Manuscript, compiled 1898-1902. Josefowitz Collection. *Racontars de Rapin* (Paris: Falaize, 1951). Transcription of original manuscript.

91. *L'Esprit moderne et le catholicisme*. 1902; manuscript. St. Louis Art Museum. First draft, from 1896-1897, included *Diverses choses* as *L'Eglise catholique et les temps modernes*. Excerpts and illustrations from the 1902 manuscript published by H. Stewart Leonard, "An Unpublished Manuscript by Paul Gauguin," *Bulletin of the St. Louis Art Museum* 34:3 (Summer 1949):41-48. English trans., 1927, with annotations and notes by Frank Lester Pleadwell on file at the St. Louis Art Museum and at the Art Institute of Chicago. See also Philippe Verdier, "Un manuscript de Gauguin: L'esprit moderne et le Catholicisme," *Wallraf-Richartz-Jahrbuch* 46 (1985):273-328.

92. *Avant et après*. 1903; manuscript written in the Marquesas Islands. Private collection. Facsimile editions: Leipzig: Kurt Wolf Verlag, 1918; Paris: Druet, 1919; Paris: Crès, 1923, transcription; Copenhagen: Scripta, 1950; Paris: Paul Carit Andersen, 1951. Taravoa: Editions Avant et Après, 1989. Condensed English ed.: *The Intimate Journals of Paul Gauguin*. Trans. by Van Wyck Brooks. Preface by Emil Gauguin. New York: Crown, 1936; Bloomington, Indiana: Indiana University Press-Midland Books, 1956. Another ed.: London: KPI Limited, 1985.

VII. Graphics Published During Gauguin's Lifetime

93. "Soyez symboliste." *La Plume* 2 (1 Jan. 1891):11.

94. "Mme la Mort." *La Plume* 2 (1 Sept. 1891):292, and in no. 145.

95. Rachilde [Marguerite Eymery Vallette]. *Théâtre, avec un dessin inédit de Paul Gauguin et une préface de l'auteur* (Paris: Savia, 1891).

96. "Mme la Mort." *Théâtre d'art* 3 (ca. 1891). Bibliothèque Arsenal, Collection Rondel.

97. "La Madeleine." *L'Ymagier* (ca. April-May, 1895), following p. 141.

98. "Manao Tupapau." *L'Estampe originale* (April-June 1894), no. 53.

99. "Hommage à Puvis." *Mercure de France* (Feb. 1895).

100. "Ia Orana Maria." *L'Epreuve* (March 1895).

VIII. Photographs

101. Vizzavona-Druet Collection. "L'Oeuvre de Paul Gauguin." Collection of photographs. Paris, Bibliothèque Nationale, DC 397b.

Contemporary Accounts and Critiques of Gauguin's Life and Work Published Through 1906

102. ADAM, PAUL. "Peintres Impressionnistes." *Revue contemporaine* 4 (April-May 1886):541-51.

103. ADAM, PAUL. "A propos de la Sixième exposition." *Revue contemporaine* (1888).

104. ANTOINE, JULES. "Glanures--au sujet de la peinture nouvelle." *L'Art moderne* (10 March 1889):77-79.

105. ANTOINE, JULES. "Impressionnistes et synthétistes." *Art et critique* 1 (9 Nov. 1889):369-71.

106. ANTOINE, JULES. "Le Carnaval d'un ci-devant." *L'Art moderne* (15 Feb. 1891):55-56.

107. ANTOINE, JULES. "Aux XX." *L'Art moderne* (19 April 1891):128-29.

108. ANTOINE, JULES. "Petite chronique." *L'Art moderne* (8 March 1891):81.

109. ANTOINE, JULES. "Le Salon de la libre esthétique." *L'Art moderne* (8 April 1894):109; see also 18 Feb. 1894:55; 7 March 1897;73-75.

110. AURIER, G.-ALBERT (pseud. Luc le Flaneur). "Enquête de choses d'art." *Le Moderniste illustré* (13 April 1889):14

111. AURIER, G.-ALBERT. "Le symbolisme en peinture--Paul Gauguin." *Mercure de France* 2:15 (March 1891):155-165.

112. AURIER, G.-ALBERT. "Concurrence." *Le Moderniste illustré* 1 (27 June 1889):2.

113. AURIER, G.-ALBERT. "Monticelli-Paul Gauguin." *Revue indépendante* 18 (March 1891):419-22.

114. AURIER, G.-ALBERT. "Paul Gauguin." *Théâtre d'art* (15 May 1891):3.

115. AURIER, G.-ALBERT. "Paul Gauguin." *La Plume* 2 (1 Sept. 1891):300.

116. AURIER, G.-ALBERT. "Les symbolistes." *Revue encyclopédique* 2:32 (1892):474-86.

117. AURIER, G.-ALBERT. *Oeuvres posthumes*. Paris: Mercure de France, 1893.

118. BARRUCAND, VICTOR. "Vers l'Océanie." *La Revue anarchiste* 1 (1-15 Dec. 1893):108-10.

119. BAUER, HENRI. "La ville et le théâtre: le bénéfice de Verlaine." *L'Echo de Paris* (23 May 1891).

120. BERNARD, EMILE. "Lettre ouverte à M. Camille Mauclair." *Mercure de France* 14:66 (June 1895):332-39.

121. BERNARD, EMILE. "Notes sur l'école dite de 'Pont-Aven'." *Mercure de France* 48:168 (Dec. 1903):675-82.

122. BIDOU, HENRI. "Paul Gauguin." *Journal des débats* (11 Sept. 1903):499.

123. CASTETS, H. "Gauguin." *Revue universelle* 3:96 (15 Oct. 1903):535-36.

124. CHRISTOPHE, JULES. *La Plume* 107 (14 Oct. 1893):416.

125. COLLEVILLE, VICOMTE DE. "Livre esthétique, Bruxelles." *La Plume* 9 (15 March 1897):189.

126. *Courrier de la Cornouaille* 3 (2 June 1894):3. News item on the fight at Concarneau, France.

127. DAURELLE, J. "Chez les jeunes peintres." *L'Echo de Paris* (28 Dec. 1891).

128. DAYOT, ARMAND. "La vie artistique: Paul Gauguin." *Figaro illustré* 12:46 (Jan. 1894):110-11.

129. DEGAS, EDGAR. "Letters, 1880-1898." 15 items including one letter on an exhibition by Gauguin. Located at The Getty Center for the History of Art and the Humanities, Santa Monica, California.

130. DELAROCHE, ACHILLE. "Les annales du symbolisme." *La Plume* 3:41 (1 Jan. 1891)14-20.

131. DELAROCHE, ACHILLE. "D'un point de vue esthétique: A propos du peintre Paul Gauguin." *L'Ermitage* 5 (Jan. 1894):35-39.

132. DENIS, MAURICE. "Définition du néo-traditionnisme." *Art et critique* (23 and 30 Aug. 1890). Reprinted in *Théories, 1890-1910, du symbolisme et de Gauguin vers un nouvel ordre classique* (Paris: Bibliothèque de l'Occident, 1912; other eds. 1913, 1920, 1964).

133. DOLENT, JEAN. "Chronique: Paul Gauguin." *Journal des artistes* (22 Feb. 1891):49.

134. DUJARDIN, JULES. *La Réforme* (26 Feb. 1897).

135. FABRICE, DELPHI. *Peintres de la Bretagne*. Paris: Editions de l'Art et ses Amateurs, 1898. 136 p. See pp. 75-80 for information on Gauguin.

136. FAGUS, FELICIEN. "Paul Gauguin et Charles Morice: 'Noa-Noa' (La Plume)." *La Revue blanche* 25(1901):637-38.

137. FENEON, FELIX. "VIIIe exposition impressionniste." *La vogue* (13-20 June 1886). Reworked for the pamphlet *Les impressionnistes en 1886*; both reprinted in *Oeuvres plus que complètes*, Joan U. Halperin, ed. Geneva: Droz, 1970 1:27-38.

138. FENEON, FELIX. "Calendrier." *Revue indépendante* 6 (Jan., Feb., March 1888):169-70, 307-08, 487-90; and (May 1888):382-83. Reprinted in *Oeuvres plus que complètes* 1:94-105.

139. FENEON, FELIX. "Autre groups impressionniste." *La Cravache Parisienne* (6 July 1889): reprinted in *Oeuvres plus que complètes* 1:175-79.

140. FENEON, FELIX. "Certains." *Art et critique* (14 Dec. 1889); reprinted in *Oeuvres plus que complètes* 1:171-73.

141. FENEON, FELIX. "Gauguin et les peintres de Pont-Aven." *Le chat noir* (23 May 1891); reprinted in *Oeuvres plus que complètes* 1:192-93.

142. FENEON, FELIX. "Expositions." *La revue anarchiste* (15 Nov. 1893); reprinted in *Oeuvres plus que complètes* 2:930.

143. FONTAINAS, ANDRE. "Art." *Mercure de France* 20 (Dec. 1896):613-14.

144. FONTAINAS, ANDRE. "Vincent van Gogh, Paul Gauguin, memento-art." *Mercure de France* 21 (Jan. 1897):221-22.

145. FONTAINAS, ANDRE. "Art moderne." *Mercure de France* 25, 29, 33, 34 (Jan. 1898, Jan. 1899, Feb. 1900, May 1900):300-07, 235-42, 522-27, 540-47.

146. FOUQUIER, HENRY. "L'avenir symboliste." *Le Figaro* (24 May 1891):1.

147. GARNIER, EDOUARD. "La céramique et la verrierie modernes." *Gazette des Beaux-Arts*, 13 (Jan. 1885):26-38.

148. G., M. "Les mois artistique: le salon d'Automne." *L'Art et les artistes* 2(1906):296-308.

149. "Gauguin et l'école de Pont-Aven." *Essais d'art libre* 4-5 (Nov. 1893):164-68.

150. GEFFROY, GUSTAVE. "Paul Gauguin." *La Justice* (22 Feb. 1891; 12 Nov. 1893):1.

151. GEFFROY, GUSTAVE. "Paul Gauguin." *Le Journal* (12 Nov. 1893).

152. GEFFROY, GUSTAVE. "L'art d'aujourd'hui: Falguière-Chauval-Gauguin." *Le Journal* (20 Nov. 1898):1-2.

153. GUERNIN, JOSEPH. "Les arts." *L'Ermitage* 28(Nov. 1903):232-34.

154. GUILLOT, FRANÇOIS, *Souvenirs d'un colonial en Océanie (1888-1891)*. Annecy: 1895.
a. 2nd ed.: Annecy: Dépollier, 1935.

155. HAVARD, HENRI. "Exposition des artistes indépendants." *Le siècle* (2 March 1882).

156. HENNEQUIN, EMILE. "Beaux-arts: les expositions des arts libéraux et des artistes indépendants." *La Revue littéraire et artistique* (1882):154-55.

157. HEPP, ALEXANDRE. "Impressionnisme." *Le Voltaire* (3 March 1882).

158. HIRSCH, CHARLES-HENRI. "Notes sur l'impressionnisme et le symbolisme des peintres." *La Revue blanche* 2 (Feb. 1892):103-08.

159. HURET, JULES. "Paul Gauguin devant ses tableaux." *L'Echo de Paris* (23 Feb. 1891):2.

160. HUYSMANS, J.-K. *L'Art moderne*. Paris: Charpentier, 1883.

161. JARRY, ALFRED. "Sixième exposition chez le Barc de Boutteville." *Essais d'art libre* 5 (Feb. 1894):40-42.

162. JENOT, Lieutenant P. "Le premier séjour de Gauguin à Tahiti d'après le manuscrit Jénot (1891-1893)." *Gazette des Beaux-Arts* 6 ser. (Jan.-April 1956; published in 1958):115-26. Reprinted in *Gauguin, sa vie, son oeuvre* (Paris: *Gazette des Beaux-Arts*, 1958.

163. KAHN, GUSTAVE. "Roger-Marx." *Mercure de France* 28:196 (Oct. 1898):43-52.

164. KALOPHILE, ERMITE (pseud.). "Chroniques: IV, les arts." *L'Ermitage* 4(1893):373.

165. KALOPHILE, ERMITE (pseud.). "Galerie Durand-Ruel: Oeuvres de M. Gauguin." *L'Ermitage* 4 (Dec. 1893):373.

166. LEBLOND, MARIUS-ARY. "La vie anarchique d'un artiste." *Dépêche de Toulouse* (1 Oct. 1903).

167. LEBLOND, MARIUS-ARY. "Gauguin en Océanie." *Revue universelle* 3:96 (15 Oct. 1903):536-37.

168. LECLERCQ, JULIEN. "Albert Aurier." *Essais d'art libre* 2 (Nov. 1892):201-08.

169. LECLERCQ, JULIEN. "Sur la peinture (de Bruxelles à Paris)." *Mercure de France* 11:53 (May 1894):71-77.

170. LECLERCQ, JULIEN. "La lutte pour les peintres." *Mercure de France* 12 (Nov. 1894)254-71.

171. LECLERCQ, JULIEN. "Exposition Paul Gauguin." *Mercure de France* 13 (Jan. 1895):121-22.

172. LOSTALOT, ALFRED DE. "Les artistes contemporains-M. Félix Bracquemond." *Gazette des Beaux-Arts* (Aug. 1884):155-61.

173. MANTZ, PAUL. "Exposition des oeuvres des artistes indépendants." *Le Temps* (23 April 1881).

174. MAUCLAIR, CAMILLE. "Les portraits du prochain siècle." *Essais d'art libre.* 4(1893):117-21.

175. MAUCLAIR, CAMILLE. "Choses d'art." *Mercure de France* 14:66 (June 1895):357-59.

176. MAUS, OCTAVE. "Le salon des XX à Bruxelles." *La Cravache* 417 (16 Feb.; 2 March 1889):1.

177. MEIER-GRAEFE, JULIUS. *Der Moderne Impressionismus.* Berlin: J. Bard, 1903. See pp. 47-65 for information on Gauguin.

178. MERKI, CHARLES. "Apologie pour la peinture." *Mercure de France* 8:42 (June 1893):139-53.

179. MERRILL, STUART. "Souvenirs sur le symbolisme." *La Plume* 16 (1 Feb. 1903):107-15.

180. MIRBEAU, OCTAVE. "Paul Gauguin." *Echo de Paris* (16 Feb. 1891):1. Reprinted in Octave Mirbeau, *Des artistes, 1885-96* (Paris: Flammarion, 1922):119-29.

181. MIRBEAU, OCTAVE. "Paul Gauguin." *L'Art moderne* (22 March 1891):92-94.

182. MIRBEAU, OCTAVE. "Retour de Tahiti." *Echo de Paris* (14 Nov. 1893):1.

183. MIRBEAU, OCTAVE. "Paul Gauguin." *Le Figaro* (18 Feb. 1891):1.

184. MONFREID, GEORGES-DANIEL DE. "Sur Paul Gauguin." *L'Ermitage* 14 (Dec. 1903):265-83.

185. MONFREID, GEORGES-DANIEL DE. "Lettre de Daniel de Monfreid au peintre Louis Bousil." *La Revue provinciale* (Toulouse) 3 (1903):383-89.

186. MONKHOUSE, COSMO. "Some Original Ceramists." *Magazine of Art* 5(1882):443-50.

187. MORICE, CHARLES. "Paul Gauguin." *Mercure de France* 9:48 (Dec. 1893):289-300.

188. MORICE, CHARLES. "L'Atelier de Paul Gauguin." *Le Soir* (4 Dec. 1894):2.

189. MORICE, CHARLES. "Le Départ de Paul Gauguin." *Le Soir* (28 June 1895):2.

190. MORICE, CHARLES. "Paul Gauguin." *Les hommes d'aujourd'hui* 9:440 (Dec. 1896). Published in abridged form in "Paul Gauguin," *Journaux des artistes* (19 April 1896).

191. MORICE, CHARLES. "La quinzaine artistique, Laertes." *La Dépêche de Toulouse* (19 Sept. 1903).

192. MORICE, CHARLES. "Paul Gauguin." *Mercure de France* 48:166 (Oct. 1903):100-35.

193. MORICE, CHARLES. "Quelques opinions sur Paul Gauguin." *Mercure de France* 48:167 (Nov. 1903):413-33.

194. NATANSON, THADEE. "Peinture." *La Revue blanche* 8 (Feb. 1895):186-88.

195. NATANSON, THADEE. "Peinture." *La Revue blanche* (1 Dec. 1896):516-18.

196. NATANSON, THADEE. "Petite gazette d'art: de M. Paul Gauguin." *La Revue blanche* 17 (Dec. 1898):544-46.

197. NOCQ, HENRI. *Tendances nouvelles*. Paris: H. Floury, 1896. 203 p. Mentions Gauguin.

198. OLIN, PIERRE-M. "Les XX." *Mercure de France* 2:16 (April 1891):236-40.

199. OLIN, PIERRE-M. "Nécrologie-Paul Gauguin." *Chronique des arts et de la curiosité* (1903):248-49.

200. OLIN, PIERRE-M. "Opinions d'artiste." *L'Escarmouche* (19 Nov. 1893):3.

201. PASSE, JEAN. "Impressionnistes et symbolistes." *Journal des artistes* (27 Dec. 1891):390.

202. REDON, ODILON. "Opinions sur Paul Gauguin." *Mercure de France* (Nov. 1903). Reprinted in *Critiques d'art* (Bordeaux: William Blake, 1987).

203. *Revue de l'exposition universelle de 1889* 2:226.

204. RIVIERE, HENRI. "Aux indépendants." *Le Chat noir* (8 April 1882).

205. ROGER-MARX, CLAUDE. "Paul Gauguin." *Le Voltaire* (20 Feb. 1891):1-2.

206. ROGER-MARX, CLAUDE. "Les arts décoratifs et industriels aux salons du Palais de L'Industrie et du Champ-de-Mars." *Revue encyclopédique* 1(15 Sept. 1891):584-89, 826-27.

207. ROGER-MARX, CLAUDE. "Exposition Paul Gauguin." *Revue encyclopédique* 4:7(1 Feb. 1894):33-34.

208. ROGER-MARX, CLAUDE. "La libre esthétique." *Revue encyclopédique* 4 (1 Nov. 1894):475-78.

209. ROTONCHAMP, JEAN DE. [pseud. Louis Brouillon]. *Paul Gauguin: 1848-1903*. Weimar: Kessler; Paris: E. Druet, 1906; reprinted Paris: Crès, 1925.

210. SEGALEN, VICTOR. "Gauguin dans son dernier décor." *Mercure de France* 50:174 (June 1904):679-85.

211. SEGUIN, ARMAND. "Paul Gauguin." *L'Occident* (March, April, May 1903):158-67, 230-39, 298-305.

212. SIGER, CARL. "Paul Gaguin colon." *Mercure de France* (August 1904):569-73.

213. SISSON, THEODORE. "Gauguin." *Le Temps* (2 Sept. 1903).

214. STRINDBERG, AUGUST. "L'Actualité: le misogyne Streinberg [sic] contre Monet." *L'Eclair* (15 Feb. 1895):1.

215. TARDIEU, EUGENE. "La peinture et les peintres-M. Paul Gauguin." *L'Echo de Paris* (13 May 1895):2.

216. VIELLIARD, FABIEN. "Paul Gauguin." *L'Art littéraire* 13 (Dec. 1893):51.

217. WAUTERS, A. J. "Aux XX." *La Gazette* (20 Feb. 1891).

218. WYSEWA, TEODOR DE. "Notes sur la peinture Wagnérienne et le salon de 1886." *La Revue Wagérienne* (8 May 1886):100-13.

219. WYZEWA, TEODOR DE. "Le nouveau salon du Champ-de-Mars." *L'Art dans les deux mondes* (13 June 1891).

220. Z., C. V. *La Gazette* (28 Feb. 1897).

Works (Oeuvre)

I. Catalogues Raisonnés (entries 221-232)
II. Gauguin's Paintings
  A. Gauguin's Paintings By Year
  B. Gauguin's Paintings Throughout the World
III. Gauguin's Ceramics
IV. Gauguin's Prints

I. Catalogues Raisonnés

The most complete and reliable catalogue raisonné to date is Georges Wildenstein's *Gauguin--Catalogue I*, edited by Raymond Cogniat and Daniel Wildentsein (Paris: Les Beaux-arts, 1964). Volume 1 covers paintings and a few watercolors and pastels. A projected volume 2, if ever published, will cover drawings. Bengt Danielsson's article, "Gauguin's Tahitian Titles," *Burlington Magazine* 9:760 (April 1967):228-33, clarifies and corrects titles of the Tahitian works.

Gauguin's ceramics are catalogued in Merete Bodelsen's *Gauguin's Ceramics* (London: Faber and Faber, 1964). For prints (woodcuts, zincographs, lithographs and etchings) see Mongan, Kornfeld and Joachim's *Paul Gauguin: Catalogue Raisonné of His Prints* (Bern: Galerie Kornfeld, 1988), among others.

The catalogues raisonnés below are listed in chronological order.

221. GUERIN, MARCEL L. *L'Oeuvre gravé de Gauguin*. Paris: Henri Floury, 1927. 2 vol., illus., pl., 600 copies.

Descriptive catalogue raisonné of Gauguin's prints.
a. Revised ed.: San Francisco: Alan Wofsy Fine Arts, 1980. 272 p., 104 illus.

222. WHITE, WIEBE ALICE. *Paintings by Paul Gauguin Owned in the United States of America, and the Hawaiian Islands*. Chicago: Art Institute, Ryerson Library, 1936, 1943. 77 p.; 18 p. supp., typescript.

Describes 85 paintings in chronological order.

223. REWALD, JOHN. *Gauguin Drawings*. New York: Thomas Yoseloff, 1958. 40 p., 126 pl.

Includes notes and reproductions of 126 drawings arranged chronologically. Many dates are based on deductions and stylistic considerations rather than known facts, since Gauguin's drawings are rarely dated. Notes and comments include references to paintings and prints in which similar elements appear.
Review: C. Kesler, *College Art Journal* 18(Spring 1959):274-77.

224. GRAY, CHRISTOPHER. *Sculpture and Ceramics of Paul Gauguin*. Baltimore: The Johns Hopkins Press, 1963. 330 p., 390 illus., 19 col. pl.

Study and catalogue raisonné of the known pieces of Gauguin's sculpture and ceramics. The text deals with Gauguin's growth as a sculptor and the artistic influences which formed his style. 150 pieces are illustrated.
Reviews: J. Hillier, *Connoisseur* 156(Aug. 1964):273; J. Arguelles, *Gazette des Beaux-Arts* 6th ser, 64 (Sept. 1964):188; W. Andersen, *Art Bulletin* 46(Dec. 1964):579-86; R. Reiff, *Art Journal* 24(Winter 1964-65):210+; D. Irwin, *Burlington Magazine* 107(Sept. 1965):477-78.

225. WILDENSTEIN, GEORGES. *Gauguin*. Edited by Raymond Cogniat and Daniel Wildenstein. Vol. 1, Catalogue. Paris: Les Beaux-Arts, 1964.

Only volume published of an anticipated complete catalogue. Details 638 paintings and other "definitive works." Revisions and a second volume on Gauguin's drawings and prints have been announced. Paintings are arranged by year and subject matter. Regarded as unreliable on the chronology of undated works and on questions of authenticity. Also criticized for the small size and poor quality of its reproductions. Numerous rectifications are proposed by Merete Bodelsen in "The Wildenstein-Cogniat Gauguin Catalogue," *Burlington Magazine* 108 (Jan. 1966):27-38; and by Bengt Danielsson in "Gauguin's Tahitian Titles," *Burlington Magazine* 109(April 1967):228-33.
Reviews: R. Pickvance, *Connoisseur* 159 (July 1965):198; J. Richardson, *Apollo* 82(Sept. 1965):255-56; M. Bodelsen, *Burlington Magazine* 108:754(Jan. 1966):27-38.

a. Revised ed.: Merete Bodelsen, ed. Paris: Flammarion, 1981. Also published in English, German, Spanish, and Italian editions.

226. AGUSTONI, FABRIZIO and GIULIO LARI. *Cataloguo completo dell'opera grafica di Paul Gauguin* [Complete Catalogue of the Printed Works of Paul Gauguin]. Introduction by Paolo Bellini. Milan: Salamon e Agustoni, 1972. 106 p., 73 illus.

Catalogue raisonné of Gauguin's printed work which comprises: lithographs and etchings from his early Breton period and wood engravings from his first and second voyages to Tahiti (1894-95, 1895-1903). Notes on the print runs are included and each illustrated work is accompanied by details of title, dimensions, printer, and state. In an introductory text, Bellini situates Gauguin's art--both his paintings and his prints--within the tradition of creative expression which seeks to evade Western intellectual culture. He proceeds to characterize the successive phases in Gauguin's oeuvre, noting in particular the development of his iconography and its pagan symbolism in the works executed in Polynesia and describing specific changes in his style during this mature phase.

227. SUGANA, GABRIELE MANDEL. *L'Opera completa de Gauguin* [The Complete Works of Gauguin]. Milan: Rizzoli, 1972. 119 p., illus. 64 col. pl.

Catalogue raisonné of Gauguin's paintings. The text includes extracts from Gauguin's letters, a survey of the critical reception of his work from 1880 to 1961, a chronology, a brief bibliography, and a collections list.
a. French ed.: *Toute l'oeuvre peinte de Gauguin*. Trans. by Simone Darses. Paris: Flammarion, 1981. 119 p., illus., some col.

228. FIELD, RICHARD SAMPSON. *Paul Gauguin: Monotypes*. Published on the Occasion of the Exhibition at the Philadelphia Museum of Art, March 23 to May 13, 1973. Philadelphia: Museum of Art, 1973. 148 p.

Exhibition catalogue, Philadelphia Museum of Art.

229. COOPER, DOUGLAS. *Gauguin; Catalogue Raisonné*. Manuscript with some photocopies. ca. 1975, ca. 2000 p. Located at The Getty Center for the History of Art and the Humanities, Santa Monica, California.

Contains unpublished material for a complete catalogue of Gauguin's work, arranged in chronological order. Folder 1 contains a Gauguin family tree and chronology by Cooper in manuscript. Douglas Cooper died in 1984.

230. GERSTEIN, MARC SAUL. *Impressionist and Post-Impressionist Fans*. Ph.D. diss., Harvard University, 1978. 385 p.

Examination of folding fans (éventail) and screen fans (écran) by prominent French Impressionist and Post-Impressionist artists. The dissertation is primarily a catalogue raisonné. Gauguin's section (pp. 266-349) describes 30 fans by Gauguin, created from 1881-1902.

231. FEZZI, ELDA. *Gauguin*. Milan: Rizzoli, 1979. 2 vol., 94 p. each.

Catalogue raisonné of the paintings of Paul Gauguin to 1889. The text gives an account of Gauguin's life, describing how he first started painting as a hobby, his friendships with other impressionist painters, including his attempt at living and working with Vincent van Gogh, and concludes that Gauguin's main inspiration were medieval icons, which provided him with the starting points for the first deliberately crude paintings in the history of modern art.
Another ed.: *Tout Gauguin*. Paris: Flammarion, 1982. 2 vol.
a. German ed.: *Paul Gauguin, das Gesamtwerk*. Trans. by Wolfgang Bensch. Frankfurt, Berlin, Wien: Ullstein GmbH, 1979. 2 vol.
b. U.S. ed.: *Gauguin: Every Painting*. Trans. by Susan Brill (vol. 1) and Jane Carroll (vol. 2). New York: Rizzoli, 1980. 2 vol.
c. English ed: *Gauguin: The Complete Paintings*. Trans. by Susan Brill and Jane Carroll. London, New York: Granada, 1981. 2 vol., 340 illus., some col.

232. MONGAN, ELIZABETH, EBERHARD W. KORNFELD, HAROLD JOACHIM. *Paul Gauguin: Catalogue Raisonné of his Prints*. Produced with the assistance of Christine E. Stauffer. Bern: Galerie Kornfeld, 1988, 283 p., illus., col. pl.

Catalogue raisonné of 78 prints, 5 rubbings from sculptures and reliefs not regarded as original prints by Gauguin, and 3 rubbings from carvings of which there is no proof that the original carvings were by Gauguin. Includes woodcuts, zincographs, lithographs and etchings. Discusses all of Gauguin's known graphic works and proposes a new chronological order. The most comprehensive and reliable publication about Gauguin's prints.
Review: P. Gilmour, *The Print Collector's Newsletter* 20(March/April, 1989):26-29.

II. Gauguin's Paintings

The Wildenstein-Cogniat Catalogue (commonly abbreviated W-C or W) lists 650 oil paintings by Gauguin. Others undoubtedly existed but were destroyed or lost before being inventoried. On Gauguin's death a number of paintings were acquired by various collectors. Sales were organized in Paris either by dealers or by those with depositions of works, such as Auguste Bauchy, the owner of the Café des Variétés. Mette Gauguin also sold nearly all of her husband's paintings that were left in Emile Schuffenecker's studio in Paris. Georges-Daniel de Monfreid sold paintings to Dr. Gustave Fayet, director of the museum of Béziers, and to Prince Emmanuel Bibesco. Parisian art dealer Ambroise Vollard held most of Gauguin's Polynesian output at the artist's death.

In April, 1903, one month before Gauguin's death, Vollard wrote Monfreid that he possessed 36 paintings, all of which were for sale. Six months later, having learned of the Gauguin's death, Vollard wrote again to Monfreid that he would purchase any Gauguin painting on hand for 250 francs, according to his 1890 contract. Vollard also sold 30 Gauguin paintings held by Bauchy in 1905. Vollard later travelled to Pont-Aven and purchased about 20 paintings from Marie Henry in Le Pouldu. Vollard's Polynesian Gauguins were eventually sold to foreign collectors primarily in the United States and Russia. Those held by Mette, the majority of which were Brittany paintings, went to collectors and museums in Scandinavia. Relatively few remained in France.

According to the Wildenstein-Cogniat catalogue, 81 paintings have disappeared and are unidentifiable. It is certain that Wildenstein-Cogniat's count of paintings executed during Gauguin's early period (1871-78; when Gauguin was 23-30 years old) is low--only 29 paintings are accounted for over eight years. Probably the majority of Gauguin's earliest works were lost.

Gauguin himself frequently underestimated the number of his paintings. In 1900 he wrote to Bibesco that he had finished about 300 paintings during his lifetime. The establishment of periods of Gauguin's art is difficult due to the instabilities of his life and career. After painting for 15 years (1871-86), the output of which is uncertain, the essential part of his career may be divided into two cycles, each with two periods: Brittany (Pont-Aven and Le Pouldu, 1886 and 1888-90) and Polynesia (Tahiti and the Marquesas, 1891-93 and 1895-1903).

These three major periods--yearly, (1871-86) Brittany, Polynesia--have about an equal numbers of paintings: around 190 for the first, 180 for the second, and 170 for the third. In addition, besides works executed in Paris, Rouen, Dieppe, and Copenhagen, there are two minor yet distinctive series: Martinique (1887) and Arles (1888). About 20 paintings exist from Martinique, and 17 from Arles.

Gauguin's period of greatest activity, according to dates established in Wildenstein-Cogniat, was his Brittany sojourn from 1888-89, when he painted 75 works in each year. In contrast, his ten years in Tahiti and the Marquesas produced the fewest paintings. The Wildenstein-Cogniat catalogue numbers known works by year.

A. Gauguin's Paintings By Year

Number of paintings by year,
according to the *Wildenstein-Cogniat Catalogue* (1964)

1871	1	1882	19	1893	15
1872	2	1883	14	1894	18
1873	2	1884	43	1895	4
1874	4	1885	49	1896	22
1875	7	1886	32	1897	12
1876	6	1887	24	1898	10
1877	4	1888	75	1899	17
1878	3	1889	75	1900	
1879	11	1890	27	1901	11
1880	11	1891	39	1902	24
1881	11	1892	49	1903	6

B. Gauguin's Paintings Throughout the World

Gauguin's paintings are widely dispersed. The Wildenstein-Cogniat catalogue lists numbers of paintings by location in 1964. Totals in the tables below include paintings held in both museums and private collections. Wildenstein (W.) numbers refer to specific paintings so identified in the Wildenstein-Cogniat catalogue. Countries and museums with the greatest number of Gauguin paintings are listed first.

Nation/City		Museums	Private Collections	Total
U.S.A.		**52**	**107**	**159**
Chicago	- Art Institute W. 300, 387, 439, 486, 513, 523, 550, 595, 615	9		
New York	- Metropolitan Museum W. 428, 442, 526, 538	4		
	- Museum of Modern Art W. 293, 499	2		
	- Brooklyn Museum W. 424 bis	1		
Boston	- Museum of Fine Arts W. 121, 406, 516, 636	4		

Nation/City		Museums	Private Collections	Total
San Antonio	- Marion Koegler Art Institute W. 333, 415, 617	3		
Washington	- National Gallery of Arts W. 323, 463, 572	3		
Cambridge	- Fogg Art Museum W. 382, 547	2		
Los Angeles	- County Museum W. 365, 404	2		
Merion	- Barnes Foundation W. 388, 464	2		
Minneapolis	- Institute of Art W. 434, 504	2		
Worchester	- Art Museum W. 98, 440	2		
Baltimore	- Museum of Art W. 449	1		
Buffalo	- Albright Art Gallery W. 327	1		
Cleveland	- Museum of Art W. 612	1		
Hartford	- Wadsworth Atheneum W. 320	1		
Honolulu	- Academy of Arts W. 456	1		
Indianapolis	- John Herron Art Institute W. 308	1		
Kansas City	- W. Rockhill Nelson Gallery W. 424	1		

Nation/City		Museums	Private Collections	Total
Miami	- Joe and Emily Lowe Gallery W. 73	1		
Northampton	- Smith Museum of Art W. 36	1		
Palm Beach	- (West) - Norton Gallery W. 326	1		
Pittsburgh	- Carnegie Institute W. 601	1		
Providence	- Rhode Island School W. 431	1		
Provincetown	- Chrysler Art Museum W. 412	1		
Saint Louis	- City Art Museum W. 298	1		
Springfield	- Museum of Fine Arts W. 363	1		
Toledo	- Museum of Art W. 441	1		
FRANCE		**35**	**32**	**67**
Paris	- Musée du Jeu de Paume W. 13, 173, 196, 269, 292, 307, 313, 315, 377, 427, 434, 468, 506, 507, 510, 511, 525, 528, 556, 559, 571, 596	22		
	- Musée du Petit Palais W. 66, 318	2		
	- Musée des Arts Décoratifs W. 282	1		
Grenoble	- Musée de Peinture W. 240, 263	2		

Nation/City		Museums	Private Collections	Total
Reims	- Musée des Beaux-Arts W. 407, 532	2		
Rennes	- Musée des Beaux-Arts W. 63, 65	2		
Le Havre	- Musée des Beaux-Arts W. 546	1		
Lyon	- Musée des Beaux-Arts W. 548	1		
Strasbourg	- Musée des Beaux-Arts W. 533	1		
Orléans	- Musée des Beaux-Arts W. 290	1		
DENMARK		**34**	**13**	**47**
Copenhagen	- Ny Carlsberg Glyptotek W. 6, 38, 39, 67, 68, 75, 78, 87, 88, 119, 141, 147, 166, 217, 252, 258, 344, 380, 420, 480, 505, 514, 530, 575, 592	25		
	- Musée des Beaux-Arts W. 123	1		
Ordrupgaard	- Collection W. Hansen W. 52, 268, 304, 311, 409, 535, 576, 628	8		
SWITZERLAND			**5**	**42**
Basel	- Kunstmuseum W. 136, 366, 454, 476, 634	5		
Zurich	- Fondation Buhrle (open to the public: 7 paintings)			

Nation/City		Museums	Private Collections	Total
GREAT BRITAIN		**14**	**16**	**30**
London	- Tate Gallery W. 516, 553, 569	3		
	- Courtauld Institute W. 557, 558	2		
	- Home House Trustees W. 352	1		
Edinburgh	- National Gallery of Scotland W. 232, 245, 573	3		
Birmingham	- Barber Institute of Fine Arts W. 271, 564	2		
Cambridge	- Fitzwilliam Museum W. 5	1		
Manchester	- City Art Gallery W. 169	1		
Newcastle	- Laing Art Gallery W. 203	1		
U.S.S.R.		**29**		**29**
Leningrad	- State Hermitage Museum W. 426, 435, 450, 461, 470, 481, 484, 501, 512, 537, 538, 540, 542, 544, 562, 565, 570, 581, 584, 585, 586, 597, 603, 629	24		
Moscow	- Museum of Modern Western Art (now in the Pushkin Museum) W. 288, 305, 589	3		
	- Pushkin State Museum of Fine Arts W. 297, 579	2		

Nation/City		Museums	Private Collections	Total
GERMANY		**12**	**5**	**17**
Essen	- Folkkwang Museum W. 349, 609, 619, 625	4		
Munich	- Staats gemälde Bayrische W. 201, 226, 541	3		
Berlin	- Staatsgemäalde Sammlungen W. 354	1		
Cologne	- Walrof Richarts-Museum W. 339	1		
Hamburg	- Kunsthalle W. 275	1		
Stuttgart	- Staatsgalerie W. 385	1		
Dresden	- Galerie d'Art Moderne W. 466	1		
THE NETHERLANDS		**11**	**3**	**14**
Amsterdam	- Van Gogh Museum W. 222, 224, 225, 239, 296, 299, 482, 529	8		
Otterlo	- Rijksmuseum Kröller-Müller W. 152, 452	2		
Rotterdam	- Boymans Museum W. 160	1		
NORWAY		**6**	**8**	**14**
Oslo	- Nasional-galleriet W. 50, 95, 134, 375, 359 593	6		

Nation/City		Museums	Private Collections	Total
JAPAN		**9**	**3**	**12**
Tokyo	- Bridgestone Gallery W. 124, 184, 261, 369	4		
	- National Museum of Western Art W. 167, 256, 340, 386	1 4		
Kurashiki	- Ohara Museum W. 455	1		
SWEDEN		**6**	**3**	**9**
Stockholm	- Nationalmuseum W. 309, 356, 623	3		
Göteborg	- Konstmuseum W. 28, 205, 248	3		
BELGIUM		**4**	**3**	**7**
Brussels	- Musées royaux des Beaux-Arts W. 250, 328, 423	3		
Liège	- Musée des Beaux-Arts W. 616	1		
BRAZIL		**3**	**1**	**4**
São Paulo	- Museu de Arte W. 534, 536, 545	3		
GREECE			**4**	**4**
ARGENTINA		**1**	**2**	**3**
Buenos Aires	- Museo de Belles Artes W. 465	1		
CANADA		**1**	**2**	**3**
Ottawa	- National Gallery W. 71	1		

Nation/City		Museums	Private Collections	Total
CZECHOSLOVAKIA		**3**		**3**
Prague	- Museum of Modern Art W. 322, 614, 622	3		
HUNGARY		**2**	**1**	**3**
Budapest	- Museum of Fine Arts W. 37, 446	2		
EGYPT		**2**		**2**
Cairo	- Egyptian Government W. 155, 335	2		
FINLAND		**2**		**2**
Helsinki	- Atheneum W. 491, 637	2		
VENEZUELA 2			**2**	
COLOMBIA			**1**	**1**
ITALY		**1**		**1**
Milan	- Galleria d'Arte Moderni W. 158	1		
YUGOSLAVIA		**1**		**1**
Belgrade	- National Museum W. 577	1		
		233	248	481
Held in Private Collections (no place given)			88	88
Disappeared or Unidentified Works			81	81
TOTALS		**233**	**417**	**650**

As the tables above indicate, the United States held 159 of 650 Gauguin paintings in 1964, nearly 25 percent. However, they were widely dispersed. France was second with 67. In terms of public works, in order the United States, France, Denmark, and the U.S.S.R. had the greatest. Gauguin's paintings executed during specific periods are most accessible at two museums, the Glyptotek Carlsberg in Copenhagen (Brittany) and the Hermitage in Leningrad (Tahitian).

III. Gauguin's Ceramics

In June, 1886, after the eighth Impressionist exhibition, Gauguin was introduced to the ceramist Ernest Chaplet (1835-1909) by the engraver Félix Bracquemond. Chaplet had served a 13-year apprenticeship at the Sèvres factory and was a master porcelain painter. Gauguin learned stoneware technique from Chaplet and found in ceramics an excellent medium for expressing his love for raw materials and his decorative sense. Of an estimated 100 ceramic objects by Gauguin, 60 or so remain. This oeuvre was catalogued by Gray in 1963 and by Bodelsen in 1964. The extreme difficulty in dating Gauguin's pieces accounts for the differences in these authors' interpretations.

Gauguin's passion for ceramics may be traced to his childhood. His mother had a collection of Peruvian pottery that was destroyed when her house in St. Cloud burned in 1871. His guardian, Gustave Arosa, also owned anthropomorphic Peruvian ceramics, which later influenced Gauguin's works. Gauguin's pieces were mostly modelled by hand. Many contain familiar Breton motifs shepherds, shepherdesses, lambs, geese, faces, and so on. His later works have no resemblance to utilitarian objects and are purely sculptural.

Gauguin's ceramic technique was highly original. He may be rightly considered one of the great revivers of stoneware art at the end of the nineteenth century. For Gauguin, the art of pottery was inextricably linked with painting. His Brittany sketchbooks show numerous motifs common to both forms and many designs for ceramics. Gauguin often depicted his ceramics in his paintings. Bodelsen demonstrated how Gauguin's ceramic technique led him to simply and highlight outlines of shapes, which brought him close to cloisonnism even before he experimented with this technique in painting. The evolution of his ceramic oeuvre is part of Gauguin's general stylistic development toward an increasingly complex symbolism.

Gauguin hoped that his ceramics would provide an income when his paintings failed to sell. Buyers were few, however, and the ceramics sold as poorly as his pictures. Yet the proceeds of a ceramics sale by Theo van Gogh (300 francs) in 1888 enabled Gauguin to pay for his trip to Arles, where he joined Vincent.

IV. Gauguin's Prints

Gauguin's printed works include lithographs and etchings from his Breton period and woodcuts from his Tahitian periods. Gauguin began working in lithography in late 1888 and quickly achieved a remarkable proficiency. The Morgan, Kornfeld and Joachim catalogue (1988) describes 78 prints and various rubbings from sculptures and carvings.

Gauguin's first graphic undertaking was an album of ten zinographs in 1889, called The Volpini Suite. Gauguin finished the set in February 1889. Approximately 50 sets were printed by Ancourt in Paris. The suite was shown in June in Volpini's cafe at the Exposition Universelle of 1889. Gauguin's portfolio shared a place in the exhibition catalogue with a set of prints by his friend Emile Bernard. Bernard was an experienced lithographer and probably worked closely with Gauguin on the project.

Gauguin's only known etching was his *Portrait of Stéphane Mallarmé*, completed in January, 1891. Only two proofs of the first state are known, and about ten of the second. According to Jean de Rotonchamp, Gauguin borrowed the necessary equipment from the painter Léon Fauché, a fellow Volpini exhibitor. Charles Chassé repeats an account by Paul Sérusier which credits Eugène Carrière with introducing Gauguin to the etching technique and varnishing the plate Gauguin used.

Gauguin's most sustained achievement in the graphic medium was the series of ten woodcut prints made for *Noa Noa* in late 1893 and early 1894. This woodcut suite was intended to illustrate his *Noa Noa* manuscript. *Noa Noa* began as a guide to Gauguin's Tahitian works but became even denser and ultimately more mythic. The earliest *Noa Noa* text, written while Gauguin worked on the woodblocks, was given to Charles Morice for amendments and alterations. It loosely follows the format of a travel journal of Gauguin's first Tahitian period (1891-93).

Gauguin engaged the Parisan printer Louis Roy to produce editions of 25 to 30 impressions of each print. Gauguin varied each impression so that no two are alike. Since none were numbered or mounted in any systematic way, there are no surviving sets of Roy-printed Noa Noa impressions. From the large number produced for the book only a few were used in the preparation of the final manuscript.

Gauguin worked on other woodblocks in Brittany in the summer of 1894 and in 1895. During the summer of 1894 Gauguin made the largest and most impressive woodblock of his career, called *Manao Tupapau*. The motif is a woman in the fetal position in an imaginary pond in the midst of a Tahitian village. The various impressions of this block which survive show the extent of Gauguin's experimentation with this medium. Many were hand colored by the artist. Woodcuts of the *Oviri* figure were created in 1895.

A suite of 14 woodcut prints from 1898-99 also exist, printed by Gauguin in Tahiti. Almost 500 impressions were sent to the dealer Ambroise Vollard in 1900. Twelve of the 14 prints can be considerd in pairs or even freizes related by size, format, mode of printing, and composition. Three were devoted to Brittany subjects.

Secondary Bibliography

I. Biography and Career
   A. Monographs (entries 233-367)
   B. Articles (entries 368-482)
II. Gauguin and Contemporaries in France
   A. Monographs (entries 483-550)
   B. Articles (entries 551-662)
III. Paul Gauguin and Vincent van Gogh
   A. Monographs (entries 663-680)
   B. Articles (entries 681-717)
IV. Gauguin in Panama and Martinique
   A. Monographs (entries 718-719)
   B. Articles (entries 720-723)
V. Gauguin in Tahiti and the Marquesas Islands
   A. Monographs (entries 724-767)
   B. Articles (entries 768-829)
VI. Oeuvre in General
   A. Monographs (entries 830-842)
   B. Articles (entries 843-864)
VII. Oeuvre--Paintings
   A. Monographs (entries 865-878)
   B. Articles (entries 879-886)
VIII. Individual Works--Paintings
   A. Monographs (entries 887-897)
   B. Articles (entries 898-999)
IX. Self-Portraits
   A. Monographs (entries 1000-1002)
   B. Articles (entries 1003-1018)
X. Oeuvre--Drawings
   A. Monographs (entries 1019-1023)
   B. Articles (entries 1024-1034)

XI. Oeuvre--Prints and Graphic Art
A. Monographs (entries 1035-1047)
B. Articles (entries 1048-1079)
XII. Oeuvre--Ceramics and Scrulpture
A. Monographs (entries 1080-1082)
B. Articles (entries 1083-1113)
XIII. Oeuvre--Miscellaneous Media
A. Monographs (entries 1114-1115)
B. Articles (entries 1116-1125)
XIV. Museums and Collections (entries 1126-1209)
XV. Technique
A. Monographs (entries 1210-1211)
B. Articles (entries 1212-1222)
XVI. Iconography
A. Monographs (entries 1223-1240)
B. Articles (entries 1241-1283)
XVII. Japonisme
A. Monographs (entries 1284-1294)
B. Articles (entries 1295-1305)
XVIII. Mentions of Paul Gauguin
A. Monographs (entries 1306-1407)
B. Articles (entries 1408-1502)
XIX. Films, Videos, Recordings and Other Media (entries 1503-1507)

I. Biography and Career

A. Monographs

233. ALEXANDRE, ARSENE P. U. *Paul Gauguin; sa vie et le sens de son oeuvre.* Paris: Bernheim-Jeune, 1930. 275 p., 92 illus., 2 col pl.

Study of the life and art of Gauguin based to a great extent on Emile Schuffenecker's recollections and on Gauguin's letters to Schuffenecker, many of which are quoted here for the first time.

234. ANDERSEN, WAYNE V. *Gauguin's Paradise Lost.* With the assistance of Barbara Klein. New York: Viking Press, 1971. 371 p., 138 illus.

Psychoanalytical biography of Gauguin that has its starting point in the views of nature and the myths which he encountered in Brittany and Tahiti. The author's main intention is to elucidate the ways in which nature and myth were incorporated into Gauguin's personal mythology, reordered by his unconscious mind, and translated into the symbolic system of his paintings.
a. English ed.: London: Secker & Warburg, 1972. 370 p.

235. ANTONY DE WITT, ANTONIO. *Paul Gauguin.* Milan: U. Hoepli, 1944. 45 p., illus., pl. In Italian.

Biography and analysis of Gauguin's paintings. Pages 30-45 include bibliographic notes by Giovanni Scheiwiller.
Review: *Emporium* 101(Jan. 1945):50.
a. 2nd ed.:1945.

236. ANTONY DE WITT, ANTONIO. *Vita e arte di Gauguin* [Life and Art of Gauguin]. Milan: All'Insegna del Pesce d'Oro, 1948. 295 p.

Biography of Gauguin published on the centenary of his birth.

237. AWAZU, NORIO. *Gogyan Gauguin.* Tokyo: Shueisha, 1970. 152 p., illus., 79 col. pl.

Text in Japanese with English captions and a list of plates in French.
a. Another ed.: 1971.

238. BAELEN, JEAN. *La vie de Flora Tristan: Socialisme et féminisme au XIXe siècle.* Paris: Editions du Seuil, 1972. 252 p.

Biographical study of Gauguin's maternal grandmother, Flora Tristan (1803-1844).

239. BARDEAU, JACQUELINE. *A la découverte de Gauguin.* Paris: Office Français des Techniques Modernes d'Education, 1972. 18 p. 16 col. slides.

240. BEAUTE, GEORGES. *Paul Gauguin vu par les photographes.* Preface by Paul-René Gauguin. Lausanne: Edita, 1988. 127 p., illus.

Pictorial biography of Gauguin replete with photographs, the majority of which are not identified.

241. BECKER, BERIL. *Paul Gauguin, the Calm Madman.* New York: Albert & Charles Boni, 1931. 348 p., 8 pl.

Popularized account of Gauguin's life in the form of an historical novel.
a. 2nd ed.: New York: Tudor, 1935.

242. BERRUER, PIERRE. *Le bon Dieu n'a pas d'oreilles: Gauguin, le roman d'une vie.* Paris: Plon, 1986. 341 p.

Fictional biography based on Paul Gauguin's life. By choosing the novel format, the author believes that he captures Gauguin's exceptional human spirit and sensuality.

243. BERTRAM, ANTHONY. *Paul Gauguin.* London: The Studio; New York: William E. Rudge, 1930. 8 p., 24 pl.

Brief biographical introduction followed by small black-and-white plates.
a. 3rd ed.: 1930.

244. BETZ, GERD. *Paul Gauguin: Leben und Werk.* Stuttgart: Belser, 1984. 93 p., illus.

Study of Gauguin's life and art.

245. BODELSEN, MERETE CHRISTENSEN. *Gauguin og Impressionisterne* [Gauguin and the Impressionists]. Copenhagen: Kunstforeningen, 1968. 196 p., 30 illus., 10 pl.

Study of Gauguin's early Impressionist works and his relationship and influence on other Impressionist painters. Covers Gauguin's earliest paintings and influences and his work in Denmark. Includes documentation and index.

246. BOLTON, LINDA. *Mieux connaître Gauguin.* Paris: Editions Atlas, 1989, 1990. 63 p., col. illus.

General introduction to Gauguin's life and works.

247. BOUDAILLE, GEORGES. *Gauguin.* Paris: Editions Aimery Somogy, 1963. 272 p. illus., col.pl.

Illustrated biography and analysis of Gauguin's works in three parts.
a. English ed.: London: Thames and Hudson, 1964. Trans. by Alisa Jaffa. 274 p.
b. U.S. ed.: New York: Tudor, 1964. 274 p.

248. BOWNESS, ALAN. *Gauguin.* London: Phaidon, 1971. 16 p., 48 col. pl.

Introduction treats Gauguin's life and development as an artist. Studies Gauguin's symbolism and primitivism.
a. 2nd ed: London: Phaidon, 1972. 16 p., 48 col. pl., cassette tape.

249. BURCHARD, L. [Article on Gauguin in *Allgemeines Lexikon der bildenden Künste*, vol. 13]. Leipzig: Seemann-Verlag, 1920.

250. BURNETT, ROBERT. *The Life of Paul Gauguin*. London: Cobden-Sanderson, 1936. 294 p., 10 illus.

Biography which reconstructs Gauguin's life from letters and manuscripts. Lacks documentation but has a detailed index. Mentions his paintings only when Gauguin wrote about them.
Review: D. Lord, *Burlington Magazine* 70 (April 1937):201-02.
a. U.S. ed.: New York: Oxford University Press, 1937. 294 p.

251. CACHIN, FRANCOISE. *Gauguin: 'ce malgré moi de sauvage'*. Paris: Découvertes Gallimard, Réunion des musées nationaux, 1989. 196 p., illus., mostly col.

Illustrated biography by the director of the Musée d'Orsay and inspector general of French national museums. Includes a section on Gauguin's writings, criticism, and contemporary observations (pp. 133-87).

252. CACHIN, FRANCOISE. *Gauguin*. Paris: Flammarion, 1990. 311 p., illus.

253. CAHN, ISABELLE. *Actualité des arts plastiques: Gauguin*. Paris: CNDP, 1988. 78 p.

254. CAHN, ISABELLE. *Gauguin et le mythe du sauvage*. Paris: Flammarion, Arthaud, 1988. 127 p.

255. CHARMET, RAYMOND. *Gauguin*. Deventer, Holland; Verviers: Marabout Université, 1965. 89 p., illus., 63 pl., 24 col. pl.

Biographical study profusely illustrated.
a. English ed.: *Gauguin*. Trans. by Haydn Barnes. London: Blandford Press, 1966. 90 p., illus.

256. CHASSE, CHARLES. *Gauguin sans légendes*. Paris: Les Editions du Temps, 1965. 169 p., illus., 8 col. pl.

Biography of Gauguin with a chronology and bibliography. The last chapter explains his influence and artistic legacy.

257. CLAVEL, BERNARD. *Paul Gauguin*. Lyon: Editions et Imprimeries du Sud-Est, 1958. 96 p., 6 pl.

258. COGNIAT, RAYMOND. *Paul Gauguin*. Paris: Braun, 1938.

259. COGNIAT, RAYMOND. *Gauguin*. Paris: Tisné, 1947. 55 p., 120 pl., some col.

Chronological biography which covers major events in Gauguin's life and career.
a. English ed.: *Gauguin*. London: House of Beric, 1947. 51 p., 120 pl.
b. U.S. ed.: *Gauguin*. Trans. by Kenneth M. Leake. New York: H. N. Abrams, 1963. 79 p., 36 col. illus.

260. COSSIO DEL POMAR, FELIPE. *Arte y vida de Pablo Gauguin (escuela sintetista)*. Paris, Madrid: Leon Sanchez Cuesta, 1930. 366 p., 56 illus., pl.

Study of the art and life of Gauguin in Spanish, illustrated by small reproductions of photographs and works.

261. COSSIO DEL POMAR, FELIPE. *El hechizo de Gauguin* [The Spell of Gauguin]. Santiago, Chile: Ediciones Ercilla, 1939. 227 p.

Life of Gauguin in Spanish.
a. Another ed.: México: Leyenda, 1944, 143 p.

262. COSSIO DEL POMAR, FELIPE. *La vida de Pablo Gauguin*. Buenos Aires: Editorial Schapire, 1945. 381 p., illus., some col.

Life of Gauguin in Spanish.

263. COURTHION, PIERRE. *Gauguin, 1848-1903; Second Collection*. London: Faber and Faber, 1963.

264. DAIX, PIERRE. *Paul Gauguin*. Paris: Lattes, 1989. 418 p.

Detailed biography and critical analysis of his works.

265. DALLET, JEAN-MARIE. *Je, Gauguin*. Paris: Robert Laffont, 1981. 190 p.

First-person narrative of the life of Gauguin based on writings, letters, and published biographies.
a. 2nd ed.: Paris: Presses-Pocket, 1985. 157 p.

266. DAMIGELLA, ANNA MARIA. *Gauguin*. Florence: Giunti, 1989. 50 p., col. illus.

Biographical and critical survey in Italian profusely illustrated by reproductions of Gauguin's works.

267. D'ANGELIS, GASTON. "L'homme." In *Gauguin*. Paris: Hachette, 1960. pp. 41-53.

268. DIEHL, GASTON. *Gauguin.*

Pictorial biography illustrated by Gauguin's paintings and drawings.
a. U.S. ed.: *Gauguin.* Trans. by Anne Ross. New York: Crown Publishers, 1967. 48 p., illus., col. pl.

269. DORRA, HENRI. "Paul Gauguin." In *Metropolitan Museum of Art Miniatures.* New York: The Museum, Book-of-the-Month Club, 1953.

Brief introduction to and study of Gauguin.

270. DORSENNE, JEAN. *La vie sentimentale de Paul Gauguin, d'après des documents inédits.* Paris: L'Artisan du Livre, 1927. 157 p., 8 pl.

Biography which relied on then unpublished letters and writings by Gauguin. Takes the position that Gauguin was a frustrated and misunderstood artist who lived a tragic life.
a. German ed.: *Paul Gauguins Lebenskampf.* Freiburg im Briesgau: Urban, 1928.

271. VAN DOWSKI, LEE [Herbert Lewandowski]. *Paul Gauguin, das abenteuerlicheg Leben des grossen Malers* [Paul Gauguin, the Adventures of the Great Painter]. Bern: Delphi-Verlag, 1948.

General biography in German.
a. Another German ed.: 1950.

272. VAN DOWSKI, LEE. [Herbert Lewandowski]. *Paul Gauguin; oder die Flucht vor der Zivilisation* [Paul Gauguin; of The Flight from Civilization]. Foreword by Henri Guillemin. Bern: Delphi-Verlag, 1948. 358 p., illus., 30 pl.

Study in German of Gauguin's life and romantic legend.
a. Excerpt: *Erste Fassung eines Oeuvre Katalog für Gauguins Gemälde* [First Version of an Oeuvre-Catalog for Gauguin's Paintings]. Bern: Delphi-Verlag, 1950 (pp. 338-58).

273. VAN DOWSKI, LEE [Herbert Lewandowski]. *Die Wahrheit über Gauguin* [The Truth about Gauguin]. Darmstadt: J. G. Bläschke, 1959. 281 p., illus., col. pl.

Study of Gauguin's life and oeuvre which attacks popular romantic legends. Relies heavily on firsthand contemporary accounts and Gauguin's writings. Includes a catalog by year of 400 paintings.
a. Other eds.: 1973.

b. English ed.: *Gauguin: The Truth.* Trans. by H. Mitchell. London: P.R. Macmillan, 1961. 196 p., 32 pl.

274. DUMONT, HENRI. *Gauguin.* Milan: Uffici Press, 195-? 36 p., illus. Biographical sketch and captions in English, French, and German.

275. ESTIENNE, CHARLES. *Gauguin.* Geneva: A. Skira, 1953. 116 p., 52 col, illus.

Collection of biographical and critical studies with a chronology, bibliography, and list of exhibitions.
a. Other eds.: Paris: Nathan, 1988. 192 p., 152 illus., 98 col.; Amsterdam: Ed. Time-Life Books, 1989. 157 p., illus.
b. English ed.: *Gauguin: Biographical and Critical Studies.* Trans. by James Emmons. Geneva: Skira, 1953. 115 p., 52 col. illus.

276. FLETCHER, JOHN GOULD. *Paul Gauguin, His Life and Art.* New York: Nicholas L. Brown, 1921. 193 p., 10 illus.

Popularized biography of Gauguin which emphasizes his primitivism and romantic legends.
Review: H.E.F., *The Arts* 1 (1921):51-53.

277. FONSMARK, ANNE-BRIGITTE. *Gauguin og Danmark.* Copenhagen: Ny Carlsberg Glyptotek, 1985. 67 p.

Examines Gauguin's stay in Denmark, from November, 1884 until June, 1885.

278. FOUCHET, MAX-POL. *Gauguin.* Paris: Henri Scrépel, 1975. 54 p., illus., 32 col. pl.

Biographical and critical introduction followed by color plates of paintings with excerpts from writings and letters.
a. U.S. ed.: *Gauguin.* Trans. by Mary Fitton. Woodbury, NY: Barron's, 1975.

279. FRANCOLIN, CLAUDE. *La vie passionnée de Paul Gauguin.* Paris: Seghers, 1958. 332 p., pl.

Novel based on Gauguin's life.

280. FUKUNAGA, TAKEHIKO. *Gogyan no sekai.* Tokyo: Shinchosa, 1972. 400 p., illus. In Japanese.

281. GATTEY, CHARLES NEILSON. *Gauguin's Astonishing Grandmother: A Biography of Flora Tristan.* London: Femina, 1970. 223 p., illus., 17 pl.

Biography of Gauguin's maternal grandmother, Flora Tristan (1803-1844). Flora Tristan was an early proponent of and activist in labor unions and feminism. In 1821, she married the artist and lithographer André Chazàl. She wrote several books, including *L'Union ouvrière* (Bordeaux, 1843), her most popular.
a. German ed.: *Flora Tristan.* Zürich: Ala Verlag, 1971. 256 p., illus.

282. GAUGUIN, PEDRO MARIA. *Gauguin's spanske arv: Fra Flora Tristan til Borgia* [Gauguin's Spanish Ancestry: From Flora Tristan to the Borgias]. Lyngby, Denmark: Bogan, 1983. 276 p., illus. 16 pl.

Genealogical study of Gauguin's maternal Spanish ancestry back to the 14th century. The first section is devoted to Gauguin's life, followed by chapters on prominent ancestors including Flora Tristan and the Borgia nobility. Written by a relative of Paul Gauguin.

283. GAUGUIN, POLA. *Paul Gauguin.* Oslo: Glydendal, 1937. 219 p., illus.

Sympathetic biography of Gauguin written in Norwegian by his son Pola (1883-). Draws on childhood memories and letters. Claims that his mother Mette admitted late in life that although she never understood the artistic side of Gauguin's nature, she felt him justified in sacrificing everything for art and asserting his individuality.
Reviews: E. Buckman, *Magazine of Art* 30(March 1937):182; J. Kraemer, *Arts & Decoration* 46 (March 1937):48; *California Arts & Architecture* 51(May 1937):37; D. Lord, *Burlington Magazine* 71(Dec. 1937):295.
a. English eds.: *My Father, Paul Gauguin.* Trans. by Arthur G. Chater. New York: A.A. Knopf; London: Cassell, 1937. 292 p., illus.
b. Swedish ed.: *Paul Gauguin.* Trans. by Cösta Olzon. Stockholm: Bonnier, 1937. 222 p., 52 pl., 4 col pl.
c. French ed.: *Paul Gauguin, mon père.* Trans. by Georges Soutreau. Paris: Editions de France, 1938. 289 p., pl.
d. German eds.: *Mein Vater Paul Gauguin.* Trans. by Elisabeth Ihle. Berlin: Henschel, 1950. 271 p.; Munich: List, 1960. 180 p.

284. GAUGUIN, POLA. *Mette og Paul Gauguin.* Copenhagen: Glydendal, 1956. 206 p., 7 pl.

Biography of his parents by Gauguin's son Paul (Pola) Rollon, born in 1883. Includes letters and reminiscences.

285. *Gauguin*. Paris: P. Tisne, 1947. 51 p., 120 pl., some col.

286. *Gauguin*. Milan: Vallardi, 1963. 36 p., pl.

287. *Gauguin*. Paris: Editions Bellevue, 1975.

288. *Gauguin*. Paris: Hachette, 1960. 283 p., illus., col. pl.

Volume in Hachette's "Collection Génies et Réalitiés" series on Gauguin. Includes essays by Henri Perruchot, "La vie"; Gaston d'Angelis, "L'homme"; Bernard Dorival, "Le Milieu"; François Nourissier, "Sa place dans la mêlée symboliste"; Maurice Malingue, "L'homme qui a réinventé la peinture"; Richard Field, "Plagiaire ou créateur?"; Claude Roger-Marx, "Ce que lui doit la peinture contemporaine"; Maurice Rheims, "La côté des Gauguin"; and René Huyghe, "Initiateur des temps nouveaux."

Other eds.: 1961, 1965, 1986, 1987.

289. *Gogyan Gauguin*. Texts by Yasushi Inoue, Shuji Takashina, Ikuo Hirayama, and Makoto Ooka. Tokyo: Chuo Koronsha, 1972. col. illus. In Japanese.
a. Abridged ed.: 1973. 100 p.

290. GOLDWATER, ROBERT JOHN. *Paul Gauguin*. New York: H.N. Abrams, 1957. 160 p., illus., 63 col. pl.

Biography and critical analysis of Paul Gauguin from the beginning to the end of his career. Includes 48 large-color plates with commentary. Goldwater was the director of the Museum of Primitive Art in New York at the time of this publication.
Reprints: New York: Abrams, 1972, 1983. 160, 126 p.; "Concise edition" London: Thames and Hudson, 1985. 126 p.
a. English ed.: London: Thames and Hudson, 1957.
b. French ed.: Trans. by Daphné Monay-Vaudover. Paris: Nouvelles Editions Françaises, 1957. 87 p., illus., 47 col. pl.
c. German ed.: Vienna: Buchgemeinschaft, 1960. 142 p.
d. Japanese ed.: Tokyo: Bijutsu Shuppansha, 1961. 144 p., illus., 47 col. pl.

291. GORHAM, CHARLES O. *The Gold of Their Bodies; A Novel about Gauguin*. New York: Dial Press, 1955. 376 p., pl.

Fanciful romantic novel based on Gauguin's life. Emphasizes "his right to paint, and for the painter's right to dare everything for the sake of art" (dust jacket).

a. German ed.: *Und das Gold ihrer Körper. Das abenteuerliche Leben Paul Gauguins*. Zurich: Buchclub Ex Libris, 1959. 247 p., pl.

292. GRABER, HANS. *Paul Gauguin, der Künster erzählt sein Leben* [Paul Gauguin, The Artist Tells His Life]. Basel: Benno Schwabe, 1939. 341 p., illus.

293. GRABER, HANS. *Paul Gauguin. Nach eigenen und fremden Zeugnissen* [Paul Gauguin. In His Own and Others' Words]. Basel: Benno Schwabe, 1939. 512 p., 60 pl.

Biography of Gauguin illustrated by his paintings. Based on letters, writings, contemporary accounts and criticism.
a. 2nd ed.: 1946, 512 p.

294. GRAVELAINE, FREDERIQUE DE. *Paul Gauguin; la vie, la technique, l'oeuvre peinte*. Lausanne: Edita, 1988. 159 p., illus., 49 col. pl.

Examination of Gauguin's life and artistic technique as revealed in his paintings.

295. HANSON, LAWRENCE and ELISABETH HANSON. *Noble Savage: The Life of Paul Gauguin*. New York: Random House, 1955. 300 p., 22 illus.

Popularized biography which stresses his life and legend over his art. Reviews: *Art Digest 29* (1 March 1955):14; *Apollo* 61(April 1955):126; *Werk* 42(July 1955): supp. 152.
a. English eds.: London: Chatto & Windus, 1955; London: Arrow Books, 1960.
b. Danish ed.: *Forgifrat Paradis* [Poisoned Paradise]. Trans. by Brita Knyphausen and Eugen Wretholm. 1955. 319 p.
c. Czech eds.: *Urozený, divoch. Zivot Paula Gauguina*. Prague: SNKLHU, 1959; 1967. 371 p., 20 pl.
d. Spanish ed.: *Gauguin*. Trans. by José C. Oliveira. 1960.
e. Chinese ed.: 1982. 181 p., 12 pl.

296. HAUTECOEUR, LOUIS. *Gauguin*. Geneve: A. Skira, 1938. 8 p., 8 col. pl.

Color plates following a short introduction.
a. Excerpts: *Beaux-Arts* (4 November 1938):5.
b. Other eds.: 1940, 1942, 1946, 1947.

297. HOOG, MICHEL. *Paul Gauguin, vie et oeuvre*. Paris: Nathan; Fribourg: Office du Livre, 1987. 333 p. 217 illus., 150 in col.

Sets Gauguin in artistic and historical perspective by examining artists who influenced Gauguin, especially Cézanne, Monet, and van Gogh. Includes chapters on Gauguin's childhood and youth in Peru; his artistic training in Martinique, and Panama; Gauguin's involvement in Parisian literary and poetic currents, particularly symbolism; Gauguin's flight from Western civilization and sojourn in Tahiti; Primitivism; his return to France and his last stay in the Marquesas; and a critical opinion of his work. Includes a chronology, bibliography, and lists of exhibitions and works. The author is the curator-in-chief at the Musée de l'Orangerie, Paris.
Review: R. Kendall, *Apollo* 129(May 1989):367-68.
a. English ed.: *Paul Gauguin: Life and Work.* New York: Rizzoli, 1987. 335 p., 217 illus., 150 col.
b. German ed.: *Paul Gauguin: Leben und Werk.* Fribourg: Office du Livre, 1987.

298. HUYGHE, RENE. *Paul Gauguin.* Paris: Hachette, 1959. 94 p., illus., some col.

Analysis of Gauguin's life and painting which argues that modern art begins with Gauguin and van Gogh.
a. Other French eds.: Paris: Hachette, 1961; Paris: Flammarion, 1967; 1988.
b. U.S. eds.: *Gauguin.* Trans. by Helen C. Slonim. New York: Crown, 1959; 1978, 1988. 96 p., 46 illus., col. pl.
c. Swedish ed.: *Gauguin.* Malmo: Allhem, 1959. 95 p.
d. Italian ed.: *Gauguin.* Milan: Uffici, 1959; A. Vallardi, 1960. 96 p., 43 pl.
e. English ed.: Naefels, Switzerland: Bonfini Press, 1977.

299. HUYGHE, RENE. "Initiateur des temps nouveaux." In *Gauguin* Paris: Hachette, 1960, pp. 237-83.

300. IKEDA, MASUO and YOSHIKAZU IWASAKI. *Gogyan.* Tokyo: Schoakukan, 1977. 158 p., illus., 54 col. pl. In Japanese.
Titles and captions also in English, French, and other languages.

301. KANTOR-GUKOVSKAYA, ASYA SOLOMONOVA. [*Paul Gauguin: Life and Work*]. Leningrad, Moscow: Publishing House "Sovetskii Khudozhnik," 1965. 183 p., 52 illus., pl. In Russian.
a. U.S. ed.: *Paul Gauguin.* Trans. by John McNair. New York: H.N. Abrams, 1977. 41 p., 25 pl., some col.
b. Another ed.: Leningrad: Aurora Art Publishers, 1987. 24 p., illus., 13 col. pl.

302. KUNSTLER, CHARLES. *Gauguin, peintre maudit.* Paris: Librairie Floury, 1934. 194 p. 63 pl., 8 col.

Biography and criticism of Gauguin, based on letters and excerpts from his writings.
Review: *L'Amour de l'art* 15: supp. 3 (October 1934).
a. Other eds.: 1937, 1942, 1947.

303. LANGER, ALFRED KARASEK. *Paul Gauguin.* Leipzig: VEB E.A. Seemann, 1963. 97 p., illus., 90 col. pl.

Biography and critical analysis in German, with an English summary on pages 94-95.
a. Another ed.: 1965.

304. LAZAR, BELA. *Gauguin.* Paris: Office Central de Libraire, 1908. 39 p.

Text of an address made at the National Gallery in Budapest on May 14, 1907, on the occasion of an exhibition of works by Gauguin.

305. LECLERC, ANDRE [pseud. for Irene Immerman]. *Gauguin.* London, New York: Hyperion Press, 1949. 47 p., illus., some col.

Chiefly illustrated biographical treatment.
a. French ed.: Paris: Hyperion, 1950. 48 p., illus.

306. LEGRAND, GERARD. *Gauguin.* Paris: Bordas, 1966. 64 p. illus., col. pl.

Largely pictorial biography illustrated by Gauguin's paintings. Includes a section on Tahiti, a chronology, and an appendix of excerpts from Gauguin's writings.

307. LEPROHON, PIERRE. *Paul Gauguin.* Paris: Grund, 1975. 415 p., 60 illus., 16 pl.

Detailed biography in two parts. The first section (pp. 1-320) covers the life and artistic output of Gauguin. The second part (pp. 322-415) is a bibliographic essay with commentaries and documents about the artist. Includes sections on numbers of paintings and disposition, exhibitions, writings by Gauguin, sites and locations, and a genealogy, chronology, and bibliography.

308. LEYMARIE, JEAN. *Gauguin.* Lausanne: J. Marguerat, 1950. 32 p., 53 pl. Pictorial biography.

309. MALINGUE, MAURICE. *Gauguin.* Monaco: Documents d'art, 1943. 168 p., illus., 111 pl., 12 col.

Biographical introduction followed by large plates.
a. Another ed.: 1944.

310. MALINGUE, MAURICE. *Gauguin: le peintre et son oeuvre.* Foreword by Pola Gauguin. Paris: Presses de la Cité, 1943. 2 vols., 253 p., illus., pl.

Review: *Formes et couleurs* 10:4 (1948):110.
a. Another ed.: 1948. 255 p., illus., pl.

311. MALINGUE, MAURICE. "L'homme qui a réinventé la peinture." In *Gauguin.* Paris: Hachette, 1960, pp. 110-37.

312. MALINGUE, MAURICE. *La vie prodigieuse de Gauguin.* Paris: Editions Buchet/Chastel, 1987. 311 p., illus.

Biographical treatment of Gauguin's life interspersed with writings and letters.

313. MARCHIORI, GIUSEPPE. *Gauguin.* Florence: Sadea/Sansoni, 1967. 39 p., 40 col. pl. In Italian.

Includes an introduction about the artist's life and works and notes on the plates.
a. English eds.: *Gauguin, the Life and Work of the Artist.* Trans. by Caroline Beamish. London: Thames and Hudson, 1967, 1984. 38 p., 79 p., col. pl.
b. U.S. ed.: New York: Grosset & Dunlap, 1967. 39 p., 80 p., col. pl.
c. French ed.: *Gauguin.* Trans. by Henriette Valot. Paris: Flammarion, 1980. 40 p., 79 p. col. pl.

314. MARKS-VANDENBROUCKE, URSULA F. *Paul Gauguin, ses origines et sa formation artisitique.* Ph.D. diss., Sorbonne, Paris, 1956.

Deals with Gauguin's artistic development, education, and influences.

315. MARTINI, ALBERTO and FRANCO RUSSOLI. *Paul Gauguin.* Milan: Fratelli Fabbri Editori, 1964. 17 p., illus., 16 col. pl. In Italian.

Includes a short introduction and notes on the color plates.
a. New ed.: 1977.

316. MITTELSTADT, KUNO. *Paul Gauguin.* Berlin: Henschel, 1963. 48 p., illus., 40 pl., some col. In German.

Pictorial treatment which includes notes on the plates, a general introduction, and a chronology.
a. Another ed.: Berlin: Henschel, 1973. 72 p., 30 illus., 17 col. pl.

317. MORICE, CHARLES. *Gauguin*. Paris: H. Floury, 1919. 235 p., illus., 62 pl., some col.

Biography and reminiscences of Gauguin's life by Charles Morice (1861-1919), an important symbolist poet and author who met Gauguin in 1889. Gauguin learned synthetist theories from Morice and had contacts with him for the rest of his life. Morice wrote newspaper articles about Gauguin and prefaces to several exhibition catalogues. He corresponded regularly with Gauguin and collaborated in 1893 on the *Noa Noa* manuscript.
a. 2nd ed.: Paris: H. Floury, 1920.

318. MIYAKAWA, ATSUSHI. *Gogyan*. Tokyo: Shinchosha, 1974. 93 p., illus., 32 col. pl.

319. MOTOE, KUNIO. *Gogyan*. Tokyo: Shueisha, 1986. 99 p., illus. In Japanese, list of plates also in French.

320. MOTOE, KUNIO and TAKESHI KASHIWA. *Gogyan*. Tokyo: Senshukai, 1978. 87 p., illus., 38 pl., 32 col. In Japanese; title also in French.

321. MULLER, JOSEPH-EMILE. *Gauguin*. Paris: F. Hazan, 1981. 37 p., 72 p. col. pl.

Life and analysis of Gauguin's oeuvre.
a. English ed.: *Gauguin*. Trans. by Jane Brenton. London: Eyre Methuen, 1982. 37 p., 60 p. col. pl.

322. NACENTA, RAYMOND. *Gauguin*. Paris: Art et Style, 1960. 8 p., illus., 35 pl., 9 col. Text in French and German.

Largely pictorial survey of Gauguin's art following a preface by Nacenta.

323. NICHOLLS, PAUL C. *Gauguin*. New York: Tudor Publishing Co., 1967. 36 p., 96 col. pl.

Pictorial treatment which includes a biographical introduction, chronology, and notes on the color plates.

324. OLMOS, PEDRO. *Gauguin*. Buenos Aires: Editorial America, 1943. 208 p., 8 pl.

Biography in Spanish.

325. *P. Gauguin*. México: Publicaciones Cruz O., 1981. 32 p., illus.

326. *Paul Gauguin*. Paris: Chêne, 1986. 238 p., illus.

327. PAYRO, JULIO E. *Paul Gauguin*. Buenos Aires: Editorial Poseidón, 1943. 66 p., 42 illus., 4 col. pl.

Life and analysis of Gauguin in Spanish illustrated by reproductions of his paintings. Includes a chronology.

328. PERRUCHOT, HENRI. *Gauguin, sa vie ardente et misérable*. Paris: Le Sillage, 1948. 332 p., illus., 8 pl.

Biography of Gauguin which stresses the romantic legend and Polynesian periods.

329. PERRUCHOT, HENRI. *La vie de Gauguin*. Paris: Hachette, 1961. 428p., illus., pl., some col.

Biography which includes a chronology, exhibitions list, and bibliography. Illustrated by reproductions of photographs and works.
a. English ed.: *Gauguin*. Trans. by Humphrey Hare, ed. by Jean Ellsmoor. London: Perpetua, 1963. 398 p., pl.
b. U.S. ed.: *Gauguin*. Trans. by Humphrey Hare, ed. by Jean Ellsmoor. Cleveland, New York: World Publishing Company, 1963. 398 p., pl.
c. German ed.: *Gauguin. Eine Biographie*. Munich: Bechtle, 1964. 478 p., pl.
d. Czech ed.: Trans. by Hanna Olédzka. Warsaw: Pánstwony Instytut Wydawniczy, 1970. 461 p., pl.

330. PERRUCHOT, HENRI. "La vie de Gauguin." In *Gauguin*. Paris: Hachette, 1960, pp. 7-39.

331. PERRUCHOT, HENRI. *Art et destin: 4. Gauguin*. 1960.

332. PETERS, ROBERT LOUIS. *Gauguin's Chair; Selected Poems, 1967-1974*. Trumansburg, NY: Crossing Press, 1977. 138 p.

Poems based in part on Gauguin's life.

333. LE PICHON, YANN. *Sur les traces de Gauguin*. Paris: Robert Laffont, 1986. 262 p., illus., some col., col. pl.

Juxtaposes color reproductions of Gauguin's paintings with black-and-white photographs--many by the painter himself--of the artist, his wife and family, his models and studio, and paintings by his favorite artists. The photographs formed "a whole little world of friends who talk to me every day," as Gauguin put it. The work covers Gauguin's life in detail. Includes a section of maps which shows Gauguin's travels in France and elsewhere.
a. English ed.: *Gauguin: Life, Art, Inspiration.* New York: Harry N. Abrams, 1987.
Trans. by I. Mark Paris. 268 p., illus., some col.

334. PIERRE, MICHEL. *Bonjour, Monsieur Gauguin.* Illustré par Philippe Moins. Paris: Casterman, 1989. 64 p., illus.

Children's story based on an 11-year-old boy finding a reproduction of a work by Gauguin in his mailbox. Follows Gauguin's life to Brittany and Oceania.

335. POOL, PHOEBE. *Paul Gauguin.* London: Knowledge Publishing Co., 1967. 33 p., 2 illus., 16 col. pl.

a. U.S. ed.: New York: Funk & Wagnalls, 1978. 33 p., illus.

336. PRATHER, MARLA and CHARLES F. STUCKEY, eds. *Gauguin: A Retrospective.* New York: Hugh Lauter Levin Associates; distributed by Macmillan, New York, and Pandemic, London; 1987. 387 p., 226 illus., 125 col.

Survey of the life and art of Gauguin through an anthology of the writings of friends, colleagues, writers, artists and critics, as well as the writings of Gauguin himself. The introduction provides an account of Gauguin's life and artistic career.
a. Another ed.: New York: Park Lane, distributed by Crown Publishers, 1989.

337. RABOFF, ERNEST LLOYD and ADELINE PETER. *Paul Gauguin.* Bradley Smith, ed. New York: Doubleday, 1974. 31 p., illus.

Children's book on Paul Gauguin. Includes a brief biographical sketch and discussion of his paintings, drawings, and designs.
a. Other eds.: New York: J.P. Lippincott, 1988; New York: Harper & Row, 1988.

338. READ, HERBERT EDWARD. *Gauguin (1848-1903).* London: Faber & Faber, 1949. 24 p., illus., pl.

a. Another ed.: 1958.

339. RENE, JEAN. *Gauguin*. Paris: Braun, 1948. 32 p., 24 col. pl. In French, English, and German.

340. REWALD, JOHN. *Gauguin*. New York: French and European Publications; Paris: Hyperion Press, 1938. 167 p., illus., 127 pl., some col.

Large plate-book with an introduction on Gauguin's life and work. Reprints Gauguin's "Notes on Painting" essay (ca. 1890), pp. 161-63, first published in 1910 by Henri Mahaut. Includes a comprehensive bibliography of works on Gauguin to 1937.
Reviews: J. Babelon, *Gazette des Beaux-Arts*, 6th ser., 21 (Feb. 1939):126; *Apollo* 51 (February 1950):58; *Connoisseur* 125 (May 1950):128; *Art Digest* 24 (July 1950):22; *Art News* 49 (October 1950):6.
Excerpts: *Beaux Arts* (7 April 1939):6.
a. Other eds.: London: William Heinemann, 1949. 167 p.; New York: Hyperion Press, 1949; New York: Macmillan, 1950. 167 p., 160 illus., 16 col. pl.

341. REWALD, JOHN. *Gauguin*. New York: Harry N. Abrams, 1954. 6 p., 16 col. pl. Also published in a smaller format, "Abrams-Pocket Library of Great Art" series, 1954, illus., 20 col. pl.

Short biography of Gauguin followed by a "Commentary" section which discusses each plate.

342. REY, ROBERT. *Gauguin*. Paris: F. Rieder, 1924. 63 p., 40 pl.

Biography of Gauguin illustrated with plates.
a. Other eds.: Paris: Rieder, 1928, 1929.
b. U.S. ed.: Trans. by F.C. de Sumichrast. New York: Dodd, Mead, 1924. 63 p., 40 pl.
c. English ed.: London: J. Lane, 1924. 63 p., 40 pl.

343. RHEIMS, MAURICE. "La côté des Gauguin." In *Gauguin*. Paris: Hachette, 1960, pp. 211-35.

344. ROGER-MARX, CLAUDE. "Ce que lui doit la peinture contemporaine." In *Gauguin*. Paris: Hachette, 1960, pp. 171-209.

345. ROTONCHAMP, JEAN DE [Louis Brouillon]. *Paul Gauguin, 1848-1903 Avec huit reproductions de tableaux de l'artiste*. Weimar: Kessler; Paris: Edouard Druet, 1906. 227 p., illus. 300 copies.

First major biography of Gauguin. Brouillon (1858-?), an art critic, wrote under the pseudonym of Jean de Rotonchamp. Emile Schuffenecker introduced the two men in 1889.
a. Another ed.: Paris: G. Crés, 1925. 264 p., 8 pl.

346. RUSSELL, JOHN. *Gauguin.* New York: American Library, 1968. 24 p., illus., 32 col. pl.

Includes a brief introduction, biography, and bibliography.
a. English eds.: London: Collins, UNESCO, 1968. 20 p., 34 illus., 32 col. pl.; Lausanne: UNESCO and Editions Rencontre, 1970. 86 p., 32 col. pl., slides.
b. French ed.: Paris: A. Michel, 1968. 32 p., 32 col. pl.

347. SABLONIERE, MARGRIT DE. *Paul Gauguin.* Amsterdam, Antwerp: Wereld-Bibliotheek, 1960. 74 p., In Dutch. 16 pl.

Study of the life and work of Gauguin with considerable information on his relationship with Vincent and Theo van Gogh.

348. SCHMIDT, GEORG. *Gauguin.* Bern: A. Scherz, 1950. 31 p., 53 pl.

a. Italian ed.: *Gauguin.* Trans. by Ervino Pocar. Milan: A. Martello, 1950. 32 p., 53 pl.

349. SCHEIWILLER, GIOVANNI. *Paul Gauguin, 1903-1948.* Milan: Espéria, 1943. 6 p., 8 pl.

350. SCHNEIDER, BRUNO F. *Gauguin.* Munich: Südwest Verlag, 1966. 28 p. (pp. 10-28 illus. with text).

Introduction to Gauguin and his art works followed by reproductions and notes on the color plates.
a. U.S. ed.: *Gauguin.* Trans. by Susan Bellamy. New York: Crown Publishers, 1966. 28 p., illus., 10 col. pl.

351. SEDLAK, JAN. *Paul Gauguin.* Prague: Odeon, 1977. 84 p., illus. In Czech.

352. SEGALEN, VICTOR. "Hommage à Gauguin." In *Lettres de Paul Gauguin à Georges-Daniel de Monfreid.* Paris: G. Crès, 1918, pp. 1-77; rev. ed. Paris: G. Falaize, 1950, pp. 11-47.
a. Other eds.: 1920, 1930.

353. TAN'O, YASUNORI. *Gogyan.* Tokyo: Kodansha, 1977. 32 p., illus. In Japanese.

a. Another ed.: 1980. 133 p.

354. TAVERNIER, M. L. and PATRICK O'REILLY. *L'écriture de Gauguin: étude graphologique*. Paris: Société des Océanistes, 1968. 52 p., illus.

Analysis of Gauguin's handwriting which concludes that it is lyrical, rhythmic, and enthusiastic. Interesting also for the documents reproduced and examined.

355. THARAUD, JEROME and JEAN. *Le gentil douanier et un artiste maudit*. Paris: Cahiers Libres, 1929. 47 p.

Brief biography of Gauguin on pp. 33-47.

356. THOMSON, BELINDA. *Gauguin*. London: Thames and Hudson, 1987. 215 p., 182 illus., 31 col.

Study of the life and work of Gauguin which pays close attention to the artist's writings and interpretations of his art. In many instances, Gauguin's creative influence continued, in the form of changes to a title or authoritative written exegeses, long after a work had left his studio. He often intervened as well in the equally important stage of public reception and critical interpretation. Demonstrates that Gauguin's belief in the ultimate triumph of his supreme acts of individualism sustained him through the bad times.

357. TOW, MARTIN. *Tainted Paradise; A Study of the Life and Art of Paul Gauguin*. New York [Camden, N.J.: Haddon Craftsmen], 1937. 170 p., 18 pl.

Fictionalized account of Gauguin's life and work.

358. UEBERWASSER, WALTER. *P. Gauguin: Sucher nach Heiligen Hainen* [Paul Gauguin: Seeker of Sacred groves]. Basel: Basler Druck- und Verlagsanstalt, 1950. 12 p., pl.

359. WALTHER, INGO F. *Paul Gauguin, 1848-1903; The Primitive Sophisticate*. Trans. by Michael Hulse. Cologne: Benedikt Taschen Verlag, 1988. 95 p., illus., some col.
a. English ed.: *Paul Gauguin, 1848-1903; the Primitive Sophisticate*. Trans. by Michael Hulse. Cologne: B. Taschen, 1988. 95 p., illus.

360. WERNER, ALFRED. *Paul Gauguin*. New York: McGraw-Hill, 1967. 47 p., illus., 19 pl., 20 slides.

Life and study of Gauguin's art, accompanied by slides and commentary. Volume in McGraw-Hill's "Color Slide Program of the Great Masters" series.

361. WIESE, ERICH. *Paul Gauguin; zwei Jahrzehnte nach seinem Tode* [Paul Gauguin; Two Decades after His Death]. Leipzig: Klinkhardt & Biermann, 1923. 16 p., 32 pl.

Biographical and critical study of Gauguin with black-and-white plates. See also *Der Cicerone* 15:14 (July 1923):635-39.

362. WILDENSTEIN, DANIEL and RENE COGNIAT. *Paul Gauguin.* Milan: Fratelli Fabbri, 1972. 95 p., illus., 30 col.

Biography of Gauguin, documented with extracts from the artist's letters and other contemporary material, which shows how his early Impressionist work of the Paris and Pont-Aven years gradually evolved into an innovative and emotive primitivism under the influence of the culture of the French West Indies after 1887, and of Tahiti where he spent much time after 1891. The symbolic and expressive use of flat color found in his Martinique paintings marked a definite move away from Impressionist naturalism, and the human figure took over from landscape as subject matter. Influenced by Emile Bernard and Symbolist ideas during a brief return to Pont-Aven in 1888, and encouraged by his use of flat, pure color areas in paintings executed during his stay with van Gogh in Arles in the same year, Gauguin reached the monumental simplicity displayed in *Where do we come? What are we? Where are we going*? (1897). A section in which his works appear in chronological order illustrates this development, and a letter from August Strindberg to Gauguin is also included, in which the writer refuses to compose the introduction to a catalogue accompanying an exhibition of Gauguin's work. Several pages are devoted to Gauguin's caricatures and forgeries.

Review: *American Artist* 38(November 1974):25-26.
a. English ed.: *Gauguin.* London: Thames & Hudson, 1973. 95 p., 212 illus.
b. U.S. eds.: Garden City, NY: Doubleday, 1974; Secaucus, NJ: Chartwell Books, 1982.
c. French ed.: Anvers: Plantyn, 1974.

363. WILDENSTEIN, GEORGES, ed. *Gauguin; sa vie, son oeuvre.* Paris: Gazette des Beaux-Arts, 1958. 211 p., illus.

Collection of texts, studies and documents on Gauguin published as a monograph by the *Gazette des Beaux-Arts* as numbers 1044-1047 (January-April 1958). Contributors include Wildenstein, Ursula F. Marks-Vandenbroucke, Haavard Rostrup, Yvonne Thirion, Jénot, Jean

Loize, and Georges Le Bronnec. Unedited and little-known documents about Gauguin are appended.

364. WISE, SUSAN. *Paul Gauguin: His Life and His Paintings*. Chicago: Art Institute of Chicago, 1980. 18 p., 16 illus., pl.

Focuses on how the sequence of events in Gauguin's life played a major role in his long drive to find a plastic expression for an intensive personal vision. "Basically defiant, it seems impossible to imagine that his works had any source other than his inability to absorb and consequently encompass accepted standards. In other words, the basic character of man and the way in which he met perpetually with criticism, hardship and contempt was transformed into the driving impetus of his creative intention." (p. 16)

365. YOSHIKAWA, ITSUJI. *Poru Gogyan/Paul Gauguin*. Tokyo: Heibonsha, 1970. 15 p., illus., 8 pl.

Short, chiefly illustrated biography of Gauguin in Japanese.

366. ZAMFIRESCU, NINA STANCULESCU, ed. *Gauguin*. Bucharest: Meridiane, 1969.

Pictorial treatment of Gauguin's works. Includes reprints of texts by contemporary artists and critics about Gauguin's life and works, and a chronology.
a. 2nd ed.: 1972.
b. English ed.: *Gauguin*. Trans. by Sylvia M. Oldfield-Florescu. London: Abbey Press, 1973. 38 p., 61 pl.

367. ZELENINA, KLAVDIIA. *Pol Gogen*. Moscow: Gos. Muzei Novogo Zapadnogo Iskusstva, 1926. 8 p.

B. Articles

368. ANGER, ISOLDE. "Paul Gauguins Leben" [Paul Gauguin's Life]. *Kunst* 48 (1950): 8-11. 5 illus.

369. ARRIETA, RAFAEL ALBERTO. "Pablo Gauguin, pintor y escritor." *Instituto popular de conferencia, Anales* 29(Buenos Aires, 1944):39-55.

370. BERNARD, EMILE. "Gauguin." *Mercure de France* (Dec. 1908).

371. BIAD, A. "Paul Gauguin." *Contemporary Review* 190(July 1956):33-37.

372. BODELSEN, MERETE CHRISTENSEN. "Gauguin, the Collector" [with a catalogue of Gauguin's collection]. *Burlington Magazine* 112:810(Sept. 1970):590-612.

373. BODELSEN, MERETE CHRISTENSEN. "En norsk Malerinde set med Gauguins ejne" [A Norwegian Woman-Painter seen by Gauguin]. *Kunst og Kultur* 62:3 (1979): 143-48. 6 illus.

Discusses the Norwegian painter Agnes Steineger and her relationship with Gauguin. Includes a facsimile of a letter and a drawing by Gauguin in August, 1886.

374. BOSMAN, ANTHONY. "Paul Gauguin." *Kroniek van Kunst en Kultur* (Amsterdam)9:5(May 1948):139-40.

375. BOURET, JEAN. "Gauguin, toujours inconnu." *Arts* 308(27 April 1951):1, 8.

376. BOWNESS, ALAN. "The Case for Gauguin." *Art News and Review*. 7(15 Oct. 1955):2.

377. BREST, R. "Gauguin." *Ver y Estimar* (Buenos Aires) (Oct.-Nov. 1948).

378. BUSER, THOMAS. "Gauguin's Religion." *Art Journal* 27:4(Summer 1968):375-80.

379. CAHN, ISABELLE. "Gauguin." *Le Petit journal des grandes expositions*. 191(1989):1-4.

380. CHABOT, C. "Paul Gauguin." *Art et vie* (1935):209-15.

381. CHAMPIGNEULLE, BERNARD. "Il y a 70 ans Gauguin." *Arts* 757(Jan. 1960):757.

382. CHASSE, CHARLES. "Beaucoup de faits nouveaux sur Gauguin." *Prisme des arts* (1957). 4 p.

383. CHASSE, CHARLES. "Le sort de Gauguin est lié au krach de 1882." *Connaissance des arts* 84(Feb. 1959):40-43. 9 illus.

Examines Gauguin's change of profession from stockbroker to painter in 1882.

384. COGNIAT, RAYMOND. "Gauguin l'inadapté." *Arts* 4(June 1948):1+.

385. COGNIAT, RAYMOND and DANIEL WILDENSTEIN. "Paul Gauguin." *Grands peintres* 17 (Sept. 1966):18.

386. COOPER, DOUGLAS. Collection of "Papers, ca. 1933-1985," which includes Cooper's files and papers on Gauguin. Contains Cooper's working papers for the unfinished catalogue raisonné for Gauguin and Cooper's work in dating and authenticating Gauguin's paintings for individuals and institutions. Also includes typescripts for lectures delivered by Cooper in London, Paris, Cambridge, and the U.S. on Gauguin's works. Douglas Cooper (1911-84) was an English art historian, critic and collector. Located at The Getty Center for the History of Art and the Humanities, Archives of the History of Art, Santa Monica, California.

387. DAMISCH, HUBERT. "L'amour m'expose." *Cahiers du Musée National d'art Moderne* 29(Autumn 1989):80-90.

388. DANTO, A.C. "Gauguin." *The Nation* 246:11(June 1988):838-40.

389. DAUBLER, THEODOR. "Gauguin." *Kunstwerk* 11(Nov.-Dec. 1957):10-13.

390. DAVIS, F. "Gauguin Through His Own Eyes." *Country Life* 150(15 July 1971):150.

391. DEVOLUY, JOHN. "Time to Think of Gauguin." *Art News* 48(1949):14-17.

392. DORIVAL, BERNARD. "Gauguin, avant qu'en lui-même." *Table ronde* 41 (1951):174-81.

393. DORSENNE, JEAN. "La vie affective de Paul Gauguin." *Mercure de France* 115(1927):305-61.

394. VAN DOWSKI, LEE [Herbert Lewandowski]. "Gauguin als Schriftsteller; Eine Studie" [Gauguin as a Writer: A Study]. *Cahiers de Frontenac* (Geneva, 1947).

395. FRANKFURTER, A.M. "Gauguin." *Art News* (March 1936):5-6.

396. GALLEGO, JULIAN. "Años de aprendizaje de Paul Gauguin." *Goya, Revista de Arte* 36 (May-June 1960):367-72. 11 illus.

397. GARDNER, J. "Paul Gauguin in the Vanguard." *National Review* 40(7 Nov. 1988):70-71.

398. GAUGUIN, PAUL. "The Wisdom of Paul Gauguin from his Letters to Georges-Daniel de Monfreid." *International Studio* 73 (1921):118-20.

399. GAUGUIN, PAUL. "Une lettre inédite de Paul Gauguin." *Labyrinthe* (Geneva) 4(15 Jan. 1945):9. Facsimile.

400. GAUGUIN, PAUL. "Une lettre de Gauguin." *Prisme des arts* 1(15 March 1956):19. Facsimile.

401. GAUGUIN, POLA. "Paul Gauguin: avant et après." *Kunsten Idag* 1(1954):20-33. illus. Summary in English.

402. "Gauguin." *Burlington Magazine* 45(1924):98-101.

403. "Gauguin." *The Studio* 16(1938):232-38.

404. "Gauguin." *Chicago Art Institute Quarterly* 53:(Feb. 1959):1-7.

405. "Gauguin." *Art et Style* 55(1960).

406. "Gauguin." *F. Magazine* (1987).

407. "Gauguin before Gauguin." *Time* 69(1 April 1957):76.

408. "Gauguin, fut-il assassiné?" *Beaux-Arts* (17 Aug. 1934):1.

409. "Gauguin: Turning Point." *Art News*, 45(1946):26-29, 67.

410. "Gauguin's Faithless Javanese." *Life* 29:11(11 Sept. 1950):112.

411. GAUNT, W. "Paul Gauguin." *London Studio* 16(Studio 116; Nov. 1938):232-38.

412. "Great Loves of Great Artists." *Life* 29(Sept. 1950):112.

413. GUIBAL, JEAN. "Gauguin blessé à Concarneau." *La Dépêche de Brest* 4(Aug. 1942).

414. HAVELAAR, JUST. "Paul Gauguin." *Elsevier's Geillustreerd Maandschrift* 44(1912):411-20.

415. HAWEIS, STEPHEN. "Paul Gauguin-Artist." *International Studio* 73(May 1921):93-98.

416. HERTZ, HENRI. "Paul Gauguin." *Art in America* 15:3(April 1927):138, 143-53. 2 pl.

417. HILDEBRANDT, HANS. "Paul Gauguin." *Aussaat* 1:12 (1947):14-18.

418. HOBHOUSE, J. "Civilized Man, Savage Artist." *Newsweek* 111(16 May 1988):78-80.

419. HUEBNER, F. M. "Briefe von Paul Gauguin" [Letters of Paul Gauguin]. *Kunstchronik* 30(11 July 1919):815-18.

420. HUGHES, ROBERT. "Unforgettable Self-Delusion." *Time* (22 March 1971):44-46.

421. IMBOURG, P. "Le bal Gauguin." *Beaux-Arts* (18 Dec. 1936): 1+.

422. JEWELL, EDWARD A. "Gauguin: Fact and Myth." *New York Times* (26 Sept. 1937).

423. KREMER, R. "Gauguin." *USA Today* 116(May 1988):70-83.

424. KUNSTLER, CHARLES. "L'évolution de Gauguin." *L'Art vivant* 7(March 1931):86-87.

425. KUNSTLER, CHARLES. "Paul Gauguin et la Révolution Espagnole." *Les Nouvelles littéraires* (9 Jan. 1937).

426. KUNSTLER, CHARLES. "Gauguin est-il mort empoisonné?" *Candide* (28 June 1934).

427. KUNSTLER, CHARLES. "Sur la mort de Paul Gauguin." *Comoedia* 16(17 July 1934).

428. LASSAIGNE, JACQUES. "Gauguin tel qu'il fut." *Revue de la pensée française* 6(June 1947):43-47.

429. LOIZE, JEAN. "Quand Gauguin se faisait critique d'art." *Le Figaro littéraire* (9May 1953):4.

430. LORMEL, LOUIS. "Gauguin." *La Revue illustrée* (1907).

431. MALINGUE, MAURICE. "Du nouveau sur Gauguin." *L'Oeil* 55-56 (July-Aug. 1959):32-39. 13 illus.

432. MALINGUE, MAURICE. "Encore du nouveau sur Gauguin. *L'Oeil* 58 (Oct. 1959): 24-33,68. 21 illus.

Primarily an interview between Malingue and Pola Gauguin, son of the painter, concerning Gauguin's family life. Includes some unpublished photographs of the family.

433. MARKS-VANDENBROUCKE, URSULA F. "Documents divers concernant Gauguin." *Gazette des Beaux-Arts* 6th ser. 47(Jan.-April 1956):209-11.

434. MARKS-VANDENBROUCKE, URSULA F. "Gauguin--Ses origines et sa formation artistique." *Gazette des Beaux-Arts* 6th ser., 47(Jan.-April 1956)[published 1958]:9-62. Reprinted in *Gauguin, sa vie, son oeuvre* (Paris, 1958).

435. MAUCLAIR, CAMILLE. "La Pintura en Francia (Homenaje a Gauguin)." *La Nacion* (18 Feb. 1934).

436. MAUCLAIR, CAMILLE. "Homenaje a Paul Gauguin." *Museo nacional de bellas artes boletin* (Buenos Aires) 1(March 1934):16.

437. MEYER-RIEFSTAHL, RUDOLF. "Paul Gauguin." *Deutsche Kunst und Dekoration* 27 (Nov. 1910):109-16.

438. MONFREID, GEORGES DANIEL DE. [Article on Gauguin in *L'Hermitage*] (Dec. 1908).

439. MORICE, CHARLES. [Article on Gauguin in *Art Moderne*] 80(1909).

440. NEMECZEK, A. "Paul Gauguin: der Aussteiger" [Paul Gauguin: the Dropout]. *Art: das Kunstmagazin* pt. 3 (March 1982):20-45. 20 illus.

441. NEWTON, E. "Gauguin." *Apollo* 59(April 1954):92-93.

442. "A Noble Rogue: Five New Books Offer Five Different Versions of the Enigmatic Paul Gauguin." *Arts & Antiques* (May 1988):118.

443. NØRREGARD-NIELSEN, HANS EDVARD. "For hundrede år siden" [A hundred years ago]. *Årsskrift-Carlsbergfondet, Frederiksborgmuseet, Ny Carlsbergfondet* (1985):135-42. 4 illus., 1 col. In Danish.

Study of Paul Gauguin's stay in Copenhagen with his Danish wife's family in the winter of 1884-85, when he painted the Impressionist-style *Skaters in Frederiksberg Garden*, (Ny Carlsberg Glyptotek, Copenhagen).

444. O'CONNELL KERR, JOHN. "Paul Gauguin, Creative Iconoclast." *The Studio* 150:752(Dec. 1955):170-75. 7 illus.

445. "On inaugure une plaque sur la maison natale de Gauguin." *Beaux-Arts* (22 Dec. 1933):6.

446. "P. Gauguin: Artist's Unhappy Life is now a Legend." *Life* 21(1946):60-64.

447. "Paul Gauguin." *London Studio* 16(1938):232-38.

448. "Paul Gauguin." *Paris-Match* 565(6 Feb. 1960):35-38. 5 illus.

449. PERL, J. "The King of Dropouts." *The New Republic* 198(13 June 1988):39-42.

450. PERRUCHOT, HENRI. "Pourquoi Gauguin avait choisi la misère." *Arts* 739(9-15 Sept. 1959):11.

451. PERRUCHOT, HENRI. "Explication de Gauguin." *Revue des deux mondes* 5 (1961): 218-30.

452. PFISTER, KURT. "Paul Gauguin." *Deutsche Kunst und Dekoration* 55(Dec. 1924):140-54.

453. PUY, MICHEL. "Paul Gauguin." *L'Art décoratif* 25(April 1911):173-88.

454. PUY, MICHEL. "Gauguin." *Les Marges* (July 1920).

455. READ, HERBERT EDWARD. "Gauguin." *Kunstwerk* 19(July 1965):5.

456. REWALD, JOHN. "Précisions sur Gauguin." *L'Amour de l'art* 19(July 1938):257.

457. REWALD, JOHN. "Le suicide de Paul Gauguin." *Marianne* (Paris)(7 Sept. 1938):9.

458. REWALD, JOHN. "The Genius and the Dealer." *Art News* 58:3(May 1959):30-31, 62-65.

Details Gauguin's business relationship with Ambroise Vollard.

459. REY, ROBERT. "Gauguin." *L'Art vivant* 3(1927):212-15.

460. REY, ROBERT. "Paul Gauguin." *L'Amour de l'art* (May 1928).

461. REYER, GEORGES. "Paul Gauguin." *Paris-Match* 493(20 Sept. 1958):46-63, 85. 9 illus.

462. ROSTRUP, HAVAARD. "Gauguin et le Danemark." *Gazette des Beaux-Arts* 6th ser., 47(Jan.-April 1956)[published in 1958]:63-82. Reprinted in *Gauguin; sa vie, son oeuvre* (Paris, 1958).

463. SABLONIERE, MARGRIT DE. "De Nalatenschap van Gauguin" [The Legacy of Gauguin]. *Kroniek van Kunst en Kultuur* (Amsterdam)11:3(March 1950):88-89.

464. "Savage from Peru." *Apollo* 93(June 1971):519-21. 2 illus.

465. SCHAPIRO, MEYER. "Gauguin: A Family Portrait." *The Nation* 145 (10 July 1937):50.

466. SOLOMON, D. "Gauguin: Savage or Sophisticate?" *Harper's Bazaar* 121(May 1988):134-37+.

467. SOUDAY, PAUL. "Gauguin" *Le Temps* 3(Nov. 1919).

468. "Special Gauguin." *L'Amateur d'art* 1(hors-série, 1989):3-48. illus.

469. SUTTON, DENYS. "P. Gauguin." *Maanblad voor beeldende Kunsten* 25(April-May 1949):106-10. Text in English.

470. TERRASSE, CHARLES. "Paul Gauguin." *L'Art d'aujourd'hui.* 4:16(Winter 1927):29-36, pl. 61-80.

471. THIIS, JENS. *Kunst og Kultur* Oslo 3(1912):27-30.

472. TSCHANN, GASPARD. "Probleme um Gauguin" [Problems Regarding Gauguin]. *Weltkunst* 43(1973):918.

473. VALLERY-RADOT, PIERRE. "Gauguin, misères et maladies." *La Presse médicale* 65(5 Jan. 1957):39-40.

474. VASSEUR, PIERRE. "Paul Gauguin à Copenhague." *Revue de l'art ancien et moderne* 67, supp. 2(March 1935):117-26. English summary.

475. VAUXCELLES, LOUIS. "About Gauguin." *Formes* 12(Feb. 1931):23-24.

476. VENTURI, LIONELLO. "Gauguin." *L'Arte* 5(March 1934):136-65.

477. VERDIER, PHILIPPE. "Un manuscrit de Gauguin: L'Esprit moderne et le catholicisme." *Wallraf-Richartz-Jahrbuch* 46(1985):273-328.

Includes the text of Gauguin's 1902 manuscript.

478. "Victorian Retrospect; Gauguin: Turning Point." *Art News* 45(April 1946):26-29+.

479. W., A. "Autour de Gauguin." *Bulletin de la vie artistique* 7(1926):332-33.

480. WIESE, ERICH. "Paul Gauguin: Zwei Jahrzehnte nach seinem Tode" [Paul Gauguin: Two Decades after his Death]. *Der Cicerone* 15(1923):635-41.

481. WILDENSTEIN, GEORGES. "Les comptes de Gauguin." *Gazette des Beaux-Arts* 6th ser., 47(Jan.-April 1956[published 1958]):187-88. Reprinted in *Gauguin; sa vie, son oeuvre* (Paris, 1958).

482. WILDENSTEIN, GEORGES. "Documents diverses concernant Gauguin." *Gazette des Beaux-Arts*. 6th ser., 47 (Jan.-April 1956[published 1958]):209-11. Reprinted in *Gauguin; sa vie, son oeuvre* (Paris, 1958).

II. Gauguin and Contemporaries in France (Paris, Pont-Aven, Le Pouldu)

A. Monographs

483. AUSTIN, LLOYD JAMES. "Mallarmé critique d'art." In *the Artist and the Writer in France: Essays in Honour of Jean Seznec.* Edited by F. Haskell, A. Levi, K. Shackleton. Oxford: Clarendon Press, 1974. 184 p., 20 pl. See pp. 153-62.

Mallarmé's art criticism (a few articles, scattered notes, remarks in letters) is less extensive than that of Baudelaire or Valéry. But, far more than they, Mallarmé had the sense of his time. His friends included his elders Manet, Degas and Whistler, his contemporaries Monet, Redon, Rodin, Renoir, Berthe Morisot and many others; he hailed van Gogh, defended *Gauguin*, mourned Seurat, collaborated with Raffaelli, honored Puvis de Chavannes, esteemed Toulouse-Lautrec and Vuillard. Apart from notes in the London *Athenaeum*, his main contributions to art criticism are his preface to the 1896 exhibition catalogue of Berthe Morisot's works, detailed comments on Redon's lithographs, and a substantial, prophetic article on "The Impressionists and Edouard Manet," published in *Art Monthly Review* in 1876, and mentioning, among others, Sisley, Pissarro, Eva Gonzalès and Cézanne. Mallarmé had great powers of analysis and synthesis. He excelled in evoking the atmosphere of the works described. His art criticism is an extension of his poetry.

484. BANTENS, ROBERT JAMES. *Eugène Carrière; His Work and His Influence*. Ph.D. diss., Pennsylvania State University, Union Park, 1975. Ann Arbor, Michigan: UMI Research Press, 1983. 271 p., 38 illus.

Examines the oeuvre and influence of the Symbolist painter Eugène Carrière (1849-1906), who exerted a significant influence on fin-de-siècle aesthetic. The final chapter concentrates on the artist's impact on Rodin, Gauguin, the Nabis and the young Picasso.

485. BERNARD, EMILE. *Souvenirs inédits sur l'artiste peintre Paul Gauguin et ses compagnons, lors de leur séjour à Pont-Aven et au Pouldu*. Preface by René Maurice. Lorient: Imprimerie du Nouvelliste du Morbihan, 1939. 24 p., illus.

Memoirs of Emile Bernard (1868-1941), French painter, poet, and art critic. Bernard painted with Gauguin and the Pont-Aven school and influenced Gauguin's cloisonnism.

486. BLANCHE, JACQUES-EMILE. *Propos de peintre; de Gauguin à la Revue nègre*. Paris: Emile-Paul Frères, 1928. 226 p.

Includes the author's account of meeting Gauguin in Dieppe. Quotes writings from other authors on Gauguin and explains Gauguin's collaboration with Charles Morice on *Noa Noa*.

487. BOYLE, CAROLINE ROSS. *Paul Sérusier*. Ph.D. diss., Columbia University, New York, 1980. 2 vol., 534 p.

Examines Sérusier's artistic career, concentrating on his stylistic development after his six years with the Nabis, which involved numerous changes and influences, including Italian Primitive painting, medieval tapestries and Egyptian sculpture. Sérusier's theoretical writings and his relationships with the three major influences in his life--Paul Gauguin, French Symbolist writers, and Father Desiderius Lenz--are discussed in detail.

488. BRETON, ANDRE. *L'Art imagique*. Paris: Club Français du Livre, 1957. 230 p., illus., col. pl.

Includes a section on Gauguin and Gustave Moreau.

489. CARLEY, LIONEL. *Delius, the Paris Years*. Rickmansworth, England: Triad Press, 1975. 96 p., illus.

Biography of Frederick Delius (1862-1934), English musical composer of German descent who moved to Paris in 1888. Gauguin, Strindberg, and Munch were among his friends. William Molard introduced Delius to Gauguin in 1894. Pages 45-52, etc. relate their contacts and friendship.

490. CHASSE, CHARLES. *Gauguin et le groupe de Pont-Aven, documents inédits*. Paris: H. Floury, 1921. 93 p., 31 illus., 1 pl.

Study of Gauguin's years and companions at Pont-Aven. Includes 11 reproductions of Gauguin's Pont-Aven works.

491. CHASSE, CHARLES. *Le mouvement symboliste dans l'art du XIXe siècle*. Paris: Librairie Floury, 1947. 215 p., 32 illus.

Includes two chapters (4-5) on Gauguin, along with information on Moreau, Redon, Carrière, Maurice Denis, Rodin, and the Pont-Aven group.

492. CHASSE, CHARLES. *Gauguin et son temps*. Paris: La Bibliothèque des Arts, 1955. 150 p., 21 pl.

Biography which emphasizes Gauguin's Pont-Aven and Le Pouldu periods.
Review: *Werk* 44:supp. (September 1957):173.

493. CHASSE, CHARLES. *Nabis et leur temps*. Paris: La Bibliothèque des Arts, 1960.

Examines the Nabi movement, which began in 1888 on the initiative of Paul Sérusier who was influenced by Gauguin's work in Brittany. The Nabis included Maurice Denis, Edouard Vuillard, and Pierre Bonnard.
a. English ed.: *The Nabis & their Period*. Trans. by Michael Bullock. London: Lund Humphries, 1969. 136 p., 44 pl., 6 col.
b. U.S. ed.: New York: Praeger, 1969. 136 p., 44 pl., 6 col.

494. CHEYRON, J. *Emile Bernard avant Paul Gauguin*. Chassiers: Impr. Hubert et fils, 1983. 16 p., illus.

495. DELOUCHE, DENISE. *Peintres de la Bretagne: découverte d'une province*. Rennes: Université de Haute Bretagne; Paris: Klineksick, 1977. 401 p., 171 illus.

Study of the Brittany region of France as represented in the work of painters. Brittany first became a popular subject for artists with Gauguin and the Pont-Aven school, and as early as 1830 painters and lithographers as well as contemporary writers flocked there to work. This study traces the developments in the pictorial vision of Brittany through the examination of the work and interaction of painters, printmakers, writers, and critics.

496. DELOUCHE, DENISE, et al. *Pont-Aven et ses peintres à propos d'un centennaire.* Rennes: Presses Universitaires de Rennes 2; Institut culturel de Bretagne, 1986. 279 p., illus., some col.

497. DELOUCHE, DENISE. *Bretagne: images et mythes.* Rennes: Presses Universitaires de Rennes 2, 1987. 237 p., illus.

498. DELOUCHE, DENISE. *Les Peintres et le paysan breton.* Baille: Ursa-Le-Chasse-Marée, 1988. 216 p., illus., some col.

499. DELOUCHE, DENISE. *Artistes étrangers à Pont-Aven, Concarneau et autres lieux de Bretagne.* Rennes: Presses Universitaires de Rennes 2, 1989. 233 p., illus., some col.

500. DELSEMME, PAUL. *Un théoricien du symbolisme: Charles Morice.* Paris: Librairie Nizet, 1958. 276 p., illus.

Biographical and critical study of Charles Morice (1860-1919). Morice was a poet and disciple of Stéphane Mallarmé, who played an important role as a critic and defender of Symbolist art following the death of Albert Aurier in 1892. Includes information on his relationship with Gauguin and Morice's collaboration on the *Noa Noa* manuscript from 1893-95. Morice later wrote several articles on Gauguin and one of the first Gauguin biographies in 1919.

501. DENIS, MAURICE. *Gauguin, ses amis, l'école de Pont-Aven et l'Académie Julian.* Paris, 1933? 30 p., illus.

502. DONNELL-KOTROZO, CAROL A. *Post Impressionism: A Critical Study.* Ph.D. diss., University of California, Los Angeles, 1972. 412 p.

Using as starting point Edward Fry's claim that the post-Impressionists can be credited with creating Expressionism as a new tradition, the author suggests several alternative interpretations of post-Impressionism: that Gauguin, van Gogh and Cézanne are not Expressionists, Symbolists, nor direct forerunners of any modern art movement, such as Cubism or Fauvism; that such assumptions are the result of the fact that post-Impressionism followed a period of scientific naturalism; and that the modern view is in direct conflict with these artists' own works and writings.

503. *Emile Bernard, 1868-1941. A Pioneer of Modern Art*. Catalogue compiled by Mary Anne Stevens, et al. Zwolle: Waanders, 1990. 384 p., 140 col. pl., illus. In English and German.

Includes an essay, "Emile Bernard and Paul Gauguin: The Avant-Garde and Tradition."
Exhibition held in 1990 at Mannheim (Staedtische Kuntshalle) and at Amsterdam (Rijksmusem Vincent van Gogh).

504. DORIVAL, BERNARD. "Le milieu." In *Gauguin*. Paris: Hachette, 1960, pp. 55-91.

505. *Essais d'art libre. Revue mensuelle*. Geneva: Slatkine Reprints, 1971. 5 vol.
Reprint of this periodical originally published in Paris which includes articles on and mentions of Gauguin. Covers Feb. 1892 to Oct. 1894.

506. FENEON, FELIX. *Oeuvres*. Introduction by Jean Paulhan. Paris: Gallimard, 1948. 478 p.

Fénéon (1861-1944), an art critic, wrote several articles on Gauguin from 1888-93, which are reprinted here.
a. Another ed.: *Oeuvres plus que complètes*. Geneva: Librairie Droz, 1970. Joan U. Halperin, ed. 2 vols., 1087 p., 9 pl.

507. FRERE, HENRI. *Conversations de Maillol*. Geneva: P. Cailler, 1956. 350 p., pl.

Mentions Gauguin's influence on Aristide Maillol (1861-1944) and other artists.

508. GAUSS, CHARLES EDWARD. *The Aesthetic Theories of French Artists, 1855 to the Present*. Baltimore: The Johns Hopkins Press, 1949. 111 p.

Chapter 5, pp. 53-68, includes information on Symbolism and Fauvism. Gauguin, Maurice Denis, and Henri Matisse are discussed.
a. Reprint: 1963.

509. GENTHON, ISTVAN. *Rippli-Rónai: Der Ungarische 'Nabi'* [Rippli-Rónai: The Hungarian 'Nabi']. Budapest: Corvina, 1958. 30 p., illus., 49 col. pl.

Study of the Nabi painter József Rippli-Rónai (1861-1927), which mentions Gauguin.

510. GERARD, JUDITH. "Den lilla flickan och gengangaren. La petite fille et le Tupapau." In Gerda E. Kjellberg, *Hänt och Sant* [Events and Truths]. Stockholm: P.A. Norstedt & Söners, 1951, pp. 53-74. 206 p., illus.

Contains information on Gauguin and William and Ida Molard, neighbors whom Gauguin befriended in December, 1893. William was a musical composer, Ida a sculptress.
a. Unpublished French trans.: Danielsson Archives, Tahiti.

511. GIDE, ANDRE. *Si le grain ne meurt.* Paris: Editions de la Nouvelle Revue Française, 1924. 3 vols.

Includes Gide's account of visiting Marie Henry's auberge in Le Pouldu. The inn's dining room was decorated from floor to ceiling by Gauguin, Meyer de Haan, and Paul Sérusier in 1889.
a. Other French eds.: Paris: 1928, 1929, 1933, 1945, 1953, 1966.
b. English eds.: *If It Die; An Autobiography.* Trans. by Dorothy Bussy. London: 1925, 1935, 1951; New York: 1935, 1957.

512. HALPERIN, JOAN UNGERSMA. *Félix Fénéon and the Language of Art Criticism.* Ann Arbor, Michigan: UMI Research Press, 1980. 243 p., 22 pl.

Included in this study of art critic Félix Fénéon (1861-1944) are references to Fénéon's articles on Gauguin, written in 1888-93.

513. HARIS, LUDWIG. *Gauguins Bretagne: ein Tagebuch* [Gauguin's Bretagne: a Diary]. Hamburg: Ellert & Richter Verlag, 1988. 88 p., illus., col. pl.

Pictorial treatment in German of Gauguin's career in Brittany, particularly in Pont-Aven. Includes photographs and quotations from diaries and letters.

514. HARTRICK, ARCHIBALD STANDISH. *A Painter's Pilgrimage through Fifty Years.* Cambridge, England: Cambridge University Press, 1939. 252 p., illus., 19 pl.

Memoirs of a British artist who studied in France and was acquainted with Gauguin, van Gogh, and other artists. Hartrick met Gauguin in Pont-Aven in 1886. Chapter 3 contains observations and impressions of Gauguin (pp. 28-38).

515. HUMBERT, AGNES. *Les Nabis et leur époque, 1888-1900.* Geneva: Pierre Caillier, 1954. 152 p., 49 pl.

Gauguin mentioned throughout this historical overview of the Nabis and their period.

516. IKEGAMI, CHUJI and KAJA OTOHIKO. *Sezanu, Goho, Gogyan.* Tokyo: Kodansha, 1974. 151 p., illus., 90 pl.

517. INBOPEN, GUDRUN. *Mallarmé und Gauguin: Absolute Kunst als Utopie* [Mallarmé and Gauguin: Absolute Art as Utopia]. Stuttgart: J.B. Metzler, 1978. 160 p., 4 illus.

Views Gauguin's work not as an isolated phenomenon, nor simply as a late product of Romanticism, but as an important manifestation within the Symbolist debate at the end of the 19th century. Gauguin became personally acquainted with Mallarmé in 1891 and was influenced by him, for both poet and painter shared an interest in the role of the symbol in art and in its relationship to the world of external reality. The author looks at Mallarmé's work in general and at *Igitur* in particular, and discuss Mallarmé's concept of the nature of the symbol. She then turns to previous theories of symbolic representation, from Goethe and Schiller, via the Schlegels, to Hegel, moving next to a consideration of Gauguin in relation to Mallarmé and discussing the role of the absolute in his painting.

518. JAWORSKA, WLADYSLAWA. *W Kregu Gauguina, Malarze Szkoly Pont-Aven.* Warsaw: Pànstwowy Instytut Wydawniczy, 1969. 377 p., illus., some col.

Study of the activity of an international group of painters in Brittany during 1886-96. Under the leadership of Paul Gauguin, they constituted a closed artistic community and eventually worked out a new formula for painting which became known as Synthetism. The gathering of new material has enabled the author to sketch a more complete collective portrait of the Pont-Aven group, to achieve greater accuracy in particulars--biographical dates, anecdote, and the authenticity of paintings not previously identified--and finally, on the theoretical plane, to draw certain conclusions from the study as a whole which have illuminated the relationship between painting and the philosophy, literature, music, and theatre of the period, and have made it possible for the author to arrive at a definition of the aesthetics of Synthetism.

a. French ed: *Paul Gauguin et l'école de Pont-Aven.* Trans. from the Polish by Simon Laks. Neuchâtel: Ides & Calendes, 1971. 261 p., 250 illus., 39 col. pl.

b. U.S. ed.: *Gauguin and the Pont-Aven School.* Trans. by Patrick Evans. Greenwich, Conn.: New York Graphic Society, 1972. 264 p., 250 illus., 39 col. pl.
c. English ed.: London: Thames & Hudson, 1972. 264 p.
Reviews: G. Bazin, *Gazette des Beaux-Arts*, ser. 6, 78 (Dec. 1971):supp. 29; T. Hilton, *Studio* 184 (Nov. 1972):197-98; J. Masheck, *Art in America* 61(Nov. 1973):138-39.

519. JULLIAN, PHILIPPE. *Les Symbolistes.* Paris, 1973.

Information on Gauguin included with other Symbolist artists.
a. English eds.: *The Symbolists.* Trans. by Mary Anne Stevens. London and New York: Phaidon, 1973. 240 p., 213 illus., col. pl.; 2nd. English ed., 1977.

520. LOEVGREN, SVEN. *The Genesis of Modernism: Seurat, Gauguin, van Gogh, & French Symbolism in the 1880's.* Ph.D. diss., University of Uppsala, 1959. Stockholm: Almqvist & Wiksell, 1959. 178 p., illus. Bloomington: Indiana University Press, 1971. 241 p., 28 illus.

Interpretative survey of the intellectual currents leading to Symbolism and the development of post-Impressionism. Examines Symbolism in literature and painting with an analysis of key works by Gauguin and others. Includes an analysis of *The Vision After the Sermon* (1888).
a. Revised ed.: New York: Hacker Art Books, 1983. 241 p., 28 illus.

521. LOIZE, JEAN. *Les amitiés du peintre Georges-Daniel de Monfreid et ses reliques de Gauguin; de Maillol et Codet à Segalen.* Paris: Jean Loize, 1951. 175 p., illus., 8 pl.

Biography of Georges-Daniel de Monfreid, which includes considerable information on his association with Gauguin. Over half of the work describes documents, letters, memorabilia, art works, photographs, and relics relating to Gauguin and other artists and writers.

522. LOPPIN, PAUL. *Louis Brouillon: le premier biographe de Gauguin.* Paris: Pierre Béarn, 1962. 70 p.

Biography of the art critic Louis Brouillon (1858-), who wrote under the pseudonym Jean de Rotonchamp. Brouillon wrote the first major biography of Gauguin, *Paul Gauguin, 1848-1903* (Weimar: Kessler; Paris: E. Druet, 1906).

523. LUCIE-SMITH, EDWARD. *Symbolist Art.* London: Thames and Hudson, 1972. 216 p., 185 illus., 24 col.

Chapter 8 deals with Gauguin, Pont-Aven, and the Nabis.
a. Reprint: 1984.
b. U.S. eds.: New York: Praeger, 1972. 216 p., illus.; New York: Oxford University Press, 1972. 216 p., illus.

524. LUGNE-POE, AURELIEN FRANÇOIS. *Le Sot du Tremplin; souvenirs et impressions de théâtre*. Paris: Gallimard, 1930. 3 vol.

La Parade, vol. 1, contains reflections and reminiscences about Gauguin.

525. MAUCLAIR, CAMILLE. *L'Art indépendant français*. Paris: La Renaissance du Livre, 1919. 170 p.

Gauguin and contemporary painters are mentioned in Chapter 2, pp. 25-37.

526. MAUNER, GEORGES L. *The Nabis: Their History and Their Art, 1888-1896*. Ph.D. diss., Columbia University, 1967; New York and London: Garland, 1978. 485 p., 159 illus., 80 pl.

Mentions Gauguin's early influence on the Nabis and Symbolist artists at Pont-Aven in the introduction.

527. MEIER-GRAEFE, JULIUS. *Entwickelungsgeschichte der modernen Kunst*. Stuttgart: Hoffmann, 1904. 3 vol., illus., pl.

Gauguin and the Pont-Aven school are discussed in vol. 1, pages 371-91.

528. MEIER-GRAEFE, JULIUS. *Der moderne Impressionismus*. Berlin: Julius Bard, 1904. 66 p., illus., 8 pl.

Gauguin's life and work are treated on pages 48-65.

529. MILNER, JOHN. *Symbolists and Decadents*. London, New York: Studio Vista; Dutton, 1971. 160 p., illus., pl.

Deals in part with Gauguin's symbolism and the Pont-Aven circle.

530. MORICE, CHARLES. *Gauguin*. Paris: H. Floury, 1919. 235 p., illus., 62 pl., some col.

Biography and reminiscences of Gauguin's life by Charles Morice (1861-1919), an important symbolist poet and author who met Gauguin in 1889. Gauguin learned synthetist theories from Morice and had contacts with him for the rest of his life. Morice wrote newspaper articles about

Gauguin and prefaces to several exhibition catalogues. He corresponded regularly with Gauguin and collaborated in 1893 on the *Noa Noa* manuscript.
a. 2nd ed.: Paris: H. Floury, 1920.

531. MORNAND, PIERRE. *Emile Bernard et ses amis: van Gogh, Gauguin, Toulouse-Lautrec, Cézanne, Odilon Redon.* Geneva: Pierre Cailler, 1957. 95 p., 10 pl., some col.

Biography and study of Emile Bernard (1868-1941), painter and co-founder of the Pont-Aven School. Examines Gauguin's relationship with Bernard and their influence on each other.

532. MULLER, JOSEPH-EMILE. *Impressionnisme.* Paris: Fernand Hazan, 1974. 31 p., 40 pl.

Presents paintings selected from the works of 12 Impressionists--Cézanne, Degas, Gauguin, Manet, Monet, Morisot, Pissarro, Renoir, Seurat, Sisley, Toulouse-Lautrec, and van Gogh. An essay briefly outlines the life and work of each artist, and provides a short description of Impressionism and Neo-Impressionism in which the author suggests that the movement was not a homogeneous one, and that the differences which exist between painters who were influenced by impressionism are as significant as the similarities, concluding that it is the personal contributions of the principal artists which require emphasis.

533. NOURISSIER, FRANÇOIS. "Sa place dans la mêlée symboliste." In *Gauguin.* Paris: Hachette, 1960. pp. 93-107.

534. LE PAUL, CHARLES-GUY and JUDY LE PAUL. *L'Impressionnisme dans l'Ecole de Pont-Aven: Monet, Renoir, Gauguin et leurs disciples.* Lausanne, Paris: La Bibliothèque des Arts, 1983. 284 p., illus., some col.

Traces Gauguin's career from Sunday painter and collector of the Impressionists to leader of the Pont-Aven painters. Gauguin arrived at Pont-Aven in June, 1886 and painted there sporadically until November, 1894. The Le Pauls devote chapters to other members of the Pont-Aven colony, who generally fell into two camps regarding Gauguin. Younger painters like Loiseau, Moret, and Bernard admired him. Established artists like Monet and Renoir loathed him.
a. English ed.: *Gauguin and the Impressionists at Pont-Aven.* New York: Abbeville Press, 1987. 285 p., illus.

535. PISSARRO, CAMILLE. *Lettres à son fils Lucien.* John Rewald, ed. Paris: A. Michel, 1950. 522 p., illus.

Includes references to Paul Gauguin.
a. English ed.: *Letters to his Son Lucien.* John Rewald, ed.; L. Abel, trans. London: Kegan Paul, Trench, Trubner, 1943.

536. PISSARRO, CAMILLE. *Correspondance.* Critical edition by Janine Bailly-Herzberg. Preface by Bernard Dorival. Paris: Presses Universitaires de France, 1980- . Vol. 1- , illus.

Volume 2 (1886-90) includes references and letters to Paul Gauguin.

537. PUIG, RENE. *Paul Gauguin, G.D. de Monfreid et leurs amis.* Perpignan: Editions de la Tramontane, 1958. 86 p., illus., pl. 300 copies.

Study of Gauguin's relationship with the painter Georges-Daniel de Monfreid (1856-1929). Relies on then unpublished sources from the Monfreid archives in Paris. Also discusses other artists and associates in Gauguin's and Monfreid's circles. Monfreid and Gauguin first met in 1889. They kept up a long correspondence during Gauguin's Polynesian sojourns, and Monfreid looked after Gauguin's affairs in Paris during his absence.

538. PUIG, RENE. *Paul Gauguin et Emile Bernard.* Lyon: Imp. Réunies de Lyon, 1960. 14 p.

Pamphlet which examines the complex relationship and cross influences between the two painters.

539. REDON, ODILON. *Critiques d'art. Salon de 1868, Rodolphe Bresdin, Paul Gauguin.* Introduction and notes by Robert Coustet. Bordeaux: William Blake, 1987. 108 p., 20 pl.

Reprints Redon's essay, "Opinions sur Paul Gauguin," first published in the *Mercure de France* (Nov. 1903). See pages 85-87, 100-01.

540. REWALD, JOHN. *Post-Impressionism from van Gogh to Gauguin.* New York: Museum of Modern Art; distributed by Simon and Schuster, 1956. 614 p., illus., col. pl.

Monumental study of Post-Impressionism from 1886-93, which includes several chapters on Gauguin. Later editions were revised and augmented for scholarly purposes. Noted for its large anthology of paintings and value as a research guide. Includes detailed bibliography with frequent annotations.
a. 2nd ed.: New York, 1962. 619 p.
b. 3rd ed.: New York, 1978. 590 p.

c. French eds.: *Le post-impressionnisme de van Gogh à Gauguin*. Trans. by Alice Rewald. Paris: A. Michel, 1961. 530 p.; Paris: Hachette-Pluriel, 1988.
d. German eds.: *Von van Gogh bis Gauguin: Die Geschichte des Nachimpressionismus*. Cologne: DuMont Schauberg, 1967, 1987. 412, 398 p., 151 illus.

541. REWALD, JOHN. *Studies in Post-Impressionism*. Edited by Irene Gordon and Frances Weitzenhoffer. London: Thames & Hudson; New York: Harry N. Abrams, 1986. 295 p., 75 illus., 8 col.

Includes Rewald's study, based on Gauguin's letters and first published in 1943, of Gauguin's relationships with the art dealer Ambroise Vollard and the critic André Fontainas (pp. 168-213).

542. ROSKILL, MARK WENTWORTH. *Van Gogh, Gauguin and the Impressionist Circle*. Greenwich, Connecticut: New York Graphic Society, 1970. 310p., 206 illus., 8 col. Unpublished supplement dated 1969.

Includes chapters on Impressionism, Japanese prints, Seurat, Emile Bernard, and van Gogh and Gauguin. Focuses on van Gogh's and Gauguin's pictorial development and influences on each other as well as their personal relationship.
Reviews: R. Lebowitz, *Arts* 45(Nov. 1970):1-8; H. Dorra, *Art Bulletin* 54(1972):560-63; V. Jirat-Wasiutynski, *Art Journal* 33(1973):78+
a. English ed.: London: Thames & Hudson, 1970. 310 p., 206 illus., 8 col.

543. SERUSIER, PAUL. *ABC de la peinture, suivi d'une étude sur la vie et l'oeuvre de Paul Sérusier par Maurice Denis*. Paris: Librairie Floury, 1942. 124 p., 35 pl., 4 col.

Style and technique manual by the artist Paul Sérusier (1863-1927), a main link between the Pont-Aven and Nabi groups. Includes several mentions of Gauguin in the section by Denis on Sérusier's life and works.
a. Another ed.: Paris: Librairie Floury, 1950. 173 p.

544. TUAL, R. *Mademoiselle Julia de Pont-Aven*. Concarneau, 1928.

Biography of Madame Julia, owner of Villa Julia, an inn in Pont-Aven which catered to visiting artists. Julia's legend grew as she became famous among artists in Paris, London, and America.

545. TYLER, PARKER. *Cézanne/Gauguin*. Garden City, NY: Doublday, 1969. 139 p., illus., 75 col. pl.

546. VENTURI, LIONELLO. *Impressionists and Symbolists*. Trans. by Francis Steermuller. New York; Scribner's Sons, 1950. 244 p., 217 pl.

547. VERKADE, WILLIBORD. *Die Unruhe zu Gott: Erinnerungen eines Malermönchs* [Uneasy with God: Memoirs of an Artist-Monk]. Freiburg in Breisgau: Herder, 1923. 247 p.

Jan Verkade (1868-1946) was a friend of Jacob Meyer de Haan and became acquainted with Gauguin and his circle in Paris and in Pont-Aven.
a. Other eds.: 1930, 1933.
b. French ed.: *Le Tourment de Dieu: Etapes d'un moine peintre*. Trans. by Marguerite Fauré. Paris: Librairie de l'Art Catholique, 1926. 283 p.
c. English ed.: *Yesterdays of an Artist-Monk*. London: Burns, Oates and Washbourne, 1930.
d. U.S. ed.: New York: P.J. Kennedy & Sons, 1930. 304 p.

548. WANG, ROBERT THEORDORE. *The Graphic Art of the Nabis, 1888-1900*. Ph.D. diss., University of Pittsburgh, 1974. 410 p.

Establishes a chronology of the early prints of the Nabis artists, and shows how their graphic experiments of the 1890s form a basis for the development of the modern single-sheet print. Illustrations for the Nabis projects are as complete as possible and include a number of unpublished prints. Examines the graphic art of Emile Bernard and Gauguin at Pont-Aven, relating such works to the earliest prints by the Nabis. The stylistic contradictions of these prints are seen in relation to both the surface effects of Impressionism and the two-dimensionality of the Synthetist style.

549. WARD, MARY MARTHA. *Camille Pissarro in the 1880s*. Ph.D. diss., Johns Hopkins University, 1983. 2 vol., 429 p., illus.

Examines the paintings of Pissarro in the 1880s as they reveal the opposing concerns of Impressionism and Neo-Impressionism. Analyzes correspondence between Pissarro and Gauguin.

550. WELSH, ROBERT P. "Sacred Geometry: French Symbolism and Early Abstraction." In *The Spiritual in Art Abstract Painting, 1890-1985*. Los Angeles: County Museum of Art. Maurice Tuchman, ed., pp. 63-87. 435 p., 36 illus., 5 col.

Traces the use of geometric signs by the Nabis and other French artists and relates this to the development of abstraction. Describes some of the sources of ideas about the symbolism of geometric signs, in particular the writings of Helena P. Blavatsky, and traces the impact of these on the Nabis, possibly through the stimulus of Gauguin whose paintings from his Brittany period encouraged a mystical conception of art in which sacred geometry figured as one component.

B. Articles

551. ALHADEFF, ALBERT. "Minne and Gauguin in Brussels: An Unexplored Encounter." *La scultura nel XIX secolo* (Bologna, 1979):177-88. 10 illus. In English.

Compares conservative critical responses to Gauguin and *gauguinisme* to those elicited by sculptures of Georg Minne in the late 1880s and early 1890s.

552. "Les amis de Paul Gauguin." *Beaux-Arts* (27 July 1934):4.

553. ANQUETIL-PLESSIER, MARIE AMELIE. "Un Nabi oublié au monastère de Beuron: Jan Verkade." *Information d'histoire de l'art* 20:5(Nov.-Dec. 1975):202-10.

Account of the life and work of Verkade, a friend of Gauguin who entered the monastery of Beuron but never lost touch with the Nabis circle or ceased to paint. Also discusses the Ecole d'art sacré at Beuron.

554. ANSIEAU, JOELLE. "Deux Sculptures de Georges Lacombe: *Isis* et le *Christ*." *Revue du Louvre et des Musées de France* (1983):287-95. 13 illus.

Examines the iconography of two wooden sculptures by the Nabi artist Georges Lacombe: *Isis* (Musée d'Orsay, Paris) and *Christ*. Discusses the influence of Egyptian art and the art of Gauguin on Lacombe's sculptural ideas.

555. AURIANT, A. "Souvenirs sur Emile Bernard." *Maintenant* 7(1948?):124-67.

556. BARTH, WILHELM. "Der unbekannte Gauguin" [The Unknown Gauguin]. *Cicerone* 20:19(Oct. 1928):620-29. 8 illus.

557. BENINGTON, JONATHAN. "From Realism to Expressionism: the Early Career of Roderic O'Conor (Paintings of Brittany with a Checklist of Works in Public Collections Dating up to 1903)." *Apollo* 121(April 1985):253-61.

558. BERNARD, EMILE. "Gauguin et Emile Bernard." *Le Point* (Oct. 1937):170-73.

559. BLANCHE, JACQUES-EMILE. "Les arts et la vie; Paul Gauguin et Charles Morice, initiateurs." *Revue de Paris* (May 1920):103-07.

560. BOUDOT-LAMOTTE, M. "Le peintre et collectionneur Claude-Emile Schuffenecker." *L'Amour de l'art* 17(Oct. 1936):284.

561. BOYLE-TURNER, CAROLINE. "Sérusier's Talisman" *Gazette des Beaux-Arts* 6th ser., 105(May-June 1985):191-96. 5 illus. In English, summary in French.

Discusses the circumstances in which Paul Sérusier's *Talisman*, 1888 (private collection) was painted. Notes that the small panel, commonly described as the top of a cigar box, shows no evidence of being other than a small panel, probably chosen for its size because time for the lesson, given by Gauguin to Sérusier, during which it was painted, was short. Discusses the significance of its unfinished state for Nabis working methods and explains the title in terms of a poem of 1889, "La montagne de doute" by Sérusier's friend Albert Aurier.

562. BOYLE-TURNER, CAROLINE. "Gauguin and the Pont-Aven Circle." *Art News* 85:8(Oct. 1986):106-9. 6 illus.

By 1888, Paul Gauguin had found in the Pont-Aven region of Brittany a culture and landscape which satisfied his need for earthiness and primitivism. Artists such as Emile Bernard (1868-1941), Armand Seguin (1869-1903), Roderic O'Conor (1860-1940), Paul Sérusier (1865-1927) and Maxime Maufra (1861-1918) gathered around Gauguin there and formed a movement known as Synthetism. The Synthetists aimed to produce a synthesis between what they felt and what they observed, and their work was a rejection of both Realism and Impressionism. The Synthetists were interested in printmaking as a medium, as well as painting, and the author concentrates on the efforts of the major Pont-Aven artists in this medium in the 1880s and 1890s.

563. BOYLE-TURNER, CAROLINE. "La Bretagne vue par les graveurs de l'Ecole de Pont-Aven." *Nouvelles de l'estampe* 101-102 (1988):15-23. 16 illus.

Studies prints of the Pont-Aven painters, including Gauguin's *Misères humaines* and *Le Drame de la mer* (both 1889). Comments on their rapid execution and asserts that the themes of peasants working and untamed countryside contribute to a savage image of Brittany.

564. BRETON, ANDRE. Three-page letter, dated 1954, by the French surrealist poet André Breton (1896-1966). Includes a draft checklist relating to an exhibition of modern art in 1954. Makes special reference

to Georges Seurat and Gauguin, and to Paul Signac's collection of art. Located at The Getty Center for the History of Art and the Humanities, Archives of the History of Art, Santa Monica, California.

565. BRINKEMANN, A. E. "Gauguin bei don Wildon." *Das Kunstwerk* 5(1949):5-8.

566. BROWN, SARA. "Un fragmento histórico". *Cuadernos Americanos* 19:6 (1960): 67-121. 6 pl.

Concerns Gauguin and Mallarmé, and his years in Oceania.

567. CARIEL. "Gauguin en Bretagne." *Le Futeur Breton* (Nov.-Dec, 1919).

568. CARIOU, ANDRE. L'Ecole de Pont-Aven au Musée des Beaux-Arts de Quimper." *La Revue du Louvre et des musées de France.* 37:2(1987):99-104.

569. CHARLES-BELLET, L. "Paul Gauguin et ses amis." *Beaux-Arts* 110(1943): 9. 4 illus.

Highlights paintings by Gauguin, Bernard, and Matisse at the Musée d'Albi.

570. CHASSE, CHARLES. "Gauguin et Mallarmé." *L'Amour de l'art* 3 (Aug. 1922):246-56. 3 illus.

571. CHASSE, CHARLES. "Le premier séjour de Gauguin à Pont-Aven." *Dépêche de Brest* (18 and 23 July 1932).

572. CHASSE, CHARLES. "Importance pour la Bretagne de l'école de Pont-Aven." *Nouvelle revue de Bretagne* (March-April 1946).

573. CHASTEL, ANDRE. "Seurat et Gauguin." *Art de France* 2(1962).

General essay which stresses the importance of Puvis de Chavannes' example to Georges Seurat and Gauguin.

574. DALEVERZE, J. "Un ami de Gauguin, Daniel de Monfreid." *L'Oeil* 250:35(May 1976):34-37. 6 illus.

Account of the friendship between the two painters, which began in 1889, with quotations from their correspondence. Monfreid acted as an informal agent for Gauguin, receiving, repairing, and trying to sell the pictures Gauguin sent from the South Seas.

575. DANIELSSON, BENGT. "När Gauguin censurerades i Stockholm" [When Gauguin Was Censored in Stockholm]. *Svenska Dagbladet* (11 Nov. 1964).

576. DAUCHOT, FERNAND. "Meyer de Haan en Bretagne." *Gazette des Beaux-Arts* 40(1952):355-58.

577. DENIS, MAURICE. "L'Epoque du symbolisme." *Gazette des Beaux-Arts* 11(March, 1934):164-79.

578. DENIS, MAURICE. "Pierre Bonnard." *Le Point* 24(1940-45):4-5.

This short notice introduces a longer article by Renée Marie entitled "Bonnard et son époque." Writing about influences on Bonnard, Denis mentions Paul Gauguin, Paul Sérusier, and Symbolism.

579. DEVERIN, EDOUARD. "Un ami de Gauguin: Schuffenecker." *Les Marges* (Jan. 1935).

580. DIETRICH, LINNEA STONESIFER. "The Redefinition of Symbolism in the Visual Arts." *Print Collector's Newsletter* 6:2(May-June 1975):34-38. 3 illus.

Argues that the aim of the Symbolist artists (Paul Cézanne, Paul Gauguin, Vincent van Gogh, Georges Seurat, and Odilon Redon) was not to elaborate a programmatic content nor to display mere technical virtuosity, but to create art that stressed the mutual interdependence of form and content. The intended effect of Symbolist art is to transmute the viewer into the Ideal. The "synthetist symbol"--be it object, image, color, etc.--creates the link between form and content and belongs to both levels. This theory is applied to Paul Gauguin's woodcuts entitled *Manao Tupapau* (*The Spector Watches over Her*) 1892, and the painting of the same title and date in the collection of A. Conger Goodyear, New York. These are related to the poetry and aesthetic theory of Stéphane Mallarmé, the Symbolist poet.

581. DONNELL, CAROL A. "The Problem of Representation and Expression in Post-Impressionist Art." *British Journal of Aesthetics* 15:3(Summer 1975):226-38.

Seeks to refute certain assumptions prevalent in criticism of Gauguin, van Gogh, and Cézanne, and proposes new interpretations of post-Impressionism.

582. DORRA, HENRI. "Emile Bernard and Paul Gauguin." *Gazette des Beaux-Arts* 6th ser., 45(April 1955):227-46, 255-60. With French translation.

583. DORRA, HENRI. "Gauguin's Unsympathetic Observers." *Gazette des Beaux-Arts*, 6th ser., 76:1223(Dec. 1970):367-72. Summary in French.

584. DORRA, HENRI. "Munch, Gauguin, and Norwegian Painters in Paris." *Gazette des Beaux-Arts* 6th ser., 88:1294(Nov. 1976), 175-80. 3 illus. Summary in French.

Argues that Munch saw Gauguin's zincographs, probably at the Café Volpini exhibition or at Théo van Gogh's gallery, in Paris in 1889, and that their influence contributed to the dramatic changes in Munch's work around 1891. Relates Munch's *Melancholy-the Yellow Boat* both to French romantic-naturalist pictures such as Jules Breton's *Evening* (Hôtel de Ville, Cruisery) and to Gauguin's zincograph, *Human Miseries*. Also traces the influence of a Gauguin drawing, *Aux roches noires*, on Munch's *Scream*.

585. DORRA, HENRI. "Extraits de la correspondance d'Emile Bernard des débuts à la Rose Croix (1876-1892)." *Gazette des Beaux-Arts* 6th ser., 96(Dec. 1980):235-42. Summary in English.

Presents excerpts from Bernard's letters of this period containing information on Gauguin, Laval, Schuffenecker, Cézanne, van Gogh, Aurier, Redon, Pissarro, and Péladan. Also reveals Bernard's admiration for the primitives, his literary opinions, and the deep effect the Romanesque frescoes in Tournai Cathedral had on him during a visit in 1890.

586. DORRA, HENRI. "Les pastilles Géraudel et les grands maîtres fin-de-siècle" [Géraudel pills and the great turn-of-the-century masters]. *Gazette des Beaux-Arts* 103(Feb. 1984):85-90. 11 illus. In French, summary in English.

Demonstrates the importance of the cartoons that appeared in *Le Courrier français*, both as stylistic influences and as compositional sources for such artists as Gauguin, Toulouse-Lautrec, Bonnard, and Vallotton.

587. VAN DOWSKI, LEE. [Herbert Lewandowski]. "Gauguin und Strindberg." *Neue Zürcherzeitung* (1948):3.

588. DUCA, G. M. LO. "De Gauguin à de Monfreid." *Emporium* 88(Dec. 1938):333.

589. "L'Ecriture et la peinture chez Sartre et le portrait de soi de Montaigne." *Papers in Romance* 3:2(Spring 1981):117-24.

590. ESTIENNE, CHARLES. "Le cinquantenaire de Gauguin et de l'Ecole de Pont-Aven." *Beaux Arts* (25 Aug. 1939):1.

591. FACY, MAURICE. "Gauguin et la Bretagne." *Brittia* (May 1914).

592. FLORISOONE, MICHEL. "Gauguin et Victor Segalen." *L'Amour de l'art* (19 Dec. 1938):384-86.

593. FOUCHET, MAX-POL. "L'innocence de Gauguin." *Galerie Jardin des arts* (France). 148(June 1975):47-53. 9 illus.

Study of Gauguin's art and his relationship to the Impressionists supported by extracts from his letters and writings. The artist's belief in art as an intellectual exercise and artists as being the epitome of high intelligence, and his interest in the use of expressive color, are emphasized.

594. GAUGUIN, PAUL. "Une lettera di Paul Gauguin." *Lettere ed Arti* (Milan)2:1(Jan. 1946):10-13.

Letter by Gauguin to Georges-Daniel de Monfreid, dated November 1901.

595. "Gauguin and the Pont-Aven Group." *Connoisseur* 161(Jan. 1966):34-35.

596. GOTTE, G. "'La moisson à Saint-Briac': Ein Landschaftsbild von Emile Bernard aus dem Jahr 1889" ['Harvest at Saint-Briac': A Landscape by Emile Bernard Dating from 1889]. *Neusser Jahrbuch* (1984): 37-40. 2 illus.

In 1984 the Clemens-Sels-Museum in Neuss, Germany, acquired the cited painting by Bernard after a visit to Gauguin in Pont-Aven at a time when Bernard was trying to free himself from the influence of his master Pissarro. The strong contours and synthesis of form and color characteristic of *cloisonnisme* attracted him, and he and Gauguin attempted to capture the symbolic content of nature by analogical visual means. Though painted from memory, *Harvest at Saint-Briac* is closer to nature than typical examples of cloisonism, as evidenced by quotations from Bernard's life, his friendship with Gauguin and van Gogh, and troubled relationship with his father, and his later influence on the Nabis, Fauves, and Cubists.

597. GRAUTOFF, OTTO. "Paul Gauguins tragisches Künstlerschicksal" [Paul Gauguin's Tragic Artistic Fate]. *Jahrbuch der Jungen Kunst* (Leipzig 1920):265-68.

598. GRIVEL, M. "Gauguin et l'Ecole de Pont-Aven." *Nouvelles de l'estampe* 101-102 (1988):35.

Note on the prints by Gauguin and other members of the Pont-Aven school shown at the Bibliothèque Nationale in Paris in 1989.

599. HAKANSSON, T. "Strindberg and the Arts." *Studio* 181(Feb. 1971):62-67.

600. HARRISON, C. "Gauguin and the Pont-Aven Group." *Studio* 171(Feb. 1966):60-61.

601. HELLER, REINHOLD. "Rediscovering Henri de Toulouse-Lautrec's *At the Moulin Rouge.*" *Museum Studies* 12:2(1985):115-35.

602. HILTON, IAN. "Brittany Revisited: Huchel, Gauguin and 'Le Pouldu.'" *Modern Languages* 64:1(March 1983):48-51.

603. HOFSTATTER, HANS-HELLMUT. "Emile Bernard-Schüler oder Lehrer Gauguins" [Emile Bernard-Schüler or The Teacher of Gauguin]. *Das Kunstwerk* 11:1(July 1957):3-10.

604. JAWORSKA, WLADYSLAWA. "Problems of Pont-Aven." *Apollo* 83(May 1966):372-77.

605. JAWORSKA, WLADYSLAWA. "Ze Studiów nad Szkola Pont-Aven," *Rocznik Historii Sztuki* 6(1966):230-85. Summary in French.

Reprints extracts from her book, *W Kregu Gauguina* (1969). The first section deals with Gauguin and Emile Bernard.

606. JODIDIO, PHILIP. "Gauguin, corps et âme." *Connaissance des arts* 443(Jan. 1989):7.

607. JOHNSTON, ROY. "Gauguin's Irish Friend." *Art & Artists* 216(Sept. 1984):26-28.

Discusses the Pont-Aven painter Roderic O'Conor (1860-1940).

608. JOHNSTON, ROY. "Roderic O'Conor: The Elusive Personality. *Irish Arts Review* 2:4(Winter 1985):31-40. 12 illus. (6 col.)

The author, who selected the paintings and prepared the catalogue for the 1985 Roderic O'Conor retrospective at the Barbican Art Gallery, London, explores evidence of the artist's life and character. Born into one of Ireland's most historically influential families, O'Conor (1860-1940) chose to pursue art rather than follow a more traditional profession. He spent the rest of his life in France and was associated with Gauguin and the Pont-Aven school in Brittany in the 1890s. O'Conor's death in relative seclusion and his work becoming available only after his wife's death 16 years after his own, contributes to his "mystery man" image. Though abrasive, his associations with artistic contemporaries gave rise to warm friendships until his father's death in 1893 and Gauguin's final departure, whereupon he withdrew into himself and his painting took on more controlled, almost naturalistic traits.

609. JOLY-SEGALEN, ANNE. "Paul Gauguin and Victor Segalen." *Magazine of Art* 45(Dec. 1952):370-74.

610. KILLER, P. "Cuno Amiet in Pont-Aven." *Du* (Switzerland) 33:391(Sept. 1973):638-41, 672. In German, summary in English. 8 illus.

Traces the effect on Amiet of his 13-month stay in Pont-Aven. He arrived some time after the departure of Gauguin and Bernard, but it was there that he saw and was intensely affected by their paintings. Amiet's stay in Brittany was a turning point in his life, since he was encouraged by his surroundings to paint regularly and thus established the foundations of his own style.

611. KNAPP, JAMES F. "Primitivism and Empire: John Synge and Paul Gauguin." *Comparative Literature* 41:1(Winter 1989):53-68.

612. KUNSTLER, CHARLES. "Emile Schuffenecker." *L'Intransigeant* (14 Feb. 1934).

613. KUSPIT, DONALD B. "Civil War: Artist Contra Critic." *Artforum* 19(Oct. 1980):60-64.

614. KUSPIT, DONALD B. "Artist and Critic: Never the Twain Shall Meet." *Structurist* (Canada)25-26(1985-86):30-36. 2 illus.

Defining the realtionship between artist and art critic as one of conflict, the author explores it with reference to the work and views of Paul Gauguin and Charles Baudelaire. Gauguin regarded critics as an oppressive force on art, guarding their culture jealously. Baudelaire regarded artists as spoiled children and held that critics were necessary to keep their work up to standard, and to keep before them the question of what is the good of art. Thus, the artist can judge his output only in egotistical, and self-referential terms, while the art critic must relate it to the values of the wider culture.

615. LEBIHAN, OLIVIER. "Chamaillard et le groupe de Pont-Aven." *Bulletin des amis du musée de Rennes* 2(1978):120-29.

616. LEVEQUE, J.J. "Puvis de Chavannes quitte le purgatoire" *Galerie Jardin des arts* 165(Jan. 1977):50-3. 6 illus.

Discusses the oeuvre of Puvis de Chavannes in light of a retrospective exhibition held in Paris at the Grand Palais. Comments on the fact that at the very moment when a young generation was preparing to revolutionize painting, Puvis de Chavannes promoted an art of antique values. Nevertheless, he influenced the generation of Symbolists to come, above all Gauguin, who was particularly sensitive to his supple, flowing, even sensual line. However, Gauguin underlined a fundamental difference when he said that Puvis de Chavannes was a Greek, whereas he himself was a savage.

617. LLOYD, C. "Camille Pissarro: Towards a Reassessment." *Art International* (Switzerland) 25:1-2(Jan. 1982):59-66. 5 illus.

Study of the importance of Pissarro's letters and art in establishing his influence in his lifetime. His personal letters (especially the now famous ones to his son Lucien) substantiate his influence on contemporary artists and friends, and reveal not only an intelligent appraisal of the main developments in French painting during the second half of the 19th century, but also a purposeful approach to art and formidable powers of self-criticism. Focusing on his paintings rather than the graphic and print work, the author looks at their importance and expanding circles of influence. Pissarro's landscapes, figure paintings, urban paintings and domestic interiors indicate his importance to French painting, and show how his work influenced contemporaries, such as Cézanne, Gauguin and van Gogh.

618. LOIZE, JEAN. "Monfreid et Gauguin." *L'Amour de l'art* 19(1938):358.

619. LOIZE, JEAN. "Monfreid, Gauguin, Maillol." *Arts* 308(1951):8.

620. LYONS, LISA. "Aristide Maillol: *Monument to Debussy*." *Toledo Museum of Art, Museum News* 17:3(1974):62-64.

Discusses Maillol's heritage and early training, Gauguin's influence on him, his career as a tapestry maker and his turn to sculpture as a result of threatened blindness. There follows a discussion of the commissison for the memorial to Claude Debussy, covering France's reaction to Debussy's death, and a detailed description of the bronze *Monument to Debussy* (Museum of Art, Toledo), dated 1930.

621. MADSEN, KARL. "Til minde om Theodor Philipsen" [In Memory of Theodor Philipsen]. *Kunstmuseets Aarsskrift* (Copenhagen 1920):82-95.

622. MANACH'H, E.M. "Gauguin et Segalen." *Nouvelle revue des deux mondes* 5(1978):331-35.

Presents the thesis that the French poet Victor Segalen's obsession with Paul Gauguin was rooted in their similar ways of viewing the world and in their common concern with an ancient, mythical society facing a 20th-century world of change.

623. MATHEWS, PATRICIA. "Passionate Discontent: the Creative Process and Gender Difference in the French Symbolist Period." *Bulletin* (Allen Memorial Art Museum, Oberlin, Ohio) 43(Summer 1988):20-30.

Discusses several Gauguin paintings: *Agony in the Garden*; *Tahitian series*; *She thinks of returning*; *Be in love and you will be happy*.

624. MATHIEU, P.L. "Puvis de Chavannes, ou le peintre et son mur." *Oeil* 256(Nov. 1976):26.

625. MAURICE, RENE. "Reflets du mouvement symboliste sur l'art en Bretagne." *La Nouvelle revue de Bretagne* (Nov.-Dec 1953).

626. METKEN, GUNTER. "Gauguin in der Bretagne." *Artis* (1962):40-45. 6 illus.

627. MIRBEAU, OCTAVE. "Lettres à Claude Monet." *Les cahiers d'aujourd'hui* 9(1922):161-76.

628. MOFFATT, F.C. "The Breton Years of Arthur Wesley Dow." *Archives of American Art Journal* 15:2(1975):2-8. 8 illus.

Dow painted in Brittany from 1885-88, during which time his work, in the plein-air mode, resembled the Barbizon School. He resided for a time at the same pension as Paul Gauguin, but gave no indication of understanding or emulating him.

629. MONFREID, GEORGES-DANIEL DE. "A la mémoire de Paul Gauguin." Woodcut, 1917. A single sheet, with an illustration featuring a portrait of Gauguin, and facing it, a design. Located at The Getty

Center for the History of Art and the Humanities, Archives of the History of Art, Santa Monica, California.

630. MORLAND, JACQUES. "Odilon Redon et le symbolisme." *Mercure de France* 249(1936):636-40.

631. "Nabis and Their Circle." *Minneapolis Institute of Art Bulletin* 51(Dec. 1962):129.

632. NEVE, C. "The Revival of Camden Town: R. A. Bevan Memorial Exhibitions." *Country Life* (U.K.)158:4074 (31 July 1975):276-77. 4 illus.

R. A. Bevan (1901-74) did much to make the work of his father (R. P. Bevan) and of fellow painters Gilman, Gore and Ginner more intelligible and accessible, principally through his bequest to the Ashmolean Museum. At exhibitions held in Oxford and Colchester, R. P. Bevan's work emphasizes that he was older than the other members of his group and mentions that he was at Pont-Aven with Gauguin in 1894-95.

633. ORTON, F. and G. POLLOCK. "Les données bretonnantes: la prairie de representation." *Art History* (U.K.) 3:3(Sept. 1980):314-44. In English. 8 illus.

Takes issue with the nature of the term "Post-Impressionism," arguing that it is part of a strategy to classify and contain diverse and complex practices, and discusses its use in art historical writings. Proceeds to examine the state of art in France in the 1880s which led to a search for a new source of imagery and meaning that is identified with the "discovery" of Brittany, notably the Pont-Aven region. The reasons for the province's attraction is analyzed with reference to contemporary writings, showing the role of the region in France's economy, its reputation as a summer holiday place, and the social implications of its regional costumes. The authors then discuss in detail the way in which Gauguin, Seurat, Bernard, and van Gogh all reacted to the region, and the ways in which art historians have interpreted this.

634. O'TOOLE, J.H. "Henri-Gabriel Ibels: 'Nabi jouraliste'." *Gazette des Beaux-Arts* 99:1356(Jan. 1982):31-38. 7 illus.

By the 1890s, Ibels "was everywhere"--his work abounded in posters, magazine and book illustration, and in the programs of the Théâtre Libre. An excellent graphic artist and colorist, he was immensely popular in Paris (especially for his circus and café concert themes) in the 1890s. A founding member of the Nabis, Ibels also produced numerous lithographs and posters in which the influence of Gauguin and the

Japanese printmakers was evident. His technique was also close to that of his friend Toulouse-Lautrec, with whom he collaborated on occasion.

635. LE PAUL, CHARLES-GUY and G. DUDENSING. "Gauguin et Schuffenecker." *Bulletin des amis des musées de Rennes* (Summer 1978):48-60.

636. LE PAUL, CHARLES-GUY. "Maurice Denis: l'inspiration et la vision bretonnes." *L'Oeil* (Switerland), 288-289 (July-Aug. 1979):38-43. 7 illus.

Discusses the life and work of Maurice Denis (1870-1943), emphasizing his primacy as a Breton artist and contemporary of Gauguin, Seurat, Bonnard, and Vuillard. The occasion for this sketch is the exhibition "Maurice Denis In Brittany" at the Musée de l'Hôtel de Ville, Pont-Aven, France.

637. PAUL, DEREK LIONEL. "Willumsen and Gauguin in the 1890s." *Apollo* 215(Jan. 1980):36-45. 12 illus.

Danish artist J.F. Willumsen (1863-1958) was influenced over a ten-year period by Gauguin and the "Pont-Aven aesthetic" after their meeting in Brittany in 1890. This influence shows most notably in three 1890 paintings--*Two Women Parting after a Chat* (North Jutland Art Museum, Aalborg), *Two Women Walking* and *Breton Woman Walking towards the Spectator* (both Willumsen Museum, Frederikssund). This influence also shows in wood-carving--*Prostitute Awaiting her Prey in 'Montagnes Russes'* (Willumsen Museum) from Gauguin's *Be in love and you will be happy* (Museum of Fine Arts, Boston), and in portrait pottery--*Family Vase* from Gauguin's *Self-portrait vase* (both Danske Kunstindustriemuseum, Copenhagen). From 1892 on two major works by Willumsen, *Jotunheim* and *The Great Relief* (both Willumsen Museum) are believed to have been inspired by Thomas Carlyle's *Sartor Resartus*, introduced to Willumsen by Gauguin's circle in Brittany.

638. "Peintres du XIXe siècle: Gauguin et Victor Segalen." *L'Amour de l'art* 15 Dec. 1938):384-86.

639. PELLEAU, PAUL T. "Saint-Pol-Roux et Paul Gauguin." *Arts* 43(23 Nov. 1945):6.

640. PENNEC, JOS and SYLVAIN-CHRISTIAN DAVID. "Jarry et Gauguin." *L'Etoile-absinthe* (1982).

641. PERUCCI-PETRI, U. "Die Schule von Pont-Aven" [The Pont-Aven School]. *Du* (Switzerland) 33:391 (Sept. 1973):606-37, 664. Summary in English. 39 illus.

Traces the mutual influences between Gauguin and Bernard while painting at Pont-Aven, their individual developments, and the effect their painting had on other contemporary painters in the district, as well as on later developments in art. In particular, the author describes Bernard's development of a style known as *cloisonnisme* and its influence on Gauguin's development, with detailed analysis of *The Vision after the Sermon* (1888). Finally, the gradual breakup of the original school, the departure of Gauguin, and Bernard's abandonment of *cloisonnisme* are considered.

642. LE PICHON, YANN. "Gauguin et ses amis." *Beaux-Arts* 29 (1985):66-71. 9 illus.

643. PLATTE, HANS. "Wegbereiter der modernen Malerei" [Trail Blazers of Modern Art]. *Artis* 3, 4, 6 (1963): 30-35, 34-37, 16-22. 25 illus.

Deals with Gauguin, Cézanne, van Gogh, and Seurat.

644. PLESSIER, GHISLAINE. "Un ami de Gauguin: Francisco Durrio (1868-1940), sculpteur, céramiste et orfèvre." *Bulletin de la société de l'histoire de l'art français* (1982):199-212. 31 illus.

Sheds light on the little-known career of Francisco ("Paco") Durrio. Notes his friendships with numerous artists in Paris, including Picasso and Gauguin, the latter presenting him with some 30 works and acting as a major influence on his art. His projects for sculpture and contributions in ceramics and jewellery to the salons are listed and discussed, and his influence on the young jeweller Manolo Hugué and the relation of his style to Art Nouveau are noted. A list of Durrio's works in the Museum of Contemporary Art in Madrid is appended.

645. REFF, THEODORE. "Degas' Sculpture, 1880-1884." *Art Quarterly* 33:3(Autumn 1970):278.

646. ROGER-MARX, CLAUDE. "Souvenirs sur Ernest Chaplet." *Art et décoration*(March 1910):89-98.

647. SALMON, ANDRE. "Chamaillard et le group de Pont-Aven." *L'Art vivant* 2(15 July 1925):15-16.

648. SCHUFFENECKER, EMILE. Letters, 1895-1898, to Jules Bois, and a three-page essay (undated) on Paul Gauguin. Schuffenecker (1851-1934) was a friend of Gauguin. Collection includes seven letters to Bois (a writer on the occult) and a brief, largely biographical essay in which Schuffenecker expresses his admiration for the work of Gauguin.

Located at The Getty Center for the History of Art and the Humanities, Archives of the History of Art, Santa Monica, California.

649. SERUSIER, PAUL. Manuscript letter (undated) to M. Ancey in which Sérusier discusses his artistic relationship with Gauguin. Included in the Paul Sérusier "Papers, 1881-1964" collection at The Getty Center for the History of Art and the Humanities, Archives of the History of Art, Santa Monica, California.

650. SOEDERSTROEM, G. "Strindberg et les cercles d'art parisiens." *Revue d'histoire du théâtre* 30:3(1978):321-33.

Examines August Strindberg's many contacts with the Parisian art world between 1876 and 1897, particularly his relationship with Paul Gauguin.

651. SOFFICI, ARDENGO. "Recapitulations: trois post-impressionistes (Gauguin, Matisse, Seurat)." *Valori plastici édition française* 2(1920):51-54.

652. SUTTON, DENYS. "Carrière and the Symbolists at the Orangerie." *Burlington Magazine* 92:564(March 1950):81.

653. SUTTON, DENYS. "Revolutionary Quartet." *Apollo* 77(June 1963):478-81.

654. SUTTON, DENYS. "Echoes from Pont-Aven." *Apollo* 79(May 1964):403.

655. THOMPSON, RICHARD. "The Sculpture of Camille Pissarro." *Source* 2:4(Summer 1983):25-28. 3 illus.

Referring to a letter of 1882 from Pissarro to Gauguin as well as to drawings by Pissarro and his son Lucien, this article draws inferences concerning Pissarro's activity as a sculptor. None of Pissarro's sculptures are known to have survived.

656. THOMSON, BELINDA. "Camille Pissarro and Symbolism: Some Thoughts Prompted by the Recent Discovery of an Annotated Article." *Burlington Magazine* 124:946(Jan. 1982):14-25. 7 illus.

An annotated copy of an article, "Le symbolisme en peinture-Paul Gauguin" by Albert Aurier in *Mercure de France*, March 1891, was recently found in the library of the Ashmolean Museum in Oxford. Annotations by Pissarro reveal his hostility to the emergent Symbolist movement. Compares Pissarro's work of the 1880s, particularly his experiments in graphic media such as *Potato Harvest* (1886) with

Gauguin and Bernard's prints of Breton life in 1889. Analyzes attitudes to Pissarro's *Haymakers*, 1889 (Private collection, West Germany).

657. "La vérité sur les relations d'Emile Bernard et de Paul Gauguin." *Art-documents* 39(1953):4-5; see also 40(1954):4-5.

658. VISSON, ASSIA R. "Georges Seurat; Camille Pissarro, Letters to his son Lucien; Paul Gauguin, Letters to Ambroise Vollard and André Fontainas." *Gazette des Beaux-Arts* ser. 6,25(Feb. 1944):127-28.

659. WALLIS, ANNE ARMSTRONG. "Symbolist Painters of 1890." *Marsyas* 1(1941):117-52.

660. WALTER, ELISABETH. "Madeleine au bois d'amour par Emile Bernard." *Revue du Louvre et des musées de France*. 28:4(1978):286-91. 8 illus.

Acquisition in 1977 by the Musées Nationaux of France of Emile Bernard's painting, *Madeleine in the Forest of Love*, Pont-Aven, 1888, occasioned a study of the personality of the model, Madeleine Bernard, Emile's sister. Documents cast light on various episodes in the young girl's life. It was learned that if she was engaged to Charles Laval, she never married him. The records of their deaths show that both died unmarried, he in Paris on 24 April 1894, and she on 19 Nov. 1895 in Cairo, where she had gone to join her brother, Emile. Also discusses her presence in Pont-Aven and Paul Gauguin's relationship to her and her brother.

661. WILDENSTEIN, GEORGES. "Gauguin in Bretagne." *Gazette des Beaux-Arts*, 6th ser. (Jan.-April, 1956)[published in 1958]:83-94. Reprinted in *Gauguin, sa vie son oeuvre* (Paris, 1958).

662. WRIGHT, WILLARD HUNTINGTON. *Modern Painting; Its Tendency and Meaning*. New York: Dodd-Mead, 1915. 26 pl.

Gauguin and the Pont-Aven School are discussed in Chapter 8 (pp. 187-206).
a. Reprints: 1927, 1930.

III. Paul Gauguin and Vincent van Gogh

A. Monographs

663. AGEE, JAMES. "Noa Noa." In *Agee on Film*, vol. 2. Five Film Scripts by James Agee. New York: McDowell, Obolensky, 1959-60. 2 vol.
a. Another ed.: New York: Grosser & Dunlap, 1969.

Includes Agee's film script, "Noa Noa," begun in 1953 under contract, with David Bradley as the director. Negotiations for the film production were interrupted by Agee's death in 1955, and "Noa Noa" was never produced. The script deals with Gauguin's short stay in Arles with van Gogh and his years in Tahiti.

664. GOGH, VINCENT VAN. *Lettres à sa mère*. Trans. by Louis Roelandt. Paris: Falaize, 1952. 116 p.

Includes mentions of and letters to Paul Gauguin. See especially pages 85-98, 101-10.

665. GOGH, VINCENT VAN. *Verzamelde brieven van Vincent van Gogh*. J. van Gogh-Bonger, ed. Amsterdam: Wereldbibliotheek, 1952-54. 4 vols., illus.

666. GOGH, VINCENT VAN. *The Complete Letters of Vincent van Gogh, with Reproductions of all the Drawings in the Correspondence*.
a. U.S. eds.: Greenwich, Conn.: New York Graphic Society, 1958; 1959; 1978.
b. French ed.: *Correspondance complète*. Trans. by M. Beerblock and L. Roelandt. Introduction by Georges Charensol. Paris: Gallimard/Grasset, 1960.
c. German ed.: *Briefe*. Berlin: B. Cassirer, 196-.

667. HANSON, LAWRENCE AND ELISABETH. *The Seekers: Gauguin, Van Gogh, Cézanne*. New York: Random House, 1963. 334 p., 39 pl. (12 pl. by Gauguin).

Biographical narrative which traces the interactions and influences of the three painters on each other.
Review: C. Mount, *Art Quarterly* 27:2(1964):250+.
a. English ed.: *The Post-Impressionists: Cézanne, Gauguin, Van Gogh*. London: Cassell, 1963. 306 p., 18 pl.

668. HAYES, DENNIS and RICHARD PAYNE. *The Yellow House at Arles: Gauguin and van Gogh*. Toronto: Playwrights Canada, 1984. 105 p.

Two-act play based on Gauguin and van Gogh's tumultuous period in Arles. It deals with the impact of poverty, the art market, and technology in the arts. Gauguin and van Gogh are the only characters.

669. JANSON, H. W. and BOGOMILA WELSH-OVCHAROV, eds. *Van Gogh in Perspective*. Englewood Cliffs, N.J.: Prentice-Hall, 1974. 178 p., 25 illus.

Collection of authoritative and interpretative essays on Vincent van Gogh, which provide aesthetic and cultural evaluations of his work. Includes an essay by Gauguin on his relationship with van Gogh.

670. JIRAT-WASIUTYNSKI, VOJTECH, et al. *Vincent van Gogh's Self-Portrait Dedicated to Paul Gauguin; an Historical and Technical Study*. Cambridge, MA: Center for Conservation and Technical Studies, Harvard University Art Museums, 1984. 38 p., 35 illus., 12 col.

Report on a study made by conservation scientists (Eugene Farrell and Richard Newman), a painting conservator (H. Travers Newton), and an art historian (Jirat-Wasiutynski). Painted by van Gogh in 1888 and given to Gauguin in exchange for his self-portrait, van Gogh's *Self-Portrait* (Fogg Art Museum, Harvard University), was badly damaged and altered between 1888 and 1911. Includes quotes from letters by Vincent that mention the painting. Describes in technical terms the condition of the painting and the nature of the damages and repairs which were already visible in a photographic reproduction of 1911. Letters from Gauguin and memoirs of the painter Judith Gérard show that Gauguin himself restored the painting and that about eight small brushstrokes of yellow-green paint were added by Gérard (Vincent did not use yellow in the background green). Examines Gauguin's recipes for this restoration noting his insensitivity to Vincent's brushwork and use of impasto. Speculates that what damage did not arise from Gauguin's restorations, namely the damaged inscription and signature, may have been inflicted by van Gogh himself. Suggests explanations and also explores the possibility of Gauguin having tried to remove them. Concludes that the damaged inscriptions and clumsy repaint should be regarded as an important part of this painting and its history, evidence of the relationship between Gauguin and van Gogh, and that they should, therefore, be left alone.

671. KODERA, TSUKASA. *Vincent van Gogh: Christianity Versus Nature*. Amsterdam/Philadelphia: John Benjamins Publishing Company, 1990. 284 p., 8 col. pl., 119 illus.

Includes a section on Gauguin (pp. 59-65), and numerous other references.

672. MATENA, DICK. *Gauguin en van Gogh*. Lombard, 1990. In Dutch.

Historical fiction based on the artists' time in Arles.

673. MAURON, CHARLES. *Van Gogh: études psychocritiques*. Paris: J. Corti, 1976. 186 p.

Discussion of van Gogh's personality, his unconscious, his relationship with his brother Theo, encounters and parallels with Gauguin, Monticelli, Maupassant and Baudelaire, aspects of his art, and his period in Arles in 1888.

674. MURINA, ELENA BORISOVNA. *Van Gogh*. Moscow: Iskusstvo, 1978. 437 p., 218 illus.

Biography which includes details of van Gogh's stay in Arles and his personal and artistic relationship with Gauguin.

675. ROSKILL, MARK WENTWORTH. *Van Gogh, Gauguin and the Impressionist Circle*. Greenwich, Connecticut: New York Graphic Society, 1970. 310p., 206 illus., 8 col. Unpublished supplement dated 1969.

Includes chapters on Impressionism, Japanese prints, Seurat, Emile Bernard, and van Gogh and Gauguin. Focuses on van Gogh's and Gauguin's pictorial development and influences on each other as well as their personal relationship.
Reviews: R. Lebowitz, *Arts* 45(Nov. 1970):1-8; H. Dorra, *Art Bulletin* 54(1972):560-63; V. Jirat-Wasiutynki, *Art Journal* 33(1973):78+
a. English ed.: London: Thames & Hudson, 1970. 310 p., 206 illus., 8 col.

676. ROSKILL, MARK WENTWORTH. *Van Gogh, Gauguin and French Painting of the 1880s; A Catalogue Raisonné of Key Works*. Ann Arbor, Mich.: University Microfilms, 1970. 342 p.

677. SABLONIERE, MARGRIT DE. *Paul Gauguin*. Amsterdam, Antwerp: Wereld-Bibliotheek, 1960. 74 p., 16 pl. In Dutch.

Study of the life and work of Gauguin with considerable information on his relationship with Vincent and Theo van Gogh.

678. STERNHEIM, CARL. *Gauguin und van Gogh*. Berlin: Die Schmiede, 1924. 72 p.

Lyrical interpretation of Gauguin's visit with van Gogh in Arles, taken from Gauguin's memoirs in *Avant et après*.
a. Dutch ed.: *Gauguin en van Gogh*. Trans. by M.C.A. Bijieveld. Amsterdam: A. Mak, 1925.

679. TRALBAUT, MARK EDO. *Van Gogh & Gauguin*. Antwerp: B. & P. Père, 1956. 42 p. 2 pl. In Dutch and French.

Discusses the two artist's influence on each other and their relationship.

680. UITERT, EVERT VAN. *Vincent van Gogh in Creative Competition: Four Essays from Simiolus*. The Netherlands: E. van Uitert, 1983. 95 p. illus.

Collection of four essays by van Uitert which first appeared in Dutch in *Simiolus, Netherlands Quarterly for the History of Art*, 1977-80. The first three essays deal with van Gogh and Gauguin: 1)"Vincent van Gogh and Paul Gauguin; A Creative Competition" (1977); 2)"Vincent van Gogh in Anticipation of Paul Gauguin"(1978-79); and 3)"Vincent van Gogh and Paul Gauguin in Competition: Vincent's Original Contribution" (1980).

B. Articles

681. BODELSEN, MERETE CHRISTENSEN. "An Unpublished Letter by Theo van Gogh." *Burlington Magazine* 99:651(June 1957):198-202.

Facsimile and discussion of a letter from Theo to Gauguin. Includes details on Gauguin's life.

682. CACHIN, FRANÇOISE. "Copenhagen. Gauguin and Van Gogh." *Burlington Magazine* 127:988 (1985): 480-83. 1 illus.

Discussion of the artists represented at two exhibitions in 1984-85 at the Ordrupgaard museum and Ny Carlsberg Glyptotek in Copenhagen.

683. CIKOVSKY, NICOLAI. "Van Gogh and a Photograph: A Note on 'La Berceuse'." *New Mexico Studies in the Fine Arts* 3(1978):23-28. 7 illus.

Notes that the *La Berceuse* is more like the photograph of van Gogh's mother in format, pose, and even appearance than are other more straightforward contemporary portraits of Mme. Roulin by van Gogh (Reinhart Collection, Winterthur) and Paul Gauguin (Saint Louis Art Museum). Claims that *La Berceuse* was painted after van Gogh's mental crisis of 1888, at a time when he desperately sought maternal comfort.

684. COLLINS, BRADLEY. "Art & Psychoanalysis--van Gogh and Gauguin on the Couch." *Art in America* 77:12(Dec. 1989):57-63.

Account of presentations at the Psychology of the Artist Symposium held at New York University on March 31 and April 1, 1989. Panelists included John Gedo, Donald Kuspit, Albert Lubin, Ziva Amishai-Maisels, Gilbert Rose, and Aaron Sheon.

685. CONSTABLE, W. G. "French Painting in Amsterdam. *Burlington Magazine* 49:284(Nov. 1926):222-33.

Mentions and reproduces Gauguin's *Portrait of van Gogh.*

686. DARRAGON, ERIC. "Van Gogh, Tartarin et la diligence de Tarascon." *Critique: revue générale des publications françaises et étrangères* 38:416(Jan. 1982):42-60.

Arriving in Arles in February 1888, van Gogh showed in his correspondence that he owned a copy of Alphonse Daudet's *Tartarin de Tarascon* (1872), his guide to understanding the Midi. His delight in the character gave rise to a painting, the *Tarascon Diligence* (Henry and Rose Pearlman Foundation), a direct evocation of a page in Daudet. In his intense work of the summer of 1888 and in the autumn, the solar illusion of the character of Tartarin returned endlessly, such as in the *Self-Portrait in the Tarascon Road* (destroyed). The final crisis which closed the encounter with Gauguin was interpreted by van Gogh himself through a page of *Tartarin in the Alps*. The whole Arles period was marked by this process of identification with a grotesque hero who sums up the Midi, a land of illusion and lies.

687. "Les deux écritures: l'une de van Gogh, l'autre de Gauguin." *France illustration* 388(21 March 1953):407.

688. DORRA, HENRI. "Gauguin's Dramatic Arles Themes." *Art Journal* 38:1(Fall 1978):12-17. 9 illus.

Discusses *Vintage at Arles-Human Miseries*, 1888 (Ordrupgaard, Copenhagen), identifying the source for the central figure as a lithograph of 1857 by Rops, *In the Ardenne--Now that Stupid Marie-Josèphe Thinks of a Child that has been Buried.* Notes the influence of Gauguin's contact with van Gogh on his work of the late 1880s.

689. GAIGNERON, A. DE. "Le pôle absolu de la couleur." *Connaissance des arts* 392(Oct. 1984):70-77. 8 illus.

A recent exhibition at the Metropolitan Museum of Art, New York, which featured van Gogh's Arles period, provided an opportunity for questioning the meaning of this period and its relationship to the rest of van Gogh's work. Citing extracts from the painter's letters to his brother, the author evokes the importance of the symbol, van Gogh's internal devastation, his friendship with Gauguin, and his interest in Japanese art, and sees this period as the culmination of van Gogh's work as a whole.

690. GOGH, VINCENT VAN. "Minnen av van Gogh och Cézanne" [Memoirs of van Gogh and Cézanne]. *Paletten* (Gothenburg)3(1952):92-93.

691. GOGH, VINCENT VAN. "Letters to Gauguin and Signac." *Art News* 57(Oct. 1958):33-34, 58-59.

692. GOGH, VINCENT W. VAN. "Van Gogh and Gauguin." *Vincent: Bulletin of the Rijksmuseum Vincent van Gogh* (Netherlands) 4:1(1975):2-7. 4 illus.

Van Gogh and Gauguin came from the same social class, the middle class of the 19th century, and both had been exposed to intellectual influences from a young age. The article traces the early career of each artist and the elements of similarity in their work. Both started with grey or dark tones, which only changed when they moved to other countries. Gauguin was influenced by the tropical colors of Martinique; Vincent by the luminosity of the Impressionist works he encountered in Paris. In Paris, both discovered the beauty of Japanese prints, and both attempted to master the flat clear color planes and simplification of design. Both reached the peak of their capabilities in foreign lands with warm climates, and each experienced nostalgia for the country of his youth. Discusses the benefit to their work of the mutual exchange of ideas, their involvement in social causes, and their differing attitudes towards plagiarism. Claims that Gauguin copied all his figures from sculptures of Gustave Arosa, of which he had a collection of photographs, but never mentioned this. Van Gogh always acknowledged the origins of his work. Their correspondence is also commented on.

693. HAMMACHER, A. M. "Vlucht uit de beschaving: Gauguin en van Gogh" ["Flight from Civilization: Gauguin and van Gogh"]. *Kroniek van Kunst en Kultur* (Amsterdam)9:9(Sept. 1948):252-54.

694. HOFFMANN, K. "Zu van Goghs Sonnenblumenbildern." *Zur Kunstgeschichte* 31:1(1968):32+.

695. HULSKER, J. "The Poet's Garden." *Vincent: Bulletin of the Rijksmuseum Vincent van Gogh* (Netherlands) 3:1(1974):22-32. 16 illus.

Debates the question of which of the paintings and drawings of the public garden in front of the "yellow house" in Arles, intended for decoration of the house in preparation for Gauguin's proposed visit, were actually included by van Gogh in the group known as *The Poet's Garden*. The term originated in a letter to Emile Bernard, but refers to an earlier letter to Gauguin in which contemplation of the plants in the public garden evokes for the painter landscapes "in which one likes to imagine the presence of Botticelli, Giotto, Petrarch, Dante and Boccaccio." Consideration of the letters and of the paintings and drawings concerned allows the author to establish four paintings, intended for Gauguin's bedroom, which van Gogh included in the *The Poet's Garden* series.

696. JOHNSON, RONALD. "Vincent van Gogh and the Vernacular: The Poet's Garden." *Arts Magazine* 53:6(Feb. 1979):98-104. 15 illus.

The vernacular tradition in European literature is traced through the troubadours, Boccaccio, and 19th-century poets known as the *Félibres*. These southern vernacular traditions influenced van Gogh's painting development in Arles and particularly *The Poet's Garden* series. The paintings of *The Poet's Garden* were to decorate Vincent's "yellow house." He associated each of the three sides of the garden across from his house with an early poet and a contemporary painter: Gauguin and Petrarch, Boch and Dante, and himself and Boccaccio. The bushes, trees, and flowers were used to symbolize the character of each painter-poet pair as well as different types of love. Through visual equivalents of the language of the vernacular, van Gogh defined his ideal of the artist as a poet-gardener and the enclosed garden as the location of the love he sought and symbolizied. These paintings, then, were earthly, humble, and yet disguised love poetry in the vernacular tradition.

697. MARAINI, ANTONIO. "Cézanne, Gauguin, van Gogh." *Dedalo* (1920):186-96.

Discusses a self-portrait by Gauguin.

698. MELLQUIST, J. "Bifurcation between Gauguin and van Gogh." *Apollo* 72(Nov. 1960):150.

699. MITERWA, K. "Gauguin i van Gogh w. Arles." *Glos Plastykou* (Dec. 1935).

700. MOFFAT, ALEXANDER. "From the Land/As a Fhearann." *Alba* (Spring 1987):10-12. 6 illus.

The exhibition "From the Land," held at the An Lanntair Gallery, Stornoway, Scotland, commemorated the centenary of the 1886 Crofting

Act and was divided into five sections: history, photography, popular images, painting, and film and television. Analyzing the content of the exhibition, the author draws a comparison between the evolution of the 19th-century French rural painters and the use of landscape by Highland artists. Van Gogh and Gauguin are adduced as figures who, despite their rejection of the urban theme, made a major contribution to modern art.

701. "Mutual Portraits." *Time* 67(2 Jan. 1956):40-43.

702. NORDENFALK, CARL. "De datum van Gauguins aankomst te Arles" [The Date of Gauguin's Arrival in Arles]. *Museumjournaal* 3:8(March 1958): 164-65, 167.

Argues that Gauguin arrived in Arles on October 24, 1888, and not on October 23, the commonly accepted date.

703. RICH, D. C. "Gauguin in Arles." *Chicago Art Institue Bulletin* 29(March 1935):34-37.

704. ROCHA, AUGUSTO DA. "Algo mas sobre van Gogh y Gauguin a proposito de su ingreso al Museo nacional de bellas artes." *Museo nacional de bellas artes boletin* (Buenos Aires) 1(July 1934):1-6.

705. ROGER-MARX, CLAUDE. "Lettres inédites de Vincent van Gogh et de Paul Gauguin." *Europe; revue mensuelle* (Paris)17:194(15 Feb. 1939):163-74.

706. SCHEMPP, T. "Did Gauguin Destroy van Gogh? With Reply by H.W. Van Loon." *Art News* 41(15 Nov. 1942):4 and (1 Dec. 1942):4.

707. SOTEMANN, A. L. "Four Traditions in Modernist Poetry and Art Theory." *Word & Image* (U.K.)4:1(Jan.-March 1988):297-302.

Discusses similarities between the basic conceptions of certain authors and painters concerning the genesis, ends, means and nature of their work. The author outlines his theory on poetics and periods in literary history before looking at analogous phenomena in the arts, noting a division between "expressive" and "objective" artists, with reference to Gauguin and van Gogh.

708. SOTH, LAUREN. "Gauguin, van Gogh and the Fishermen of Iceland." *Burlington Magazine* 131(April 1989):296-97.

Discusses Gauguin's two *Les Drames de la mer* zincographs (1889).

709. SPANUDIS, T . "Cézanne, Gauguin e van Gogh." *Habitat* 83(May 1965):31-35.

710. SUND, JUDY. "Favoured Fictions: Women and Books in the Art of van Gogh." *Art History* 11(June 1988):255-67.

711. UITERT, EVERT VAN. "Vincent van Gogh and Paul Gauguin: A Creative Competition." *Simiolus* 9:3(1977):149-68. 4 illus.

Examines the controversy between the two artists following their collaboration at Arles in 1888. Investigates sources of Gauguin's theory of art and the influence in Brittany on his personal development. Also deals with the reasons for the attitude adopted by van Gogh.

712. UITERT, EVERT VAN. "Vincent van Gogh in Anticipation of Paul Gauguin." *Simiolus* 10:3-4(1978-79):182-99. 10 illus.

Discusses the decoration and paintings by van Gogh for the yellow house in Arles which he rented after 1888 when he was visited by Gauguin; influence of Gauguin on van Gogh especially on paintings of *The Poet's Garden* for Gauguin's bedroom; and the interaction and relationship of the two painters.

713. UITERT, EVERT VAN. "Vincent van Gogh and Paul Gauguin in Competition: Vincent's Original Contribution." *Simiolus* 11:2(1980):81-106. 13 illus.

Study of the effect on Vincent van Gogh of his collaboration with Paul Gauguin in 1888. Discusses the relationship of form to content in the paintings of both artists, and the artistic rivalry between them that resulted from their different attitudes to freedom of representation.

714. "Une lettre inédite de Van Gogh." *Beaux-Arts* (10 March 1939):1.

715. "Van Gogh, rapports avec Gauguin." *L'Amour de l'art* 18(April 1937):35.

716. VATTIER, SUZANNE. "La condition de l'artiste van Gogh-Gauguin." *Arts de France* 8(1946):83-89.

717. "Vincent van Goghs Wahnsinn und Ende" [Vincent van Gogh's Insanity and End]. *Genius* (Munich)1(1919):46-50.

Article based in part on excerpts from Gauguin's *Avant et après* manuscript.

IV. Gauguin in Panama and Martinique, April to October, 1887

A. Monographs

718. CUCCHI, ROGER. *Gauguin à la Martinique: Le musée imaginaire complet de ses peintures, dessins, sculptures, céramiques, les lettres, les catalogues d'expositions*. Vaduz: Calivran Anstalt, 1979. 93 p., 24 illus., 4 col.

Contents: présentation de M. Malingue; chronologie de la vie de Gauguin; lettres écrites pendant le voyage à la Martinique; extraits du livre, d'A. Alexandre sur Paul Gauguin, édité par Bernheim; article Gauguin à Bruxelles d'Octave Maus; article la presse et la vente de l'hôtel Drouot, Octave Mirbeau; reproduction pages du catalogue Wildenstein; reproduction liste oeuvres de Gauguin dans le catalogue Wildenstein; reproduction liste oeuvres de Gauguin dans le catalogue Salon d'automne de 1906, préface par Charles Morice; reproduction catalogue de l'exposition Gauguin à Leicester Galleries, Londres, juillet 1924; reproduction catalogue de l'exposition de la collection Durrio d'oeuvres de Gauguin à la Leicester Galleries, Londres, mai-juin 1931; oeuvres de Gauguin exposées à l'exposition du Tricentenaire du rattachement des Antilles à la France (Oct. 1935); Centre d'art Musée Paul Gauguin.

719. POPE, KAREN KRISTINE RECHNITZER. *Gauguin and Martinique*. Ph.D. diss., University of Texas, Austin, 1981. 395 p., 167 illus.

Study of Gauguin's Martinique period and the paintings which resulted from his trip to the Caribbean in 1887. Establishes that Gauguin made the trip at a crucial time in the development of his art, that the Martinique experience stimulated the production of large-figure paintings, and that the Martinique works contain early statements of themes and imagery which reappear, recast and clarified, in Gauguin's later works. Appendices examine the works of Gauguin's companion, Charles Laval, and the attribution problems which have complicated study of Gauguin's Martinique period.

B. Articles

720. COOPER, DOUGLAS. "An Important Gauguin Discovery." *Burlington Magazine* 123:937(April 1981):195-97. 1 illus.

Recounts the events and documentary evidence leading to and confirming the rediscovery of one of the 12 canvases painted by Gauguin in 1887 during his stay in Martinique. This trip proved to be almost a total disaster for him, since through illness he found little strength to paint except for five weeks in June-July, 1887, and during the 10 days just before he left the island. The paintings he managed to finish radiate a mood of spiritual contentment--colorful, lively landscapes, which mark the beginning of his creative liberation as an artist. The rediscovery of *Paysage de la Martinique*, previously know as *Allées et venues*, new in the collection of Baron Heinrich Thyssen-Bornemisza, is described.

721. GOGH, VINCENT VAN. "Enkele notities over Gauguin op Martinique" [Some Notes About Gauguin in Martinique]. *MJ, Museum Journaal voor Moderne Kunst* 6(1960):15-16.

722. JOYAU, AUGUSTE. "Paul Gauguin à la Martinique." *La Revue française de l'élite européenne* 117(April 1960):78-81. illus.

723. PLANET, GEORGES. "Gauguin à la Martinique." *Syndicat intercommunal d'aménagement touristique du nord, bulletin d'information* (Fort-de-France) 2(Jan. 1973):25-31.

V. Gauguin in Tahiti and the Marquesas Islands

A. Monographs

724. AGEE, JAMES. "Noa Noa." In *Agee on Film*, vol. 2. Five Film Scripts by James Agee. New York: McDowell, Obolensky, 1959-60. 2 vol.
a. Another ed.: New York: Grosser & Dunlap, 1969.

Includes Agee's film script, "Noa Noa," begun in 1953 under contract, with David Bradley as the director. Negotiations for the film production were interrupted by Agee's death in 1955, and "Noa Noa" was never produced. The script deals with Gauguin's short stay in Arles with van Gogh and his years in Tahiti.

725. AGOSTINI, JULES. *Tahiti*. Paris: J. André, 1905.

Mentions Gauguin's years and work in Tahiti.

726. AQUINO, RICARDO BIGI DE. *Paul Gauguin, Robert Louis Stevenson and the South Pacific: A Study in Humanistic Geography*. M.A. thesis, University of Victoria, 1975. 177 p.

Studies Gauguin's and Stevenson's differing literary views of the South Pacific.

727. BOMPARD, PIERRE. *Ma mission aux Marquises, Paul Gauguin*. Paris: Editions des Deux Miroirs, 1962. 139 p., 4 pl.

Narrative by Bompard (1890-1962), a painter, of his journey to Tahiti and the Marquesas in 1957. Following in Gauguin's wake, Bompard shares impressions of Gauguin's South Pacific experiences. Includes conversations with Gauguin's descendants and visits to Gauguin's houses, tomb, and other sites.

728. BROOKE, RUPERT. *The Letters of Rupert Brooke*. Geoffrey Keynes, ed. London: Faber and Faber, 1968. 709 p., 16 pl.

The poet Rupert Brooke (1887-1915) spent three months in Tahiti in early 1914. Part of the time was spent searching for "lost Gauguins." Brooke failed to find any but considered Tahiti an ideal place to work. For letters which mention Gauguin, see pp. 523, 535, 544, 550, 568-69. Brooke's visit is also treated in Robert Langdon's *Tahiti: Island of Love* (London: Cassell, 1959), chapter 48.
a. U.S. ed.: New York: Harcourt, Brace & World, 1968. 709 p.

729. DALLET, JEAN-MARIE. *Gauguin; ou, l'atelier du tropique, roman*. Paris: Editions Saint-Germain-des-Pres, 1976. 141 p.

French novel based on Gauguin's years in Tahiti.

730. DANIELSSON, BENGT. *Söderhavets glömda öar. Reseskildring fram Marquesasorna* [Forgotten Islands of the South Seas. Travel Description Through the Marquesas]. Stockholm: Tidens Forlag, 1952.

Mentions Gauguin's years and art in Tahiti and the Marquesas.
a. English ed.: *Forgotten Islands of the South Seas*. London: Allen & Unwin, 1957. 204 p.

731. DANIELSSON, BENGT and MARIE-THERESE DANIELSSON. *Gauguin à Tahiti et aux îles Marquises*. Pape'ete: Publications du Pacifique, 1975. 327 p., 16 pl.

Study of Gauguin's years and artistic output in Tahiti and the Marquesas.
a. Revised ed.: 1988. 372 p. See also 783.
Review: M. Sanson, *Gazette des Beaux-Arts* 6th ser. 88(July-Aug. 1976):3-4.

732. DANIELSSON, BENGT. *Gauguins Söderhavsár* [Gauguin's South Pacific]. Stockholm: Forum, 1964. 301 p., col. pl.

Account of the last 12 years of Gauguin's life, ten of which were spent in Tahiti and the Marquesas. Describes geographical, cultural and social conditions of the time. Attempts to explain Gauguin's actions, lifestyle, difficulties, griefs and triumphs in the South Pacific.

Reviews: W. Townsend, *Studio* 171(March, 1966):122; P. Yates, *Arts & Architecture* 83(July, 1966):36.
a. English ed.: *Gauguin in the South Seas*. Trans. by Reginald Spink. London: Allen & Unwin, 1965. 310 p., 66 illus., 16 col. pl.
b. U.S. ed.: New York: Doubleday, 1966. 336 p., illus., col. pl.
c. Russian ed.: Moscow, 1968. 280 p., illus.
d. French eds.: *Gauguin à Tahiti et aux îles Marquises*. Pape'ete: Editions du Pacifique, 1975. 327 p., illus., 16 pl.; Pape'ete, 1988. 372 p.; Paris: Presses-Pocket, 1988. 372 p.

733. DANIELSSON, BENGT and PATRICK O'REILLY. *Gauguin journaliste à Tahiti & ses articles des "Guêpes."* Paris: Société des Océanistes, 1966. 53 p., 10 pl.

Study of Gauguin's journalist career in Tahiti from 1899-1901. Includes information and articles he wrote for *Le Sourire* (The Smile) and *Les Guêpes* (The Wasps). These publications were critical of the French administration and missions. Gauguin wrote and edited articles for both and supplied occasional illustrations.

Les Guêpes ran from March, 1899 to August, 1900. It was a monthly at first although it later became erratic. Nine issues of the four-page *Le Sourire*, Gauguin's own satirical journal, exist. It ceased publication in April, 1900.

734. DANIELSSON, MARIE-THERESE and BENGT DANIELSSON. *Gauguin à Tahiti*. Paris: Société des Océanistes, 1973. 30 p., illus., some col.

Overview of Gauguin's years and art in Tahiti.
a. English ed.: *Gauguin in Tahiti*. Paris: Société des Océanistes, 1973. 30 p., illus., some col.

735. DAWS, GAVAN. *A Dream of Islands*. New York: Norton, 1980. 289 p., 6 pl.

Subtitled "Voyages of Self-Discovery in the South Seas," Daws includes a section (pp. 216-70) on Gauguin's years and work in Tahiti and the Marquesas. Portrays Gauguin as an extreme case of a man at war with society and with himself.

736. *Dossier de la succession Paul Gauguin*. Pape'ete: Société des Etudes Océaniénnes, 1957. 43 p.

Documents which detail Gauguin's final days in the Marquesas and events after his death.

737. FEZZI, ELDA and FLORELLA MINERVINO. *Noa Noa e il primo viaggio a Tahiti di Gauguin: Studi storico-filologici*. Introduction by Marc Sanson. Milan: Rizzoli, 1974. 163 p., illus., 37 pl.

Historical and philological study of Gauguin's first stay in Tahiti (1891-93) and his *Noa Noa* manuscript.

738. FIELD, RICHARD SAMPSON. *Paul Gauguin: The Paintings of the First Trip to Tahiti*. Ph.D. diss., Harvard University, 1963; New York & London: Garland, 1977. 532 p., 87 illus., 44 pl.

The first study to establish a chronology for Gauguin's Tahitian paintings of the years 1891-93, based on a detailed catalogue utilizing all known data, including letters, sketchbooks, and stylistic evidence. The catalogue itself is included as an appendix to the volume. Gauguin's paintings of 1891-93 are rather uneven and do not manifest a single-minded pursuit of stylistic innovation. They are often allegorical in nature. Gauguin's work is seen as the outgrowth of a complicated effort to recreate a Tahitian past that was an equivalent for contemporary European preoccupations with the psychological past. The Tahitian woman became the vehicle for Gauguin's own need to objectify his unconscious. With the exception of one or two works of late 1892, which transcend the multi-determined nature of most of the Tahitian oeuvre and broach a proto-Fauvist style, Gauguin is seen as a captive of the rather confused sytlistic situation of the 1890s.

739. GORSKY, BERNARD. *Trois tombes au soleil: Robert Louis Stevenson, Paul Gauguin, Alain Gerbault*. Paris: Albin Michel, 1976.

Section on Gauguin (pp. 123-234) deals with his years in Tahiti and the Marquesas. Includes excerpts from letters and other writings in this largely biographical treatment.

740. GRAY, FREDERIC CHARLES. *Four Visions of Tahiti in Twentieth-Century French Literature: Gauguin, Segalen, Chadourne, t'Serstevens*. M.A. thesis, University of Hawaii, 1964. 71 p.

741. GUILLOT, FRANÇOIS. *Souvenirs d'un colonial en Océanie*. Annecy, 1935.

Includes reminiscences of Gauguin in Tahiti.

742. HAMON, RENEE. *Gauguin, le solitaire du Pacifique. A Tahiti et aux îles Marquises*. Preface by Robert Rey. Paris: Vigot Frères, 1939. 47 p., illus., 41 photogs.

Account of Gauguin's years in Tahiti and the Marquesas, illustrated by photographs of places and people he knew. The author visited the islands in the late 1930s and recorded her impressions and conversations with French and Tahitians who knew Gauguin.
a. Excerpts: *L'Amour de l'art* 17(July 1936):246-50; *Beaux-Arts* (25 February-25 March, 1938).

743. JARRY, ALFRED. *Oeuvres complètes*. Michel Arrivé, ed. Paris: Gallimard, 1972.

Includes Jarry's "three poems after and for Paul Gauguin" (Trois poèmes d'après et pour Paul Gauguin): "Ia Orana Maria," "L'Homme à la hache," and "Manao Tupapau"(see pp. 252-55).
a. Another ed.: 1988, 1113 p.

744. LANGDON, ROBERT. *Tahiti: Island of Love*. London: Cassell, 1959. 276 p., illus.

Chronological story and narrative of Tahiti. Includes information on Gauguin and visits by Rupert Brooke (1914) and Somerset Maughan (1916) to Tahiti looking for "lost Gauguins."
a. Other eds.: London: Harborough, 1960; Sydney: Pacific Publicaitons, 1968 and 1979.

745. LEBLOND, MARIUS-ARY. *Peintres de race*. Brussels: G. Van Oest, 1909. 238 p., illus., 28 pl.

Final chapter discusses Gauguin's work in Tahiti and the Marquesas. Deals with his "Polynesian style," exoticism, nudes, and symbolism.
a. 2nd ed.: Paris: Librairie Générale des Sciences, Arts & Lettres, 1912.
b. Reprint: Geneva: Slatkine, 1981.

746. LOIZE, JEAN. *Gauguin écrivain, ou, les sept visages de "Noa Noa."* Paris: Musée de l'Homme, Société des Océanistes, 1949. 26 p. 320 copies.

Text of an address on Gauguin's different versions of *Noa Noa* delivered by Loize on July 1, 1948 at the Musée de l'Homme. Includes bibliographic details and an index of names cited.

747. LUCAS, CHRISTOPHER. *Tiki and the Dolphin; The Adventures of a Boy in Tahiti*. New York: Vanguard Press, 1974. 163 p.

Fictional story for children which includes an imaginary friendship between a boy and Paul Gauguin in Tahiti.

748. MAUGHAM, W. SOMERSET. *The Moon and Sixpence*. New York: Doubleday, 1919. 341 p.

Fictionalized biography loosely based on Gauguin's life which portrays the character of the true artist as a man of renunciation. Maugham's fictional character, Charles Strickland, is a bored stockbroker who escapes to a painter's life in Tahiti. Themes of escape, material repudiation, and self-destruction are emphasized over artistic pursuits. Borrows numerous details from Gauguin's life with significant variations.
Other eds.: 1919 (English), 1935, 1944.

749. MORTEVEILLE, BRIGITTE. *Le mythe de la Nouvelle-Cythère dans la littérature française de Bougainville à Gauguin*. Paris, 1982. 138 p.

Discusses the treatment of Tahitians and Tahitian culture in French literature, including a section on Gauguin's writings.

750. O'REILLY, PATRICK. *Tahiti et la Polynésie française, 1768-1964*. Lettres manuscrits et documents depuis les premières missions. Rares impressions polynésiennes. Importantes lettres autographes de Paul Gauguin. Livres et autographes de Pierre Loti et illustrations pour ses oeuvres. Vente aux enchères publiques à Paris le 2 juin 1969. Paris, 1969. 1 vol., illus.

Auction sales catalogue with a preface by O'Reilly. Includes a list of estimated prices.

751. PERRUCHOT, HENRI. *Gauguin; Tahiti*. Paris: Hazan, 1958. 16 p., 4 illus., 15 pl., 14 col.

a. English ed.: London: Methuen, 1958. 14 p., 15 pl.
b. U.S. ed.: New York: Tudor, 1958.

752. PERRUCHOT, HENRI. *Gauguin, sa vie ardente et misérable*. Paris: Le Sillage, 1948. 332 p., illus., 8 pl.

Biography of Gauguin which stresses the romantic legend and Polynesian periods.

753. PIERRE, JOSE. *Gauguin aux Marquises, roman*. Paris: Flammarion, 1982. 253 p.

Novel in journal and dramatic form which covers Gauguin's last two years in the Marquesas (1901-03).

754. REY, ROBERT. *Onze menus de Paul Gauguin, menus propos.* Geneva: Gérald Cramer, 1950. 123 p., 11 pl., some col.

Study and facsimile reproductions of 11 menus produced and illustrated by Gauguin in Tahiti in the 1890s. These impromptu works are decorated by drawings and watercolors. Also summarizes Gauguin's years in Tahiti and his conflicts with French authorities.

755. ROBERTS, KEVIN. *Stonefish and Other Poems.* Lantzville, British Columbia: Oolichan Books, 1982. 77 p.

Poems by an Australian writer living in Canada. The first section, "Stonefish," has poems based on Gauguin's life and art in the South Pacific.

756. ROHDE, PETRA-ANGELIKA. *Paul Gauguin auf Tahiti: Ethnographische Wirklichkeit und künstlerische Utopie* [Paul Gauguin on Tahiti: Ethnographic Reality and Artistic Utopia]. Ph.D. diss., Freiburg (Breisgau) University, 1987. Rheinfelden: Schäuble Verlag, 1988. 210 p., 64 pl.

Concentrates on Gauguin's Polynesian periods and paintings. Includes three chapters on Tahitian culture and society, chapters on Gauguin's life and years in Tahiti and the Marquesas, and Gauguin's primitivism. Probes Gauguin's understanding and use of native mythology and symbolism in his works.

757. SCHNEEBERGER, PIERRE-FRANÇOIS. *Gauguin à Tahiti.* Lausanne: International Art Book Collection, 1961. 64 p., 27 col. illus.

Study of Gauguin's years and work in Tahiti and the Marquesas. Captions to the plates are taken from Gauguin's letters and other writings.
a. German ed.: *Gauguin, Tahiti.* Munich, Vienna: Andermann, 1962. 62 p.
b. U.S. ed.: *Gauguin: Tahiti.* Trans. by Diana Imber. New York: French & European Publications, 1963. 62 p., 28 col. pl.

758. SEGALEN, VICTOR. *Les immémoriaux.* Paris: Plon, 1956. 278 p., 65 illus., pl.

Ethnographical study of ancient Tahitian religion and culture. All of the illustrations except one are of works by Gauguin.
Reprint: Paris: Plon, 1977.

759. SEGALEN, VICTOR. *Gauguin dans son dernier décor, et autres textes de Tahiti.* Montpellier: Fata Morgan, 1974. 144 p.

Collection of journal excerpts, letters, and other writings by Segalen, who visited Gauguin's residences in Tahiti and in the Marquesas in 1903-04.
a. Reprints: 1980, 1986.
b. German ed.: *Paul Gauguin in seiner letzten Umgebung. Die zwei Gesichter des Arthur Rimbaud.* Frankfurt am Main: Qumran, 1982.

760. SEGALEN, VICTOR. *Essai sur l'exotisme, une esthétique du divers* (notes). Paris: Fata Morgana, 1978. 91 p.

Segalen (1878-1919), a marine physician and writer, visited the South Pacific in 1903-04. The 1986 edition includes a section (pp. 95-155) on Gauguin in Tahiti and the Marquesas.
a. New ed.: Augmented with (subtitle) *Textes sur Gauguin et l'Océanie, précédé de Segalen et l'exotisme par Gilles Manceron.* Paris: Livre de Poche, 1986. 157 p.

761. STADLER, WOLFGANG. *Paul Gauguin: Südseezauber* [Paul Gauguin: South Sea Magic]. Introduction by Wolf Stadler. Freiburg, Basle, Vienna: Herder, 1985. 48 p., 24 col. illus.

Presents 24 paintings by Gauguin, portraying the people and landscapes of the islands of Tahiti and Mataiea, with an essay on the artist's life and work. Interprets the paintings and quotes extensively from Gauguin's letters and other writings.

762. TAMARIT CRESPO, RAFAEL. *Adiós a Noa-Noa; Poemas 1975.* Badalona: JES Artes Grãf, 1975. 50 p.

Collection of poems inspired by Gauguin's life and work, particularly his years in Tahiti.

763. TEILHET-FISKE, JEHANNE H. *The Influence of Polynesian Culture and Art on the Works of Paul Gauguin, 1891-1903.* Ph.D. diss., University of California, Los Angeles, 1975. 405 p. Ann Arbor, Mich.: UMI Research Press, 1983. 303 p., 94 illus.

Examines the depth of Gauguin's understanding of Tahitian and Marquesan myths, superstitions, customs, and behavioral characteristics between 1891 and 1903, as well as placing in perspective what influence Polynesian art and religion had on Gauguin's works. Also explores how Gauguin incorporated Polynesian art and religious ideas into his Symbolist-Theosophical works. Views Gauguin as an informed lay-anthropologist and credits him with being the first Western artist to recognize the aesthetic merit and contextual meaning of Polynesian art.

a. Revised ed.: *Paradise Reviewed: An Interpretation of Gauguin's Polynesian Symbolism.* Ann Arbor, Mich.: UMI Research Press: Bowker, 1983.

764. TUGENDKHOLD, I. AKOV ALEKSANDROVICH. *Zhizn i Tvorchestvo Polia Gogena. Noa-Noa Puteshestvie na Tahiti.* Moscow: D.I.A. Makovskii, 1918.

765. VANCE, MARY LYNN ZINK. *Gauguin's Polynesian Pantheon as a Visual Language.* Ph.D. diss., University of California, Santa Barbara, 1983. 662 p., 225 illus.

Shows that the myths concerning the ancient Polynesian deities Taaroa, Hina, Tefatou, Oro, and Vairaumati provided Gauguin with subject matter that he developed into a symbolic visual language. In accordance with his theory of the visual parable, Gauguin intended this language to be mysterious, and even incomprehensible; on a literal level and yet explicit and profound on a symbolic level. Gauguin's manuscripts, articles, and letters reveal that he synthesized his understanding of the religion from his experiences and from his reading of quasi-anthropological texts, religious treatises, novels and poems. He developed image-types for the deities to symbolize the philosophical principles he felt they embodied: the principle of creation, the equivalence of the religions, the immortality of the supreme being, the interaction of the forces of life and death, the triumph of the resurrection of the spirit over the mortality of the body, ferocity in warfare, enthusiasm for sexual pleasure, and feminine beauty.

766. VOLLARD, AMBROISE. *Recollections of a Picture Dealer.* Translated from the Original French Manuscript by Violet M. Macdonald. London: Constable, 1936. 326 p., pl.

Memoirs of Ambroise Vollard (1867-1939) the successful Parisian art dealer who purchased his first Gauguin painting in 1893. In March, 1900 Gauguin agreed to contract with Vollard for 24 paintings a year at 200-250 francs, in return for a monthly salary of 300 francs. Vollard raised the advance and picture price in February, 1901.
a. U.S. eds.: Boston: Little, Brown, 1936. 326 p., 32 pl.; New York: Hacker Art Books, 1978. 326 p; New York: Dover, 1978. 326 p.
b. French eds.: *Souvenirs d'un marchand de tableaux.* Paris: Albin-Michel, 1937, 1948, 1959, 1984.

767. WILSON, T. L. RODNEY. *Van der Velden (1837-1913).* Wellington, New Zealand: A.H. & A.W. Reed, 1976. 184 p., 198 illus.

Intended as initial presentation of material eventually to be expanded into a catalogue raisonné. In this book the author accounts for the influence of Van der Velden on New Zealand painting, indicating in turn the influence of New Zealand on Van der Velden. In the introduction he compares the roles of Gauguin and Van der Velden as European artists with established reputations who lived and worked in the Southern hemisphere.

B. Articles

768. "L'atelier de Gauguin à Atuona; photograph." *Art et artist* 38(July 1939):360.

769. ATKIN, PARK. "Noa noa by Paul Gauguin...marées society." *The Arts* 13(1928):68+.

770. AUSTIN, FLORENCE. "Noa noa." *L'Objet d'art* 13(Dec. 1988-Jan. 1989):62-69. illus.

771. BOREL, PIERRE. "Les derniers jours et la mort mystérieuse de Paul Gauguin." *Pro Arte* (Sept. 1942): 13-16. 2 illus.

772. BOUGE, L.J. "Traduction et interprétations des titres en langue tahitienne inscrits sur les oeuvre océaniennes de Paul Gauguin." *Gazette des Beaux-Arts* 6th ser., 47(Jan.-April 1956[published 1958]):161-64. Reprinted in *Gauguin; sa vie, son oeuvre* (Paris, 1958).

773. LE BRONNEC, GUILLAUME. "La vie de Gauguin aux îles Marquises." *Bulletin de la Société des Etudes Océaniennes* 9:5 (March 1954): 198-211.

774. LE BRONNEC, GUILLAUME. "Les dernières années." *Gazette des Beaux-Arts* ser. 6, 47(Jan.-April 1956 [published 1958]):189-204. Reprinted in *Gauguin, sa vie, son oeuvre* (Paris, 1958).

Includes an inventory of Gauguin's personal effects on his death.

775. BROWN, SARA. "Un fragmento histórico." *Cuadernos Americanos* 19:6 (1960): 67-121. 6 pl.

Concerns Gauguin and Mallarmé, and Gauguin's years in Oceania.

776. CHASSE, CHARLES. "Les démêlés de Gauguin avec les gendarmes et l'évêque des îles Marquises." *Mercure de France* 288(15 Nov. 1938):62-75.

777. CHERONNET, L. "P. Gauguin à Tahiti." *France illustration* 5(5 Feb. 1949):132-34.

778. COLLINS, R.D.J. "Paul Gauguin et la Nouvelle Zélande." *Gazette des Beaux-Arts* 6th ser., 90(Nov. 1977):173-76. 9 illus.

During his return journey to Tahiti in 1895, Gauguin spent 10 days--19 to 29 August--in Auckland, New Zealand. Drawings of New Zealand Maori art which he may have done while there still exist. Attention is drawn to the presence in a painting of 1896, *Te Tamari no Atua* (Bayerische Staatsgemäldesammlungen, Munich) and of elements that may have been borrowed from New Zealand art.

779. DANIELSSON, BENGT. "Gauguin's Tahitian Titles." *Burlington Magazine* 9:760(April 1967):228-33.

780. DANIELSSON, BENGT. "The Exotic Sources of Gauguin's Art." *Expedition* 11:4(Summer 1969):16-26. 19 illus.

781. DANIELSSON, BENGT. "Gauguins Söderhavsår" [Gauguin's Years in the South Seas]. *Louisiana Revy* (Denmark) 23:1(Oct. 1982):4-19. 31 illus.

Describes Gauguin's early life, his travels to South America, his visit to Panama, his marriage to Mette Gad, his friendships with other artists, and the periods spent in Paris, Copenhagen, and Brittany. Focuses on his life in Tahiti. Concludes that, as far as Gauguin's art is concerned, his main contribution to history is not the introduction of new exotic subjects, but the destruction of existing conventions, dogmas, and academic taboos of his time.

782. DANTO, A. C. "Gauguin's Tahitian Daze." *Art News* 87(Summer 1988):128-32.

783. DAVIDSON, MARSHALL B. "The Enigmatic Islands of Paul Gauguin." *Horizon* 2:3(Jan. 1960):32-40. 6 col. pl.

Brief introduction by Davidson followed by color reproductions.

784. "Gauguin the Great Painter of Tahiti and the Hero of the Moon and Sixpence." *The Touchstone* (Feb. 1920).

785. GREGG, F. J. "Gauguin in the South Seas." *Art Review* 1(Dec. 1921):17, 27.

786. HAMON, RENEE. "Sur les traces de Gauguin en Océanie." *L'Amour de l'art* 17(July 1936):246-50.

787. HAMON, RENEE. "Le solitaire du Pacifique." *Beaux-Arts* (Feb.-March 1933).

788. HAMON, RENEE. "The Recluse of the Pacific: Paul Gauguin's Life in Tahiti and the Marquesas." *The Geographical Magazine* 8(1939):263-76.

789. HAUPT, D.E. and V. MUSE. "P. Gauguin: The Painters Paradise, Then and Now." *Life* 11(July 1988):46-52.

790. HOURS, MADELEINE. "Macrophotographies d'après quelques oeuvres de Gauguin exposées à Papéari (Tahiti)." *Bulletin du laboratoire du Musée du Louvre/Revue de Louvre* supp. 10(1965):39-55. 15 illus.

791. HUYGHE, RENE. "Gauguin et la fiction de *Noa-Noa*." *Arts* (15 June 1951):1.

792. IZERGINA, A. "Kartina Polja Gogena 'sem' ja taitjan." [Gauguin's Tahitian Family]. *Soob. gos Ermitaza* (Leningrad) 20(1961):44-46. 1 illus.

793. JACQUIER, HENRI. "Histoire locale: le dossier de la succession Paul Gauguin." *Bulletin de la Société des Etudes Océaniennes* 10(Sept. 1957):673-711.

794. KEABLE, ROBERT. "Bohemian and Rebel in the World's Garden: How Stevenson Found a Brother in the Tahitian and Gauguin Sought in Him Living Art." *Asia* 24(Nov. 1924):892-97.

795. LA FARGE, HENRY. "John La Farge and the South Sea Idyll." *Journal of the Warburg and Courtauld Institues* 7(1944):34-39.

796. "La langueur des Marquises." *Paris-Match* 2110 (2 Nov. 1989).

Article on Captain Paul-Emile Miot's visit to the Marquesas in 1869-70 and the photographs he took there and in Tahiti. Illustrated by Gauguin's painting *Te Arii Vahine* (1896).

797. LARSON, K. "Stranger than Paradise." *New York* 21(23 May 1988):63-64.

798. LEITHAUSER, BRAD. "Gone Native (Looking Back at the Reality Behind Paul Gauguin's Luminous Dreams of Tropical Innocence)." *Arts & Antiques* (May 1988):66-75, 108. 7 col. illus.

Account of Gauguin's life in Tahiti, noting that while he found much of interest there, he did not find peace and quiet. Compares Gauguin's response to the South Seas with that of Robert Louis Stevenson, who died in Samoa in 1894. Concludes that Gauguin's vision of paradise was not fulfilled by the reality of Tahiti.

799. LEMASSON, HENRI. "La vie de Gauguin à Tahiti." *Encyclopédie de la France et d'outremer* (Feb. 1950):18-19.

800. LOO, ESTHER VAN. "Gauguin et Tahiti." *Géographia* (Paris) 90(March 1959):25-33.

801. MENARD, PAUL. "Painter of Polynesia." *Vogue* 108(15 Oct. 1946):300-05.

802. MENARD, WILMON B. "Gauguin's Tahiti Son." *Saturday Review of Literature* (30 Oct. 1954):34-40.

803. MENARD, WILMON B. "Gauguin: New Facts Come to Light on Tahitian Journey." *Look* 20(21 Aug. 1956):46-48+.

804. MORILLOT. "Gauguin et Tahiti." *Jazz* (Paris) 1(Dec. 1928):18-20. 2 illus.

805. MORILLOT. "Gauguin of Tahiti." *La Pluma* (Montevideo) 2(1931):46-48.

806. NEVERMANN, HANS. "Polynesien und Paul Gauguin." *Baessler-Archiv* 4 (1956):221-31.

807. O'BRIEN, FREDERICK. "Gauguin in the South Seas." *The Century* 100:2(June 1920):225-35.

808. O'REILLY, PATRICK. "Paul Gauguin, peintre de la vierge en Océanie." *Missions des Iles* (Paris) 21(1949):108-09.

809. O'REILLY, PATRICK. "'Les amours d'un vieux peintre aux Marquises,' ou Paul Gauguin héro d'une comédie en vers écrite de son vivant." *Journal de la Société des Océanistes* 18:18 (Dec. 1962):113-20.

810. O'REILLY, PATRICK. "La mort de Gauguin et la presse française." *Le Vieux papier* (Paris: Société archéologique, historique et artistique) 24:212(April 1965):225-47.

811. PERRUCHOT, HENRI. "Gauguin et la Pacifique." *Réalités* 70 (Nov. 1951):84-92. 9 illus.

812. PERRUCHOT, HENRI. "La fin de Gauguin." *Revue de Paris* (Sept. 1961): 122-36.

813. PERRUCHOT, HENRI. "Les archives Gauguin du fonds Monfreid." *Jardin des Arts* 83(1961): 15-24. 19 illus.

Describes Georges-Daniel de Monfreid's collection of Gauguin's works and documents, especially important for understanding his Polynesian periods.

814. PIERRE, JOSE. "Fragments d'un 'Gauguin aux Marquises'" [Fragments of a 'Gauguin in the Marquesas']. *Opus international* (France) 81 (Summer, 1981):26-32. 5 illus.

Imaginary account of a film crew attempting to create a fictional account of Gauguin's last years on the Marquesas Islands. The author, identifying himself totally with Gauguin and speaking for him, assimilates sexual and creative energy and advocates painting as the pursuit of sensual delight. Excerpts from the scenario are interposed with the text, in which "Gauguin" makes such statements as that Pollock's drip technique resembles urination, the lack of animal presence in the work of Cézanne and van Gogh represents their refusal to make love with nature, Munch expressed his sexuality "nocturnally" and Gauguin "sunnily." One scenario extract deals with Gauguin's desire to reinvent nature in his works. "Gauguin" also discusses American puritanism.

815. RAMSDEN, ERIC. "Death of Paul Gauguin's Tahitian Mistress." *Pacific Islands Monthly* 6:14(16 Jan. 1944):22-23.

816. REUTERSWARD, PATRIK. "Gauguin och den tahitiska kvinnan" [Gauguin and the Women of Tahiti]. *Konsthistorisk Tidskrift* 53:2(1984):79-85. 5 illus. In Swedish, summary in English.

Distinguishes three pictorial approaches to Tahitian women in Gauguin's paintings and three corresponding attitudes toward the women and their culture. Gauguin first focused on their racial characteristics and suggested the primitive nature of their society. Second, by emphasizing surface pattern and intense color, he presented a poetic but inaccurate image of a highly sophisticated oriental culture, an appraoch developed to address the public in Paris. Gauguin's third, more mature and realistic approach exalted the Tahitian woman's power of thought and reflection.

817. REY, ROBERT. "Dernier décor de la demeure de Gauguin aux îles Marquises." *Revue des arts* 3:2(June 1953):115-21. 8 illus.

818. ROSE, B. "Gauguin's Wild Kingdom." *Vogue* 178(May 1988):290-93+.

819. RUGIERE, PAUL. "Tahiti et Gauguin." *Mercure de France* 151(1921):686-96.

820. SEGALEN, VICTOR. "Journal des îles, Océanie, 1903-1904." *Mercure de France* (May-June 1956).

Segalen, a ship's surgeon, and writer, visited French Polynesia in 1903-04. He saw Gauguin's studio in Atuona, Marquesas, after the artist's death. He purchased 24 Gauguin "relics" (books, photographs, albums, etc.) for 178.25 francs at the public auction in Pape'ete on September 2, 1903. Gauguin's palette, for example, sold for 2 francs.

821. SIEMER, L. "Paul Gauguin, Strandlandschaft auf Tahiti" [Paul Gauguin, Beach Landscape on Tahiti]. *Der Kunsthandel* 47(1955):13.

822. TOKUDA, Y. "The Locus of Madness: 9. Paul Gauguin." *Mizue* (Japan) 861(Dec. 1976):78-87. In Japanese, summary in English. 11 illus.

The unfolding of Gauguin's nature and art in the later years on Tahiti is considered to be related to three elements: his secret longing for barbarism, the author tracing this to his ancestry and his childhood experiences in Lima; his abandonment of Impressionism for synthetism in which he was influenced by the art of the Far East; and his attempt to create an art with a quality of symbolism opposed to the rationalism of Western civilization. Refers to Kretschmer's theory that Gauguin suffered from cyclothymia, evident in his use of colors which closely reflected his state of mind at the time of creation. His themes and subjects also reflect a subconscious concern with time and man's future.

823. T'SERVTEVENS, A. "Aux Marquises sur les traces de Gauguin." *Les Nouvelles littéraires* (13 Oct. 1949):1, 5.

824. VIEL, PHILIPPE. "Gauguin dans ses meubles à Tahiti." *Revue des messageries maritimes lors de l'inauguration du musée Gauguin.* 4 p.

825. VILLARET, BERNARD. "Les dernières années de Gauguin." *Revue de Paris* (Feb. 1953):116-25.

826. WEDEWER, R. "Neuer Exotismus" [New Exoticism]. *Kunstwerk* 33:5(1980):3-34. 29 illus.

Examines the modern tendency of artists to embrace non-European cultures in a quest for "pan-ethnic subjectivity." The author considers some psychological reasons for this attraction to the strange and wild, illustrating the ultimate impossibility of discarding one's ethnic identity by the example of Gauguin, for whom the South Seas were an experience not so much of a strange culture than of distance from his own.

827. WILDENSTEIN, GEORGES. "Inventaire des biens de Gauguin, 27 mai, 1903." *Gazette des Beaux-Arts* 6th ser., 47(Jan.-April 1956 [published 1958]):201-04. Reprinted in *Gauguin; sa vie, son oeuvre* (Paris, 1958).

828. WILDENSTEIN, GEORGES. "Le premier séjour de Gauguin à Tahiti, d'après le manuscript Jénot (1891-1893)." *Gazette des Beaux-Arts*, 6th ser., 47(Jan.-April, 1956[published 1958]):115-26). Reprinted in *Gauguin; sa vie, son oeuvre* (Paris, 1958).

829. WILDENSTEIN, GEORGES. "Vente des oeuvres d'art, livres et objets ayant appartenu à Gauguin -- 2 Septembre 1903." *Gazette des Beaux-Arts*, 6th ser., 47(Jan.-Apr. 1956 [published 1958]):205-08. Reprinted in *Gauguin, sa vie, son oeuvre* (Paris, 1958).

VI. Oeuvre in General

A. Monographs

830. CACHIN, FRANCOISE. *Gauguin*. Paris: Livre de Poche, 1968. 377 p., 198 illus.

Study of the life and work of Gauguin centered around 80 paintings, drawings, and sculptures considered to be major works in the artist's development. Includes a chronology, bibliography, and a list of paintings in major museums.
Reprints: Paris: Flammarion, 1988, 311 p., 317 illus., 105 col.; Paris: Hachette, 1989, 273 p., illus., 8 col. pl.

831. DONNELL-KOTROZO, CAROL A. "Gauguin and the Art of Reintegration" in *Critical Essays on Postimpressionism*, pp.37-55. East Brunswick, N.J.; London; Toronto: Associated University Presses for the Art Alliance Press, Philadelphia, 1983. 183p., 51 illus., 6 col. pl.

Collection of five essays in which the author analyzes the phenomenon of Post-Impressionism and some of the critical interpretations which have influenced contemporary misconceptions about it. Her Gauguin essay argues that Gauguin achieved reintegration between the world of the senses and the world of the mind, and thus maintained a permeable boundary between the ego and the world.

832. ELGAR, FRANK, ed. *Gauguin*. Paris: F. Hazan, 1949. 15 p., 24 pl.

833. ESTIENNE, CHARLES. *Gauguin*. Geneva: A. Skira, 1953. 116 p., 52 col. illus.

Collection of biographical and critical studies with a chronology, bibliography, and list of exhibitions.
a. Other eds.: Paris: Nathan, 1988. 192 p., 152 illus., 98 col.; Amsterdam: Ed. Time-Life Books, 1989. 157 p., illus.
b. English ed.: *Gauguin: Biographical and Critical Studies*. Trans. by James Emmons. Geneva: Skira, 1953. 115 p., 52 col. illus.

834. FIELD, RICHARD SAMPSON. "Plagiaire ou créateur?" in *Gauguin*. Paris: Hachette, 1960, pp. 139-69.

835. GAUGUIN, PAUL. *Paul Gauguin*. Introduction by Per Amann. Ramerding, Germany: Berghaus Verlag, 1978. 76 p., 65 pl., chiefly col.

Pictorial treatment with a brief biographical introduction.
Reprint: Ramerding: Berghaus, 1980. 76 p., 65 pl.
a. English ed.: *Paul Gauguin*. Trans. by Stephen Gorman. Avon, England: Artline Editions, 1987. 104 p., illus.

836. GOLDWATER, ROBERT JOHN. *Paul Gauguin*. New York: H.N. Abrams, 1957. 160 p., illus., 63 col. pl.

Biography and critical analysis of Paul Gauguin from the beginning to the end of his career. Includes 48 large-color plates with commentary. Goldwater was the director of the Museum of Primitive Art in New York at the time of this publication.
Reprints: New York: Abrams, 1972, 1983. 160, 126 p.; "Concise edition" London: Thames and Hudson, 1985. 126 p.
a. English ed.: London: Thames and Hudson, 1957.
b. French ed.: Trans. by Daphné Monay-Vaudover. Paris: Nouvelles Editions Françaises, 1957. 87 p., illus., 47 col. pl.
c. German ed.: Vienna: Buchgemeinschaft, 1960. 142 p.
d. Japanese ed.: Tokyo: Bijutsu Shuppansha, 1961. 144 p., illus., 47 col. pl.

837. HAMILTON, FLORENCE WIGGIN. *The Early Work of Paul Gauguin, from Impressionism to Synthetism*. Ph.D. diss., Yale University, 1948.

838. HILL, AUDREY LEIGH. *The Re-evaluation of Gauguin as an Artist, 1889 to 1980.* M.A. thesis, California State University, Long Beach, 1981. 118 p.

Examines changes in the critical views of Gauguin published in English from 1889 to 1980. The author believes that the assessment of Gauguin as a painter has undergone major changes since his death in 1903. Many external factors influenced these perceptions, particularly the occurrence and acceptance of later schools of art; increasing awareness in critical circles of theories in the fields of psychology and philosophy; and museum and gallery exposure. Finds that Gauguin was ultimately seen to have perceived the canvas as a plane covered with paint, and to have been primarily concerned with the expression of ideas.

839. HOOG, MICHEL. *Paul Gauguin, vie et oeuvre.* Paris: Nathan; Fribourg: Office du Livre, 1987. 333 p. 217 illus., 150 in col.

Sets Gauguin in artistic and historical perspective by examining artists who influenced Gauguin, especially Cézanne, Monet, and van Gogh. Includes chapters on Gauguin's childhood and youth in Peru; his artistic training in Martinique, and Panama; Gauguin's involvement in Parisian literary and poetic currents, particularly symbolism; Gauguin's flight from Western civilization and sojourn in Tahiti; Primitivism; his return to France and his last stay in the Marquesas; and a critical opinion of his work. Includes a chronology, bibliography, and lists of exhibitions and works. The author is the curator-in-chief at the Musée de l'Orangerie, Paris.
a. English ed.: *Paul Gauguin: Life and Work.* New York: Rizzoli, 1987. 335 p., 217 illus., 150 col.
b. German ed.: *Paul Gauguin: Leben und Werk.* Fribourg: Office du Livre, 1987.

840. ROUSSEAU, THEODORE. *Theodore Rousseau: Selections from his Writings.* New York: The Metropolitan Museum of Art, 1979. 91 p., 6 col. pl.

Tribute to and collection of writings by the former Curator-in-Chief of the Metropolitan Museum of Art. Chapter 5 (pp. 70-91) reprints his introduction to the exhibition catalogue, *Gauguin: Paintings, Prints, Sculpture* (New York: The Metropolitan Museum of Art, 1959).

841. STEINBERG, BARBARA HOPE. *Understanding Gauguin: An Analysis of the Work of the Legendary Rebel Artist of the 19th Century.* New York and London: A & W Visual Library, 1976. 32 p., illus., some col.

Pictorial biography and analysis of Gauguin's works. Deals with his use of color, composition, symbolism, and works in various media. Includes a biographical outline and a list of museums with major works.

842. WADLEY, NICHOLAS. *Gauguin: 116 reproductions*. Oxford, England: Phaidon, 1978: 112 p., illus., 96 pl.
a. French ed.: *Gauguin: 116 oeuvres*. Paris: SACELP, 1986. 112p., illus., 96 pl.

Includes reproductions of paintings and drawings.

B. Articles

843. BADT, KURT. "Die Gestalt Gauguins." *Zeitschrift für bildende Kunst* 32(May-June 1921):120-28.

844. BODELSEN, MERETE CHRISTENSEN. "Gauguin Studies." *Burlington Magazine* 109:769 (April 1967):217-27.

845. "Contributions to Gauguin Studies." *Burlington Magazine* 109:769 (April 1967):216-46. 36 illus.

Includes "Gauguin Studies" by M. Bodelsen; "Gauguin's Tahitian Titles," by B. Danielsson; "Some Unknown Blocks for Woodcuts by Gauguin," by T. Gottheiner; "Gauguin and a Peruvian Mummy," by W. V. Andersen; and "Meaning of Gauguin's *Oviri* Ceramic," by B. Landy.

846. "Echo from Elysium." *Time* 62:(14 Dec. 1953):84+.

847. "Et sur Gauguin." *L'Amour de l'art* (1938): 257.

848. "Gauguin: The Hidden Tradition." *Art News* 65(Summer 1966): 26-29.

849. "Heat Wave" [cover story; special section] *House & Garden* 160 (May 1988): 142-55.

850. "Homenaje a Gauguin." *Ver y Estimar* (Buenos Aires) 2:8 (Oct.-Nov. 1948): 73-88.

Includes an inventory of works by Gauguin in Buenos Aires (pp. 73-79) and a bibliography (pp. 80-88).

851. HOPPE, RAGNAR. "Paul Gauguin och hans målnigar: National-Museum och andra nordiska samlingar" [Paul Gauguin and His Paintings: The National Museum of Sweden and Other Nordic Collections]. *Nationalmusei Arsbok* 8 (1926): 65-103.

852. HUGHES, ROBERT. "Seeing Gauguin Whole at Last." *Time* 131 (9 May 1988): 76-77.

853. KAHN, GUSTAVE. "Paul Gauguin." *L'Art et les artistes* (Nov. 1925).

854. KERR, JOHN O'CONNELL. "Paul Gauguin, Creative Iconoclast." *The Studio* 150 (Dec. 1955): 170-75.

855. KUNSTLER, CHARLES. "L'art de Gauguin" *Beaux-arts* (23 Feb. 1934): 2.

856. LASSAIGNE, JACQUES. "Le centenaire de Gauguin." *Revue de la pensée française* 8 (1949): 45-49.

857. LOIZE, JEAN. "Il faut réhabiliter Gauguin." *Arts* (8 May 1953): 11-12.

858. "Paul Gauguin." *Gazette des Beaux-Arts* 6th ser., 47 (Jan.-April 1956) [published 1958]: 5-211. English summaries. 70 illus., 4 col. pl.

Includes "Arbre généalogique: Gauguin--ses origines et sa formation artistique" by U.F. Marks-Vandenbroucke; "Gauguin en Bretagne: L'influence de l'estampe japonaise dans l'oeuvre de Gauguin" by Y. Thirion; "Le premier séjour de Gauguin à Tahiti, 1891-1893" by Jénot; "L'idéolgie et l'esthétique dans deux tableaux-clés de Gauguin" by G. Wildenstein; "Traduction et interprétation des titres en langue tahitienne inscrits sur les oeuvres océaniennes de Paul Gauguin" by L. J. Bouge; "Gauguin sauvé du feu" by J. Loize; "Les comptes de Gauguin" by G. Wildenstein; "Les dernières années" by G. Le Bronnec; "Inventaire des biens de Gauguin, 27 mai 1903;" "Vente des oeuvres d'art, livres et objets ayant appartenu à Gauguin, 2 septembre 1903;" and "Documents divers concernant Gauguin communiqués par Mme. Vandenbroucke."

859. PERRUCHOT, HENRI. "Les archives Gauguin du fonds Monfreid." *Jardin des arts* 83(Oct. 1961): 14-24. 19 illus.

Describes Georges-Daniel de Monfreid's collection of Gauguin's works and documents, especially important for understanding his Polynesian periods.

860. SANDSTROM, SVEN. "Présence médiate et immédiate." *Archives de l'art Français* 25(1978): 407-17. 8 illus.

Examines the extent to which a painted portrait can replace a written description, with particular reference to the work of Odilon Redon and Paul Gauguin. The author assesses the ability of each artist to capture the character of their subjects, to portray the complete person rather than merely a visual likeness.

861. SOMMER, CLEMENS. "New Ways to Gauguin." *Magazine of Art* 31(Sept. 1938):514-21. 10 illus.

862. VITALI, LAMBERTO. "Una nuova fonte dell' arte di Gauguin" [A New Source of Gauguin's Art]. *La Biennale di Venezia* 23 (Jan. 1955): 18-19.

863. WEISBERG, GABRIEL P. "Gauguin Reconsidered: Symbol, Decoration, and the Unification of the Arts." *Arts Magazine* 63:9(Sept. 1988):44-51.

864. ZEGERS, PETER and DOUGLAS DRUICK. "The Gauguin Research Project at the Art Institute of Chicago." *The Print Collector's Newsletter* 19 (May-June 1988): 56.

VII. Oeuvre - Paintings

A. Monographs

865. ABE, NOBUO and KIMIO NAKAYAMA. *Gogyan: Rakuen no Maboroshi*. Tokyo: Sankei Shinbun, 1987. 37 p.

866. ALLEY, RONALD. *Gauguin*. London: Spring Books, 1961. 95 p., illus., 48 col. pl.

Includes an introduction to Gauguin's life and works, an outline biography, and notes and commentary on the paintings reproduced.
Review: R. Pickvance, *Apollo* 79 (1964): 249.
a. Other eds.: London: Spring Books, 1963; 1966; 1968.
b. U.S. ed.: New York: Marboro Books, 1961.

867. BOLTON, LINDA. *Gauguin*. Seacaucus, N.J.: Chartwell Books, 1987. 64 p., illus., col. pl.

Analysis of ten paintings which traces Gauguin's development from his Impressionist beginnings in 1875 through his Tahitian periods. Outlines the major events in Gauguin's life and explains important influences on his work, both social and artistic.

868. CADORIN, PAOLO, MONIQUE VEILLON, and BRUNO MUHLETHALER. "Décoloration dans la couche picturale de certains tableaux de Vincent van Gogh et de Paul Gauguin." In *ICOM Committee for Conservation: 8th Triennial Meeting*. Sydney, Australia,

6-11 September 1987, vol. 1, pp. 267-73. (Marina del Rey, California: Getty Conservation Institute, 1987). Kirsten Grimstad, ed. 3 vol., 1230 p., 10 illus. Summary in French.

Examination of two canvases painted at the same time, one by van Gogh and the other by Gauguin, in an attempt to document the disappearance of a pink color over large areas of both paintings. Chemical analysis established that the pink pigment was an Eosin lake produced and sold after 1871. As a result, new considerations on the paintings' original color are presented.

869. VAN DOWSKI, LEE [Herbert Lewandowski]. *Paul Gauguin: Paintings*. Basel: Amerbach, 1947. 14 p., illus., 24 pl.

Short biographical introduction followed by black-and-white plates.
a. French ed.: *Paul Gauguin, tableaux: vingt-quatre reproductions*. Basel: Amerbach, 1947. 11 pl, 24 pl. 1947.

870. *Paul Gauguin*. Milan: Fratelli Fabbri Editori, 1964. 7 p., 16 pl., some col.

871. GIRIEUD, PIERRE. *Paul Gauguin: 24 phototypes*. Paris: Librairie de France, 1928. 7 p., 24 pl.

Album of black-and-white plates of some of Gauguin's most famous paintings, with a short biographical introduction.

872. GRAVELAINE, FREDERIQUE DE. *Paul Gauguin; la vie, la technique, l'oeuvre peinte*. Lausanne: Edita, 1988. 159 p., illus., 49 col. pl.

Examines Gauguin's life and artistic technique as revealed in his paintings.

873. HOURS, MADELEINE. "Macrophotographies d'après quelques oeuvres de Gauguin exposées à Papéari (Tahiti)." *Bulletin du laboratoire du Musée du Louvre/Revue de Louvre* supp. 10(1965):39-55. 15 illus.

874. MASCIOTTA, MICHELANGELO. *Paul Gauguin*. Firenze: Nardini, 1978.

Miniature book which includes a short introduction, chronology, and tiny color plates.
a. U.S. ed.: *Paul Gauguin, The Paintings*. Woodbury, New York: Barron's, 1979. 157p., illus., col. pl.

875. RAYNAL, MAURICE. *Gauguin; Masterpieces of French Painting*. Geneva, Paris: Albert Skira; New York: Transbook Company, 1950. 6 p., 10 col. pl.

876. TARALON, JEAN. *Gauguin; Peintures*. Paris: Editions du Chêne, 1949. 25 p., illus., 17 col. pl.
a. Another ed.: 1953. 18 p., 16 col. pl.

Brief biography and study of Gauguin's major paintings followed by mounted color plates.

877. TONO, YOSHIAKI and KANKOKAI ZAUHO. *Gogyan*. Tokyo: Kawade Shobo, 1964. 137 p., 94 pl. In Japanese.

878. WHITE, WIEBE ALICE. *Paintings by Gauguin Owned in the United States of America, and the Hawaiian Islands*. Chicago: Art Institute, Ryerson Library, 1936, 1943. 77 p., 18 p. supp., typescript.

Describes 85 paintings in chronological order.

B. Articles

879. BODELSEN, MERETE CHRISTENSEN. "Gauguin's Cézannes." *Burlington Magazine* 710 (May 1962):204-11.

880. BODELSEN, MERETE CHRISTENSEN. "The Dating of Gauguin's Early Paintings with a Summary of Marie Heegaarrd's Letters from Paris, October 1872-October 1873." *Burlington Magazine* 107:747(June 1965):306-13. Reply with rejoinder, J.W. Goodison, 107:752(Nov. 1965):579-80.

881. COATSWORTH, ELIZABETH J. "Daughters of the Morning. Paintings by Paul Gauguin. Poems by Elizabeth J. Coatsworth." *Asia* 21(April 1921):321-28.

882. COOPER, DOUGLAS. "Not all Painted with the Same Brush." *Times Literary Supplement* (19 Aug. 1965):712.

883. "Gauguin Paintings Inspire Fashions." *Design* 49 (March 1948):11.

884. KANDINSKY, WASSILY. "Gauguin." *Appolon* (Oct.-Nov. 1910).

885. Moscow, Museum of Modern Western Art. "Oeuvres dans le Musée d'art moderne occidental à Moscou." *Cahiers d'art* 25:2(1950):341.

886. RUHMER, EBERHARD. "Paul Gauguin: Eau mystérieuse." *Die Kunst und das Schöne Heim* 58(1960):281-83. 4 illus.

Discusses Gauguin's painting of 1893 and the studies which preceeded them.

VIII. Individual Works - Paintings

A. Monographs

887. ADOLPHE, HELEN. "Wrestling with the Angel: Rilke's 'Gazing Eye' and the Archetype." In *Perspectives in Literary Symbolism*, ed. Joseph Strelka. University Park: Pennsylvania State University Press, 1968. 257 p.

Mention of Gauguin's *The Vision after the Sermon* (1888) on page 31.

888. BARSKAIA, ANNA G., MARINA BESSONOVA, et al. *Impressionist and Post-Impressionist Paintings in Soviet Museums*. New York: Facts on File, 1985. 408 p., 294 col. pl.

Includes 29 paintings by Gauguin, plates 119-148, accompanied by notes and description.
English ed.: Oxford: Phaidon; Leningrad: Aurora, 1985. 406 p.

889. BLANTON, CATHERINE W. "Notes on a Portrait by Gauguin in the Chester Dale Collection." In *Report on Studies in the History of Art, National Gallery of Art*. Washington, D.C.: GPO, 1967. I:89-98.

890. FRASER, DONALD HAMILTON. *Donald Hamilton Fraser on Gauguin's 'Vision after the Sermon-Jacob Struggling with the Angel.'* London: Cassell, 1969. 31 p., illus., 1 col. pl.

Analysis of Gauguin's painting of 1888. *The Vision after the Sermon* is viewed as Gauguin's first image in the new style of synthetism, and for which Gauguin was recognized as the leader of Symbolism.

891. Marie Harriman Gallery, New York. *D'où venons-nous? Que sommes-nous? Où allons-nous*? New York: The Gallery, 1936. 8 p., 4 pl. 1,000 copies printed.

Includes letters by Gauguin and excerpts from writings on Gauguin by Arsène Alexandre, Charles Morice and Roger Fry.

892. JACOBSON, EGBERT. "*Mahana no Atua*" in *Basic Color*. Chicago: P. Theobald, 1948. 207 p., illus.

See pages 181-83 for a discussion of Gauguin's painting (*Day of the Gods*, 1894).

893. NASH, STEVEN A., et al. *Albright-Knox Art Gallery. Painting and Sculpture from Antiquity to 1942.* New York: Rizzoli, 1979. 576 p., ca. 500 illus, 34 in col.

A fully illustrated volume cataloguing about half of the works in the permanent collection of the Albright-Knox Art Gallery, part of the Buffalo Fine Arts Academy. Gauguin's *The Yellow Christ*, (1889), *Spirit of the Dead Watching* (1892), and *Carved 'Coco de Mer'* (1901-03) are discussed on pp. 222-29.

894. PLATTE, HANS, ed. *Paul Gauguin. Ta Matete, Der Markt.* Stuttgart: Philipp Reclam, 1959. 32 p., 15 illus.

Treatise on Gauguin's Tahitian market scenes, specifically the painting *Ta Matete* (1892). Discusses sources and critical reception.

895. VENTURI, LIONELLO. "Una 'invocazione' di Gauguin," in *Scritti di Storia dell'Arte in Onore di Mario Salmi*. Rome: De Luca, 1963. 3 vol., 3 illus.

Brief discussion (III:467-70) of an unpublished watercolor by Gauguin entitled *Invocation*.

896. VIIRLAID, HELLE KAJA. *The Concept of Vision in Paul Gauguin's 'Vision After the Sermon.'* Ph.D. diss., National Library of Canada, Ottawa, 1980. 270 p., illus.

897. VINCENT, MADELEINE. *La peinture des XIXe siècles; catalogue du Musée de Lyon*. Lyon: Editions de Lyon, 1946-56 pl. 7 vol.

Volume 7 (pp. 223-28) includes a description of Gauguin's painting *Nave Nave mahana* (1896).

B. Articles

898. ALDEN, ROBERT. "Part of a Gauguin Hidden since 1894." *New York Times* (8 June 1958).

899. AMISHAI-MAISELS, ZIVA. "Gauguin's 'Philosophical Eve.'" *Burlington Magazine* 115:843(June 1973):373-82. 12 illus.

Gauguin's painting *Parau na te Varua Ino* (1892) can be compared with earlier canvases on the theme of the temptation of Eve, for example the

Volpini Eve. The 1892 canvas, a Tahitian version of the theme, shows an Eve who, unlike the earlier figure, had absorbed the guiltless sexual freedom of the Tahitians. Gauguin used this theme to express his reaction to events in his personal life. The significance of the 1892 canvas can only be realized by a detailed examination of the iconography of the work, the relationship of the finished work to the sketches made for it, and the relationship of this work to others on the same subject. It seems from this examination that Gauguin wished to show the opposition between life and rebirth and death. His use of the figure of the fallen Eve as a symbol of life develops from his interpretation of the yielding Eve as a symbol of life and fertility. Gauguin's symbolism therefore mixes biblical and Tahitian themes with European and primitive art.

900. ANDERSEN, WAYNE V. "Gauguin's Calvary of the Maiden." *Art Quarterly* 34:1 (Spring 1971): 86-104. 24 illus.

901. BAZIN, GERMAIN. *Arts* (8 May 1953).

Article on Gauguin's *Village sous la neige* (1894), mistakenly believed by Victor Segalen to be his last work. Bazin argues that the painting was retouched after its execution, and that the colors used correspond to those on Gauguin's last palette.

902. BEGUIN, SYLVIE. "Arearea." *La Revue du Louvre et des musées de France* 11:4-5 (1961):215-22. 6 illus.

903. BIRNHOLZ, ALAN C. "Double Images Reconsidered: A Fresh Look at Gauguin's Yellow Christ." *Art International* 26:5 (Oct.-Nov. 1977):26-34. 12 illus.

Focuses on two themes: first, contends that Gauguin's *Yellow Christ* of 1889 (Albright-Knox Art Gallery, Buffalo) includes a double image of a face in Christ's loincloth. This face relates to Gauguin's use of the symbol of the serpent and the fox during the late 1880s. Second, deals with double imagery in general and the criteria needed to prove that such images do exist in particular works of art. This discussion of methodology seems especially valuable given the intense, and frequently irrational, distaste of many historians for the very subject of double images.

904. BLANTON, CATHERINE W. "Notes on a Portrait by Gauguin in the Chester Dale Collection." *Report and Studies in the History of Art* (1967):89-98, illus.

Concerns Gauguin's *Portrait de Madame Kohler*.

905. BODELSEN, MERETE CHRISTENSEN. "Gauguin's Bathing Girl." *Burlington Magazine* 101:674(May 1959):186-90.

906. CAMOIN, CHARLES. "Ce Gauguin, La Belle cabaretière d'Arles, est de Camoin." *Arts* (Jan. 1948):1+; Discussion: *Arts* (6 Feb. 1948):1+.

907. CATEFORIS, D. "Joseph and Potiphar's Wife in a Drawing by Prud'hon." *Stanford Museum* (1986-87):9-13. 4 illus.

Examines a newly acquired drawing by Prud'hon in 1793 which, the author believes, clearly inspired Gauguin's painting of Joseph and Potiphar's wife a century later (private collection).

908. CLARK, ELIOT. "Considerations on Modernistic Aesthetics." *Art in America* 9(1921):210-20.

Mentions Gauguin's *Maternity*.

909. COETZEE, S. "A Study in Iconology: Gauguin's Yellow Christ." *Lantern* (South Africa) 27:1(Nov. 1976):52-57. 11 illus.

Analyses the sources of Gauguin's painting *The Yellow Christ* (1889) and the religious feeling behind it, noting its precursors as Emile Bernard's *Breton Women on a Sunday Afternoon* and Gauguin's *Vision After the Sermon* (1888). The author states that the primitive beliefs and mystical religion of the Breton peasants captured Gauguin's imagination, and *The Yellow Christ* has a flatness and lack of perspective which blend the figure of Christ into the landscape in a manner that reflects Breton religious life. The way in which theosophy influenced Gauguin is discussed, with particular reference to this painting in which Christ was depicted as a mythical, not an historical figure, a symbol of his own suffering and sense of betrayal.

910. COLLINS, R.D.J. "Paul Gauguin et la Nouvelle Zélande." *Gazette des Beaux-Arts* 6th ser., 90(Nov. 1977):173-76. 9 illus.

During his return journey to Tahiti in 1895, Gauguin spent 10 days--19 to 29 August--in Auckland, New Zealand. Drawings of New Zealand Maori art which he may have done while there still exist. Attention is drawn to the presence in a painting of 1896, *Te Tumari no Atua* (Bayerische Staatsgemäldesammlungen, Munich) and of elements that may have been borrowed from New Zealand art.

911. COOPER, DOUGLAS. "An Important Gauguin Discovery." *Burlington Magazine* 123:937(April 1987):195-97.

Concerns Gauguin's painting *Allées et venues*.

912. DAUCHOT, FERNAND. "Le Christ jaune de Gauguin." *Gazette des Beaux-Arts* 6th ser., 44(July-Aug. 1954):65-68,80. English summary.

913. "Decorative Landscape" [Attributed work]. *Burlington Magazine* 102(Sept. 1960):397.

914. DORRA, HENRI. "Ia Orana Maria. *Metropolitan Museum of Art Bulletin* 10(May 1952):254-60.

915. DORRA, HENRI. "A Suburban Landscape by Gauguin." *Smith College Museum of Art Bulletin* 33(1953):2-4.

916. DORRA, HENRI. "Gauguin's Dramatic Arles Themes." *Art Journal* 38:1(Fall 1978):12-17. 9 illus.

Discusses *Vintage at Arles-Human Miseries*, 1888 (Ordrupgaard, Copenhagen), identifying the source for the central figure as a lithograph of 1857 by Rops, *In the Ardenne--Now that Stupid Marie-Josèphe Thinks of a Child that has been Buried*. Notes the influence of Gauguin's contact with van Gogh on his work of the late 1880s.

917. FIERENS, PAUL. "Le portrait de Suzanne Bambridge par Gauguin." *Bulletin des musées royaux des beaux arts* (Brussels)6:1(March 1957):7-14.

918. "$15 Gauguin Art Put up at $50,000." *New York Times* (17 March 1960).

919. "Fine Post-Impressionist Painting: Gauguin's Street in Tahiti." *Toledo Museum Notes* 87(Sept. 1939): 9-11.

920. "Forgotten Gauguin; South Seas Scene [*Man with an Axe*] by French Painter Turns up after 57 Years." *Life* 37:24(13 Dec. 1954):127.

921. FRAENKEL, MICHAEL. "A New Paul Gauguin." *Virginia Quarterly Review* 4(1928):1-12.

922. FRANCIS, HENRY S. "L'appel by P. Gauguin." *Bulletin of the Cleveland Museum of Art* 31(Jan. 1944):3-5.

923. FRY, ROGER E. "On a composition by Gauguin: Que sommes-nous? D'où venons-nous? Où allons nous?" *Burlington Magazine* 32(March 1918):84-85.

924. "Un Gauguin retrouvé et perdu: Portrait d'Atiti mort." *Prométhée* 20(April 1939):81.

925. "Un Gauguin sconosciuto (La Perte du pucelage)." *Emporium* 109(April 1949):184-85.

926. GERSTEIN, MARC SAUL. "Paul Gauguin's Arearea." *Bulletin, The Museum of Fine Arts Houston* 7:4(Fall 1981):2-20. 18 illus.

Study of Paul Gauguin's fan-shaped painting *Arearea* (ca. 1894) in the Houston Museum of Fine Arts. This article, the first study devoted to Gauguin's fans, considers the *Arearea* fan within the context of Gauguin's other 26 known works in the fan format and examines its formal and iconographic relationships with the work produced during and after his first voyage to Tahiti. The *Arearea* fan is discussed both as a formal experiment within the process of Gauguin's artistic development and as a refined and compelling image notable for its visual harmony and allure.

927. GILL, IAN DICKSON. "Composing the Picture: Gauguin's *Nevermore*, 1897." *Artist* (U.K.) 102:12(Dec. 1987):34-5. 2 illus.

Analyzes the cited painting for its ability to go beyond the mere copying of nature, and its expression of emotions. Sets the painting in the context of Gauguin's suicidal state in 1897, and assesses Gauguin's influence as a catalyst for other painters.

928. GINIES, LOUIS. "Histoire d'un portrait inconnu de Gauguin." *Marseille Matin* (21 Dec. 1937).

929. GIOSEFFI, DECIO. "La favola ignota di Gauguin." *Venice* (1948):12. "Numero speciale dedicato all XXIV Biennale."

930. GIRY, MARCEL. "Une source inédite d'un tableau de Gauguin." *Bulletin de la Société d'Histoire de l'Art Français* (1970 [published 1972]):181-87. 3 illus.

Gauguin's use of photographs, and the work of other artists, is well established but in the case of *Manao Tupapau* (Spirit of the Dead Watching) of 1892, it has normally been accepted that Gauguin's description of the genesis of the picture in a letter to his wife provided sufficient explanation. It is here argued that an 1801 engraving by Humbert de Superville provides an exact parallel of the components of Gauguin's painting and that he had this engraving in mind at some stage of the composition. There is not, however, any concrete evidence that Gauguin knew the engraving.

931. GOLDWATER, ROBERT JOHN. "Gauguin's *Yellow Christ.*" *Gallery Notes* (Buffalo, NY)11:3(June 1947):2-13.

932. GORDON, DONALD E. "Marc and Friedrich Again: Expressionism as Departure from Romanticism." *Source* 1:1(Fall 1981):29-32. 3 illus.

In view of previous literature relating Expressionism to Northern Romanticism, and Franz Marc specifically to Caspar David Friedrich, it is important to note that Marc's *Blue Horse II*, 1911 (Kunstmuseum, Bern) was derived anatomically and compositionally not from a German source but instead from Paul Gauguin's *Tahitian Women Bathing*, 1891-92 (Metropolitan Museum of Art, New York) which Marc saw in Munich in August, 1910.

933. GORDON, DONALD E. "Content by Contradiction [Nietzche's Bequest to the German Expressionists]." *Art in America* 70:11(Dec. 1982):76-89. 12 illus.

Attempts to define and interpret German Expressionism. Contends that meaning in Expressionist art resides in the artist's reaction against the meaning with which he started. Discusses the ambivalence in terms of Expressionism's relation to Symbolism, in terms of the progression from Gauguin's *Spirit of the Dead Watches*, 1892 (Albright-Knox Art Gallery, Buffalo) to Marc's *Reclining Nude Among Flowers*, 1910 (private collection), to Marc's *Reclining Dog in the Snow*, 1911 (Stadelsches Kunstinstitut, Frankfurt). Cites Nietzche as the chief model for this ambivalence in Expressionist art.

934. GOWING, LAWRENCE. "Paul Gauguin." *Burlington Magazine* 91(Dec. 1949):354.
Published letter which discusses Gauguin's *D'où venons-nous?* cycle.

935. HAUTECOUR, LOUIS. "La conception de la nature chez les artistes modernes." *Gazette des Beaux-Arts* (Nov. 1936):176-87).

Mentions Gauguin's *Landscape in Brittany* (1890).

936. HENNING, E. B. "Looking at Art: The *Woman in the Waves.*" *Art News* 83:3(March 1984):104-06. 3 illus.

Discusses three paintings by Gauguin in the Cleveland Museum of Art: *Woman in the Waves* (*Ondine*), painted in Brittany, 1889; *Te Ra'au Rahi*, Tahiti, 1891; and *L'Appel*, Marquesas, 1902. Discusses the works in context of Gauguin's interest in synthetism, cloisonnism, and Symbolism and argues that *Woman in the Waves* was painted in early 1889.

937. HERBAN, MATTHEW B. "The Origin of Paul Gauguin's *Vision After the Sermon: Jacob Wrestling with the Angel* (1888)." *Art Bulletin* 59(September 1977):415-20. 8 illus. Reply with Rejoinder by Vojtech Jirat-Wasiutynski. 60:2(June 1978):397-98.

By means of a thorough investigation into the religious iconographic context of Paul Gauguin's *The Vision After the Sermon: Jacob Wrestling with the Angel*, 1888 (National Gallery, Edinburgh), especially its Breton aspects, a specific location (the chapel of S. Nicodème), date (5-6 August 1888), setting (the ripe, vermillion-red buckwheat field beside the chapel with the apple tree and the river Blavet beyond), and activities (blessing of cows, descent of an angel, and wrestling matches) are found to be the inspiration for the painting.

938. "Hidden treasure: Gauguin's *Actor*." *Time* 61(20 April 1953):81.

939. HIND, CHARLES LEWIS. "Paul Gauguin: Reflections on his *Red Dog Landscape*." *Colour* 6(April 1917):95,98.

940. HOFMANN, WERNER. "Reflexions sur l'iconisation à propos des *Demoiselles d'Avignon*." *Revue de l'Art* 71(1986):33-42.

Includes a discussion and illustration of Gauguin's *La Lune et la terre; Tahitienne* (1893).

941. HOHL, REINHOLD. "Gauguin's *Man with an Axe*." *Source: Notes in the History of Art* 2:2(Winter 1983):30-32. 1 illus.

Painted soon after he arrived in Pape'ete in June 1891, *Man with an Axe* is Gauguin's first major symbolist painting from his first Tahitian period. The author examines the work, with reference to a text in which Gauguin explained the meaning of the painting, written for an exhibition of his works held in Paris in 1893.

942. HOOP SCHEFFER, D. DE. "Ia Orana Maria (Ikgroet U, Maria), een Monotype van Paul Gauguin (1848-1903)" [Ave Maria, a Monotype by Paul Gauguin]. *Bulletin van het Rijksmuseum* (Netherlands) 20:4(Dec. 1972):171-76. Summary in English. 4 illus.

One of the first paintings Gauguin executed during his visit to Tahiti was the celebrated *Ia Orana Maria*, which is signed and dated 1891 and was one of his own favorite works. The Rijksmuseum's Print Room has just acquired a monotype of the same subject. Gauguin was in the habit of working up his colored monotypes with watercolors, and in this one it is difficult to tell which colors are printed and which are painted. Some colors may even have been painted over printed colors. The relationship of this and two other prints to the painting is difficult to determine, though it may be suggested that the Rijksmuseum monotype was a study for the painting and that the others were made later.

943. "Ia Orana Maria." *Life* (1939):384.

944. JACOBS, JAY. "Anatomy of a Masterpiece: Gauguin's *Where do we come from? What are we? Where are we going?*" *Horizon* 11:3(Summer 1969):52-65. 11 illus.

945. JOHNSON, LINCOLN F. "The Beginnings of Modernism." *Honolulu Academy of Arts Journal* (1978):19-38. 13 illus.

Places the beginnings of modernism in the 10 or 15 years on either side of 1900. Considers Thomas Eakins' *William Rush and His Model*, Monet's *Water Lilies*, van Gogh's *Wheatfield*, Gauguin's *Two Nudes on a Tahitian Beach*. Bonnard's *Flowers on the Mantelpiece*, and Picasso's *Pipe and Glass*. All works are in the collection of the Honolulu Academy of Arts.

946. KANE, WILLIAM MACGIBBON. "Gauguin's *Le Cheval blanc*: Sources and Syncretic Meanings." *Burlington Magazine* 108:760(July 1966):352-62. 8 illus.

947. LACKER, D. "Notes sur des symboles jaunes." *Peintre* (France) 567(15 June 1978):10-14.

Discusses the symbolic images conjured up by the color yellow--the color of gold, of lemons, of sulphur. Among specific works analysed, the author compares Gauguin's *Christ jaune* (1889) with Chagall's *Martyr*. Also comments on van Gogh's love of yellow and the Japanese use of yellow chrysanthemums as symbols of the living emperor.

948. LOIZE, JEAN. "Gauguin sauvé du feu." *Gazette des Beaux-Arts*, ser.6, 47 (Jan.-April, 1956):165-86.

949. LORD, DOUGLAS. "Le paysage à travers les âges." *Burlington Magazine* 73(July 1938):38.

Mentions Gauguin's *Les Bords de la Seine sous la neige*.

950. "Lure of the South Seas; Excerpts from Letters on the Subject of his Picture, *Where do we come from, what are we, where are we going?*" *Arts and Decoration* 44(Aug. 1936):14-15+.

951. MACDONALD, J. "Gauguin's *Te Burao*." *Bulletin of the Art Institute of Chicago* 17(May 1923):51-52.

952. "Mahana no Atua (Day of the Gods)." *Chicago Art Institute Bulletin* (Jan. 1946-Dec. 1949):32.

953. MATHEWS, PATRICIA. "Passionate Discontent: the Creative Process and Gender Difference in the French Symbolist Period." *Bulletin* (Allen Memorial Art Museum, Oberlin, Ohio) 43(Summer 1988):20-30.

Discusses several Gauguin paintings: *Agony in the Garden*; *Tahitian series*; *She thinks of returning*; *Be in love and you will be happy.*

954. MATTISON, D. M. "Brittany Landscape." *John Herron Institute Bulletin* 31(April 1944):9-11.

955. MAUNER, GEORGES L. "Gauguin or School of Pont-Aven: Concerning the Attribution of Two Panels in Stockholm." *Gazette des Beaux-Arts* 74(Nov. 1969):305-10. 7 illus. Summary in French.

956. MENARD, WILMON B. "Author in Search of an Artist" [Somerset Maugham's research on Gauguin]. *Apollo* 114:234(Aug. 1981):114-17. 6 illus.

An account of Somerset Maugham's visit to Tahiti in 1917 and his discovery of the glass panel by Gauguin, *Woman with Fruit* (P. Berman collection).

957. "Monet and Gauguin *Why are you sorrowful?*" *Scrapbook of Art & Artists of Chicago & Vicinity* (1957):19.

958. "Nature Morte Recently Sold." *Art News* 34(1 Feb. 1936):7.

959. "Nineteenth-Century Masterpieces." *Burlington Magazine* 66 (June 1935):294-97.

Mentions Gauguin's *Three Tahitians* (1896). See also *Burlington Magazine* 57:333 (Dec. 1930):1-23.

960. "Notable Works of Art Now on the Market: *Un village Breton.*" *Burlington Magazine* 67:supp. 3 (Dec.)

961. "Notable Works of Art now on the Market." *Burlington Magazine* 109:supp. 12 (Dec. 1967).

962. "Painting: *We greet you, Mary*, 1891." *Fortune* (Dec. 1938).

963. PALMER, FREDERICK. "Drawing with Colour: Painting with Oils." *The Artist* (Tenterden, England) 104(March 1989):21-23.

Discusses Gauguin's painting technique in *The Vision After the Sermon* (1888).

964. PEARSON, ELEANOR. "Three Paintings by Gauguin: Evidence in a Letter from Daniel de Monfreid." *Burlington Magazine* 119:896(Nov. 1977):773-74.

Letter of 11 Nov. 1989 from Monfreid to the artist supports the view that *Trois Tahitiennes*, 1896 (private collection, New York) was sold to Dr. Gouzer, not to a Dr. Nolet. Letter also mentions two unidentified paintings sold to the Parisian dealer Ambroise Vollard.

965. "Petites Bretonnes au bord de la mer." *Mizue* 651 (Aug. 1959):11.

966. PLAUT, J. S. "Gauguin Masterpiece; Entitled *D'où venons nous; que sommes-nous; où allons-nous*?" *Bulletin of the Boston Museum of Fine Arts* (June 1936):33-38.

967. "Portrait de Mallarmé" [Attributed work]. *Connaissance des arts* 370(Dec. 1982):121.

968. POULAIN, GASTON. "Une peinture inconnue de la jeunesse de Paul Gauguin." *Revue de l'art ancien et moderne* 65 (March 1934):76.

Discusses Gauguin's *Roses in a Glass*.

969. "Renoir's *Lise* and Gauguin's *Still Life with Apples and Grapes*." *Connoisseur* 148(Dec. 1961):297-99.

970. REWALD, JOHN. "Camille Pissarro; His Work and Influence." *Burlington Magazine* 72(June 1938):280-90.

Discusses Gauguin's *La Route à Osny*.

971. REY, ROBERT. "Le Manuscrit de Noa-Noa et le Cheval blanc." *Beaux-Arts* 5(15 Feb. 1927):55-56.

972. REY, ROBERT. "La Belle angèle de Paul Gauguin." *Beaux-Arts* 5:7(April 1927):105-06.

973. "Riders on the Shore." *Vogue* 96(1 Oct. 1940):62.

974. ROLLIN, LOUIS. "Un lépreux de Gauguin." *Beaux-Arts* (13 Nov. 1936):1+.

975. ROSENTHAL, G. "Gauguin's *Woman with Mango* Formerly in Collection of Edgar Degas." *Baltimore Museum News* 15(1952):1-6.

976. SAFIN-CRAHAY, F. "Neuf chefs-d'oeuvre du musée de Liège." *Beaux Arts* 7(Nov. 1983):58-63. 10 illus.

Traces the growth and history of the Musée de Liège, Belgium, giving details of its collections and illustrating with notes nine works, including Gauguin's *The Magician* (La Dominque, 1902).

977. SALMON, ANDRE. "Joseph Bernard--ouvrages inconnus de Gauguin." *L'Europe nouvelle* 2 (18 Oct. 1919):2017-18.

978. "Seascape in Brittany by Gauguin." *Springfield Museum Bulletin* 14(Oct. 1947):1-3.

979. "Seated Tahitian Figure" [Attributed work]. *Apollo* 88(Dec. 1968):98.

980. SECKER, HANS. "Ein Bild und sein Vorbild bei Gauguin" [A Picture and its Example with Gauguin]. *Atlantis* 4(July 1932):445-57.

981. SLOAN, THOMAS L. "Paul Gauguin's *D'où venons-nous? Que sommes-nous? Où allons-nous*?: A Symbolist Philosophical Leitmotif." *Arts Magazine* 53:5(Jan. 1979):104-09. 1 illus.

Claims that Gauguin's painting *D'où venons-nous? Que sommes-nous? Où allons-nous?* (1897), Boston Museum of Fine Arts, pays homage to the Symbolists, while at the same time expressing Gauguin's uncertainties about his own life. The painting expresses Gauguin's realization that there are no limits to human frailties, frustrations, and disillusionments. The primordial, metaphysical and symbolist levels of meaning of Gauguin's painting are the aggregate of his intensely personal statement.

982. STEADMAN, DAVID W. "French Painting--Romanticism to Surrealism." *Apollo* 109:204(Feb. 1979):150-56. 12 illus.

Discusses 19th and 20th century French paintings, including Gauguin's *Two Nudes on a Tahitian Beach* (1891) in the collection of the Honolulu Academy of Arts, Hawaii.

983. "Street Gauguin Once Trod Comes to Toledo: *Street in Tahiti*." *Art Digest* 14(1 Oct. 1939):7.

984. "Studies of his son Emile." *Burlington Magazine* 100:662(May 1958):181.

985. SUTTON, DENYS. "*La Perte du pucelage* by Paul Gauguin." *Burlington Magazine* 91:(April 1949):102-05.

986. "*Te Burao.*" *Chicago Art Institute Newsletter* (Dec. 1921-Dec. 1923):145, 191.

987. "*Tehura,* a New Gauguin for America." *Vogue* 89(15 Feb. 1937):55.

988. "Te Tumari no atua." *Prisma* 1:10(Aug. 1947):pl. IV.

989. "Unknown Gauguin." *Life* 28:18 (1 May 1950):93.

990. "Vision après le sermon par Paul Gauguin." *L'Estampille* 222(Feb. 1989):61-62. illus.

991. W., R. "A Portrait Head by Paul Gauguin, French, 1848-1903." *Bulletin of the Worcester Art Museum* 12(July 1921):22-23, 25.

992. W., R. "*La Femme accroupie*, Paul Gauguin, 1848-1903." *Bulletin of the Worcester Art Museum* 13(April 1922):1-3.

993. WALKER, R. W. and V. F. BROOKS. "$6 Million Man" [Man with the Axe, sold]. *Art News* 81(Oct. 1982):7.

994. WEBB, GEOFFREY. "Ingres to Cézanne." *Burlington Magazine* 46:267(June 1925):283-88.

Mentions Gauguin's *Two Nudes (Tahiti)*.

995. WEHLE, HARRY B. "A Tahitian Landscape by Paul Gauguin." *Bulletin of the Metropolitan Museum of Art* 35(March 1940):56-57.

996. WEINBERG, J. "Anty-'kalejdoskop', czyli o twórczosci Andrzeja Szonerta" [Anti-'kaleidoscope' or on the work of Andrzej Szonert]. *Sztuka* (Poland) 6(1978):13-16, 61, 63. Summaries in Russian and English. 5 illus.

With reference to an exhibition of Andrzej Szonert's work in the Galerija Balucka, Lódz, Poland (Oct. 1977), the author discusses the affinities of Szonert's paintings to posters and the diverse influences on Szonert's writings on art and artistic output, which range from Toulouse-Lautrec, Gauguin, Bonnard and Malczewski to Strzeminski and Pop Art.

997. WILDENSTEIN, GEORGES. "L'idéologie et l'esthétique dans deux tableaux-clés de Gauguin." *Gazette des Beaux-Arts* 6th ser., 47(Jan.-Apr. 1956):127-64. English summary.

Discusses works in the *Where do we come from*?" cycle and *Faa Thethe (Pastorale Tahitienne).*

998. WYKES-JOYCE, MAX. "British Impressionism: Equal of the French." *Antique Dealer and Collectors Guide* (U.K.) 40:10(May 1987): 30-34. 11 illus.

Account of some of the British painters who worked in the Impressionist style, comparing them with their French counterparts in an attempt to show that they are their equal. Among others, *Girl on a Settle* by Albert Chevallier Tayler (1857-1926) is compared with *Interior with Aline Gauguin* by Gauguin.

999. ZINK, MARY LYNN. "Gauguin's Poèmes Barbares and the Tahitian Chant of Creation." *Art Journal* 38:1(Fall 1978):18-21. 3 illus.

The symbolic meaning of Paul Gauguin's painting *Poèmes barbares* of 1896 (Fogg Art Museum, Cambridge) is elucidated in reference to the Tahitian Chant of Creation.

IX. Self-Portraits

A. Monographs

1000. ANDRONIKOVA, MANANA IRSKLIEVNA. *Ob Iskusstve Portreta* [On the Art of the Portrait]. Moscow: Iskusstvo, 1975. 327 p., 139 illus.

Surveys the evolution of the Western and Russian portrait from pre-Renaissance times until the present. The approach is a synthetic one and, in order to develop a "theory of the portrait," the author draws on interdisciplinary comparisons. Analyzes portraits (often self-portraits) by Botticelli, Rembrandt, Repin, Rubens, Sar'yan, Serov, Velàzquez, and others. Observations on late 19th-century portraiture present parallels between examples such as Gauguin's self-portrait (1893) and his photo-portrait (1891), and Repin's studies for his *Religious Procession in Kursk District* (1880-83) and the final painting.

1001. MITTELSTADT, KUNO. *Die Selbstbildnisse Paul Gauguin* [The Self-Portraits of Paul Gauguin]. Berlin: Hanschelverlag, 1966. 78 p., illus., 36 pl.

Detailed study of Gauguin's self-portraits. Includes notes on each in the Catalogue section, pp. 51-67.

a. Another ed.: Vienna, Munich: Langen-Müller, 1968. 78 p., illus., 36 pl.
b. English ed.: *Paul Gauguin, Self-Portraits*. Trans. by E. G. Hull. Oxford: Bruno Cassier, 1968. 67 p., 37 illus., 76 pl., some col.

1002. ROTHSCHILD, RUTH DEBORAH. *A Study in the Problems of Self-Portraiture: The Self-Portraits of Paul Gauguin*. Ph.D. diss., Columbia University, 1961. 321 p., 76 pl.

Investigates Gauguin and his contemporaries' attention to the self-portrait as a reflection of the general interest in the self-image in France in the late nineteenth century. Argues that self-portraiture enabled Gauguin to demonstrate pride in himself and in his profession. Finds Gauguin's self-images provide new information about his character and self-knowledge.

B. Articles

1003. "Autoportrait" [Attributed work]. *Gazette des Beaux-Arts* 6th ser. 1, 77(Feb. 1971):93.

1004. B, D. "Chroniques d'art, Amsterdam." *Art Flamand et Hollandais* 18(Nov. 1912):163-66.

Mentions and reproduces a self-portrait by Gauguin.

1005. CANUDO, RICCIOTTO. "Correspondenze ester: Francia." *Vita d'Arte* 1(1908):128-30.

Mentions and reproduces Gauguin's *Portrait of the Artist.*

1006. DIEHL, GASTON. "Dans l'intimité de Gauguin." *Beaux-Arts* 66(1942):7. 3 illus.

Includes a reproduction of one of Gauguin's self-portraits.

1007. VAN DOWSKI, LEE. [Herbert Lewandowski]. "Gauguin im Spiegel seiner Selbstbildnisse" [Gauguin in the Mirror of his Self-Portraits]. *Der Bogen* 9(1948):89-91.

1008. GANN, LOUISE GEBHARD. "Gauguin's Image of Himself." *International Studio* 81(May 1925):118-23.

1009. "Gauguin." *Habitat* (São Paulo)5(1952):71.

Discusses a self-portrait in the São Paulo Museum.

1010. HOFFMAN, EDITH. "Edvard Munch." *Burlington Magazine* 93(Dec. 1951):390-94.

Mentions a self-portrait by Gauguin.

1011. VAN HOOK, KATRINA. "A Self-Portrait by Paul Gauguin from the Chester Dale Collection." *Gazette des Beaux-Arts* 6th ser., 22(Dec. 1942):183-86.

Also discusses Gauguin's *Design for a Plate* zincograph (1889).

1012. JIRAT-WASIUTYNSKI, VOJTECH. "Vincent van Gogh's Magical Conception of Portraiture and Paul Gauguin's *Bonjour, Monsieur Gauguin.*" *RACAR, Revue d'art canadienne. Canadian Art Review* 3:1(1976):65-67. 2 illus.

Gauguin's self-portrait *Bonjour, Monsieur Gauguin*, 1889 (National Gallery, Prague) rephrases Courbet's *Meeting* (Musée Fabre, Montpellier), which Gauguin and van Gogh saw in Montpellier in December 1888, in terms of Gauguin's Breton experience. The painting also reflects van Gogh's belief in a magical resemblance among the portraits of like-minded artists and patrons from Rembrandt to Delacroix and Courbet, and his identification of Gauguin as "the man come from afar".

1013. JIRAT-WASIUTYNSKI, VOJTECH. "Paul Gauguin's Self-Portraits and the Oviri: the Image of the Artist, Eve, and the Fatal Woman." *Art Quarterly* 2 (Spring 1979):172-90. 14 illus.

This article, based on research carried out for the author's Ph.D. thesis, *Paul Gauguin in the Context of Symbolism* (Princeton University, 1975), explores the central concept of self-sacrifice in the paintings and ceramics of Gauguin. Gauguin's numerous self-portrayals in the guise of Christ relate to his paintings of Eve as the "crucified maiden", and symbolize man victimized by a fatal woman. These self-sacrificial images led to his final tragic image of creation, the *Oviri* ceramic, a depiction of the Tahitian androgynous goddess Hina which is symbolic of the artist's own ideas of artistic creation and personal rebirth.

1014. JIRAT-WASIUTYNSKI, VOJTECH. "Paul Gauguin's Self-Portrait with Halo and Snake: The Artist as Initiate and Magus." *Art Journal* 46:1(Spring 1987):22-28. 9 illus.

Reading of Gauguin's *Self-Portrait with Halo and Snake* (1889) based on esoteric doctrine, which aims to demonstrate the importance of esotericism as a key to identifying and relating the major themes of Gauguin's oeuvre. After a summary of critical work on this question, the author shows how Gauguin depicts himself in the painting as a fallen angel, not in a pose of Romantic Satanism, but in the guise of a magus. The painting is also situated in the context of the decoration of Marie Henry's inn at Le Pouldu, which was based on imagery of the Fall and the resultant cycle of life and death.

1015. LIPMAN, JEAN. "Great Portraits from Impressionism to Modernism." *Art in America* 26(July 1938):138.

Mentions a self-portrait by Gauguin.

1016. MARAINI, ANTONIO. "Cézanne, Gauguin, van Gogh." *Dedalo* (1920):186-96.

Discusses a self-portrait by Gauguin.

1017. NORDSTOM, GERT Z. "Zemiotik och Mångsyntagmatiska Konstverk" [Semiotics and Polysyntagmatic Works of Art]. *Paletten* (Sweden) 3(1987):p. 32-33. 3 illus.

Explains syntagms as combinations (of words, musical notes, elements in a picture, etc.) and semiotics as the interpretation of syntagms. To illustrate polysyntagmatism, he analyzes the *Gauguin* self-portrait which incorporates a picture of Emile Bernard, showing how the acts of creation and interpretation are both dynamic and how the picture can be conceived of as a concrete act of linguistic communication.

1018. SCHMIDT, GEORG. "Paul Gauguins Letzes Selbstbildnis? [Paul Gauguin's Last Self-Portrait?]" *Öffentliche Kunstsammlung Jahresberichte* Basel (1941-45):251-61.

X. Oeuvre - Drawings

A. Monographs

1019. KANE, WILLIAM MACGIBBON. *Mes Secrets: The Earlier Drawings of Paul Gauguin (1873-1891).* Ph.D. diss., Boston University, 1975. 3 vol., 1658 p., illus.

Analyzes the role of drawing in Gauguin's development during his formative and early mature years. Contemporary definitions of drawing and Gauguin's own rare statements are cited, as well as the contrasting stimuli of academic and independent attitudes and the beginning of the reductive approach to drawing which became his most advanced mode. The *Stockholm Sketchbook*, the *Mahaut-Hammer Sketchbook*, the *Album Briant*, and all published drawings on separate sheets are discussed. The unsigned *Album Walter* in the Louvre, heretofore largely unpublished, is ascribed to Gauguin on the basis of stylistic analysis and comparison to his other work of the crucial period 1888-1891 and later. His life history is summarized. A catalogue of published drawings on separate sheets is provided, as well as an appendix of works owned by Gustave Arosa, and a comprehensive bibliography.

1020. LEYMARIE, JEAN, ed. *Paul Gauguin, aquarelles, pastels et dessins de couleur.* Basel: Phoebus, 1959. 98 p., illus., col. pl.

Plate book with introduction and commentaries by Jean Leymarie. Review: M. Bodelsen, *Burlington Magazine* 105 (June 1963):285.
a. Reprint: Geneva: Skira, 1988.
b. English ed.: *Paul Gauguin: Watercolours, Pastels and Drawings in Colour.* Trans. by Robert Allen.
c. U.S. eds.: *Gauguin: Watercolors and Pastels.* New York: Harry N. Abrams, 1962. 16 p., 24 col. pl.; New York: Rizzoli, 1989. 98 p., illus.

1021. LONGSTREET, STEPHEN, ed. *The Drawings of Gauguin.* Alhambra, Calif.: Borden Publishing Co., 1965. 46 p., illus.

1022. PATACKY, DENES. *Master Drawings from the Collection of the Budapest Museum of Fine Arts; 19th and 20th Centuries.* New York: Abrams, 1959. 27 p., 94 pl.

Includes two Tahitian drawings by Gauguin.

1023. PICKVANCE, RONALD. *The Drawings of Gauguin.* London, New York, Sydney, Toronto: Paul Hamlyn, 1970. 44 p., illus., 116 pl.

Includes an essay on Gauguin's drawings and notes on the plates. The drawings are interpreted to include his pastels, fans, lithographs, woodcuts and monotypes. Explores Gauguin's methods and techniques, poses, motifs, and use of various media.
a. U.S. ed.: Feltham, N.Y.: Hamlyn, 1970. 44 p., illus., 132 pl.

B. Articles

1024. AMISHAI-MAISELS, ZIVA. "A Gauguin Sketchbook: Arles and Brittany." *Israel Museum News* 10 (1975):68-87.

1025. ARNOLD, MATTHIAS. "Die Postimpressionisten als Zeichner" [The Post-Impressionist Painters as Draftsmen]. *Weltkunst* 58:2 (15 Jan. 1983):120-24. 9 illus. (4 col.)

Includes reflections on drawings and watercolors by Paul Gauguin, George Seurat, Paul Signac, Vincent van Gogh, Emile Bernard, Henri de Toulouse-Lautrec, Pierre Bonnard, Edouard Vuillard and Paul Cézanne.

1026. "A Double Masterwork." *Life* 46:10(9 March 1959):91-92.

Concerns sketches recently discovered on the back of a pastel by Gauguin owned by John Cowles.

1027. BODELSEN, MERETE CHRISTENSEN. "Gauguin and the Marquesan God" [with French summary]. *Gazette des Beaux-Arts* 6th ser., 57:1106(March 1961):167-80. 17 illus., 2 pl.

1028. FRANCIS, HENRY S. "Drawing: Head of a Tahitian Woman." *Cleveland Museum of Art Bulletin* 37(Oct. 1950):178. 1 illus.

1029. "Finds Gauguin Manuscript." *Art Digest* 7(August 1933):13.

1030. "Gauguin Drawing Found." *Connoisseur* (U.S.) 143(June 1959):83.

1031. MONNIER, G. "Dessins de Degas, Cézanne, Gauguin." *Revue du Louvre* (1980):180-82. 6 illus.

Discusses Gauguin's drawings for *Hiva* and *Oà*, part of a gift of Suzanne and Henri Baderou to the Musée de Rouen.

1032. OPRESCO, O. "Dessins français du XIX siècle au Musée Britannique." *Revue de l'art ancien et moderne* 54:301(Dec. 1928):235-54.

1033. ROSKILL, MARK WENTWORTH. " An Unexpected Gauguin Discovery: Preliminary Drawing for Still Life with Flowers and Fruit of 1894." *Boston Museum of Fine Arts Bulletin* 62:328(1964):81-88.

1034. ROSTRUP, HAAVARD. "Eventails et pastels de Gauguin." *Gazette des Beaux-Arts* 6th ser., 56:1100(Sept. 1960):157-64. 11 illus.

XI. Oeuvre - Prints and Graphic Art

A. Monographs

1035. BAAS, JACQUELYNN. *Auguste Lepère and the Artistic Revival of the Woodcut in France*. Ph.D. diss., University of Michigan, Ann Arbor, 1982. 356 p., 146 illus.

Traces the transformation of the French woodcut from a reproductive into an original art medium during the last quarter of the 19th century. Includes a chapter entitled "Some Aspects of the Woodcut and Symbolism: Bernard, Denis, Gauguin, Alfred Jarry and Rédé Gourmont." A brief chronology of the woodcut revival in France is appended.

1036. BARTH, WILHELM. *Paul Gauguin*. Basel: Benno Schwabe, 1929. 166 p., 50 illus. In German.

Biography and analysis of Gauguin's works.

1037. CATE, PHILLIP DENIS and SINCLAIR HAMILTON HITCHINGS. *The Color Revolution: Color Lithography in France 1890-1900*. Santa Barbara, Salt Lake City: Peregrine Smith, 1978. 136 p., 101 pl., some col.

Brief mention of Gauguin's printmaking.
a. Another ed.: New Brunswick, N.J.: Rutgers University Art Gallery, 1978. 146 p., illus., some col.

1038. CHADOURNE, MARC and MAURICE GUIERRE. *Marehurehu, entre le jour et la nuit. Croyances, légendes, coutumes et textes poétiques des Maoris d'O-Tahiti avec quatorze illustrations de Gauguin*. Paris: Librairie de France, 1925. 102 p., illus.

Work on ancient Tahitian life and customs illustrated with 14 woodcuts by Gauguin.

1039. DARAGNES, JEAN-GABRIEL. "Les bois gravés de Paul Gauguin." *Arts et métiers graphiques* 49(15 Oct. 1937):35-42. 10 illus.

1040. DAVIDSON, MARSHALL B. "Notes: the Cover Design of this Issue." *Metropolitan Museum of Art Bulletin* 17(May 1959):240.

Detail of Gauguin's woodcut print *Auti te pape* (The Fresh Water is in Motion, 1893-94).

1041. EDWARDS, HUGH. *Gauguin Prints at the Art Institute of Chicago and the Metropolitan Museum of Art.* 32 p., illus.

1042. GAUGUIN, PAUL. *Paul Gauguin; 10 gravures sur bois. D'après les bois originaux par Pola Gauguin.* Copenhagen: Chr. Cato, 1921.

Portfolio of 10 woodcuts in an edition of 100 numbered copies, including 8 prints of the *Noa Noa* series. Pola Gauguin (Gauguin's son) printed these prints with the help of a book press and two cylinders, one of moistened rubber and one of hard leather. The black-and-white prints are extremely legible.

1043. *Gauguin; A Portfolio of 12 Color Woodblocks from the Collection of the Museum of Fine Arts, Boston.* Introduction by W. G. Russell Allen. New York, London: American Studio Books, 1947. 14 p., 12 col. pl.

Reprints of 12 Tahitian-theme woodcuts, ten of which were made at Pont-Aven in the fall of 1894, after Gauguin's return from his first trip to Tahiti. Editions of 30-50 impressions of each subject were made by Louis Roy in Paris.

1044. GRAHAM, RIGBY A. *Paul Gauguin: Woodcutter and Private Printer.* Wymondham, England: Brewhouse Press, 1969. 8 p., illus.

Short study of Gauguin's woodcuts, printmaking, and private press in Tahiti. Discusses Gauguin's work on two Tahitian newspapers, *Les Guêpes* and *Le Sourire.*

1045. HARTRICK, ARCHIBALD STANDISH. *Lithography as a Fine Art.* London: Oxford University Press, 1932. 98 p., illus., 15 pl.

Mentions Gauguin's contributions to lithography and his influence on other artists.

1046. SYKOROVA, LIBUSE. *Gauguin Woodcuts.* Trans. by Till Göttheiner. London: Paul Hamlyn, 1963. 20 p., illus.

Study of Gauguin's woodcuts. Introduction relates the woodcuts to his other works. Catalogue portion describes 28 original woodcuts mostly made by Gauguin during his second sojourn in Oceania (1895-1903).
a. Revised ed.: Feltham, England: P. Hamlyn, 1968.
b. French ed.: *Les gravures sur bois de Paul Gauguin.* Prague: Artia, 1963. 22p., 15 pl.

1047. TARBELL, ROBERTA K. "Direct Carving." In *Vanguard American Sculpture, 1913-1939*. Jeffrey Wechsler, R.K. Tarbell, J. M. Marter, eds. New Brunswick, N.J.: Rutgers University, 1979, pp. 45-66, 27 illus.

Discussion of the role of direct carving in the development of avant-garde sculpture in the U.S. from 1913 to 1930. Describes in part the work of some of its leading European exponents such as Gauguin. *Vanguard American Sculpture, 1913-39* was an exhibition held at Rutgers University Art Gallery in 1979.

B. Articles

1048. ANTREASIAN, GARO Z. "Some Thoughts about Printmaking and Print Collaboration." *Art Journal* 39:3 (Spring 1980):180-88. 11 illus.

Discusses the genesis and practices of modern collaborative and non-collaborative printmaking ideology, using as examples works by Thomas Moran, Paul Gauguin, James McNeill Whistler, Stanley William Hayter, Pablo Picasso and others.

1049. ASKELAND, JAN. "Omkring tre Norske Grafikere" [On Three Norse Graphic Artists]. *Kunsten Idag Hefte* 17(Winter 1951):23-37, 58-59. English summary.

1050. BOYLE-TURNER, CAROLINE ROSS. "La Bretagne vue par les graveurs de l'Ecole de Pont-Aven." *Nouvelles de l'estampe* 101-102 (1988):15-23. 16 illus.

Studies prints of the Pont-Aven painters including, Gauguin's *Misères humaines* and *Les Drames de la mer* (both 1889). Comments on their rapid execution and asserts that the themes of peasants working and untamed countryside contribute to a savage image of Brittany.

1051. CARY, ELISABETH LUTHER. "The Color Prints of Paul Gauguin." *New York Times* (3 May 1936).

1052. "Fakes and Forgeries: A Problem Poser Forgery." *Print Collector* (Italy) (Autumn-Winter 1972):72-72. 5 illus.

An article intended to help the layman recognize re-issues of etchings printed recently from the original cancelled plates and yet described as being examples of the first edition. There is particular reference to *The Portrait of Mallarmé*, by Gauguin, tracing the history of the plate and showing where the cancellation lines are still visible.

1053. "'La femme aux figues' Etching by P. Gauguin and A. Séguin." *Print Collector* (Italy) (Autumn-Winter 1972):71. 1 illus.

Discusses the authorship of the etching *La Femme aux figues*, once thought to have been prepared by Gauguin and overdrawn and completed by Séguin, but now found to be a joint piece of work, with the figure and still life entirely by Gauguin and the background by Séguin.

1054. FIELD, RICHARD SAMPSON. "Gauguin's Noa Noa Suite." *Burlington Magazine* 110:786(Sept. 1968):500-11.

1055. FIELD, RICHARD SAMPSON. "Gauguin's Woodcuts." *Expedition* 11:4(Summer 1969):27-29. 12 illus.

1056. FIELD, RICHARD SAMPSON. "Gauguin's Monotypes." *Print Collector's Newsletter* 3:5(Nov.-Dec. 1972):97-100. 4 illus.

1057. FIELD, RICHARD SAMPSON. "Gauguins Traesnit" [Gauguin's Woodcuts]. *Louisiana Revy* 23:1(Oct. 1982):28-34. 7 illus.

Analyses the primitive elements in Gauguin's art, emphasizing the *Noa Noa* print series, stating that Gauguin's allegories remained basically European in character and that the South Seas influence was only an accompaniment to an interior monologue.

1058. FORMAN, NESSA. "Gauguin's Experiments with Monotype." *Art News* 72(Summer 1973):84.

1059. FRANCIS, HENRY S. "Woodcut by Gauguin: *Nave Nave fenua* (Terre délicieuse)." *Bulletin of the Cleveland Museum of Art* 21(June 1934): 96-98. See also *Art Digest* 8(Aug. 1934):20.

1060. "Gauguin as a Printmaker." *Minneapolis Institute of Fine Arts Bulletin* 39(22 April 1950):77-78.

1061. GOLDWATER, ROBERT JOHN. "A Unique Gauguin: Marquesan Elements in a Woodcut in the Metropolitan Museum in New York." *Magazine of Art* 30(Jan. 1937):24-26, 54-55.

1062. GRIVEL, M. "Gauguin et l'Ecole de Pont-Aven." *Nouvelles de l'estampe* 101-102 (1988):35.

Note on the prints by Gauguin and other members of the Pont-Aven school shown at the Bibliothèque Nationale in 1989.

1063. VAN HOOK, KATRINA. "A Self-Portrait by Paul Gauguin from the Chester Dale Collection." *Gazette des Beaux-Arts* 6th ser., 22(Dec. 1942):183-86.

Also discusses Gauguin's *Design for a Plate* zincograph (1889).

1064. KEABLE, ROBERT. "From the House of Gauguin: Reproduction of a Woodcut by Paul Gauguin." *The Century Magazine* 106(Sept. 1923):765-72. See also *London Mercury* 8(1923):578-85.

1065. KORNFELD, EBERHARD W. "Meister der Grafik des 19. und 20. Jahrhunderts" [Masters of the Print in the 19th and 20th Centuries]. *Du* (Switzerland) 36:420(Feb. 1976):26-51. 21 illus.

An illustrated and chronological summary of 21 print artists, from Goya to Lissitzky. The masters chosen include Gauguin, Daumier, Toulouse-Lautrec, Munch, Picasso, Klée, and Kandinsky, among others.

1066. LASS, H. "Gauguin Woodblocks Rediscovered in Prague." *American Artist* 29(May 1965):36-41+. 13 illus.

1067. LINDBERG-HANSEN, JACOB. "Discovering Paul Gauguin the Woodcarver." *College Art Journal* 12:2(Winter 1953): 117-20.

1068. "Masters in the Art News." *Art News* 65:6(Oct. 1966):25.

Discusses Gauguin's woodcut *Maruru* (1892).

1069. MAYER, DOLORES A. "Gauguin's *L'Univers est crée*: a Creative Vision." *Porticus; The Journal of the Memorial Art Gallery of the University of Rochester* 1(1978):41-45. 3 illus.

Discusses a wood engraving of 1893-94.

1070. PHILLIPS, M. "Monotype." *Artist's Proof* 8(1968):53.

1071. REY, ROBERT. "Paul Gauguin, graveur." *Byblis* 7:26(Summer 1928):43-48.

1072. "*Te Atua*: The Gods (first state): The William McCallin McKee Memorial Collection(first state). Relief Impression, the Joseph Brooks Fair Collection (fourth state). Roy Edition (duplicate print fund)." *Chicago Art Institute Bulletin* (Jan. 1942-Dec. 1945):67-68.

1073. SIMON, T. F. "Stefánik in Search of Gauguin on Tahiti." *Hollar* 13.

Simon, a Czech graphic artist, lived in Paris in 1904. At M. R. Stefánik's request, Simon made prints from Gauguin's Tahitian woodcut blocks.

1074. SOTH, LAUREN. "Gauguin, van Gogh and the Fishermen of Iceland." *Burlington Magazine* 131(April 1989):296-97.

Discusses Gauguin's two *Les Drames de la mer* zincographs (1889).

1075. "An Unpublished Wood Engraving by P. Gauguin." *Print Collector* (Italy) (Autumn-Winter 1972):70. 1 illus.

Examines of Paul Gauguin's newly discovered wood engraving of the crucifixion and the religious feeling behind it.

1076. VARENNE, GASTON. "Les bois gravés et sculptés de Paul Gauguin." *L'Art décoratif* 13(Jan. 1911):37-38.

1077. VARENNE, GASTON. "Les bois gravés et sculptés de Paul Gauguin." *La Renaissance de l'art français* 10:12(Dec. 1927):517-24.

1078. "With Gauguin We Come to a Different Type of Mind; Woodcut *Auti te pape* by Paul Gauguin." *Metropolitan Museum of Art Bulletin* 16(July 1921):157-58.

1079. "Zinc Plate Engraving." *Kunsten Idag* (Oslo)11:3(1949).

XII. Oeuvre - Ceramics and Sculpture

A. Monographs

1080. BODELSEN, MERETE CHRISTENSEN. *Gauguin Ceramics in Danish Collections*. Copenhagen: Munksgaard, 1960. 36 p., illus.

Study of Gauguin's ceramic sculptures in Danish collections.
Review: M. Strauss, *Burlington Magazine* 105 (June 1963):286.

1081. BODELSEN, MERETE CHRISTENSEN. *Gauguin's Ceramics; A Study in the Development of His Art*. London: Faber & Faber Ltd., in association with Nordisk Sprog-og Kulturforlag, Copenhagen, 1964. 330 p., 14 illus., 19 col. pl.

1082. CHADWICK, HELEN WHITNEY. *Chaplet and Gauguin: A Contribution to the Rise of Art Nouveau*. M.A. thesis, Pennsylvania State University, 1968. 68 p.

Studies the collaboration between the ceramist Ernest Chaplet (1835-1909) and Paul Gauguin in 1886-88, which produced a collection of ceramics later regarded as early examples of French Art Nouveau.

B. Articles

1083. AMISHAI-MAISELS, ZIVA "Gauguin's Early Tahitian Idols." *Art Bulletin* 60:2(June 1978):331-41. 19 illus.

Two of Gauguin's Tahitian sculptures, the *Idol with a Shell* and the *Crucifixion* (both in the Agnès Huc de Monfreid collection, Corneille de Conflant), are redated to 1891 on the basis of the dates of his copies of these statues in *Ancien culte mahorie* (Louvre, Paris) and *Vairaumati tei Oa* (Hermitage, Leningrad). This redating throws new light on two major aspects of Gauguin's art. First, it permits a clear view of the development of the influence on him of primitive art. This aspect is examined in detail by means of the development of images on the *Idol with a Shell* from their sources through his work of 1891-1903. Secondly, it indicates the manner in which Gauguin built up his dream of ancient Tahitian life through a syncretic merging of images and ideas from Christian, Buddhist and Polynesian art and religion.

1084. "Art News of Paris: Unknown Gauguin Wood Sculpture of a Leper." *Art News* 35(5 Dec. 1936):20.

1085. BARTH, WILHELM. "Eine Unbekannte Plastik von Gauguin" [An Unknown Sculpture of Gauguin]." *Das Kunstblatt* 13(June 1929):182-83.

1086. BERRYER, ANNE-MARIE. "A propos d'un vase de Chaplet décoré par Gauguin." *Bulletin des Musées Royaux d'art et d'histoire* 3rd ser., 16:1-2(Jan.-April 1944):13-27.

1087. BODELSEN, MERETE CHRISTENSEN. "Gauguin Ceramics in Danish Collections." *Danske Kunstindustrimuseum Virksomhed* (1954):91-124.

1088. BODELSEN, MERETE CHRISTENSEN. "Paul Gauguin som Kunsthåndvaerker" [Paul Gauguin as an Artisan]. *Kunst og Kultur* 47(1964):141-56.

1089. BRAUN, BARBARA. "Paul Gauguin's Indian Identity: How Ancient Peruvian Pottery Inspired his Art." *Art History* 9:1(March 1986):36-54. 48 illus., 6 pl.

Examines the influence of the forms and motifs of pre-Columbian pottery on Gauguin's ceramic sculpture and subsequently on his painting and relief sculpture.

1090. CACHIN, FRANÇOISE. "Un bois de Gauguin: Soyez mystérieuses." *La Revue du Louvre et des Musées de France* 29:3 (1979):215-18.

Describes the polychromatic wooden relief by Paul Gauguin, *Soyez mystérieuses*, recently acquired by the Louvre. It was made at Le Pouldu in Brittany, in the autumn of 1890. A letter to Emile Bernard, written in Sept. 1890, dates the work precisely. The relief reveals aspects of the artist's style that were absorbed in his Tahitian works, being inspired by the painting *Ondine* (1889) as well as by the techniques of popular sculpture in wood and by Japanese reliefs.

1091. CHARLIER, HENRI. "L'esprit sculptural." *L'Art sacré* (1936):175-80.

1092. CLARK, G. "The Liberation of Clay: the Roots of Modern Ceramic Art." *Studio Potter* 2(1978):63-70. 13 illus.

Describes the advent of the artist-potter in France in the late 19th and early 20th centuries. The author discusses the work of the 19th-century pioneers and the major contributions of Ernest Chaplet (1835-1909), Paul Gauguin (1848-1903), Auguste Delaherche (1857-1940), and Jean Carries (1855-1894).

1093. D'ALBIS, JEAN. "La céramique impressionniste à l'atelier de Paris-Auteuil (1873-1885)." *Cahiers de la céramique, du verre et des arts du feu* 41(1968):32-42.

1094. "Gauguin Chiseled His Hatred in Wood: The Bishop of Pape'ete as 'Père Paillard'." *Art Digest* 2(1May 1928):24.

1095. HUNEKE, A. "Plastiken von Malern" [The Sculptures of Painters]. *Bildende Kunst* 6(1979):289-94. 12 illus.

Many important developments in modern sculpture came about due to the efforts of artists who were known primarily for their work as painters. In this connection the author looks at sculptures by Daumier, Degas, Renoir, Gauguin, Matisse, Picasso, Braque, Boccioni, Derain, Ernst, Modigliani, Schmidt-Rottluff, Nolde, Schwitters, and Schlemmer. He concludes with a closer look at the work of two German "realist" painter-sculptors, Käthe Kollwitz and Otto Pankol.

1096. KJELLBERG, P. "Les pirates de la sculpture." *Connaissance des arts* 230(April 1971):9.

1097. LAKS, CLAUDIE. "Gauguin, la céramique d'un sauvage." *La Revue de la céramique et du verre* 48(Sept.-Oct. 1989):12-15. illus.

1098. LANDY, BARBARA J. "The Meaning of Gauguin's *Oviri* Ceramic." *Burlington Magazine* 109:769(April 1967): 242-46.

1099. LINDBERG-HANSEN, JACOB. "Discovering Paul Gauguin, the Woodcarver." *College Art Jounal* 12:2(1953):119.

1100. MASTAI, M. L. D. "My House . . . of Sculptured Wood." *Apollo* 75(Nov. 1961):148-49.

1101. PALLUCCHINI, RODOLFO. "Que sommes-nous? Un panneau sculpté par Gauguin." *Arts* (12 Sept. 1947):1+.

1102. PITTS, GREG. "Paul Gauguin." *American Ceramics* 7:3(1989):26-33.

Discusses *Vase Decorated with Three Breton Girls* (1886-87), *Portrait Vase of Mme. Schuffenecker*, and the *Oviri* (1894) statue.

1103. REY, ROBERT. "Les Bois sculptés de Paul Gauguin." *Art et décoration* (Feb. 1928):57-64. illus.

1104. RINUY, P. L. "1907: Naissance de la sculpture moderne? Le renouveau de la taille directe en France." *Histoire de l'art* 3 (1988):67-76. 5 illus. English summary.

Traces Gauguin's influence on sculptures executed in 1906-07 by Picasso, Derain, Brancusi, Matisse, Bernard and others. Claims that early 20th century sculpture was also affected by French sculptors in the 1880s: Jean Dampt, Georges Lacombe, and Aristide Maillol.

1105. "Sculpture." *Volné Smery* 27:4-6 (1929):134-35.

1106. "Sculpture de Paul Gauguin." *Zolotoe Runo* 10(1909):5-14. Reply by Charles Morice, *Zolotoe Runo* 10(1909):47-52.

1107. SIZERANNE, ROBERT DE LA. "Chaplet et la renaissance de la céramique." *Revue des deux mondes* 57(May 1910):157-71.

1108. TRALBAUT, MARK EDO. "Rond een pot van Gauguin" [A Guaguin Pot]. *Mededelingenblad Vriende van de Nederlandske Ceramiek* 18(April 1960).

1109. VARENNE, GASTON. "Les Bois gravés et sculptés de Paul Gauguin." *L'Art décoratif* 13(Jan. 1911):37-38.

1110. VARENNE, GASTON. "Les Bois gravés et sculptés de Paul Gauguin." *La Renaissance de l'art français* 10:12(Dec. 1927):517-24.

1111. VAUXCELLES, LOUIS. "A propos des bois sculptés de Paul Gauguin." *L'Art décoratif* 13(Jan. 1911):37-38.

1112. VAUXCELLES, LOUIS. "La sculpture de Paul Gauguin." *L'Art décoratif* (1935).

1113. VERDIER, PHILIPPE. "Les céramiques de Gauguin." *Cahiers de la céramique, du verre et des arts du feu* 41(1968):43-54.

XIII. Oeuvre - Miscellaneous Media

A. Monographs

1114. GERSTEIN, MARC SAUL. *Impressionist and Post-Impressionist Fans*. Ph.D. diss., Harvard University, 1978. 385 p.

Examination of folding fans (éventail) and screen fans (écran) by prominent French Impressionist and Post-Impressionist artists. The dissertation is primarily a catalogue raisonné. Gauguin's section (pp. 266-349) describes 30 fans by Gauguin, created from 1881-1902.

1115. REY, ROBERT. *Onze menus de Paul Gauguin, menus propos*. Geneva: Gérald Cramer, 1950. 123 p., 11 pl., some col.

Study and facsimile reproductions of 11 menus produced and illustrated by Gauguin in Tahiti in the 1890s. These impromptu works are decorated by drawings and watercolors. Also summarizes Gauguin's years in Tahiti and his conflicts with French authorities.

B. Articles

1116. BEGUIN, SYLVIE. "Arearea." *La Revue du Louvre et des musées de France* 11:4-5(1961):215-22. 6 illus.

1117. "By Gauguin . . . Discovery of Two Important Frescoes by Paul Gauguin, Pouldu." *Art Digest* 1(1 March 1927):12.

1118. "Gauguin Frescoes Found." *The Palette and Chisel* 8:3(March 1931):6

1119. "Gauguin Frescoes Found in Pouldu. 'Jeanne d'Arc' Fresco." *Art News* 24(19 June 1926):2.

1120. "Gauguin Settee Sells at Auction for $375." *Art Digest* 4(1 Dec. 1929):13.

1121. "Gauguin's Frescoes." *Art Digest* 5(15 Jan. 1931):17.

1122. GERSTEIN, MARC SAUL. "Paul Gauguin's Arearea." *Bulletin, The Museum of Fine Arts Houston* 7:4(Fall 1981):2-20. 18 illus.

Study of Paul Gauguin's fan-shaped painting *Arearea* (ca. 1894) in the Houston Museum of Fine Arts. This article, the first study devoted to Gauguin's fans, considers the *Arearea* fan within the context of Gauguin's other 26 known works in the fan format and examines its formal and iconographic relationships with the work produced during and after his first voyage to Tahiti. The *Arearea* fan is discussed both as a formal experiment within the process of Gauguin's artistic development and as a refined and compelling image notable for its visual harmony and allure.

1123. REY, ROBERT. "A propos des peintures murales exécutées par Gauguin au Pouldu." *Bulletin de la Société de l'histoire de l'art français* (1926):37-40.

1124. ROSTRUP, HAAVARD. "Eventails et pastels de Gauguin." *Gazette des Beaux-Arts* 6th ser., 56:100(Sept. 1960):157-64. 11 illus.

1125. "Unknown Gauguin: Mural Painted in a French Inn Turns up in New York." *Life* 28(1 May 1950):93.

XIV. Museums and Collections

Entries in this section are arranged alphabetically by museum and collection name.

1126. Musée d'Albi, Paris. CHARLES-BELLET, L. "Paul Gauguin et ses amis." *Beaux-Arts* 110(1943):9. 4 illus.

Highlights paintings by Gauguin, Bernard, and Matisse at the Musée d'Albi.

1127. Albright-Knox Art Gallery, Buffalo. "Recently Acquired in the Albright Gallery: *Yellow Christ.*" *Art Quarterly* 9:4(1946):350,355.

1128. Albright-Knox Art Gallery, Buffalo. "Albright Art Gallery Acquires One of Paul Gauguin's Best Known Canvases, *The Yellow Christ*." *Pictures on Exhibit* 9(Feb. 1947):56-57.

1129. Albright-Knox Art Gallery, Buffalo. GOLDWATER, ROBERT JOHN. "Gauguin's *Yellow Christ*." *Buffalo Gallery Notes* 11 (June 1947):2-13.

1130. Albright-Knox Art Gallery, Buffalo. "Buffalo Acquires *Yellow Christ*." *Art News* 46(Aug. 1947):20.

1131. Albright-Knox Art Gallery, Buffalo. "*Yellow Christ* Acquired by Albright Art Gallery." *Art Digest* 21(Sept. 1947):13.

1132. Albright-Knox Art Gallery, Buffalo. ADLMANN, J. VON. "Noix sculptée: fruit des îles 1901-02." *Albright-Knox Gallery Notes* 28(Fall 1965):16-18.

1133. Albright-Knox Art Gallery, Buffalo. NASH, STEVEN A., et al. *Albright-Knox Art Gallery. Painting and Sculpture from Antiquity to 1942*. New York: Rizzoli, 1979. 576 p., ca. 500 illus, 34 in col.

A fully illustrated volume cataloguing about half of the works in the permanent collection of the Albright-Knox Art Gallery, past of the Buffalo Fine Arts Academy. Gauguin's *The Yellow Christ*, (1889), *Spirit of the Dead Watching* (1892), and *Carved 'Coco de Mer'* (1901-03) are discussed on pp. 222-29.

1134. Belgium Museums. JANSON, C. *La peinture française dans les musées de Belgique*. Brussels, 1947.

For Gauguin's works, see pp. 56-57.

1135. Bernheim-Jeune Collection, Paris. BERNHEIM-JEUNE, JOSSE. *L'Art moderne et quelques aspects de l'art d'autrefois; 173 planches d'après la collection privée de MM. J. G. Bernheim-Jeune. Poèmes de Henri de Régnier*. Paris: Bernheim-Jeune, 1919. 2 vols., 173 pl.

1136. Boston Museum of Fine Arts. FRANKFURTER, A. M. "Boston Acquires a Gauguin Masterwork, *D'où venons nous, que sommes nous, où allons nous*? Its First Showing in New York." *Art News* 34(25 April 1936):5.

1137. Boston Museum of Fine Arts. "Gauguin in Philosopher's Role, Appears in Boston's New Picture, *Where do we come from, what are we, where are we going?*" *Art Digest* 10(1 May 1936):5.

1138. Boston Museum of Fine Arts. "Paul Gauguin. New Acquisitions of the Boston Museum on View in New York." *London Studio* 12(1936): 52.

1139. Boston Museum of Fine Arts. "Boston: New Acquisitions." *Art News* 57(Feb. 1959):47+.

1140. Boston Museum of Fine Arts. "Gauguin's *La Guerre et la paix* Acquired by Boston Museum of Fine Arts." *Burlington Magazine* 107(March 1965):164-67.

1141. Ny Carlsberg Glyptotek, Copenhagen. FONSMARK, ANNE-BRIGITTE. "Paul Gauguin. To nyerhvervelser fra hans tidlige år" [Paul Gauguin. Two New Acquisitions of this Year]. *Meddelelser fra Ny Carlsberg Glyptotek* 43 (1987):29-58. 19 illus. English summary.

Analyses Gauguin's carved medallion of Valéry Roumy, *La Chanteuse* (1880), and a painting, *Route de Rouen II* (1885), given to a Danish painter-friend, Theodor Philipsen.

1142. Chicago Art Institute. For works by Gauguin exhibited at the Institute, see the following exhibition catalogs (listed by year, date, catalog number, and page):

1912-1913, March 24-April 16, 1913, no. 10, p. 50.
1929, May 2-June 2, no. 10, p. 49.
1932, April 6-Oct. 9, no. 5, pp. 14-15, 40.
1933, Nov. 1, no. 5, pp. 50-52, 91, 184.
1937, March 18-May 16, no. 10, p. 7.
1940, April 17-June 2, no. 13, p. 1.
1941, April 10-May 20, no. 6, pp. 18, 19, 44, 91, 94, 97, 109.

1143. Chicago Art Institute. "Gauguin Given to Art Institute. Portrait of a Tahitian Woman with Children . . . Given to the Art Institute of Chicago by Frederic Clay Bartlett." *Art News* 25(17 Sept. 1927):7.

1144. Chicago Art Institute. "Three Great Masters of the Later Nineteenth Century--Gauguin, Seurat and Toulouse-Lautrec Will Share a Single Gallery." *Chicago Art Institute Bulletin* 27(April-May 1933):67.

1145. Chicago Art Institute. SCHNIEWIND, CARL O. "Two Woodcuts by P. Gauguin: *Noa Noa* and *Te Faruru*." *Chicago Art Institute Bulletin* 34(Dec. 1940):112.

1146. Chicago Art Institute. "*Tahitian Woman.* Drawing in Pencil, Charcoal and Pastel." *Masterpiece of the Month, Notes and Bibliography* 54(Jan. 1946-Dec. 1949).

1147. Chicago Art Institute. SCHNIEWIND, CARL O. "Paul Gauguin: Woodcuts Acquired by the Institute." *Chicago Art Institute Bulletin* 43(Sept. 1949): 43-51. 10 illus.

1148. Chicago Art Institue. "The Helen Birch Bartlett Memorial Collection." *Museum Studies* 12:2 (1985-86):222-34. 12 illus.

Description of 24 paintings by 14 artists, including Gauguin, formerly in the Bartlett collection.

1149. Cleveland Museum of Art. "*L'Appel.* Gift of the Hanna Fund." *Cleveland Museum of Art Bulletin* (Jan. 1944).

1150. Cleveland Museum of Art. "Gauguin's *L'Appel* Given to Cleveland." *Art Digest* 18(15 Jan. 1944):8.

1151. Cleveland Museum of Art. "*Woman in the Waves* (Ondine)." *Cleveland Museum of Art Bulletin* (Jan. 1979/Oct. 1984).

1152. Courtauld Collection. SUTTON, DENYS. "Review of 'The Courtauld Collection' by Douglas Cooper." *Burlington Magazine* 91(1954):292-94.

1153. Chester Dale Collection. VAN HOOK, KATRINA. "A Self-Portrait by Paul Gauguin from the Chester Dale Collection." *Gazette des Beaux-Arts* 6th ser., 22(Dec. 1942):183-86.

1154. Chester Dale Collection. BLANTON, CATHERINE W. "Notes on a Portrait by Gauguin in the Chester Dale Collection." *Report and Studies in the History of Art* (1967):89-98. illus.

Concerns Gauguin's *Portrait de Madame Kohler.*

1155. Essen, Museum Folkwang. KOHN, HEINZ. *Neuere Meister aus dem Museum Folkwang zu Essen.* Cologne: E. A. Seemann, 1952. 14 p.

Discusses works by Gauguin and others.

1156. Gustave Fayet Collection, Paris. GOULINAT, J.G. "Les Collections Gustave Fayet." *L'Amour de l'art* (1925):131-42.

1157. Fogg Museum, Cambridge, Massachusetts. WATSON, FORBES. "The Fogg Museum Celebrates." *The Arts* 15(1929):229-38, 296-303, 356.

1158. Frick Collection, New York. "Frick's Gauguin: Tahitian Landscape Purchased." *Art Digest* 15(1 Dec. 1940):9.

1159. Frick Collection, New York. "The Frick Gauguin" [From a news release prepared by the Frick Collection]. *Art Quarterly* 3(1940): p. 389-90.

1160. Frick Collection, New York. "Frick Gauguin Tahitian Landscape." *Art Quarterly* 3:4(1940):382, 389-90.

1161. Frick Collection New York. COMSTOCK, H. "Gauguin's Tahitian Landscape for the Frick Collection." *Connoisseur* 107:(Feb. 1941):77.

1162. Gauguin Museum, Papeari, Tahiti. *Le Musée Gauguin*. Paris: La Fondation Singer-Polignac, 1965, 59 p., illus.

Inauguration program dated June 15, 1965: "Cette plaquette éditée par les soins de la Fondation Singer-Polignac pour conserver un souvenir de l'auguration du Musée Gauguin, 15 juin 1965." Includes the text of speeches by Professor Roger Heim and Governor Jean Sicurani.

1163. Gauguin Museum, Papeari, Tahiti. *Le Musée Gauguin*. Pape'ete: Polynésie Française, 1965. 56 p., illus.

Guidebook published soon after the museum's opening.

1164. Gauguin Museum, Papeari, Tahiti. O'REILLY, PATRICK. *Catalogue du musée Gauguin, Papeari, Tahiti*. Paris: Fondation Singer-Polignac, 1966. 142 p., illus.

Catalogue of the Gauguin Museum in Tahiti, founded near Mataiea in 1964. Includes a museum guide, introduction, and descriptions of 475 Gauguin-related objects (books, photographs, letters, sculptures and carvings, and other artifacts). Exhibits trace Gauguin's life from birth to death.

1165. Gauguin Museum, Papeari, Tahiti. O'REILLY, PATRICK. "Un musée Gauguin à Tahiti" [with English trans.]. *Museum* (Unesco) 20:2(1967):77-89.

1166. Gauguin Museum, Papeari, Tahiti. ARTUR, GILLES. "Notice historique du Musée Gauguin de Tahiti suivie de quelques lettres inédites de Paul Gauguin." *Journal de la Société des Océanistes* 38:74-65(1982):7-17.

1167. Gauguin Museum, Papeari, Tahiti. *The Gauguin Museum, Tahiti*. Papeari: The Museum, 1984. 32 p., illus.

Guidebook in English.

1168. Gauguin Museum, Papeari, Tahiti. *Le Sourire*. Nov. 1985-. Vol. 1-. Serial publication of the Gauguin Museum in Tahiti. Irregular, mostly semi-annual.

1169. German Museums. WALDMANN, E. "Das Folkwangmuseum." *Kunst und Kunstler* 6(1907-08):247+.

1170. German Museums. TIETZE, HANS. "Les peintres français du XIXe siècle dans les musées allemands." *Gazette des Beaux-Arts* 17:784(1928):105-18.

1171. German Museums. "Bericht über Galerie und Kupferstich kabinett." *Öffentliche Kunstsammlung, Basel, Jahresberichte* (1941-1945):1-28.

1172. Helmut Goedeckemeyer Collection. RIESTER, R. "Die Sammlung Helmut Goedeckemeyer" [Helmut Goedeckemeyer's Collection]. *Graphische Kunst* 9:2(1977):38-44. 12 illus.

Describes how Goedeckemeyer built his collection and discusses the various works it contains, including paintings by Gauguin.

1173. Hamburg, Museum für Kunst und Gewerbe. RIEDL, PETER ANSELM. "Erwerbungen für die Gemälde-Galerie und die Sammlung neuerer Plastik im Jahre 1962." *Jahrbuch Hamburger Kunstsammlung* 8(1963):143-52.

Includes reproductions of paintings by Gauguin acquired by the museum in 1962.

1174. Hamburg, Museum für Kunst und Gewerbe. *Stiftung zur Förderung der Hamburgischen Kunstsammlungen: Erwerbungen 1978-79* [Foundation for the Promotion of Art Collection in Hamburg; Acquisitions 1978-79]. Foreword by Wolfgang Tarnowski. Hamburg: Die Stiftung, 1979. 48 p., 31 illus., 4 col.

Catalogue raisonné of art work acquired by the Kunsthalle and the Museum für Kunst und Gewerbe, Hamburg, in 1978 and 1979. Works highlighted include a wooden display cabinet by Paul Gauguin.

1175. Wilhelm Hansen Collection. DUMONTHIER, ERNEST. "La Collection Wilhelm Hansen." *Revue de l'art ancien et moderne* 42(Dec. 1922):331-43.

1176. Hermitage and Pushkin Museums, Leningrad and Moscow. *Paul Gauguin: Musée de l'Ermitage, Musée des Beaux-Arts Pouchkine.* Introduction by Asya Kantor-Gukovskaya. Commentaries by Anna Barskaia and Marina Bessonova. Paris: Editions Cercle d'Art, 1988. 186 p., 188 illus, 78 col.

Catalogue raisonné of 30 Gauguin paintings at the Pushkin Museum of Fine Arts in Moscow and at the Hermitage Museum in Leningrad.

1177. Honolulu Academy of Arts. "Honolulu gets Tahitian Work by Gauguin." *Art Digest* 8(Sept. 1934):7.

1178. Musée de Liège. SAFIN-CRAHAY, F. "Neuf chefs-d'oeuvre du musée de Liège." *Beaux Arts Magazine* (France), 7 (Nov. 1983):58-63. 10 illus.

1179. Louvre, Paris. F. F. "L'Entrée de Gauguin au Louvre." *L'Amour de l'art* 8(March 1927):90.

1180. Louvre, Paris. "Gauguin's *La Belle angèle* for Louvre. *La Belle angèle* by Paul Gauguin. Courtesy of the Louvre, Paris." *Art Digest* 1:5(15 April 1927):5.

1181. Louvre, Paris. STERLING, CHARLES and HELENE ADHEMAR. *Peintures: Ecole française, XIXe siècle, Musée National du Louvre.* Paris: Editions des Musées Nationaux, 1958-1961. 4 vol., illus.

1182. Louvre, Paris. "Il museo del Louvre ha avuto il suo diciottesimo Gauguin." *Domus* 377(April 1961):54.

1183. Louvre, Paris. HUBERT, G. "Buste de Madame Emile Schuffenecker par Gauguin entré au musée du Louvre." *Revue du Louvre* 11:1(1961):40-41.

1184. Louvre, Paris. VIATTE, G. "Nouvelles acquisitions des musées de province depuis 1960: peintures et desseins du XIXe siècle." *Revue du Louvre* 14(1964):291.

1185. Musée de Lyon. VINCENT, MADELEINE. *La peinture des XIXe siècles; catalogue du Musée de Lyon.* Lyon: Editions de Lyon, 1946-56 pl. 7 vol.

1186. Somerset Maugham Collection. JEUDWINE, W. R. "Somerset Maugham Collection." *Apollo* 64(Oct. 1956):104-06.

1187. Paul Mellon Collection, Richmond, Virginia. NEAR, PINKNEY L. *French Paintings in the Collection of Mr. and Mrs. Paul Mellon in the Virginia Museum of Fine Arts*. Introduction by John Rewald. Richmond, Virginia: Virginia Museum of Fine Arts, distributed by University of Washington Press, Seattle and London, 1985. 146 p., 69 col. illus.

Catalogue includes works by Gauguin, among others.

1188. Metropolitan Museum of Art, New York. "Gauguin's Tahitian Landscape for the Metropolitan." *Art News* 38(6 April 1940):28-29.

1189. Minneapolis Institute of Arts. "A Tahitian Scene by Gauguin." *Minneapolis Institute Bulletin* 31(4 April 1942):45-49.

1190. Minneapolis Institute of Arts. "Minneapolis Buys Serene Gauguin Work *I raro te oviri*" [Under the pandanus]. *Art Digest* 16(15 April 1942):19.

1191. Minneapolis Institue of Arts. DAVIS, R. S. "Gauguin Landscape [*Paysage Tahitien*, 1891-93] Purchased from Eliel Memorial Fund." *Minneapolis Institute of Fine Arts Bulletin* 39(1 April 1950):62-66. 4 illus.

1192. Moscow. Museum of Modern Western Art. "Oeuvres dans le Musée d'art moderne occidental à Moscou." *Cahiers d'art* 25:2(1950):341.

1193. Marczell de Nemes Collection. MOUREY, GABRIEL. "La Collection Marczell de Nemes." *Les arts* 12(1913):1-32.

1194. Neue Pinakothek, Munich. STEINGRABER, ERICH. *Die Neue Pinakothek München*. Munich: Thiemig, 1981. 167 p., 121 illus., 118 col.

Issued on the occasion of the re-opening of the Neue Pinakothek, Munich, destroyed during World War II. Contains a summary of the history of the collection and an overview of 19th-century paintings in the museum, including several by Gauguin.

1195. Phillips Memorial Gallery, Washington, D.C. PHILLIPS, DUNCAN. *A Collection in the Making*. New York: E. Weyhe; Wash., D.C.: Phillips Memorial Gallery, 1926. 112 p.

1196. Pushkin Museum, Moscow. *Gogen: Obrazi Tsvet*. Moscow: Izdatel-stvo Sovetskii Khudozhnik, 1969. 28 p., col. illus.

Catalogue of works in the Pushkin Museum.

1197. Musée des Beaux-Arts, Quimper. CARIOU, ANDRE. "L'Ecole de Pont-Aven au Musée des Beaux-Arts de Quimper." *La Revue du Louvre et des musées de France* 37:2(1987):99-104.

1198. Edward G. Robinson Collection. SETON, MARIE. "Edward G. Robinson Collection." *The Studio* 118(1939):236-41.

1199. Russian Museums. OSBORN, MAX. "Die junge Kunst in den russischen Museen und Sammlungen." *Der Cicerone* 16(1924):899-906.

1200. Russian Museums. BESSONOVA, MARINA. *Gogen, vzgliad iz Rossii: Albom-Katalog; Moscow, Leningrad, 1989.* Moscow: Sovetskii Khudozhnik, 1989. 363 p., illus.

1201. National Gallery of Scotland, Edinburgh. "An Outstanding Gift for Scotland." *Museums Journal* 59(1960):290.

1202. Sara Lee Corporation Collection, Chicago. BRETTELL, RICHARD R. *An Impressionist Legacy: The Collection of the Sara Lee Corporation.* Introduction by David Finn. New York: Abbeville, distributed in the U.K. and Europe by Pandemic, London, 1986. 127 p., 80 col. illus.

Catalogue raisonné of the collection of paintings and sculpture on permanent display at the Chicago headquarters of the Sara Lee Corporation, which were acquired from the personal collection of the company's founder, Nathan Cummings. They are principally French and include works by Gauguin.
a. 2nd ed.: New York: Abbeville, 1987. 127 p.

1203. Smith College Art Museum, Northampton, Massachusetts. "Gauguin's *Banlieue Parisienne* in the Smith College Museum of Art." *Art Quarterly* 16:3(1953):269-70.

1204. Soviet Museums. *Paul Gauguin in Soviet Museums.* Introduction by Asya Kantor-Gukovskaya. Notes by Anna Barskaya and Marina Bessonova. Trans. by Ashkhen Mikoyan. Leningrad: Aurora Art Publishers, 1988. 186p., illus.
a. German ed.: *Paul Gauguin in den Museen der Sowjetunion.* Trans. by Holger Lange. Düsseldorf: Brücken-Verlag; Leningrad: Aurora Art Publishers, 1989. 186 p., illus.

1205. John T. Spaulding Collection. POPE, ARTHUR. "French Paintings in the Collection of John T. Spaulding." *Art News* 28(1930):97-128.

1206. St. Louis Art Museum. LEONARD, H. STEWART. "An Unpublished Manuscript by Paul Gauguin, *L'Esprit moderne et le catholicisme*." *Bulletin of the City Art Museum of St. Louis* 34:3(Summer 1949):39-50.

1207. St. Louis Art Museum. "Gauguin Mss. to St. Louis." *Art Digest* 23:(Aug. 1949):14.

1208. St. Louis Art Museum. COWART, JACK. "Acquisitions: Two Paintings by Paul Gauguin." *Saint Louis Art Museum Bulletin* 11:1(Jan.-Feb. 1975):1-5. 2 illus.

Discusses the Pont-Aven and Japanese influences in Gauguin's portrait of *Madame Roulin* (1888), and the qualities of his Polynesian landscape *Tahiti*, executed in 1891 during Gauguin's first Tahitian period.

1209. St. Louis Art Museum. "Impressionist and Post-Impressionist Paintings." *Saint Louis Art Museum Bulletin* 16:2(Winter 1982):3-35. 23 illus., 9 col.

First of a series of catalogues of the collection of French 19th-century paintings in the St. Louis Art Museum. Includes works by Gauguin, Cézanne, van Gogh, Monet, Pissarro, Renoir, Seurat, and Sisley.

XV. Technique

A. Monographs

1210. GRAVELAINE, FREDERIQUE DE. *Paul Gauguin; la vie, la technique, l'oeuvre peinte*. Lausanne: Edita, 1988. 159 p., illus., 49 col. pl.

Examines Gauguin's life and artistic technique as revealed in his paintings.

1211. HALE, CHARLOTTE. *A Study of Paul Gauguin's Correspondence Relating to His Painting Materials and Techniques*. London: Courtauld Institute Diploma Project, 1983.

B. Articles

1212. BODELSEN, MERETE CHRISTENSEN. "The Missing Link in Gauguin's Cloisonnism." *Gazette des Beaux-Arts* 6th ser., 101:1084-1085(May-June 1959):329-44. 16 illus.

1213. CANNON-BROOKES, PETER. "Cézanne, Gauguin and a Picture Frame." *International Journal of Museum Management and Curatorship* 8(March 1989):94.

1214. CHASSE, CHARLES. "De quand date le synthétisme de Gauguin?" *L'Amour de l'art* 19(April 1938):127-34.

1215. DAULTE, FRANÇOIS. "L'art de 'transposer' le sujet chez Gauguin." *Connaissance des arts* 84(Feb. 1959):44-47. 10 illus.

1216. DONNELL, CAROL A. "Representation Versus Expressionism in the Art of Gauguin." *Art International* 19:3(March 1975):56-60.

Argues that while Gauguin's work prefigures certain concepts in modern painting, the case for this tremendous legacy is usually given at the expense of his role as a representational painter.

1217. HELLER, REINHOLD. "Concerning Symbolism and the Structure of Surface." *Art Journal* 45:2(Summer 1985):146-53. 4 illus.

Examines paintings by Gauguin, Degas, Munch, and Khnopff, and argues that many late 19th-century artists consciously emphasized qualities of medium and support in order to draw attention to the work of art as a physical object, and that in so doing they were able to affirm the non-illusionistic, symbolic role of the work of art in the subjective expression of "ideas." Relates the tenets of Symbolist theory to 19th-century philosophy.

1218. PALUE, PIERRE. "Techniques des anciens: Gauguin." *Techniques des arts* 18(May-June, 1989):12-22. illus.

1219. RODDON, G. "Colour and its Application to Painting." *Artist* (U.K.) 95(May 1980): 13-16. 5 illus.

Describes the liberation of color from the role of naturalistic representation by the Impressionists. States that Cézanne used color as a means of organizing the picture surface. Gauguin and van Gogh used violet color as a means of expression. Matisse finally made color itself an expression with his cut-outs, which achieved a completely satisfying balance of color areas.

1220. SCHLEE, N. "Gauguin's Approach to Painting." *Artist* (U.K.) 85(June 1973):107-9. 4 illus.

In Gauguin's view, "painting should seek suggestion more than description." He obtained this end by using colors and lines to make purely abstract patterns and harmonies which subconsciously arouse feelings. Each painting has a "literary" and a "musical" level of meaning. Details four steps Gauguin took in painting his pictures.

1221. TILLIM, SIDNEY. "Gauguin and the Decorative Style." *Artforum* 5:2(Oct. 1966):36-38.

1222. WERNER, ALFRED. "Gauguin and the Decorative Style." *Arts Magazine* 40 (June 1966):25-27.

XVI. Iconography

A. Monographs

1223. AMISHAI-MAISELS, ZIVA. *Gauguin's Religious Themes.* Ph.D. diss., Hebrew University, Jerusalem, 1969. New York, London: Garland, 1985. 541p., 221 illus.

Analyzes Gauguin's religious iconography through an examination of such themes in his paintings, sculptures and writings as his self-portraits as Christ, the Devil, Eve, Death, the Tree of Knowledge, the Madonna and Child, and Tahitian mythology. Discusses Gauguin's iconography as an expression of events in his private life and of the ideas on art and religion current in the Symbolist milieu.

1224. ANDERSEN, WAYNE V. *Gauguin's Paradise Lost.* With the assistance of Barbara Klein. New York: Viking Press, 1971. 371 p., 138 illus.

Psychoanalytical biography of Gauguin that has its starting point in the views of nature and the myths which he encountered in Brittany and Tahiti. The author's main intention is to elucidate the ways in which nature and myth were incorporated into Gauguin's personal mythology, reordered by his unconscious mind, and translated into the symbolic system of his paintings.
a. English ed.: London: Secker & Warburg, 1972. 370 p.

1225. DELVOY, ROBERT L. *Journal du symbolisme.* Geneva: Albert Skira, 1978.

The Symbolist movement is studied as a dominant force in European art and literature from 1870 to 1900, and as arising in opposition to the spirit of realism which had produced both Impressionism and naturalism. Influenced by Pre-Raphaelitism, the operas of Wagner, and the poetry of Baudelaire, Mallarmé and Maeterlinck, Symbolist painters aimed at imaginative suggestions of emotion through symbolic allusions of death, eroticism, and luxuriant decorative form. The change in the interpretation of Symbolism is charted through examination of the work and ideas of the artists who created it, from forerunners such as Gauguin and the Pre-Raphaelites, to its major exponents.

a. English ed.: *Symbolists and Symbolism*. London: Macmillan, 1978. 247 p., 311 illus.

b. U.S. eds.: *Symbolists and Symbolism*. Trans. by Barbara Bray, et al. New York: Skira, 1978; New York, Geneva: Skira/Rizzoli, 1982.

1226. DENIS, MAURICE. *Théories, 1980-1910, du Symbolisme et de Gauguin vers un nouvel ordre classique*. Paris: Bibliothèque de l'Occident, 1912. 270p.

General study of Symbolism and Gauguin's contributions.

a. Other French eds.: 1912, 1913; Paris: L. Rouart et J. Watelin, 1920; *Du Symbolisme au classicisme. Théories*, ed. Olivier Revault d'Allonnes. Paris: Hermann, 1964. 181 p., illus.

1227. DIETRICH, LINNEA STONESIFER. *A Study of Symbolism in the Tahitian Painting of Paul Gauguin, 1891-1893*. Ph.D. diss., University of Delaware, 1973. 296 p.

Traces through his Tahitian paintings Gauguin's development of the "analogical symbol," a device employed to integrate literary, metaphysical or philosophical ideas into a painting without disrupting the integrity of the pictorial surface. Gauguin's method and its influence are also described.

1228. GOLDWATER, ROBERT JOHN. *Primitivism in Modern Painting*. New York and London: Harper & Brothers, 1938. 210 p., 58 pl.

Chapter 3, Romantic Primitivism, deals in part with Gauguin and the School of Pont-Aven. Examines Gauguin's symbolist theory, copying of Marquesan art motives, confusion of the naive and the primitive, and simplification of forms.

a. Revised ed.: New York: Vintage Books, 1967. 291 p.

1229. HADLEY, SUZANNE HANEY. *Gauguin and the Symbolists*. 1962. 56 p.

1230. HALSEY, BRIAN ELLIOT. *Paul Gauguin: A Study of the Christ Theme in His Art and Thought.* Ph.D. diss., Tallahassee: Florida State University, 1972. 292 p., 89 illus.

Demonstrates the importance that the Christ theme played in Gauguin's art and thought by cataloguing over 50 works in which he treated this subject and by analyzing his writings on the motif. Gauguin's use of tradition is examined, with reference to the Brittany calvaries, and to religious expressions from a variety of different cultures. The uniqueness of Gauguin's interpretation of religious themes is stressed.

1231. HERBAN, MATTHEW B. *Maurice Denis' 'nouvel ordre classique' as Contained in his 'Théories' (1890-1910).* Ph.D. diss., Philadelphia: University of Pennsylvania, 1972. 298 p.

Examination of Denis' classical aesthetic--a synthesis of elements of Neo-Classicism, Romanticism and Realism--and a study of his use of a Symbolist definition of painting in the identification of classical achievement in the paintings of Gauguin, van Gogh, and Cézanne.

1232. JIRAT-WASIUTYNSKI, VOJTECH. *Paul Gauguin in the Context of Symbolism.* Ph.D. diss., Princeton University, 1975. New York and London: Garland, 1978. 2 vol., 467 p., 164 illus.

Examines Gauguin's theoretical writings and his use of themes, imagery and formal devices. Establishes him as a proto-Symbolist artist. Begins by discussing the intellectual context in which Gauguin's ideas and art matured from 1885 to 1890. Proceeds to examine Gauguin's stylistic sources and his relation to Impressionism and Neo-Impressionism. Special attention is given to the role of syntheses, abstraction, and the technique of working from memory. Gauguin's 1888-1891 Symbolist mode is characterized by its high degree of "consciousness of style" and visual ambiguity. Discusses Gauguin's 1884-1891 imagery of women including such themes as vanity, sterility, androgynous perfection, the *femme fatale*, and the Fall. Studies the theme of the Earthly Paradise and contemporary Symbolist concepts of decadence, primitivism and death-rebirth. Links Gauguin's self-portraits to contemporary Symbolist images, metaphors of creation, and artists' biographies.

1233. LANDY, BARBARA J. *Paul Gauguin: Symbols and Themes in his Pre-Tahitian Works.* Barbara J. Landy, 1968. 219 p., illus.

1234. MERLIN, ANGELO. *Gauguin e l'esotismo* [Gauguin and exoticism]. Padova: CEDAM, 1943. 76 p., col. pl.
Review: G. Labo, *Emporium* 98 (Nov.-Dec. 1943):182-83.

1235. PINCUS-WITTEN, ROBERT. *Occult Symbolism in France; Joséphin Péladan and the Salons de la Rose-Croix.* Ph.D. diss., University of Chicago, 1968. New York and London: Garland, 1976. 291 p., 68 illus.

Clarifies the central issues of the Symbolist movement as they were then understood. The modern view of Symbolism emphasizes the role played by such artists as Gauguin and Redon; yet much of the meaning of their work can be understood only in light of the occult and esoteric revival of the late 19th century. The central figure of this revival was Joséphin Péladan, a critic, historian, aesthetician, dramatist, novelist, and occultist--one of the period's leading thinkers and one of its most flamboyant characters.

1236. ROOKMAKER, HENDRIK ROELOF. *Synthetist Art Theories; Genesis and Nature of the Ideas on Art of Gauguin and His Circle.* Ph.D. diss., Amsterdam University, 1959. Amsterdam: Swets & Zeitlinger, 1959. 284 p.

Deals mainly with the synthetist theory of art as developed from 1885 to 1890. Nineteenth century precursors of the synthetists are discussed as well as Symbolism. Chapters 6 and 9 deal specifically with Gauguin. Reviews: L.D. Steefel, *Journal of Aesthetics* 20(1961):104; *Art Bulletin* 45 (1963):168-69.
a. 2nd ed.: *Gauguin and 19th Century Art Theory.* Amsterdam: Swets & Zeitlinger, 1972. 362 p.

1237. SCHMALENBACH, WERNER. *Die Kunst der Primitiven als Anregungsquelle für die europaische Kunst bis 1900.* Ph.D. diss., University of Basel, 1955. Cologne: Dumont-Schauberg, 1961. 279 p.

Includes a long section on Gauguin's primitivism, pp. 111-233.

1238. VARNEDOE, KIRK. "Gauguin." In *Primitivism in 20th Century Art: Affinity of the Tribal and the Modern.* William Rubin, ed. New York: Museum of Modern Art, 1984. 2 vol., 689 p., illus.

Essay on Gauguin's primitivism (I:177-209), argues that Gauguin is a better model for modern artistic primitivism when he is taken whole--ideas and art together--with all the contradictions included. Accordingly, Gauguin gives new meaning to the commonplace notion that primitivism is an integral aspect of the modernity it seems to reject.
a. German ed.: *Primitivismus in der Kunst des Zwanzigsten Jahrhundrets.* Munich: Prestel, 1984. 742 p.
b. French ed.: *Le Primitivisme dans l'art du XXe siècle.* Paris: Flammarion, 1987.

1239. VETTER, EWALD M. "Sens Figuratif und Sens Figuré bei Gauguin." In *Festschrift Wolfgang Braunfels*. Friedrich Piel and Jörg Traegor, eds. Tübingen: Wasmuth, 1977. 439 p., illus.

Study of Gauguin's symbolism.

1240. WELSH, ROBERT P. "Sacred Geometry: French Symbolism and Early Abstraction." In *The Spiritual in Art Abstract Painting, 1890-1985*. Los Angeles: Country Museum of Art. Maurice Tuchman, ed., pp.63-87. 435 p., 36 illus., 5 col.

Traces the use of geometric signs by the Nabis and other French artists and relates this to the development of abstraction. Describes some of the sources of ideas about the symbolism of geometric signs, in particular the writings of Helena P. Blavatsky, and traces the impact of these on the Nabis, possibly through the stimulus of Gauguin whose paintings from his Brittany period encouraged a mystical conception of art in which sacred geometry figured as one component.

B. Articles

1241. AMISHAI-MAISELS, ZIVA. "Gauguin's Early Tahitian Idols." *Art Bulletin* 60:2(June 1978):331-41. 19 illus.

Two of Gauguin's Tahitian sculptures, the *Idol with a Shell* and the *Crucifixion* (both in the Agnès Huc de Monfreid collection, Corneille de Conflant), are redated to 1891 on the basis of the dates of his copies of these statues in *Ancien culte mahorie* (Louvre, Paris) and *Vairaumati tei Oa* (Hermitage, Leningrad). This redating throws new light on two major aspects of Gauguin's art. First, it permits a clear view of the development of the influence on him of primitive art. This aspect is examined in detail by means of the development of images on the *Idol with a Shell* from their sources through his work of 1891-1903. Secondly, it indicates the manner in which Gauguin concocted his dream of ancient Tahitian life through a syncretic merging of images and ideas from Christian, Buddhist and Polynesian art and religion.

1242. ANDERSEN, WAYNE V. "Gauguin and a Peruvian Mummy." *Burlington Magazine* 109:769(April 1967):238-42.

1243. ANDERSEN, WAYNE V. "Gauguin's Motifs from Le Pouldu: Preliminary Report." *Burlington Magazine* 112:810(Sept. 1970):614-20. 13 illus.

1244. BERNARD, EMILE. "Le symbolisme pictural: 1886-1936." *Mercure de France* 268 (15 June 1936):514-30.

1245. BODELSEN, MERETE CHRISTENSEN. "Gauguin and the Marquesan God" [with French summary]. *Gazette des Beaux-Arts* 6th ser., 57:1106(March 1961):167-80. 17 illus., 2 pl.

1246. BRAUN, BARBARA. "Paul Gauguin's Indian Identity: How Ancient Peruvian Pottery Inspired His Art." *Art History* 9:1(March 1986):36-54. 48 illus., 6 pl.

Examines the influence of the forms and motifs of pre-Columbian pottery on Gauguin's ceramic sculpture and subsequently on his painting and relief sculpture.

1247. CASTEL, JANE. "Gauguin to Moore: Primitivism in Modern Culture." *RACAR, Revue d'art canadienne, Canadian Art Review* 9(1982):94-98.

1248. CHASTEL, ANDRE. "Gauguin: érotisme et féerie." *Médecine de France* 7(1949):41-48.

1249. CHEETHAM, MARK A. "Mystical Memories: Gauguin's Neoplatonism and 'Abstraction' in the Late Nineteenth-Century French Painting." *Art Journal* 46:1(Spring 1987):15-21. 2 illus.

Referring to Gauguin's discussion in letters of his *Self-Portrait, 'Les Misérables'* (1888), the author argues for a strongly Neoplatonic theory of artistic practice in Gauguin's thinking, the metaphysics and mysticism of which encouraged a transcendence of material appearances in a way that prefigures the abstraction of Kandinsky, Mondrian and Malevich. The basic ideas are the Platonic theme of dissatisfaction with terrestrial existence, and an emphasis on painting from memory as a self-consciously inward turn to the soul and rejection of external appearances. The most likely sources for Gauguin's Neoplatonism were Swedenborg, via Balzac, and Schopenhauer, via the literary Symbolists. Gauguin's ideas are similar to those of Aurier and Bernard and reflect a general popularity of Neoplatonism in late 19th century France.

1250. DEMONT, BERNARD. "L'ambiguité dans la peinture de Gauguin entre 1885 et 1894." *L'Oeil* 356(March 1985):32-39. 9 illus.

Discusses Gauguin's use of ambiguity. The author looks at the post-Romantic idea of suggestion and mystery, and studies the motifs of Gauguin's 1888 paintings and the effects of his stay at Pont Aven in terms of plastic and symbolic ambiguity. Synthetism, and Gauguin's notion of the "emblem", are considered with reference to several of the works. The author concludes by examining the self-referential nature of ambiguity in the works produced by Gauguin in Tahiti.

1251. DENIS, MAURICE. "De Gauguin et de van Gogh au classicisme." *L'Occident* 90(May 1909):187-202. Reprinted in *Théories, 1890-1910, du symbolisme et de Gauguin vers un nouvel ordre classique* (Paris 1912, 1913, Paris 1920, 1964,etc.).
a. German trans.: "Von Gauguin and Van Gogh zum Klassizismus." *Kunst and Künstler* 8(1910):86-101.

1252. DIETRICH, LINNEA STONESIFER. "The Redefinition of Symbolism in the Visual Arts." *Print Collector's Newsletter* 6:2(May-June 1975):34-38. 3 illus.

Argues that the aim of the Symbolist artists (Paul Cézanne, Paul Gauguin, Vincent van Gogh, Georges Seurat, and Odilon Redon) was not to elaborate a programmatic content nor to display mere technical virtuosity, but to create art that stressed the mutual interdependence of form and content. The intended effect of Symbolist art is to transmute the viewer into the Ideal. The "synthetist symbol"--be it object, image, color, etc.--creates the link between form and content and belongs to both levels. This theory is applied to Paul Gauguin's woodcuts entitled *Manao tupapau* (*She Thinks of the Spirit of the Dead*) 1892, and the painting of the same title and date in the collection of A. Conger Goodyear, New York. These are related to the poetry and aesthetic theory of Stéphane Mallarmé, the Symbolist poet.

1253. DIETRICH, LINNEA STONESIFER. "Gauguin: The Eve of My Choice." *Art Criticism* 4:2(1988):47-60.

States that Gauguin's vision of women from European gender-stereotypes is part of his larger vision of humans as whole, integrated beings embracing both thinking and feeling, nature and culture, and matter and spirit. Gauguin's achievement was not only the emancipation of painting but the emancipation of humanity from a dualism which separates and subordinates.

1254. DORIVAL, BERNARD. "Sources of the Art of Gauguin from Java, Egypt and Ancient Greece." *Burlington Magazine* 93:577(April 1951):118-23. 5 illus. See also "Further Observations on Sources of the Art of Gauguin." *Burlington Magazine* 93(July 1951):237.

1255. DORRA, HENRI. "The First Eves in Gauguin's Eden"[with French trans.]. *Gazette des Beaux-arts* 6th ser., 41(March 1953):189-202, 225-27.

1256. DORRA, HENRI. "More on Gauguin's Eves." *Gazette des Beaux-Arts* 6th ser., 69(Feb. 1967):109-12.

1257. DORRA, HENRI. "Gauguin's Dramatic Arles Themes." *Art Journal* 38:1(Fall 1978):12-17. 9 illus.

Discusses *Vintage at Arles-Human Miseries*, 1888 (Ordrupgaard, Copenhagen), identifying the source for the central figure as a lithograph of 1857 by Félicien Rops, *In the Ardenne--Now that Stupid Marie-Josèphe Thinks of a Child that has been Buried*. Notes the influence of Gauguin's contact with van Gogh on his work of the late 1880s.

1258. DORRA, HENRI. "Le 'Texte Wagner' de Gauguin." *Bulletin de la Société de l'histoire de l'art français* (1984):281-88. 2 illus.

On a text by Gauguin in the Bibliothèque Nationale, Paris, made up of quotations and paraphrases from Richard Wagner's writings. Discusses the origin of these passages, some of which were written by Gauguin, Sérusier, and Meyer de Haan on the walls of an inn in Le Pouldu, France, in Oct. 1889. The various texts advocate the union of all the arts, the sacredness of artistic creation, the need for unity among artists sharing the same ideals, and contempt for the material side of artistic execution. Wagner also provided Gauguin with an important theme, that of Eve becoming conscious of her fall.

1259. DUNKEL, GUNTER. "Zwischen Sozialem Realismus und utopischem Entwurf" [Between Social Realism and Utopian Sketch]. *Tendenzen* (F.R.G.) 26:152(Oct.-Dec. 1985):p. 57-63. 9 illus.

Discusses six paintings and one sculpture by Auguste Renoir, Auguste Rodin, Félicien Rops, Hans von Marées, Toulouse-Lautrec, Paul Gauguin, and Théophile Alexandre Steinlen, all from the end of the 19th century. Compares their treatment of the female figure with that of the academic painters, arguing that the nonacademic works are more relevant than the academic and bourgeois image of women.

1260. FISCHER, F. W. "Zur Symbolik des Geistigen in der modernen Malerei" [Towards a Spiritual Symbolism in Modern Painting]. *Zeitschrift für Ästhetik und allgemeine Kunstwissenschaft* 29:1(1984):5-18.

Citing Kandinsky's belief that the spiritual principle in the world history has achieved prominence in modern paintings, the author discusses attempts to represent the spiritual in art. Ranging over the work and intentions of modern painters, including Cézanne, Gauguin, and Kandinsky, the author concludes that Mondrian was the artist most committed to an uncompromised attempt to deal with the spiritual in painting.

1261. FLAM, JACK D. "The Spell of the Primitive; in Africa and Oceania Artists Found a New Vocabulary." *Connoisseur* (Sept. 1984):124-31. 10 illus., 6 col.

Examines European interest in primitive art in the late 19th and early 20th centuries and traces its influence on French artists, especially Gauguin, Matisse, and Picasso. Written in connection with the exhibition *"Primitivism" in 20th Century Art: Affinity of the Tribal and the Modern*, held at the Museum of Modern Art, New York, 27 Sept. 1984-15 Jan. 1985; and the opening of the Center for African Art in New York.

1262. GLYNN, E. "Desperate Necessity: Art and Creativity in Recent Psychoanalytic Theory." *Print Collector's Newsletter* 8:2(May-June 1977):29-6. 32 illus.

Outlines the ways in which the application of psychoanalytic theory to art can be made more valuable as a vehicle for analysis if recent developments in psychoanalytic thought are taken into account. The Freudian view of the artist as a person adept at "exploiting his knack for disguising his daydreams of gratification," Kris's notion of "regression in the service of the ego," and Phyllis Greenacre's studies of the effect of the heightened sensibility of the artist upon the development of his personality are discussed and compared. Particular reference is made to the work of Egon Schiele, Mondrian, Gauguin, and van Gogh.

1263. HELLER, REINHOLD. "Concerning Symbolism and the Structure of Surface." *Art Journal* 45:2(Summer 1985):146-53. 4 illus.

Examines paintings by Gauguin, Degas, Munch, and Khnopff, and argues that many late 19th-century artists consciously emphasized qualities of medium and support in order to draw attention to the work of art as a physical object, and that in so doing they were able to affirm the non-illusionistic, symbolic role of the work of art in the subjective expression of "Ideas". Relates the tenets of Symbolist theory to 19th-century philosophy.

1264. HENNING, E. B. "Looking at Art: The *Woman in the Waves*." *Art News* 83:3(March 1984):104-06. 3 illus.

Discusses three paintings by Gauguin in the Cleveland Museum of Art: *Woman in the Waves* (*Ondine*), painted in Brittany, 1889; *Te Ra'au Rahi*, Tahiti, 1891; and *L'Appel*, Marquesas, 1902. Discusses the works in context of Gauguin's interest in Synthetism, Cloisonism, and Symbolism and argues that *Woman in the Waves* was painted in early 1889.

1265. HERBAN, MATTHEW B. "Narrative Content in and Linkage Between the Works of Paul Gauguin, 1886-1887." *Southeastern College Art Conference Review* 10:3 (1983):162.

1266. JIRAT-WASIUTYNSKI, VOJTECH. " Paul Gauguin's Paintings, 1886-91: Cloisonism, Synthetism and Symbolism." *RACAR, Revue d'art canadienne. Canadian Art Review* 9:1-2(1982):35-46. 9 illus. In English, summary in French.

Examines the role of Gauguin in the development of Symbolism; his relationship to Emile Bernard and Cloisonism; the relationship of works by Bernard, Anquetin and van Gogh to Gauguin's; and the meaning of the terms Cloisonism, Synthetism and Symbolism in relation to these artists.

1267. JOCKLE, CLEMENS. "Das Christusbild des 19. und frühen 20. Jahrhunderts" [The Image of Christ in the 19th and Early 20th Centuries]. *Münster* 41:2(1988):119-26. 14 illus.

Surveys the representation of Christ by Ingres, Overbeck, Delacroix, Friedrich, Veit, Holman Hunt, Millais, Max Liebermann, Fritz von Uhde, Daumier, Manet, van Gogh, Gauguin, Peter Lenz, and Emile Bernard. Examines the influence on such paintings of "l'art pour l'art" and the artists' private religious feelings which, rather than a general wave of religious enthusiasm, lay behind the pictures, with results varying from devotional pieces to historical and genre paintings, causing artists to invoke the past and anticipate the future in their approaches.

1268. KANE, WILLIAM MACGIBBON. "Gauguin's *Le Cheval blanc*: Sources and Syncretic Meanings." *Burlington Magazine* 108:760(July 1966):352-62. 8 illus.

1269. KUSPIT, DONALD B. "The Pathology and Health of Art: Gauguin's Self-Experience." *Psychoanalytic Perspectives on Art* 2(1987): 171-86.

Studies Gauguin's ideal of the primitive and its relationship to art. For Gauguin art had to express an emotion aimed at the most intimate part of the soul. Art was an instrument to perceive the feeling beyond the dead matter celebrated by the Impressionists, a means of consciously experiencing the unconscious. This gave rise to a paradox in Gauguin's thinking, in that art's subservience to the depiction of the unconscious meant that art itself tended to disappear. A similar paradox is apparent in the way Gauguin perceived primitive signs in apparently cold and skillful masters from the past. In conclusion, the author argues that the history that began with Gauguin, and the struggle between life and death, has today ended and primitivism has become impossible.

1270. LACKER, D. "Notes sur des symboles jaunes." *Peintre* (France) 567(15 June 1978):10-14.

Discusses the symbolic images conjured up by the color yellow--the color of gold, of lemons, of sulphur. Among specific works analysed, the author compares Gauguin's *Christ jaune* (1889) with Chagall's *Martyr*. Also comments on van Gogh's love of yellow, and the Japanese use of yellow chrysanthemums as symbols of the living emperor.

1271. VAN LIERE, E. N. "Solutions and Dissolutions: The Bather in Nineteenth-Century French Painting." *Arts Magazine* 54(May 1980):112+.

1272. MICHAUD, ERIC. "La 'fin' de l'iconographie." *Méthodologie iconographique* (1978):125-36. 4 illus.

Analyzes the "crisis" of representation in the last third of the 19th century when artists such as Gauguin, van Gogh and Maurice Denis sought to produce an immediate effect on the viewer through the direct action of lines and colors, rather than by evoking historical or literary themes.

1273. READ, HERBERT EDWARD. "Gauguin: Return to Symbolism." *Art News Annual* 15(1956):122-58. 40 illus., 22 col.

1274. READ, HERBERT EDWARD. "Paul Gauguin und die moderne Malerei." *Universitas* (Stuttgart) 16 (1961): 53-60. 2 illus.

Concerns Gauguin's symbolism.

1275. REVERSEAU, JEAN-PIERRE. "Pour une étude du thème de la tête coupée dans la littérature et la peinture dans la seconde partie du XIXe siècle." *Gazette des Beaux-Arts* 6th ser., 80(Sept. 1972), 173-84.

1276. ROGER-MARX, CLAUDE. "Gauguin et la naïveté en art." *Revue de Paris* (October 1960): 122-30. 1 illus.

1277. SCALABRIN, NICOLETTA. "Dal Wagnérisme a Paul Gauguin" [From Wagnerism to Paul Gauguin]. *Critica d'arte* 51:10(July-Sept. 1986):62-74. 4 illus. In Italian, summary in English.

Traces the impact of Wagner's visit to Paris in 1860 on music, authors, and artists, focusing on Gauguin. Underlines Gauguin's sensitivity to the relationship between music and painting, and notes parallels between his life and Wagner's.

1278. SERRITSLEV PETERSEN, LISE. "Arabesk versus Anekdote: Mallarmé, Fénéon, Gauguin og teorien om den ornamentale struktur" [Arabesque Versus Anecdote: Mallarmé, Fénéon, Gauguin and the Theory of Ornamental Structure]. *En Bog om Kunst til Else Kai Sass* (1977):390-98.

Analysis of the ornamental principle in French Symbolist aesthetics. Focuses on the Symbolist notion of the arabesque, and the connection between arabesque-shaped patterns and artistic structure is accentuated. Texts by Stéphane Mallarmé, Félix Fénéon, and Paul Gauguin constitute the material selected for examination. The article stresses the contrast between the artistic or "musical" nature of the arabesque and the non-artistic character associated with such categories of expression as "anecdote" (Fénéon), "littérature" (Gauguin) and "l'universel reportage" (Mallarmé). Finally, it is shown that Gauguin's theory of the arabesque and of visual "décor" in general is related to, and in some measure influenced by, fundamental ideas in Mallarmé's poetics.

1279. SLATKINS, W. "Maternity and Sexuality in the 1890s." *Woman's Art Journal* 2:1(Spring-Summer 1980):13-19. 5 illus.

During the 1890s there was a fascination with fertility, sexuality, and maternity in the arts, and many artists turned to archetypical depictions of "woman", including Paul Gauguin, Paula Modersohn-Becker, Edvard Munch, Gustav Klimt and Egon Schiele. Examines this attraction of artists to the iconography of female fertility, commenting on the analogy between a woman's power to create life and artistic creativity, but concluding that male artists sought to define the essence of women, whether out of unease or fear, in a way which deprived her of her individuality, intellect, and political rights.

1280. TEILHET, JEHANNE H. "Te Tamari no Atua: An Interpretation of Paul Gauguin's Tahitian Symbolism." *Arts Magazine* 53:5(Jan.1979):110-11. 1 illus.

Examines the accuracy of Gauguin's understanding of Tahitian beliefs, traditions and legends as expressed in *Te Tumari no Atua* (Neue Pinakothek, Munich). Discusses the iconography of this work in relation to the birth and subsequent death of Gauguin's child by Pahura in December, 1896.

1281. WEISBERG, GABRIEL P. "Vestiges of the Past: the Brittany 'Pardon' of Late Nineteenth Century French Painters." *Arts Magazine* 55:3(Nov. 1980):134-38. 12 illus.

One significant theme which attracted realist, naturalist and symbolist painters of the late 19th century was that of the Brittany *pardon*. It was seen at first as a continuation of medieval religious fervour on the part of the populace of Brittany by realist painters such as Jules Breton (during the 1860s) who used the theme to record the continuation of traditional events as part of an interest in folklore and regional life. Later painters, including Pascal Dagnan-Bourveret, saw the *pardon* in accurate, lifelike terms and situated the theme within the life of the region. The subject was utilized by both Paul Gauguin in his *Vision After the Sermon: Jacob Wrestling with the Angel*, 1888 (National Gallery of Scotland, Edinburgh) and by Emile Bernard to suggest personal mysticism and the elevation of the spirit.

1282. WIVEL, M. "Forsvindingspunkter: Paul Gauguin og vejen til det primitive" [Vanishing Points: Paul Gauguin and the Way to the Primitive]. *Louisiana Revy* 26:3(May 1986):6-13, 56. Summary in English. 10 illus.

The starting point of this article is Gauguin's carving during his stay in Copenhagen of a shrine containing the body of a young woman who appears to be not dead but in a troubled sleep--the symbol of his own spiritual reawakening. This was inspired by Danish Bronze Age coffins which he had seen, and which aroused his interest in the immediacy of primitive art which resulted in his work in the South Seas. Although he admired Impressionism, Gauguin felt that Western ideas of perspective were merely "fiction" and sought in Polynesia the inspiration for a new kind of painting as a gift to Western culture. After comparing Gauguin's *Oviri* (1894) statue, his Tahitian paintings and Botticelli's *Venus*, the author concludes that Gauguin painted dreams as if they were reality, and with such insight that that is their effect on the viewer.

1283. ZERVOS, CHRISTIAN. "Idéalisme et naturalisme dans la peinture moderne . . . Gauguin." *Cahiers d'art* 2:10(1927):329-30.

XVII. Japonisme

A. Monographs

1284. BOUILLON, JEAN-PAUL. "Remarques sur le Japonisme de Bracquemond" in *Japonism in Art, An International Symposium*. Edited by the Society for the Study of Japonism. Tokyo: Committee for the Year 2001, 1980, pp. 83-108. Illus.

Notes that there are many ways to approach the question of *Japonisme*: formalistic, historic, cultural, social, even political, and that until now one has prevailed--a combined anecdotal and formalistic approach which emphasizes the finding of new information about dates and explores the influence of one category of objects on another. Mentions Gauguin's contributions in resolving problems of traditional illusionistic perspective in three-dimensional space.

1285. IVES, COLTA FELLER. *The Great Wave: The Influence of Japanese Woodcuts on French Prints*. New York: The Metropolitan Museum of Art, 1974. 112 p., illus., pl.

Concerns an exhibition held in New York at the Metropolitan Museum of Art from January 14-March 9, 1975. In her introduction to the catalogue "Impressionism and Ukiyo-e," the author reviews the arrival of Japanese art in France. She argues that while artists such as Edouard Manet, Edgar Degas, Paul Gauguin, and others were rebelling against French academicism, they might not have realized that the *ukiyo-e* artists they prized had fought a similar battle.

1286. KLONER, JAY MARTIN. *The Influence of Japanese Prints on Edouard Manet and Paul Gauguin*. Ph.D. diss., New York: Columbia University, 1968; Ann Arbor; Michigan: University Microfilms, 1971. 485p., 165 illus.

Examines the nature of artistic Japonisme during the second half of the nineteenth century in France with emphasis on Manet and Gauguin. Finds that Gauguin not only exploited *ukiyo-e* patterns and colors in arriving at a synthetist style, but also used them as a Symbolist to express meaning. Part III (pp. 141-217) deals specifically with Gauguin.

1287. NEEDHAM, GERALD. "Japonisme Influence on French Painting 1854-1910" in *Japonisme: Japanese Influence on French Art 1854-1910*. Cleveland: The Cleveland Museum of Art, 1975, pp. 115-131, illus.

Noting that the Japanese influence on French painting was "intense and longlasting," Needham questions why, among the huge number of books published about 19th-century art, none are devoted to the subject. He sees two phases in *Japonisme* which correspond to the division in nineteenth-century art before and after the crisis in Impressionism. In the first phase of *Japonisme*, Needham examines the impact it had on the "Open-Air Impressionists of the 1860s and 1870s." He believes that it is the least appreciated, and that while mention is made of Edouard Manet and Edgar Degas, there is little reference to open-air painters. Japanese artistic characteristics thought to have influenced French painters are changes in perspective, the range and brightness of color, and also the themes of prints which intrigued French painters who were representing similar scenes in their paintings. In the second phase of *Japonisme*, which covered Post-Impressionism and Symbolism, as artists rejected naturalism to search for forms and colors, they also turned to Japanese art to find inspiration and confirmation of their own interests.

Needham notes that this phase of *Japonisme* is better known. He examines the works of Paul Gauguin and other Pont-Aven painters, the Nabis, Georges Seurat and the Pointillists, Vincent van Gogh, Odilon Redon, and Claude Monet after 1880.

1288. OSHIMA, SEIJI. *Japonisme: Autour de l'Impressionnisme et Ukiyo-e.* Tokyo: Bijutsukoronsha, 1980, illus.

General survey of *Japonisme* which examines the main French 19th-century painters from Edouard Manet to Paul Gauguin. Mention is made of the importance of the successive Universal Exhibitions and of the work of art critics. Siegfried Bing's role in the development of *Japonisme* is discussed in one chapter, and especially his publication *Artistic Japan*. Includes a lengthy bibliography of Japanese sources published before 1979.

1289. REIDEMEISTER, LEOPOLD. *Der Japonismus in der Malerei und Graphik des 19. Jahrhunderts.* Berlin: Staatliche Museen, 1965. 52 pp., illus.

Catalogue of a small exhibition of Japonisme in painting and the graphic works of some late 19th-centruy artists, including Paul Gauguin. The catalogue introduction briefly recalls the historical background which led to the discovery of Japanese art and to the dissemination of this material among artists.

1290. SUSUMU, S. and H. TORU. *Japanese Sense of Beauty: Source and Inspiration for Japonaiserie.* Tokyo: Metropolitan Teien Art Museum, 1985, 140 pp., illus.

Exhibition of Japanese porcelain, drawings, fans, and other designs which were collected in the West and were influential to the development of the fascination for all things Japanese. Describes the interest in *Japonisme* among writers and artists of the 19th century, concentrating his examination on France, and discusses specific works by Gauguin, Whistler, Monet, and van Gogh.

1291. THIRION, YVONNE. *De l'influence de l'estampe japonaise sur la peinture française dans la seconde moitié du XIXe siècle (au temps du 'Japonisme').* Ph.D. diss., Paris: Ecole du Louvre, 1947. 179 p., illus.

Japonisme's influence on Paul Gauguin is mentioned along with a detailed history of the diffusion of Japanese art in France.

1292. WEISBERG, GABRIEL P. and YVONNE M. L. WEISBERG. *Japonisme: An Annotated Bibliography.* New York and London:

Garland Publishing Co., Co-published with The International Center for Japonisme, 1990. 445 p., illus.

Annotated bibliography divided into books, catalogues, and articles. Subject index lists 18 citations for Paul Gauguin.

1293. WHITFORD, FRANCIS PETER. *Japanese Prints and Western Painters*. London: Studio Vista; New York: Macmillan, 1977. 264 p., 190 illus, 30 col.

Study of Japanese woodblock prints, the history of their development, their technique and subject matter, as well as an attempt to place them against the background of Japanese political and cultural history. The second part is concerned with the introduction of the prints to Europe and the extent and nature of their influence on major 19th century painters, concentrating on figures such as Gauguin, Manet, Degas, Whistler, Monet, Seurat, and van Gogh.

1294.WICHMANN, SIEGFRIED. *Japonismus: Ostasien und Europa, Begegnungen in der Kunst des 19. und 20. Jahrhunderts*. Schuler Verlagsgesellschaft, 1980.

Monumental survey of the influence of Japanese art on Western art, published to coincide with a major exhibition of Japanese art held in London at the Royal Academy of Arts during the winter of 1981-82. Concentrates on European Symbolism and Art Nouveau but also examines Abstract Expressionism and Tachism which are related to Zen ideas of spontaneity. The second section deals with individual artists, including Paul Gauguin. In the remainder of the book the subject matter of the works is used to study Japanese influences.
a. English ed.: *Japonisme: The Japanese Influence in Western Art Since 1858*. London: Thames and Hudson, 1981. 432 p., illus.
b. U.S. ed.: *Japonisme: The Japanese Influence on Western Art in the 19th and 20th Centuries*. New York: Harmony Books, 1981. 432 p., 1100+ illus., 225+ col.

B. Articles

1295. BAZAROV, KONSTANTIN. "The Floating World." *Art and Artists* 13:4(August 1978):28-33.

Discusses the meaning of *ukiyo-e* prints and especially their reflection of the "floating world" as the world of pleasure and entertainment which existed in Japanese cities between 1603 and 1868. Bazarov examines the erotic nature of many of the prints and puts them in an artistic and historical context. He believes that they had a great influence on modern

Western art in the works of Paul Gauguin, Claude Monet, Edgar Degas, Vincent van Gogh, and Aubrey Beardsley.

1296. HILLIER, JACK. "The Western Taste for Japanese Prints." *Storia dell'arte* 27(May-Aug. 1976):113-20. 48 illus.

Although Japanese prints had reached Europe prior to the 1860s, it was only from that time that they were collected and began to exercise an influence upon Western art. Initially this influence was superficial. There were borrowings of what might be called the subject matter of Japanese art, but the real strength of Japanese art was not yet understood. More informed taste was created largely by French collectors and the art critics, Duret, Gonse, and Edmond de Goncourt. Artists most strongly affected by Japanese art were Pissarro, van Gogh, Gauguin and particularly Toulouse-Lautrec. Judging from Parisian exhibitions of the 1910s, Utamaro was the artist who attracted the most interest, although Hokusai and Hiroshige were also widely appreciated.

1297. IKEGAMI, CHUJI. "Paul Gauguin et la vogue des japonaiseries en France." *Bijutsushi* 17:1(June 1967):1-32. In Japanese with French summary.

Studies how Gauguin became aware of Japanese art and how it affected him. Notes the Japanese objects in Gauguin's paintings and the references about Japan which appear in his letters. Also documents that Gauguin owned some Japanese prints and drawings. Argues that the latter have been overlooked and are found in the *Cabinet des dessins* at the Louvre. Some are from Hokusai's *Manga*. With these drawings is a manuscript by Gauguin replete with drawings by Japanese artists (among them Hokusai) and reproductions of images by Daumier, Forain, and Giotto. Ikegami studies the influence of Japanese art on Gauguin's painting and ceramics created between 1887 and 1888, in particular *Jacob Wrestling with the Angel* (1888). Sees this painting as the beginning of Gauguin's mature synthetist style.

1298. INAGA, S. "La réinterprétation de la perspective linéaire au Japon 1740-1830 et son retour en France 1860-1910." In *Actes recherches sciences sociales* 49 (1983), "La peinture et son public," pp. 29-46. 26 illus. English summary.

Examines Western linear perspective in Japan and its reemergence in France with Gauguin and van Gogh.

1299. IVES, COLTA F. "The Great Wave: Translation from the Japanese." *Art News* 74:3(March 1975):30-35.

Analyzing works by Paul Gauguin, Mary Cassatt, Pierre Bonnard and Henri de Toulouse-Lautrec, the author examines the stylistic peculiarities -- flattened figures, lack of shadows and modelling -- inherent in traditional Western art, the new viewpoints and use of perspective, the use of overall pattern and distortions found in the works of these artists, and discusses their debt to the influence of *ukiyo-e* prints. Ives notes that the views of the world of entertainment and scenes of daily life are close to the aims of Impressionist art.

1300. MALTESE, CORRADO. "Gauguin e la pittura giapponese." *Emporium* (Bergamo)105:625(Jan. 1947):2-10.

1301. MULLALY, TERENCE. "French Painting and the Japanese Print." *Apollo* 62:370(Dec. 1955):192-96.

Contends that the discovery of Japanese prints by some French painters, including Gauguin, had a significant influence on the development of modern painting. The discovery of the prints paralleled Western questioning of artistic concepts and opened new vistas for looking at the world.

1302. SCHEYER, ERNST. "Far Eastern Art and French Impressionism." *Art Quarterly* 6:2(Spring 1943):116-43.

Most likely the first comprehensive synthetic study of *Japonisme* published in the twentieth century and a seminal work for much that followed. Scheyer provides a short history of the appearance of Japanese art in the West, recalling the importance of Bracquemond, the World's Fairs, and the critics and collectors. He investigates the impact Japanese art had on Edouard Manet, Claude Monet, Edgar Degas, and others. With Paul Gauguin, Scheyer believes *Japonisme* comes to an end. Argues that the generation that followed van Gogh and Gauguin, essentially the Fauves, abandoned *Japonisme* for primitivism.

1303. TANAKA, HIDEMICHI. "Japonisme: Ukiyo-e Influence on Western Painting." *Bessatsu Taiyo* 21(Winter 1977):165-71.

General survey of the influence of Japanese prints on French nineteenth-century art, with special attention to Edouard Manet's *Portrait of Emile Zola*, the works of Edgar Degas, Vincent van Gogh, Paul Gauguin, and Paul Cézanne.

1304. THIRION, YVONNE. "L'Influence de l'estampe japonaise dans l'oeuvre de Gauguin." *Gazette des Beaux-Arts* 6th ser., 47(Jan.-April 1956): 94-114. Reprinted in *Gauguin, sa vie, son oeuvre* (Paris, 1958).

Examines how Japanese prints influenced Gauguin. Points out changes in Gauguin's handling of perspective and notes his use of bird's-eye perspective. Questioning the validity of her own assertions about the importance of the influence of Japanese prints, Thirion refutes her own doubts by mentioning different events which could have influenced Gauguin just at the moment when *Japonisme* was at its height. She mentions the importance of Siegfried Bing, his print exhibition of 1888, and his publication of *Artistic Japan*. Thirion also reiterates the role of van Gogh, who, in his letters to Gauguin, made numerous allusions to Japanese art. After examining several individual images by Gauguin which show a Japanese influence, Thirion concludes that, in spite of other influences on Gauguin's art, such as the images of Epinal, Japanese prints caused him to rethink his direction. While van Gogh saw them as "models to imitate," Gauguin found in Japanese prints an indication of the path he should follow. Their influence stimulated his own tendency toward a break with the Impressionist aesthetic and naturalism; the prints helped him embrace the new Symbolist aesthetic. In short, Gauguin discovered in Japanese prints a suggestion of abstract art. Finally, Thirion argues that at a time when everyone thought of the Japanese as leading designers, Gauguin discovered the formula for a more decorative style.

1305. THIRION, YVONNE. "Le japonisme en France dans la seconde moitié du XIXe siècle à la faveur de la diffusion de l'estampe Japonaise." *Cahiers de l'association internationale des études françaises* 13(1960):117-30.

XVIII. Mentions of Paul Gauguin in Monographs and Articles

A. Monographs

1306. ARGUELLES, JOSE A. *The Transformative Vision: Reflections on the Nature and History of Human Expression*. London, Berkeley: Shambhala Publications, distributed by Random House, 1975. 364 p., 3 illus.

Defining his purpose as primarily to present a "history of the human psyche and its forms of expression," the author explains that his ideas are the result of a combination of "psychophysical aesthetic and perennial philosophy." Concentrates on the visual arts, covering such topics as Blake's artistic vision; caricature as an expression of the truth; the "outcast" vision of van Gogh and Gauguin; the revolution in artistic expression caused by photography; impressionism; Cubism and Abstract Art; the American avant-garde; and discussing the various effects of such religious techniques as Christianity, the Hopi faith, theosophy, and of modern drugs such as LSD.

1307. BAZIN, GERMAIN. *L'Univers impressionniste.* Paris: Somogy, 1981. 320 p., 365 illus.

Argues for the far-reaching influence of the Impressionist movement on modern art, both in its new appraoch to light and mass and in its sense of *joie de vivre* which, Bazin maintains, infected European art until the onset of the First World War. The Impressionist movement is traced from its origins in the 1850s through the formation of the schools at Argenteuil and Pontoise and the first exhibitions to the movement's various later manifestations in Neo-Impressionism, Symbolism (as practiced especially by Gauguin), Rose + Croix, and the styles of a wide range of French artists inspired schools which emerged in Britain, Germany, Italy, Belgium, Hungary, Spain, the U.S., Canada and Australia.
a. 2nd ed.: Paris: Somogy, 1982. 351 p., illus.

1308. BEATTY, JOHN WESLEY. *The Modern Art Movement.* Pittsburgh: Carnegie Institute, 1924. 17 p., illus.

Gauguin's painting style and designs are discussed on pages 8-12.

1309. BELL, MARY. *The Little Book of Masterpieces.* New York: The Studio Publications, 1942 . 63 p., col. illus.

Gauguin mentioned on pages 54-55.

1310. BENET, RAFAEL and JORGE BENET AURELL. *Simbolismo.* Barcelona: Ediciones Omega, 1953.

1311. BILLY, ANDRE. *L'Epoque contemporaine, 1905-1930.* Paris: Tallandier, 1956. 365 p.

Mentions Gauguin's influence on early 20th-century artists.

1312. BLANCHE, JACQUES-EMILE. *Les arts plastiques.* Preface by Maurice Denis. Paris: Editions de France, 1931. 529 p.

Gauguin mentioned on pages 238-45 of this historical overview.

1313. BURGER, FRITZ. *Cézanne und Hodler, Einführung in die Probleme der Malerei der Gegenwart.* Munich: Delphin-Verlag, 1913. 2 vols., 180 p., 84 pl.

Other eds.: 1918, 1919, 1920, 1923.

1314. CABANNE, PIERRE. *La Nuit aussi est un soleil.* Paris: Robert Laffont, 1960.

Includes essays on Gauguin, van Gogh, and other artists.
a. English ed.: *Outlaws of Art*. London: Elek Books, 1963. 196 p.

1315. CARLEY, LIONEL and ROBERT THREFALL. *Delius: A Life in Pictures*. Oxford: Oxford University Press, 1977. 99 p., 240 illus., 10 col. pl.

Pictorial biography of the musician Frederick Delius (1862-1934), who numbered among his friends in Paris the painters Gauguin and Munch. 2nd ed.: London: Thames; New York: Universe, 1983. 99 p., illus.

1316. CHRISTOFFEL, ULRICH. *Malerei und Poesie; Die symbolistische Kunst des 19. Jahrhunderts*. Zurich: Scientia, 1948. 146 p., pl.

Another ed.: Vienna: Gallu-Verlag, 1948.

1317. COELLEN, LUDWIG. *Die neue Malerei*. 1912.

Gauguin and Matisse discussed on pages 58-61.

1318. *Collection des maîtres, série I*. Paris: Editions Braun, 193?.

1319. COQUIOT, GUSTAVE. *Des peintres maudits*. Paris: André Delpuech, 1924. 218 p.

Gauguin is discussed on pages 45-61.

1320. DAULTE, FRANÇOIS. *Aquarelle française au XIXe siècle*. Fribourg: Office du Livre, 1968. 142 p., col. illus.

Mentions Gauguin's art and influence.
a. English ed.: *French Watercolours of the 19th century*. Trans. by Frances Bap and David Joyce. London: Thames and Hudson, 1968. 143 p., 56 illus., 50 col.
b. U.S. ed.: New York: Viking Press, 1970. 140 p., pl.
c. Russian ed.: Moscow: Iskusstvo, 1981. 175 p., col. illus.

1321. DAVAL, JEAN-LUC. *La peinture à l'huile*. Geneva: Skira, 1985. 126 p., illus.

Traces the development of oil painting in the West over five centuries, from Jan van Eyck in the 15th century. Artists discussed in the later chapters include Gauguin.
a. English ed.: *Oil Painting from Van Eyck to Rothko*. London: Weidenfeld & Nicolson, 1985. 126 p., 102 illus.
b. U.S. ed.: New York: Rizzoli, 1985. 126 p., illus.

1322. DELL'ACQUA, G. A. *Gli impressionisti francesi*. Bergamo: Instituto Italiano d'Arti Grafiche, 1955. 102 p., col. pl.

1323. DOLENT, JEAN. *Les monstres*. Lithography by Eugène Carrière. Paris: Alphose Lemerre, 1896.

1324. DORIVAL, BERNARD. *Les Etapes de la peinture française contemporaine*. Paris: Gallimard, 1943-48. 4 vol.

Gauguin is mentioned frequently in vol. 1, *De l'impressionnisme au fauvisme (1889-1905)*. See especially pages 67-102.

1325. DUTHUIT, GEORGES. *Les Fauves: Braque, Derain, Van Dongen, Dufy, Friesz, Manguin, Marquet, Matisse, Puy, Vlaminck*. Geneva: Editions des Trois Collines, 1949. 254 p., illus., some col.

Discusses the Fauves in relation to van Gogh and Gauguin (see pp. 35-51).
a. English ed.: *The Fauvist Painters*. Trans. by Ralph Manheim. New York: Wittenborn, Schultz, 1950.

1326. DVORAK, FRANTISEK. *Twentieth Century Painters--The Paris School*. Trans. by G. Theiner. London: Spring, 1960. 37 p., 64 pl.

Includes three plates of paintings by Gauguin.

1327. ELGAR, FRANK. *The Post-Impressionists*. Oxford, England; Phaidon Press; New York: E.P. Dutton, 1977. 64 p., 48 col. pl.

1328. ESCHOLIER, RAYMOND. *La peinture française, XX siècle*. Paris: H. Floury, 1937. 152 p., illus., col. pl.

Mentions Gauguin's influence and legacy in the introductory chapter.

1329. FARR, DENNIS, ed. *100 Masterpieces: Bernardo Daddi to Ben Nicholson: European Paintings and Drawings from the 14th to the 20th Century*. London: Courtauld Institute of Art Fund, 1987. 216 p., 101 col. illus.

Selection of 100 paintings and drawings from the collections of the Courtauld Institute, London, including works by Gauguin. There is a short analytical and descriptive essay of each and a general introduction tracing the growth of the collection.

1330. FATHKE, B. "Marianne Werefkin und ihr Einfluss auf den Blauen Reiter" [Marianne Werefkin and her Influence on the Blaue

Reiter] in *Marianne Werefkin: Gemälde und Skizzen*, ed. by Sigrid Russ. Wiesbaden: Magistrat, 1980. 151 p., illus., some col.

Exhibition catalogue which examines the work of Marianne Werefkin based on letters and writings by the artist or by her associates, particularly after 1900. Pages 14-34 discuss the influence of Gauguin, van Gogh, and Matisse on her work after 1906 and her visit to Paris to the Matisse Art School.

1331. FENEON, FELIX. *Les impressionnistes en 1886*. Paris: Vogue, 1886.

1332. FENEON, FELIX. *Au delà de l'impressionnisme*. Françoise Cachin, ed. Paris: Hermann, 1966. 187 p., illus.

Collection of writings on Impressionism by the art critic Fénéon (1861-1944), including articles on Gauguin from 1886-91.

1333. FERNANDEZ, JUSTINO. *Prometeo*. México, D. F.: Editorial Porrua, 1945.

Gauguin is discussed on pages 9-14.

1334. FOCILLON, HENRI. *La peinture aux XIXe et XXe siècles; du réalisme à nos jours*. Paris: H. Laurens, 1928. 524 p., 210 illus.

Art history textbook which includes several references to Gauguin.

1335. FRANCASTEL, PIERRE. *L'impressionnisme; les origines de la peinture moderne de Monet à Gauguin*. Paris: Librarie Les Belles Lettres, 1937. 271 p., 12 pl.

Gauguin's primitivism's mentioned on pages 245-59.

1336. FRANCES, JOSE and GEORGES GUILLARD. *Album de pintura moderna*. Barcelona, 1935.

1337. FRANZKE, A. "Kachina in der Kunst des 20. Jahrhunderts" [The Kachina Cult in 20th Century Art] in *Kachina Figures by the Pueblo Indians of North America from the Horst Antes Collection*, ed. by Horst Antes. Karlsruhe: Badisches Landesmuseum, 1981. 176 p., illus., some col.

Examines the European fascination with "primitive art" and traces its integration into the paintings of Gauguin(see pages 5-19), the Cubists and the German Brücke movement. Provides background information on the first exhibitions of Kachina figures in Europe and describes how this interest was maintained and developed.

1338. FREIXA, MIREIA, ed. *Las Vanguardias del siglo XIX* [Avant-garde Movements in the 19th century]. Barcelona: G. Gili, 1982. 471 p.

Collection of texts and documents illustrating the development of modernism in Europe and the U.S. organized in the following categories: theoretical texts, legal stipulations, artistic techniques, artists' biographies and descriptions, and iconography. Includes text by Gauguin.

1339. GEFFROY, GUSTAVE. *La vie artistique*. Paris: E. Dentu, 1892-1903. 8 vols., illus.

Study of the lives of major artists. For sections on Gauguin, see II:382(1893); III:xi(1894); VI:221-29 (1900, but written in 1893).
a. Another ed.: Paris: H. Floury, 1903.

1340. GEIST, SIDNEY. *Brancusi/The Kiss*. New York; London: Harper & Row, 1978. 111 p. 66 illus.

Study of Brancusi's *The Kiss* (1907-08) which considers the sculpture within the framework of his developing oeuvre and situates it thematically in relation to other notable treatments of the subject, from early Greek and ethnic art examples to the work of Rodin. The formal and technical inspiration of the work is discussed in relation to Brancusi's acquaintance with Gauguin's relief *Hina and te Fatou* and André Derain's *Crouching Figure*.

1341. GOLDWATER, ROBERT JOHN. *Symbolism*. London: A. Lane, 1979. 286 p. 185 illus.

Traces the history of the Symbolist movement as a consistent evolution, beginning with Gauguin's revolutionary paintings of the 1880s and ending with the last outposts in Vienna, Holland, and Scotland.
a. U.S. ed.: New York: Harper & Row, 1979. 286 p., 185 illus.

1342. GORDON, JAN. *Modern French Painters*. New York: Dodd-Mead, 1923. 188 p., 39 illus., 18 col. pl.

Chapter 6, pp. 59-64, discusses Gauguin.
a. Reprints: 1926, 1929, 1936, 1938; Freeport, New York: Books for Libraries, 1970.
b. English ed.: London: Land, 1929.

1343. *Grand Collection of World Art*. Tokyo: Kodansha, 1974- . In Japanese.

Series which includes works by Gauguin. Lists owners in their original languages.

1344. HAUTECOEUR, LOUIS. *Littérature et peinture en France du XVIIe au XXe siècle*. Paris: A. Colin, 1942. 328 p., 50 pl.
a. 2nd ed.: Paris, 1963. 358 p., 50 pl.

1345. HERBERT, ROBERT L. *Seurat's Drawings*. New York: Shorewood, 1962. 194 p., illus., some col.

Includes observations about Seurat and Gauguin.
English ed.: London: Studio Vista, 1982. 194 p., illus., some col.

1346. HESS, WALTER. *Farbe in der modernen Malerei*. 1950.

Discusses Gauguin on pages 61-73.

1347. HESS, WALTER. *Das Problem der Farbe: In den Selbstzeugnissen der Maler von Cézanne bis Mondrian* [The Problem of Color: Statements by Painters from Cézanne to Mondrian]. Munich: Prestel, 1953. 194 p., illus.

Traces and interprets the struggle with the problem of color taken from texts by several late 19th and early 20th-century painters, including Gauguin.
a. 2nd ed.: Mittenwald: Mäander, 1981. 203 p., illus.

1348. HIND, CHARLES LEWIS. *The Post Impressionists*. London: Methuen, 1911. 94 p., illus., 23 pl.
a. U.S. reprint: Freeport, N.Y.: Books for Libraries Press, 1969.

1349. HODIN, J. P. *Edvard Munch, der Genius des Nordens*. Stockholm: Neuer Verlag, 1948. 140 p., 214 illus., 8 col. pl.
a. Another ed.: Berlin: F. Kupferberg, 1963. 214 p., illus., col. pl.

1350. HOFMANN, WERNER. *Das irdische Paradies; Kunst in neunzehnten Jahrhundert*. Münich. Prestel-Verlag, 1960. 411 p., 235 illus., 16 col. pl.

Mentions Gauguin's life and artistic output.
a. 2nd ed.: 1974. 306 p., illus.
b. English ed.: *The Earthly Paradise: Art in the Nineteenth Century*. Trans. by Brian Battershaw. London: Faber and Faber, 1961. 436 p. 234, illus., 16 col. pl.

c. U.S. ed.: New York: G. Braziller, 1961. 436 p.

1351. HOLMES, CHARLES JOHN. *Notes on the Post-Impressionist Painters, Grafton Galleries, 1910-11.* London: Philip Lee Warner, 1910. 40 p.

Impressions and criticism about post-Impressionism based on an exhibition at the Grafton Galleries in London, 1910-11. Comments on eight paintings by Gauguin.

1352. HUNEKER, JAMES GIBBONS. *Promenades of an Impressionist.* New York: C. Scribner's Sons, 1910.

Gauguin mentioned on pages 269-76.

1353. HUNEKER, JAMES GIBBONS. *Ivory, Apes and Peacocks.* New York: C. Scribner's Sons, 1932. 326 p.

This work on authors, poets, musicians, and artists includes a section on Gauguin.

1354. HUYSMANS, JORIS-KARL. *L'Art moderne.* Paris: G. Charpentier, 1883. 277 p.

Reprints articles by this art critic which first appeared in *Le Voltaire*, *La Réforme*, and the *Revue littéraire et artistique*. Covers important exhibitions in Paris from 1879-82. Mentions Gauguin's early exhibited paintings (see p. 264, for example).
a. Other eds.: Paris: P. V. Stock, 1902; Paris: Plon-Nourrit, 1908, 1911, and 1923, 301 p.; Paris: Union Générale d'Editions, 1975 and 1986. 337 p.
b. English ed.: Westmead, England: Gregg International, 1969. 277 p.

1355. *Ideas: Boletín de las Alianzas Francesas en México.* México: Alianzas Francesas, 1950. 27 p.

Mentions Gauguin.

1356. *The Impressionists and Some of their Contemporaries.* Basel: Editions Beyeler, 1970. 177 p., illus., col. pl.

Includes artists' statements and biographical notes on various French artists, including Gauguin.

1357. JOHNSON, RONALD. *The Early Sculpture of Picasso 1901-1914.* Ph.D. diss., University of California, Berkeley, 1971. New York: Garland, 1976. 248 p., 112 illus.

Studies Picasso's schooling under the influence of Gauguin and Rodin and his emergence as a sculptor, with reference to his work before the First World War. The general view that Picasso's painting is more innovative than his sculpture is challenged. Picasso's chosen themes, including blindness (linked to his "blue" period in the paintings) and jesters and pierrots (linked to the "rose" period) are discussed in detail. Picasso's change in style from that influenced by Rodin to that influenced by Gauguin is analyzed.

1358. KELDER, DIANE. *The Great Book of Post-Impressionism.* New York: Abbeville, 1986. 383 p., 413 illus., 236 col.

Gauguin, Bernard, and van Gogh are covered in Chapter 4, pp. 154-83.

1359. KLEIN, JEROME. *Modern Masters from Manet to Gauguin; Brief Histories of Their Artistic Development.* New York: Grosset & Dunlap, 1938. 28 p., illus., col. pl.

Information on Gauguin and reproductions of his work are contained on pages 24-28.

1360. KOESTLER, ARTHUR. "Farewell to Gauguin: A Joyless Traveller's Guide to the South Pacific" in *The Heel of Achilles; Essays 1968-1973*, pp. 173-82. London: Hutchinson, 1974.

1361. LAVER, JAMES. *French Painting and the Nineteenth Century.* London: R.T. Batsford, 1937. 120 p., 141 pl., some col.

Includes information on and reproductions by Gauguin.

1362. LEINZ, GOTTLIEB. *Die Malerei des 20, Jahrhunderts* [20th Century Painting]. Freiburg, Balse, Vienna: Herder, 1988. 380 p., 362 illus., 361 col.

Working on the principle of "comparative seeing," concentrates on the artists, groups and movements of the 20th century in chronological sequence, from Gauguin, Rousseau, van Gogh, Cézanne, Ensor and Munch through the Fauves. Expressionism, Cubism, Dadaism and Surrealism to Pop art, Beuys and the "Neue Wilden" are also discussed. The principles, developments and trends behind the changing face of art are set out in detail.

1363. LETHEVE, JACQUES. *Impressionnistes et symbolistes devant la presse.* Paris: Armand Colin, 1959. 302 p., illus.

Reprints contemporary criticism of Gauguin's paintings on pages 135-43.

1364. LIEDHOLM, ALF-ANTON FREDRICK. *Konstnärens värld. En studie i konstnärenspsykologi. I: Från Delacroix till Gauguin* [The Artist's World. A Study in the Artist's Psychology. From D. to G.]. Lund: 1932.

1365. *I Maestri del colore*. Milan: Fratelli Fabbri Editori, n.d.

1366. MAROIS, PIERRE. *Des goûts et des couleurs*. Introduction by André Lhôte. Paris: A. Michel, 1947. 189 p., pl.

1367. MAUCLAIR, CAMILLE. *Servitude et grandeur littéraires*. Paris: 1922.

1368. MICHAUD, GUY. *Message poétique du symbolisme*. Paris: Nizet, 1947. 3 vols.

1369. MUEHSAM, GERD, ed. *French Painters and Paintings from the Fourteenth Century to Post-Impression*. New York: Ungar, 1970. 646 p., 158 illus.

Pages 537-52 discuss Gauguin. Includes a brief biography and excerpts of letters and criticism from contemporaries.

1370. MULLER, JOSEPH-EMILE. *Fauvism*. New York, Washington D.C.: Frederick A. Praeger, 1967. 260 p., illus.

Includes research and quotations concerning color theory by Gauguin and others.

1371. MULLINS, EDWIN, ed. *Great Paintings in Themes of: The Magic of Light, the Language of Colour, Adoration, The Elements, Hunting, War, Cities, Touch, Bathing, Outdoor Life*. London: British Broadcasting Corporation, 1981. 344 p., 307 illus.

Based on the television series "100 Great Paintings," this book shares its aim which is the examination of a single painting at a time with a view to exploring it in depth with the aid of supplementary pictures where relevant. Analyses of Gauguin's paintings are included in the "Language of Colour" chapter.
a. U.S. ed.: New York: St. Martin's Press, 1981. 344 p., illus.

1372. NASGAARD, ROALD. *Willumsen and Symbolist Art, 1888-1910*. Ph.D. diss., New York University, 1973. 463 p., illus.

Examines the Danish artist J. F. Willumsen in the context of international Symbolist art. Willumsen is shown to have been fostered by the same 1880s realism which dominated European centres outside

Paris, and to have been influenced at first by the French avant garde, particularly Gauguin, Pissarro and Seurat.

1373. NATANSON, THADEE. *Peints à leur tour.* Paris: Albin Michel, 1948. 388 p. 32 pl.

Essay on Gauguin on pages 79-85.

1374. NOCHLIN, LINDA. "Eroticism and Female Imagery in Nineteenth-Century Art" in *Woman as Sex Object: Studies in Erotic Art, 1730-1970.* Thomas B. Hess and Linda Nochlin, eds. New York: *Art News Annual* 38(1972). 257 p., illus., col. pl.

Gauguin mentioned on pages 9-15.

1375. NOVOTNY, FRITZ. *Die grossen französischen Impressionisten--Ihre Vorläufer und ihre Nachfolger.* Vienna: Anton Schroll, 1952. 67 p., illus. col. pl.

1376. OPPLER, ELLEN CHARLOTTE. *Fauvism Reexamined.* Ph.D. diss., Columbia University; New York, London: Garland, 1976. 413 p., 112 illus.

Argues that the Fauves were not the embattled revolutionaries of popular story. They admired rather than rejected Impressionism and they had been studying the work of Gauguin and Cézanne long before the alleged impact of 1907. Draws on primary sources (including French newspapers, literary texts, and pictorial materials) and places the movement within the larger cultural and historical context. Documents the contradictory aspects of Fauvism, analyzes its stylistic tranformations in relation to Impressionist and post-Impressionist traditions, and explains the artistic and personal reasons for its brief life span.

1377. PAYRO, JULIO E. *Héroes del color: vida, obra, teorías y gravitación de los maestros postimpresionistas fundadores del arte contemporáneo.* Florida: Librería "El Ateneo" Editorial, 1951. 197 p., 28 pl., 11 col. pl.

Discussion of the post-Impressionists, including Gauguin.
a. 2nd ed.: *Cézanne, Gauguin, Van Gogh y Seurat; los héroes del color y su tiempo.* Buenos Aires: Nova, 1963. 199 p., 12 col. pl.

1378. PLATTE, HANS. *Die Maler des grossen Lichtes: Meisterwerke der französischen Malerei des 19. Jahrhunderts* [The Painters of the Great Light: Masterpieces of 19th-Century French Painting]. Braunschweig: Westermann, 1967. 191 p., illus., 83 pl.

a. English ed.: Diane Kelder, *The French Impressionists and Their Century*. London: Pall Mall Press, 1970.

1379. PRESTON, STUART. "Gauguin" in *Les peintres célèbres*. Bernard Dorival, ed. Geneva: L. Mazenod, 1948. 423 p., illus.

Gauguin is discussed on pages 300-03.

1380. PUY, MICHEL. *L'effort des peintures modernes*. Paris: A. Messein, 1933. 158 p.

1381. RAPHAEL, MAX. *Von Monet zu Picasso: Grundzüge einer Asthetik und Entwicklung der modernen Malerei* [From Monet to Picasso: Characteristics of an Aesthetic and the Development of Modern Painting]. Foreword by Klaus Binder. Munich: Delphin-Verlag, 1913. 130 p., pl.

Traces the development of modernism from Impressionism through post-Impressionism, focusing in part on paintings by Gauguin.
a. Other eds.: Munich: Delphin-Verlag, 1913. 127 p., pl.; Frankfurt-am-Main, Paris: Qumran, 1983. 219 p., illus.

1382. READ, HERBERT EDWARD. *The Philosophy of Modern Art*. New York: Horizon Press, 1952. 309 p.

Includes an essay on Gauguin's color theory.

1383. READ, HERBERT EDWARD. *The Tenth Muse: Essays in Criticism*. London: Routledge and Kegan Paul, 1957. 300 p., pl.

Includes essays on Gauguin, Gabo, Wright, Hepworth, DeStijl, Sutherland, and Kokoschka.

1384. REFF, THEODORE. *Degas: The Artist's Mind*. New York: The Metropolitan Museum of Art; Harper & Row, 1976. 352 p.

Biography and critical analysis of Degas which includes references to Gauguin (see index).
a. English ed.: London: Thames and Hudson, 1976. 352 p.
b. Another ed.: Cambridge, Mass.: Belknap Press of Harvard University Press, 1987.

1385. REWALD, JOHN. *The History of Impressionism*. New York: The Museum of Modern Art, 1946. 474 p., illus., col. pl.

Classic study and guide to resources. Gauguin information is mostly in chapters 12-15.

a. Other eds.: 2nd, 1955; 3rd, 1961; 4th, 1973, 1980.
b. German ed.: Köln: DuMont, 1979.

1386. REY, ROBERT. *La Renaissance du sentiment classique dans la peinture française à la fin du XIXe siècle.* Paris: Les Beaux-Arts, 1931. 162 p., 33 pl.

Part III deals with Gauguin's life and art. Argues that he drew inspiration from the classical past and from Poussin, Ingres, Delacroix, and Corot.

1387. RIVIERE, JACQUES. *Etudes.* Paris: Nouvelle Revue Française, 1911. 264 p.

Gauguin is mentioned on pages 52-57, in an essay written in 1910.

1388. ROGER-MARX, CLAUDE. *Maîtres d'hier et d'aujourd'hui.* Paris: Calmann-Lévy, 1914. 342 p.

Includes a chapter on Gauguin, pp. 323-33.

1389. ROH, FRANZ. *Der verkannte Künstler. Studien zur Geschichte und Theorie des kulturellen Missverstehens* [The Misinterpreted Artist. Studies in the History and Theory of Cultural Misunderstanding]. Munich: Ernst Heimeran, 1948. 403 p.

See pages 280-92 for information on Gauguin.

1390. ROSTRUP, HAAVARD. *Franske Billedhuggere fra det 19. og 20. Aarhundrede* [French Sculptors of the 19th and 20th Centuries]. Copenhagen: Levin & Munksgaard, 1938. 80 p., illus.

1391. ROSTRUP, HAAVARD. *Histoire du Musée d'Ordrupgaard 1918-1978: d'après des documents inédits.* Copenhagen: Gyldendal, 1981. 103 p., 42 illus., 24 col. In Danish. Summary in French and English.

Gives the history of one of the best collections of French and Danish art from the 19th century in Scandinavia (Delacroix, Corot, Courbet, Manet, Pissarro, Monet, Sisley, Degas, Cézanne, Gauguin, Matisse etc.). The founder, Wilhelm Hansen, was an insurance magnate and a great art collector. Hansen's collection is now a state museum.

1392. RUDEL, JEAN. *Panorama des arts.* Introduction by René Huyghe. Paris: L. Amiel, 1974.

General survey of the history and development of art. Devotes a chapter to Gauguin and the Nabis.
a. English ed.: *Panorama of the Arts: From Megaliths to Op Art*. London: Harrap, 1974. 200 p., 758 illus.

1393. RUSAKOVA, A. A., comp. *Borisov-Musatov*. Leningrad: Aurora Art Publishers, 1975. 224 p., 65 col. illus. In English, French, and Russian.

Covers the carreer of the Russian symbolist painter Viktor Borisov-Musatov (1870-1905) and includes several works not previously reproduced in color. The introduction summarizes the artist's life, and mentions his interest in Gauguin, Denis, and others.

1394. RUTTER, F. *Revolution in Art*. London: 1910.

1395. SCOTTI, ROLAND. *Kunst + Dokumentation 9 in der Internationalen Kunst-Ausstellung 1907 in Mannheim*. [Art + Documentation 9 in the International Art Exhibition 1907 in Mannheim]. Mannheim: Städtische Kunsthalle, 1985. 90 p., 79 illus.

Analysis of the International Art Exhibition held in Mannheim in 1907, with the intention not of reconstructing the exhibition but of elucidating certain details that have previously remained unclear, or that can be seen to have been of particular significance in determining subsequent developments in 20th century art. Traces the history to the exhibition and surveys the range of exhibited paintings, including works by Gauguin.

1396. SIMON, M. *Post-Impressionists*. New York: Wood Books, 1980. 36 p., 13 illus.

Discussion of the post-Impressionist movement, followed by sections on 12 painters, including Gauguin. Biographical sketch, analysis of the artist's oeuvre, and commentary on a selected illustrated work are included.

1397. SOFFICI, ARDENGO. *Rete mediterranea*. Florence, 1920

Gauguin is discussed on pp. 364-65.

1398. SOFFICI, ARDENGO. *Trenta artisti moderni italiani e stranieri*. Florence: Vallecchi, 1950. 393 p., 189 illus.

1399. STEIN, MEIR. *Idé og Form; Fransk Kunst: Fra Barok til Impressionisme* [Idea and Form in French Art: From Baroque to

Impressionism]. Copenhagen: Krohns Bogrykkeri, 1981. 263 p., 66 illus.

Studies French art and its national character. Discusses Gauguin's *Noa Noa*.

1400. THOMSON, BELINDA. *The Post-Impressionists*. Oxford: Phaidon, 1983. 192 p., 180 illus.

Reappraisal of the term and period of post-Impressionism. States that the last 20 years of the 19th century did not produce a coherent school of artists whose work grew directly out of Impressionism. Concludes that the period must be judged for its diversity as well as for its richness. Gauguin is viewed as a temporary hero with a unique style, but not an altogether suitable model.
a. U.S. eds.: Secaucus, N.J.: Chartwell, 1983; New York: Universe Books, 1990.

1401. VENTURI, LIONELLO. *La via dell' Impressionismo da Manet a Cézanne*. Introduction by Nello Ponente. Torini: Giulio Einaudi, 1970. 327 p., 201 pl.

1402. WELSH, ROBERT P. *Revue de l'art*. 1988.

1403. WERTH, LEON. *Quelques peintres*. Paris: G. Crès, 1923. 214 p., 12 pl.

Includes a chapter on Gauguin, pages 85-89.

1404. WHITE, BARBARA EHRLICH, ed. *Impressionism in Perspective*. Englewood Cliffs, N.J.: Prentice-Hall, 1978. 165 p., 26 illus., pl.

1405. WILENSKI, REGINALD HOWARD. *French Painting*. London: The Medici Society, 1931. 350 p., 156 pl., 12 col.

Discusses Gauguin on pages 288-95.
a. Other eds.: 1937, 1949
b. U.S. eds.: Boston: Hale, Cushman & Flint, 1936; Boston: C.T. Branford, 1949; New York: Dover, 1973.

1406. WILENSKI, REGINALD HOWARD. *Modern French Painters*. London: Faber & Faber, 1940. 424 p., 96 illus.

Includes a biography and critical analysis of Gauguin.
a. Other eds.: 1944, 1947, 1963.

b. American eds.: New York: Reynal & Hitchcock, 1940; New York: Harcourt, Brace 1949, 1954, 1963. New York: Vintage Books, 1960.

1407. ZERVOS, CHRISTIAN. *Histoire de l'art contemporain.* Paris: Cahiers d'Art, 1938. 447 p., illus.

Mentions Gauguin's life, style, and artistic contributions.

B. Articles

1408. BENDER, B. "Hanging Stephen Crane in the Impressionist Museum." *Journal of Aesthetics and Art Criticism* 35: 1 (Fall 1976): 47-55.

Argues that analogies between literature and painting are particularly misleading if made in terms of technique. In Crane's case, his personal association with painters and the desire of commentators to find historical parallels between the arts have led to his characterization as a "literary impressionist." Such parallels are treacherous and in this case misconceived. If analogies with painters must be made, they could more aptly be made with van Gogh and Gauguin, whose uses of color are comparable to Crane's visual evocations for symbolism.

1409. BIERMANN, GEORGE. "Das Stilleben in der deutschen und franzosischen Malerei" [Still Life in German and French Painting]. *Cicerone* (1927):148-53.

1410. BLANCHE, JACQUES-EMILE. "L'exposition de l'art français à Londres, 1932; le XIXe siècle." *Gazette des Beaux-Arts* (Jan. 1932):77-96.

1411. BURGESS, GELETT. "The Wild Men of Paris." *The Architectural Record* 27(May 1910):401-14.

1412. BURROUGHS, ALAN. "Making History of Impressionism." *The Arts* 1(1921):16-23.

1413. CHIRICO, ROBERT. "Cave to Café: Artists' Gatherings." *Arts Magazine* 55:1(Sept. 1980):100-03. 10 illus.

Whereas the artist has often been studied as a creator of designs for public festivities, this essay is a very broad summary of the private celebrations given by and for artists themselves. Explores the variety of gatherings, including Gauguin's farewell dinner in a Paris café in 1891.

1414. CLARK, ELIOT. "Considerations on Modernistic Aesthetics." *Art in America* 9(1921):210-20.

Mentions Gauguin's *Maternity*.

1415. COGNIAT, RAYMOND. "Le retour à la terre latine." *L'Amour de l'art* 14(1933):171.

1416. CORK, R. "Postmortem on Post-Impressionism." *Art in America* 68(Oct. 1980):90-94.

1417. DAULTE, M. "Larionov et l'art néo-primitif russe." *Oeil* (Switzerland) 287(June 1979):44-51. 15 illus.

Stresses the importance of Gauguin, Matisse and Douanier Rousseau for Larionov.

1418. DAVIS, F. "Talking about Salerooms: The Slick and the Tender." *Country Life* 160(2 Sept. 1976):586-87.

1419. DESARROIS, ANDRE. "L'art français à Londres." *Revue de l'art ancien et moderne* 61(Feb. 1932):73-104.

1420. DIEGO, ELISEO. "Por los extraños pueblos y otros poemas." *Ciudad hispanoamericanas* 15(1950):457-63.

Poetry of a Cuban poet illustrated with a painting by Gauguin.

1421. DUNSTAN, B. "Looking at Paintings." *American Artist* 46[44](Aug. 1980):56-57.

1422. FRANCE, S. "Modern French Painting: Collecting in the 1920s." *Apollo* 115:242(April 19820:276-81. 16 illus.

In March, 1921 an exhibition, *Paintings by Modern French Masters: The Post Impressionists and their Predecessors* opened at the Brooklyn Museum, New York and was of great significance for the museum's own collection of French painting. Describes the process of acquisition of several French paintings, including works by Gauguin.

1423. FISCHEL, L. "Von der Bildform der franzosischen Impressionisten." *Jahrbuch der Berliner Museen* 15(1973):58-154.

1424. FOCILLON, HENRI. "Les Salons de 1926, I. Trente ans d'art indépendant." *Gazette des Beaux-Arts* 13(May 1926):257-80.

1425. FORGES, M. T. DE "Un Nouveau tableau de Puvis de Chavannes au Musée du Louvre: *Jeunes filles au bord de la mer* panneau décoratif." *Revue du Louvre* 20:4-5(1970):252.

1426. FORWOOD, GILLIAN. "Roger Kemp and the Example of Rupert Bunny." *Art and Australia* 24:3(Autumn 1987): p. 357-63. 9 illus., 4 col.

Deals with the influence of the painter Rupert Bunny on Australian artist Roger Kemp in the 1930s. Bunny acted as a conduit for European avant-garde influence on Kemp. Examines Bunny's work and its debt to Gauguin, music, and ballet.

1427. "Gauguin." *Carreau* (Lausanne) 3(Feb. 1950):3.

1428. GEORGE, W. "Cent ans de peinture française." *L'Amour de l'art* 3(1922):101-04.

1429. GEORGE, W. "Paris Letter." *Creative Art* 8(April 1931):285. See also *Apollo* 19(1934):210.

1430. GERSTEIN, MARC SAUL. "Degas' Fans." *Art Bulletin* 64:1(1982):105-18.

1431. GOLDWATER, ROBERT J. "Some Aspects of the Development of Seurat's Style." *Art Bulletin* 23(June 1941):117-30.

1432. GOLDWATER, ROBERT J. "The Genesis of a Picture: Theme and Form in Modern Painting." *Critique* 1(Oct. 1946):5-12.

1433. GORDON, JAN. "Common Sense and Contemporary Art." *The Studio* 127(1944):1-12.

1434. GREET, ANNE HYDE. "Conversations in Arcady: Vergil, Maillol and Kessler, *Eclogues* I, II, V and VI." *World & Image* (U.K.) 3:4(Oct.-Dec. 1987):225-47. 13 illus.

In 1908, Aristide Maillol and his patron Count Harry Kessler agreed to collaborate on an illustrated edition of Vergil's *Ecologues*. The typography chosen for the bilingual edition was a Jenson roman, reflecting Kessler's admiration for William Morris. The team chosen by Kessler to produce the book was international, showing the European humanist spirit which pervaded the venture. Maillol's woodcuts show the influence of various artists, but chiefly Puvis de Chavannes and Gauguin.

1435. HAMILTON, GEORGE HEARD. "The Philosophical Implications of Impressionist Landscape Painting." *Houston Museum of Fine Arts Bulletin* 6:1(Spring 1975):2-17. 9 illus.

1436. HAMMACHER, A. M. "Vlucht mit de Beschoving." *Kronich von Kunst en Kultur* 9(1948):252-54.

1437. HAUTECOEUR, LOUIS. "La conception de la nature chez les artistes modernes." *Gazette des Beaux-Arts* (Nov. 1936):176-87).

Mentions Gauguin's *Landscape in Brittany* (1890).

1438. HERBERT, ROBERT L. "Seurat in Chicago and New York." *Burlington Magazine* 100(1958):146-55.

1439. HERBERT, ROBERT L. "City vs. Country: The Rural Image in French Painting from Millet to Gauguin." *Artforum* 8(Feb. 1970):44-55.

1440. HERRMANN, CURT. "Der Kampf um den Stil" [The Struggle for Style]. *Kunst und Kunstler* (1910-11):102-05.

1441. HUNEKER, JAMES GIBBONS. "Masters of Hallucination: Kubin, Munch, Gauguin." *New York Times* (11May 1913):13.

Discusses the works of these three artists shown at the Armory show in New York in 1913.

1442. HUYGHE, RENE. "Les origines de la peinture contemporaine: genèse et position de l'art moderne." *L'Amour de l'art* 14(1933):7-16.

1443. IVES, COLTA FELLER. "French Prints in the Era of Impressionism and Symbolism." *The Metropolitan Museum of Art Bulletin* 46(Summer 1988):4-57.

1444. JAMOT, PAUL. "L'art français en Norvège." *La Renaissance de l'art français* 12(1929):68-106.

1445. JAMOT, PAUL. "French Painting, I and II." *Burlington Magazine* 59:345(Dec. 1931):267-322; 60:346(Jan. 1932):3-72.

1446. JOHNSON, RONALD. "Primitivism in the Early Sculpture of Picasso." *Arts Magazine* 49:10(June 1975):64-68. 15 illus.

Primitivism in the early sculpture of Picasso drew heavily on Gauguin as well as primitive sculpture from the South Seas and ancient Iberia.

1447. JOHNSON, RONALD. "The Demoiselles d'Avignon and Dionysian Destruction." *Arts Magazine* 55:2(Oct. 1980):94-101.

First of a two-part essay examining the cultural and conceptual context of Picasso's violent masterpiece, *Demoiselles d'Avignon* (1906). Claims that the painting is indebted to the conceptions of Cézanne and the ambiance of primitivism Picasso absorbed from Gauguin.

1448. JONES, H. "Sur les origines de l'expressionnisme en peinture." *Vie des arts* (Canada) 27:108 (Autumn 1982):p. 16-18. 5 illus.

"Expressionism" is here defined, after W. Wundt's *Psychologie Physiologique* (1908), as a concern not with the object perceived, as in Impressionism, but with the subject who perceives it. The roots of Expressionist painting are traced throughout Europe, with the main focus on the 19th century. Precursors discussed, who tend towards the caricatural and the tragic, include: Goya, Daumier and Hogarth; Manet and Naturalism; van Gogh and, to a lesser extent, Gauguin.

1449. KOZLOFF, M. "The Anatomy of Disruption: European and American Painting 1880-1906." *Artforum* 19:4(Dec. 1980):p. 62-69. 12 illus.

Panoramic survey of the motivating concepts, themes and pictorial means in post-Impressionist painting in Europe and the U.S. from 1880 to 1906, in which the author aims to reveal the attitudes the artists sought to discard and the new ideals they replaced them with. Individual artists discussed include Gauguin.

1450. LANGE, ELEONARE H. "Portraiture Through the Ages." *Art in Australia* 4:1(1914):10-22.

1451. LARSON, PHILIP. "Brücke Primitivism: The Early Landscape Woodcuts." *Print Collector's Newsletter* 6:3(July-Aug. 1975):61-64. 4 illus.

Argues that Brücke woodcuts during 1909 to 1913 extend the inventions of Gauguin and Munch to their limit.

1452. LASCAULT, GILBERT. "Kinjo, and the Eye of the Elephant." *Cimaise* 36(June-Aug. 1989):73-84.

Discusses Ladislas Kinjo's painting "Retour à Tahiti: Hommage à Gauguin."

1453. LASSEN, ERIK. "Nyere Dansk Keramisk Kunst" [Recent Danish Ceramic Art]. *Keramik* (Copenhagen, 1956):356.

1454. LAUKOMSKI, GEORGES. "Les musées d'état et l'activité artistique dans la Russie nouvelle." *La Revue de l'art ancien et moderne* 47(1925):247-56.

1455. LEBLOND, MARIUS-ARY. "Les idées nouvelles sur le romantisme." *Mercure de France* 75(1908):561-78.

1456. LETHEVE, JACQUES. "La connaissance des peintres préraphaélites anglais en France." *Gazette des Beaux-Arts* 53(May-June, 1959):315-28.

1457. LORD, DOUGLAS. "The Impressionists at the Palais des Beaux Arts, Brussels." *Burlington Magazine* 67(Aug. 1936):84-88.

Mentions Gauguin's *D'où venons-nous*? cycle.

1458. MANSON, J. B. "Two Modern French Painters." *Apollo* 5(1927):32.

1459. MARTENSEN-LARSEN, BRITTA. "Folkekunstens betydning før Kandinsky: med henblik på hans mobler i bondestil" [The Importance of Folk Art for Kandinsky, with Reference to his Peasant-Style Furniture]. *Cras: Tidsskrift før Kunst og Kultur* 35(1983):80-94. 14 illus. In Danish.

On Kandinsky's interest in folk art, especially Bavarian glass paintings, during the years 1909-16. Discusses Kandinsky's contact with Russian folk art, Dutch national costume, Persian art, Oriental art, ethnic art, and the art of Gauguin.

1460. MASHECK, JOSEPH. "The Carpet Paradigm: Critical Progomena to a Theory of Flatness." *Art Magazine* 51:1(Sept. 1976):82-109. 16 illus.

1461. MATHIEU, P. L. "Huysmans, inventeur de l'impressionnisme." *Oeil* (Switzerland) 341(Dec. 1983):43-44.

1462. MCGEE, C. "Daniel Brennan: A Fantasy World Exploding with Color." *Southwest Art* 11:4(Sept. 1981):102-7. 9 illus.

Citing statements made by Brennan in an interview, the author describes his painting background in Kansas and his approach to his art which blossomed after a journey to México. Brennan's style was influenced by Gauguin, among others.

1463. METKEN, S. "Die verkehrte Welt; Wenn Bilderbogen Kunst anregen" [The Topsy-Turvy World; When Picture-Sheets Inspire Art]. *Kunstwerk* 24(Sept. 1971):4.

1464. NEFF, JOHN HALLMARK. "Matisse and Decoration: The Shchukin Panel." *Art in America* 63:4(July-Aug. 1975):38-48. 19 illus. (5 col.).

Comments on Gauguin's influence, underestimated according to the author, on Matisse.

1465. NEVE, C. "Garden-City Fretwork: Spencer Frederick Gore (1878-1914)." *Country Life* 173:4461(17 Feb. 1983): p. 378-79. 4 illus.

Though Spencer Gore appeared to be an unambitious and popular member of the Camden Town Group in London, the author claims that his painting became far more advanced than that of his fellow members. From 1912 until his death, Gore was freed of their inhibiting influences and produced boldly drawn and coloured pictures of landscapes and towns, releasing his own long-felt admiration for Fauvsim, Gauguin and Kandinsky.

1466. ORMOND, LEONEE. "The Soames Forsyte Collection: a Study in Fictional Taste." *Burlington Magazine* 119:896 (Nov. 1977):752-56. 4 illus.

Soames Forsyte, the central figure of John Galsworthy's novel sequence, *The Forsyte Saga*, is a picture collector, and the article is a study of this aspect of the novels, concentrating on Soames' collection of French 19th and early 20th century paintings. Soames is shown to be a remarkably astute and far-sighted collector, and his purchases of Gauguin, Matisse and Picasso in particular, are placed in the context of contemporary taste. Soames is compared to other collectors, including Sir Hugh Lane and Samuel Courtauld.

1467. "Personalities of the Modern Movement." *London Studio 5, Studio* 105(April 1933):230.

1468. PETERSEN, CARL V. Article in *Afhandlinger* (1939):253-67.

1469. POPE, KAREN KRISTINE RECHNITZER. "SR Fashion." *Saturday Review* 10(Nov./Dec. 1984):103-07.

1470. POULAIN, GASTON. "Faut-il croire?" *Comoedia* 16(6 July 1934).

1471. PRAT, V. "Extrait du roman d'un collectionneur." *Connaissance des arts* 358 (Dec. 1981):102-07. 7 illus.

Brief insights into the life and activities of collector Jacques Dubourg, who died on April 3, 1981, indicating the extent of his work as a dealer and exhibition organizer, and his friendships with artists--especially Nicolas de Staël. Remarks on some highlights of Dubourg's collection of over 600 works, including paintings by Gauguin.

1472. RATCLIFF, C. "In Detail: Matisse's *Dance*." *Portfolio* 4(July-Aug. 1981):38-45.

Notes that in both versions of *Dance*, Matisse reinvents one of Western painting's most powerful themes--a pastoral setting that is itself an art historical convention which originated in Classical times and was revived by Renaissance humanists. Modernist precedents were Gauguin's Tahitian arcadies, and van Gogh's attempts to see a golden age in the golden wheat fields of Provence. Like Matisse, both drew on Puvis de Chavannes.

1473. REBERSCHAK, S. F. "Un sogno incollato sui muri" [A dream stuck on the walls]. *Bolaffiarte* (Italy) 11:96(March 1980):48-51. 6 illus.

Discussion of the art nouveau poster artist, Alphonse Mucha (1860-1939), on the occasion of an exhibition of his work at the Musée d'Orsay, Paris. Notes particularly the artist's exclusive contract to design theatre posters for the actress Sarah Bernhardt, and his successful career in both Paris and his native Czechoslovakia. Also briefly describes some of the influences on Mucha's carreer, including Japanese prints, Gauguin's cloisonnisme and symbolist theories.

1474. REDLOW, THEODOR. "George Stefanescu." *Arta* (Romania) 35:3(1988):10-11. In Roumanian. 8 illus. (5 col.)

Short consideration of the work of Roumanian painter George Stefanescu, whose jovial calm is reflected in his style, which also shows the influence of neo-primitivism and early modernists like Gauguin and van Gogh.

1475. REFF, THEODORE. "Pissarro's Portrait of Cézanne." *Burlington Magazine* 109:776(Nov. 1967):627-33.

1476. REFF, THEODORE. "Degas: A Master among Masters." *Metropolitan Museum of Art Bulletin* 34:4(Spring 1977):29+.

1477. REWALD, JOHN. "Camille Pissarro; His Work and Influence." *Burlington Magazine* 72(June, 1938):280-90.

Discusses Gauguin's *La route à Osny*.

1478. REWALD, JOHN. "Modern Fakes of Modern Pictures." *Art News* 52(March 1953):17-18.

1479. REWALD, JOHN. "Theo van Gogh, Goupil, and the Impressionists." *Gazette des Beaux-Arts* 6th ser., 81(Jan.-Feb. 1973):1-108. Reprinted in Rewald, 1986:7-115.

1480. ROGER-MARX, CLAUDE. "L'organisation du tableau et la mémoire visuelle chez Vuillard." *Arts* (7 Sept. 1945):3.

1481. ROI, V. "Era il nostro van Gogh: geniale e folle" [He was our van Gogh: genial and crazy]. *Arte* (Italy) 14:143(July-Aug. 1984): p. 34-41, 103. 7 illus.

Traces Gino Rossi's artistic career, stressing the impact of van Gogh's and Gauguin's work, of the Fauves, of the Viennese secession, and later of Cézanne and the Cubists on his development.

1482. ROMM, A. "Les tendances dominantes dans la sculpture occidentale contemporaine." *Iskusstvo* 2(1936):125-150. In Russian, French summary, p. 186.

1483. ROWLANDS, J. "Treasures of a Connoisseur: The César de Hauke Bequest." *Apollo* 88(July 1968):50.

1484. SAURE, WOLFGANG. "Hohe Tradition und das Klassische: das Werk von André Derain" [High Tradition and the Classical: the Work of André Derain]. *Kunst* 7(July 1987):580-86. 9 col. illus.

Traces Derain's development from his early contact with Matisse in Paris and his visit to London in 1906 to his mature style of painting, in which he represents living forms rather than reproducing them, and his stage designs. The influence of Turner, Gauguin, Cézanne and van Gogh is described, as well as the main events of Derain's life and the central contrast between the fascinations which the avant-garde and ancient art exerted on him.

1485. "Selbstbildnis, Moskau, Museum Moderner Kunst. Abt. Schtachuken. Ea Haere ia oe. Moskau. Museum Moderner Kunst. Abt. Morosoff" [Self-Portraits in the Moscow Museum of Modern Art]. *Cicerone* 16: 19(Sept. 1924): 903-04, 907-08, 911.

1486. SERRITSLEV PETERSEN, LISE. "Baudelaire, Ingres og begrebet om skoenhed" [Baudelaire, Ingres and the Idea of Beauty]. *Cras: Tidsskrift før Kunst og Kultur* 35(1983):72-79. 3 illus. In Danish.

Presents an examination of Baudelaire's attitude towards the art of Ingres. Baudelaire's characterization of Ingres's draughtsmanship is compared to a passage about Cimabue and Ingres in Gauguin's *Racontars d'un rapin* manuscript.

1487. SHAPIRO, BARBARA and MICHEL MELOT. "Les monotypes de Camille Pissarro." *Nouvelles de l'estampe* 19(Jan.-Feb. 1975):16-17.

1488. SHIKES, RALPH E. and STEVEN HELLER. "The Art of Satire: Painters as Caricaturists and Cartoonists." *Print Review* 19(1984):8-125.

Mentions Gauguin's *Soyez symboliste* and *Magot de la Guadeloupe*.

1489. SILL, L. M. "Paris Notes." *American Magazine of Art* 21 (Nov. 1930):665-66.

1490. THORNTON, ALFRED and RONALD GORDON. "Art in Relation to Life-I." *Burlington Magazine* 39(July 1921):23-28.

Mentions Gauguin's *D'où venons-nous*? cycle.

1491. TRINTZIUS, RENE. "Les Trésors de la ville Musée ou 'Prenez garde à la peinture!'" *Journal de Rouen* (28 June 1932):2.

1492. VALSECCHI, MARCO. "Su existencia fué un largo viaje." *Cultura Peruana* 13(Dec. 1953):44-46.

1493. VERNON, M. and M. L. BAUGHMAN. "Art Madness, and Human Interaction." *Art Journal* 31:4(Summer 1972):416.

1494. VITRY, PAUL. "L'art français en Scandinavie." *Beaux-Arts* (1926):155-56.

1495. WALKER, JOHN A. "Art and the Peasantry." *Art & Artists* 13(Jan. 1979):26-35.

1496. WATKINS, C. LOW. "Emotional Design in Painting." *Magazine of Art* 33(1940):280-87.

1497. WATSON, E. W. "Borrowings of the Masters." *American Artist* 24(Feb. 1966):40-42.

1498. WEBB, GEOFFREY. "Ingres to Cézanne." *Burlington Magazine* 46(1925):286-88.

1499. WERNER, ALFRED. "Artists who Write." *Art Journal* 24:4(Summer 1965):344-47.

1500. WERNICK, R. "Opening the Door to the Art of the 20th Century." *Smithsonian* 19(May 1988):58-66+.

1501. YOUNG, M. S. "Letter from U.S.A." *Apollo* 87(June 1968):472.

1502. YOUNG, V. "Report from Copenhagen." *Arts Magazine* 32(March 1958):24.

XIX. Films, Videos, Recordings and Other Media

1503. DAGMAR-HENNING DAM KARGAARD. *The Wolf at the Door*. Copenhagen, 1986. 102 min., sound, color. 16 mm. In French and Danish.

Film which concentrates on the final Parisian period in the artist's life, from September, 1893 to June, 1895, beginning with his return to Paris from Tahiti and ending with his trip back to the tropics. Finding no critical success in Paris, and dejected by a series of failed love relationships, Gauguin decided to return to the islands. *Wolf at the Door* was released in 1986 in Copenhagen and was entered in the Venice Film Festival. It was released in the U.S. in 1987. Directed and produced by Henning Carlsen, it stars Donald Sutherland as Gauguin, Valarie Merea as Annah-la-Javanaise, Max von Sydow as August Strindberg, Sofie Grabol as Judith Molard, and Merete Voldstedlund as Mette Gauguin.

1504. DANIELSSON, BENGT. *Gauguin in Tahiti: The Search for Paradise*. New York: CBS News, 1967. 54 min., sound, color. 16mm.

Study of the life and art of Paul Gauguin which examines why he went to the South Pacific and how his painting was influenced by what he found there. Based on Danielsson's book *Gauguin's Söderhavsår* (1964), translated *Gauguin in the South Seas* (1965). Originally telecast as a CBS News special on June 6, 1967.

1505. HOME VISION. *Paul Gauguin: Te Oviri Rerioa. The Savage Dream*. Chicago: Home Vision, 1988. A Malone Gill producttion in association with the National Gallery of Art, Washington D.C. 45 min., sound, color. Video cassette (VHS), 1/2 inch.

Portrays Gauguin's search for a "savage" alternative to his own culture in the islands of the South Pacific.

1506. KARDOS, ISTVAN. *Noa Noa (after Gauguin). For Violin, Viola, Violoncello.* Hastings-on-Hudson, NY: General Music Publishing Co., 1973. 3 p. Musical score for three parts, 6-minutes in duration.

1507. MAZIERE, FRANCIS. *The Gauguin Years; Songs & Dances of Tahiti.* New York: Nonesuch, 196- . Program notes by Jane Sarnoff. Recorded on location. 45 min., sound disc, 33 1/3 rpm, stereo, 12 inch.

Exhibitions

I. Individual Exhibitions During Gauguin's Lifetime (1884-1903)
II. Group Exhibitions Before His Death in which Gauguin Participated (1876-1903)
III. Retrospective and Individual Exhibitions After Gauguin's Death (May 8, 1903)
IV. Group Exhibitions After Gauguin's Death (1903)

I. Individual Exhibitions During Gauguin's Lifetime (1884-1903)

1884, Autumn	Christiania [Oslo], Norway. *Kunstudstillingen* [Fine Arts Exhibition]. 2 paintings, 2 watercolors.
1885, April	Copenhagen, 51 Nørregade. *Exhibition of the Society of the Friends of Art*. Private exhibition closed after five days by order of the Academy. See Gauguin's letter to Emile Schuffenecker, 24 May 1885 (Malingue, ed. *Letters*, 22).
1887, November	Paris, Galerie Boussod & Valadon (Goupil's) 19 bd. Montmartre. Ceramics.
1888, early November	Paris, Galerie Boussod & Valadon (Goupil's), 19 bd. Montmartre, organized by Theo van Gogh. First one-man show. Works on exhibit throughout the year and exhibition in the basement in November. Ceramic works and paintings from Brittany and Martinique. See Merete Bodelsen, "An Unpublished Letter by Theo van Gogh," *Burlington Magazine* 99:651 (June 1957):198-202.

1889-90	Paris, Galerie Boussod et Valadon (Goupil's), 19 bd. Montmartre. Works on exhibit throughout these years.
1889, 31 October-11 November	Copenhagen, Kunstforeningen [Society of the Friends of Art]. *Nordiske og Franske Impressionister* [Scandinavian and French Impressionists]. See Havaard Rostrup, *Meddelselser fra Ny Carlsberg Glyptotek* 13 (1956):72.
1891, 22-23 February	Paris, Hôtel Drouot, exhibition-sale. 30 paintings. *Catalogue d'une vente de 30 tableaux de Paul Gauguin.* (Paris: Grande Imprimerie, 1891). Catalogue preface by Octave Mirbeau. See also *L'Echo de Paris* (16 February 1891):1. Reprinted in Octave Mirbeau, *Des artistes* (Paris: Flammarion, 1922):119-29.
1892, September	Paris, Galerie Boussod & Valadon (Goupil's). Exhibits *Vahine no te tiare*, one of his first Tahitian works.
1893, 4 November-1 December	Paris, Galerie Durand-Ruel. *Exposition d'oeuvres récentes de Gauguin.* Catalogue preface by Charles Morice. 20 p. 41 paintings, 2 sculptures. Reprinted in *Exhibitions of Symbolists and Nabi.* New York & London: Garland, 1981, no. 5.
1894, December	Paris. Exhibition in Gauguin's studio, 6 rue Vercingétorix. Woodcuts, monotypes and some paintings. See Julien Leclercq, "Exposition Paul Gauguin," *Mercure de France* 13 (1895):121-22.
1895, 18 February	Paris, Hôtel Drouot, second sale. Catalogue preceded by a letter from Auguste Strindberg, with Gauguin's response. 49 paintings, drawings, prints.

II. Group Exhibitions Before His Death in Which Gauguin Participated (1876-1903)

1876, 1 May	Paris, Salon, Palais des Champs Elysées. 1 painting, *Undergrowth at Viroflay* [Seine-et-Oise].
1879, 10 April-11 May	Paris, *IV*^{e} *exposition impressionniste* [fourth impressionist exhibition]. 28 avenue de l'Opéra. 1 sculpture.
1880, 1-30 April	Paris, *V*^{e} *exposition impressionniste* [fifth impressionist exhibition]. 10 rue des Pyramides. 7 paintings, 1 marble bust.
1881, 2 April-1 May	Paris, *VI*^{e} *exposition impressionniste* [sixth impressionist exhibition]. 35 bd. des Capucines. 8 paintings, 2 sculptures.
1882, 1 March	Paris, *VII*^{e} *exposition impressionniste* [seventh impressionist exhibition]. Salon du Panorama de Reichshoffen. 12 paintings, 2 pastels, 1 marble bust.
1884, Summer	Rouen, Hôtel Dauphin et d'Espagne. *Exhibition of the Murer Collection*. 1 painting.
1884, August	Rouen, *Exposition municipale des Beaux-Arts*. 1 pastel, 1 sculpture.
1886, 15 May-15 June	Paris, *VIII*^{e} *exposition impressionniste* [eighth impressionist exhibition]. 1 rue Laffitte. 19 paintings.
1886-7, 10 October-15 January	Nantes, *Exposition des Beaux-Arts*, Palais du Cours St-André. 2 works.
1889, March	Brussels, Salon des XX. *Sixième exposition annuelle*. Catalogue preface by Octave Maus. 12 works, including *Vision after the Sermon*.
1889, June	Paris, Champs de Mars. *Exposition du groupe impressionniste et synthétiste*, Café Volpini. 17 paintings and pastels, album of lithographs. Facs. ed., Paris: Rouvart et Watelin, ca. 1970.

1891, February	Brussels, Salon des XX. *Huitième exposition annuelle.* 2 vases, statuette of enamelled stoneware, several faïences, wood-reliefs (including *Be Mysterious*).
1891, 15 May	Paris, Salon de la Société Nationale des Beaux-Arts, Champ-de-Mars. 3 ceramics, 1 wood-relief.
1891, 27 May	Paris, Vaudeville Theatre. *Théâtre d'Art.* Exhibition in the foyer. Benefit for Gauguin and Paul Verlaine.
1891	Paris, Galerie Le Barc de Boutteville. *Peintres impressionnistes et symbolistes.*
1892, July	Paris, Galerie Le Barc de Boutteville. *Deuxième exposition des peintres impressionnistes et symbolistes.*
1892, November	Paris, Galerie Le Barc de Boutteville. *Troisième exposition des peintres impressionnistes et symbolistes.* 1 work shown without Gauguin's knowledge.
1893, March	Copenhagen, Kleis Gallery. *Martsudstillingen* [The March Exhibition of the Nabi and Symbolist Art]. 7 paintings, 6 ceramics.
1893, March-April	Copenhagen, *Den frie udstilling* [Center for Free Exhibition of Modern Art]. 50 paintings, sculptures, drawings.
1893, Summer	Paris, Galerie Le Barc de Boutteville.
1893	Paris, Galerie Le Barc de Boutteville. *Cinquième exposition des peintres impressionnistes et synthétistes.*
1893	Paris, Galerie Le Barc de Boutteville. *Portraits du prochain siècle.*
1894, February-March	Brussels, *Exposition de la libre esthétique.* 5 paintings.
1894, 1-2 June	Paris, Hôtel Drouot. *Vente Mme. Vve. Tanguy.*

1894	Paris, Galerie Le Barc de Boutteville. *Sixième exposition des peintres impressionistes et symbolistes.*
1895, March	Paris, Galerie Ambroise Vollard. Brittany canvases. See *Mercure de France* 13 (1895):358-59.
1895	Paris, Salon de la Société Nationale des Beaux-Arts, Champ-de-Mars.
1896, March-April	Paris, Librairie de l'art indépendant, 11 rue de la Chaussée d'Antin. See *Chronique des arts* (28 March 1896):124.
1896	Brussels, *Troisième exposition de la libre esthétique.* 1 ceramic.
1896	Paris, Galerie Ambroise Vollard.
1896, 12 November	Paris, Petit Théâtre Français.
1897, February-March	Brussels, *Quatrième exposition de la libre esthétique.* 6 paintings.
1897	Paris, Galerie Le Barc de Boutteville. *Quinzième exposition des peintres impressionnistes et symbolistes.* 6 paintings from Tahiti.
1898, May-October	Stockholm, Swedish Academy of Arts. *Exhibition of Modern French Art.*
1898, November-December	Paris, Galerie Ambroise Vollard. See Thadée Natanson, "Petite gazette d'art: de M. Paul Gauguin," *La Revue blanche* 17 (December 1898):544-46.
1900	Paris, Exposition Universelle. 1 Martinique landscape.

III. Retrospective and Individual Exhibitions After Gauguin's Death (May 8, 1903)

1903, 31 October-6 December	Paris, Petit Palais. *Salon d'Automne.* First retrospective. 9 works (4 landscapes, 4 studies and a self-portrait belonging to Maurice Denis).
1903, 4-28 November	Paris, Galerie Ambroise Vollard, 6 rue Laffitte. *Exposition Paul Gauguin.* 50 paintings, 27 drawings. See Charles Morice, "Les Gauguins du Petit Palais et de la rue Laffitte," *Mercure de France* 49 (1904):386-96.
1906, 6 October-15 November	Paris, Grand Palais. *Salon d'Automne* (fourth). *Catalogue de peintures. Oeuvres de Gauguin.* Introduction by Charles Morice. Retrospective organized by Georges-Daniel de Monfreid. 227 works. Review: P. Jamot, *Gazette des Beaux-Arts* (Dec. 1906): 456-84; (Jan. 1907): 43-63.
1909, April-May	Paris. Galerie Ambroise Vollard. *Oeuvres de Paul Gauguin.*
1909, early May	Paris, Galerie Druet, 20 rue Royale. *Tableaux de Paul Gauguin.*
1910	Paris, Galerie Ambroise Vollard. *Exposition d'oeuvres de Paul Gauguin.*
1912, March-April	Zurich, Kunstsalon Wolfsberg. *Ausstellung von Werken Paul Gauguins.* 9 paintings.
1917, 7-31 March	Paris, Galeries Nunès et Fiquet, 88-90 avenue Malakoff. *Exposition-Paul Gauguin.* Catalogue preface by Louis Vauxcelles. 37 works (paintings, watercolors, drawings, lithographs, wood sculptures, bronzes, plasters, ceramics).
1917	Copenhagen, Kleis Gallery. *Paul Gauguin i dansk besiddelse, Udstillet paa hostudstillingen.* 35 works.

1919, 10-30 October	Paris, Galerie Barbazanges. *Paul Gauguin: Exposition d'œuvres inconnues*. Catalogue preface by Francis Nargelet.
1923, 16 April-11 May	Paris, Galerie L. Dru. *Exposition rétrospective de P. Gauguin (1848-1903)*. Catalogue preface by Georges-Daniel de Monfreid. 68 works (paintings, watercolors, pastels, drawings, engravings, wood sculpture, ceramics).
1924, July-August	London, Leicester Galleries. *Exhibition of Works by Paul Gauguin Catalogue*, by Archibald S. Hartrick. Includes a biographical note and personal reminiscences by Hartrick. 35 p., 69 works.
1926, April	Oslo, Nationalmuseum. *Foreningen Fransk Konst: Paul Gauguin*. 16 p.
1926, 17 December	Paris, Association Paris-Amérique Latine. *Exposition rétrospective: hommage au génial artiste Franco-Péruvian*. Study by Felipe Cossio del Pomar, catalogue preface by Georges-Daniel de Monfreid. 25 p., 135 works. Review: H. Focillon, *Gazette des Beaux-Arts* 13 (May 1926): 257-80.
1926	Moscow, Pushkin Museum. *Paul Gauguin 1848-1903*.
1927, April-15 May	Boston, Museum of Fine Arts. *Prints by Gauguin*. Review: H.P. Rossiter, *Bulletin of the Museum of Fine Arts* 25:148 (April 1927):19-22.
1928, January-February	Paris, Musée du Luxembourg. *Gauguin, sculpteur et graveur*. Catalogue by Charles Masson and Marcel Guérin. 24 p. 107 works.
1928, February	London, Leicester Galleries. *Exhibition of Drawings, Lithographs, and Woodcuts by Paul Gauguin*. Catalogue

1928, July-August	Basel, Kunsthalle. *Paul Gauguin 1848-1903*. Preface and catalogue by Wilhelm Barth. 33 p. 254 works. Reviews: G. Tschann, *L'Amour de l'art* 9 (Dec. 1928):460-64; W. Barth, *Basler Kunstverein, Jahresbericht* (1928):1-20; W. Barth, *Basler Nachrichten* (1 Sept. 1928); W. Barth, *Kunst für Alle* 44 (1928):82-88.
1928, October	Berlin, Thannhauser Gallery. *Paul Gauguin, 1848-1903. Gauguin-Ausstellung*. Preface and catalogue by Wilhelm Barth. 63 p. 230 works.
1928	Venice, Biennial, Pallazo dell'esponsizione. *Mostra retrospettiva di Paul Gauguin* [Gauguin Retrospective]. 42 works.
1931, 7-28 February	Paris, Galerie le Portique, 99 bd. Raspail. *Exposition Gauguin*. Catalogue preface by Robert Rey. Paintings, sculptures.
1931, 26 May-14 June	Paris, Galerie de la Pléiade. *Gauguin, oeuvres gravées*. Introduction and catalogue by Henri M. Petiet. 12 p.
1931, May-June	London, Leicester Galleries. *Exhibition of the Durrio Collection of Works by Paul Gauguin*. Catalogue. Francisco Durrio, a Spanish sculptor, was a friend of Gauguin who invited him to travel to Tahiti. This collection came into Durrio's possession before Gauguin's second South Pacific journey.
1931	London, A. Tooth & Sons Gallery. *Modern French Paintings by Matisse, Gauguin, etc.*
1936, 20 March-18 April	New York, Wildenstein Gallery. *Paul Gauguin 1848-1903: A Retrospective Loan Exhibition for the Benefit of Les Amis de Gauguin and the Penn Normal Industrial and Agricultural School*. 57 p., 46 works. Review: E. Benson, *American Magazine of Art* 29 (1936):324-25. Also shown at the Fogg Art Museum, Cambridge, Massachusetts, 1-21 May 1936; and at the Baltimore Museum of Art.

1936, 22 April-9 May	New York, Marie Harriman Gallery. *Where Do We Come From, What Are We, Where Are We Going?* 16 p.
1936, 24 May-5 June	Baltimore, Museum of Art. *Paul Gauguin: A Retrospective Exhibition of his Paintings.* Catalogue preface by Henri Focillon. 34 p., 29 paintings.
1936, 5 September-4 October	San Francisco, Museum of Art. *Paul Gauguin: Exhibition of Paintings and Prints.* Preface and catalogue by G. L. McCann Morley. 28 p., 26 pl. 139 works.
1936, November	Paris, Gazette des Beaux-Arts. *La vie ardente de Paul Gauguin.* Preface by Henri Focillon, biographical text and catalogue by Raymond Cogniat. 198 works, documents. Reviews: G. Lo Duca, *Emporium* 85(May 1937):277-79; R. Barotte, *Plaisir de France* 4(1937): 40-41.
1937, 8-20 February	Edinburgh, Whytock and Reid Galleries. *Paul Gauguin. An Exhibition of the Original Works and Colour Prints and of Polynesian Art.* Introduction by David C. Scott-Moncrieff and Pola Gauguin. 15 p. 72 works.
1938, June-October	New York, Brooklyn Museum. *The Complete Graphic Work of Paul Gauguin.* Review: *Art Digest* 12(1 July 1938):24.
1939, 3-14 January	New York, Bignou Gallery. *Gauguin: First Trip to Tahiti.* Also shown at the Lefvre Gallery, London, in June. Foreword by Carl O. Schniewind. 4 p., 21 works. Review: *Art Digest* 13(15 Jan. 1939):24.
1940, 16-30 September	Los Angeles, Dalzell-Hatfield Galleries. *Gauguin.* 4 p., 11 works.
1942, 15 May-13 June	Paris, Galerie Marcel Guiot. *Gauguin: Aquarelles, monotypes, dessins, Tahiti, 1891-93.* Foreword by Marcel Guiot, catalogue by Marcel Guérin.
1945	New York, Kleemann Galleries. *Paul Gauguin.* 20 woodcuts, 3 paintings. 4 p. catalogue.

1946, 3 April-4 May	New York, Wildenstein Gallery. *A Loan Exhibition of Paul Gauguin for the Benefit of the New York Infirmary.* Foreword by Georges Wildenstein, preface by Somerset Maugham, essay "The Fiery Life of Paul Gauguin" by Raymond Cogniat, pp.15-62. Catalogue by Vladimir Visson and Daniel Wildenstein. 78 p. 91 works.
1947, April-May	Washington D.C., National Gallery of Art. *Gauguin and Edvard Munch.* Prints.
1948, May-June	Copenhagen, Ny Carlsberg Glyptotek. *Paul Gauguin, 1848-1903: Retrospektiv udstilling i anledning af hundredaaret for hans fødsel* [Retrospective on the Occasion of the Centenary of Paul Gauguin's Birth]. Preface and catalogue by Haavard Rostrup. 40 p., 129 works.
1949, July	Paris, Orangerie des Tuileries. *Gauguin, exposition du centenaire.* Preface by René Huyghe, catalogue by Jean Leymarie. 104 p., 101 works, 15 documents. Reviews: J. Leymarie, *Musées de France* 5(June 1949): 109-14; D. Sutton, *Burlington Magazine* 91(Oct. 1949): 283-88; R. Barotte, *Plaisir de France* 16(1949):55-57; M. Cazzullo, *Emporium* 110(Nov. 1949):194-201; S.J., *Paragone* 1(1950): 54-55.
1949, October-November	Chicago, Art Institute. 71 prints. Reviews: J. Devoluy, *Art News* 48(Sept. 1949):14-17, 47; *Art Digest* 24(1 Oct. 1949):17; D. Sutton, *Burlington Magazine* 91(Oct. 1949):283-86.
1949-50, 26 November-29 January	Basel, Kunstmuseum, Öffentliche Kunstsammlung. *Ausstellungen Paul Gauguin zum 100. Geburtsjahr.* Catalogue by Georg Schmidt. 64 p., 153 works. Review: *Werk* 37 supp. 1(Jan. 1950):1.
1949	Oslo, Galleri Per. *Exhibition of Coloured Woodcuts.* Review: *Kunsten Idag* (Oslo) 10:2(1949):56-57.

1950, 16 February-16 April	Lausanne, Musée Cantonal des Beaux-Arts. *Gauguin: Exposition du centenaire*. Review: H. W., *Emporium* (Bergamo) 111:666(June 1950):278-79, 281.
1950, April-May	Minneapolis, Institute of Arts. *Gauguin in Tahiti*.
1950, 16 December	Rome, Obelisco Galleria. *Paul Gauguin*. Text by Umbro Apollonio. 12 p., 15 works.
1951, 25 April-27 May	Paris, Musée National d'Art Moderne. *Collection G.D. de Monfreid*. Introduction by Jean Cassou. 8 p., 16 works.
1954, 27 March-25 April	Houston, Museum of Fine Arts. *Paul Gauguin: His Place in the Meeting of East and West*. Text by Lee Malone and Henri Dorra. 33 p., 99 works. Reviews: *Time* 63 (12 April 1954):88-90; H. Dorra, *Art Digest* 28 (15 March 1954):12-13; 28 (15 April 1954):36.
1955, 30 September-26 October	London, Tate Gallery, and Edinburgh, The Royal Scottish Academy. *Paul Gauguin: An Exhibition of Paintings, Engravings and Sculptures*. Texts by Philip James, Douglas Cooper. 40 p., 80 works. Reviews: D. Sutton, *Burlington Magazine* 98 (March 1955):84-89; D. Cooper, *Burlington Magazine* 58 (Aug. 1955):283-84; M. Tralbaut, *Het Vaderland* (22 Oct. 1955); M. Tralbaut, *Museum Journal* 1 (1955):93-98; E. Newton, *New York Times* (30 Oct. 1955).
1955, 11 November-1 December	Oslo, Kunstnerforbundet. *Paul Gauguin*. Introduction by Sigurd Willoch. 16 p., 60 works.
1956, 4 February-4 March	Palm Beach, Florida. The Society of the Four Arts. *Paul Gauguin*. Also shown at Lowe Gallery, Coral Gables. 31 p., 69 works.
1956, 5 April-5 May	New York, Wildenstein Gallery. *Loan Exhibition: Gauguin*. Introduction by Robert J. Goldwater, essay "The Woodcuts of Paul Gauguin" by Carl O. Schniewind. 64 p., 104 works. Reviews: R. Charmet, *Arts* 565(25 Apr.-1 May 1956):14; J. Mellow, *Arts Magazine* 30(May 1956):50; *Emporium* 124:7(Aug. 1956):75-80.

1957	Rome, Galleria Nazionale d'Arte Moderna. *Paul Gauguin*. Catalogue by Jacopo Rempero.
1959, 12 February-29 March	Chicago, Art Institute. *Gauguin: Paintings, Drawings, Prints, Sculptures*. Also shown Metropolitan Museum of Art, New York, 21 April-31 May. Forewords by James J. Rorimer and Allan McNab. Introduction by Théodore Rousseau, Jr., catalogue by Samuel J. Wagstaff, Claus Virch. 90 p. Reviews: E. Clark, *Studio* 158 (Aug. 1959):61; J. Richardson, *Burlington Magazine* 101 (May 1959): 188-92.
1959	Chicago, Art Institute. *Gauguin Prints*. Also shown Metropolitan Museum of Art, New York. Essay by Hugh Edwards. 32 p. catalogue. Reviews: J. Richardson, *Burlington Magazine* 101:674(May 1959):188-192; A. Werner, *Art News and Review* 11:15(15 Aug. 1959):2, 10; *Scrapbook of Art and Artists of Chicago and Vicinity* (1960):6.
1960, 1 April-29 May	Munich, Haus der Kunst. *Paul Gauguin*. Essay, "Gauguin oder Klassizimus durch Revolte," by Germain Bazin; note "Zur Graphik Gauguins," by Harold Joachim; catalogue by Jürgen Klaus, Klaus Demus. Reviews: F. Roh, *Kunstwerk* 13(June 1960):17-22; F. Roh, *Werk* 47:Supp. 137(July 1960); E. Diem, foreword by Raymond Nacenta, *Artis* (1960):16-19; *Weltkunst* 30 (1960):13-14.
1960, 7 June-31 July	Vienna, Osterreichische Galerie im Oberen Belvedere. *Paul Gauguin, 1843-1903*. 48 p., 47 pl. 142 works.
1960	Paris, Galerie Charpentier. *Cent œuvres de Gauguin*. R. Charmet, *Arts* 758(20-26 Jan. 1960):9; Introduction and preface by Jean Leymarie, catalogue by Maurice Malingue. 73 p., 100 works. Reviews: B. Champigneulle, *Arts* 757(13-19 Jan. 1960):16. P. Guéguen, *Aujourd'hui* 25(1960):38-39; A. Michelson, *Arts* 34(April 1960);23; K. Morand, *Burlington Magazine* 102(1960):128-31; G. Charensol, *Revue des deux mondes* 1(1960):712-19. P. Schneider, *Art News* 59(March 1960):48; A. Watt, *Studio* 159(May 1960):172-74, 180.

1961, 1 July-15 September	Vannes, Musée de Limur. *Hommage à Gauguin, vision d'outre-mer.*
1963	Prague, Narodni Gallery. *Paul Gauguin.*
1964	Lausanne, Musée Cantonal des Beaux-Arts. Reviews: D. Sutton, *Apollo* 79(June 1964):499; A. Frankfurter, *Art News* 63(Sept. 1964):64.
1965	New York, Wildenstein Gallery.
1966, 7 January-13 February	London, Tate Gallery. *Gauguin and the Pont-Aven Group.* Introduction by Denys Sutton, catalogue by Ronald Pickvance. 48 p., 73 works. Also shown at Kunsthaus, Zurich.
1966, 5 March-11 April	Zurich, Kunsthaus. *Pont-Aven:Gauguin und sein Kreis in der Bretagne.* 89 p.
1969	Philadelphia, University Museum, University of Pennsylvania. *Gauguin and Exotic Art.* Essays by Bengt Danielsson, William H. Davenport, Richard S. Field. 34 p.
1969, 23 August-7 December	Japan. *Gauguin.* Traveling exhibition, Tokyo, 23 Aug.-30 Sept.; Kyoto, Seibu Department Store, 5 Oct.-7 Nov.; Kyoto, Fukuoka Cultural Centre, 13 Nov.-7 Dec. Catalogue in French and Japanese. Includes essays, exhibitions lists, and bibliography.
1970	Bern, Kornfeld and Klipstein.
1970	Stockholm, Etnografiska Museet Nationalmuseum. *Gauguin i Söderhavet* [Gauguin in the South Seas]. Catalogue by Patrik Reuterswärd. 114 p., 155 works.
1971, 23 February-18 April	New York, Metropolitan Museum of Art. *Prints by Paul Gauguin.* Introduction by Colter Feller Ives. 14 p., 54 works.
1971, 18 March-26 April	Cincinnati, Cincinnati Art Museum. *The Early Work of Paul Gauguin, Genesis of an Artist.* Introduction by Richard J. Boyle. 35 p., 31 works.

1973, 23 March-13 May	Philadelphia, Museum of Art. *Gauguin-Monotypes*. Catalogue by Richard S. Field. 148 p.
1973	Chicago, Art Institute, *Paul Gauguin-His Life and Paintings*.
1978	Paris, Salon d'Automne. *Paul Gauguin*. Essay by Pierre Leprohon.
1978-79, 29 November-28 February	Munich, Museum Villa Stuck. *Paul Gauguin: Das druckgraphische Werk*. Also shown Dusseldörf, Kunsthandel Wolfgang Wittrock. Catalogue by Amine Haase, Wolfgang Wittrock, Richard S. Field. 110 p., 68 illus., 59 pl. 49 prints.
1981, October-November	Paris, Musée Marmottan. *Gauguin et les chefs d'oeuvre de l'Ordtupgaard de Copenhague*. Text by Yves Brayer. 42 p.
1982-83, 16 October-16 January	Humlebaek, Denmark, Louisiana Museum. *Gauguin pa Tahiti* [Gauguin in Tahiti]. Edited by Knud W. Jensen, Hans Erik Wallin. 63 p. 92 works including paintings, sculptures, drawings, prints, letters, and artifacts from Gauguin's years in Tahiti and the Marquesas.
1985, 11 January-10 March	Copenhagen, Ny Carlsberg Glyptotek. *Gauguin og Danmark: En udstilling i anledning of 100-året for Paul Gauguin's ophold: Danmark vinteren 1884-85* [Gauguin and Denmark: An Exhibition on the Centenary of Gauguin's Stay in Denmark during the Winter of 1884-85]. Text by Anne-Brigitte Fonsmark. 68 p. 40 works. Review: F. Cachin. *Burlington Magazine* 127:988 (1985):480-83.
1986, 28 June-30 September	Pont-Aven, Musée de Pont-Aven. *1886-1896: Cents ans: Gauguin à Pont-Aven*. Essays by Catherine Puget and Wladyslawa Jaworska. 80 p., 115 illus., 20 col. Paintings, sculptures, drawings, prints, and letters by 28 artists, including 8 Breton paintings by Gauguin.

1987, 6 March-17 May	Tokyo, National Museum of Modern Art. *Gogyan ten/Paul Gauguin.* Also shown at the Aichi Prefectural Museum, Nagoya. Catalogue by Kunio Motoe, Koji Takahashi, Ronald Pickvance. 193 p. In English and Japanese.
1988-89, 1 May-20 April	Washington, D.C., National Gallery of Art. *The Art of Paul Gauguin.* Also shown at the Art Institute of Chicago, 17 Sept.-11 Dec.; and at Grand Palais, Paris, 10 Jan.-24 April 1989. Catalogue by Richard Brettell, Françoise Cachin, Claire Frèches-Thory, Charles F. Stuckey, et al. 519 p. 280 works. Includes detailed chronology, list of exhibitions and sales, bibliography. Another publication: *Album Gauguin*, Claire Frèches-Thory and Isabelle Cahn. 48 p. Reviews: C. Frèches-Thory, *Revue du Louvre et des Musées de France* 38:5-6(1988):442-43 and *Connaissance des arts* 443(Jan. 1989):48-51; V. Jirat-Wasiutynski and H. Newton, *Burlington Magazine* 130(Sept. 1988):719-22; D. Schaff, *Art International* 5(Winter 1988):108-09; R. Field, *The Print Collector's Newsletter* 19(Sept./Oct. and Nov./Dec. 1988):130-38, 188; *Ceramics Monthly* 37(Oct. 1989):38-41; D. Sutton, *Gazette des Beaux-Arts* ser.6,113(March 1989):143-46; N. Bowe, *Apollo* 129(April 1989):275-76; B. Thompson, *Apollo* 129(April 1989):273-75; F. Hamer, *Ceramic Review* 117(May/June 1989):14;

IV. Group Exhibitions After Gauguin's Death (1903)

1904, 24 February-29 March	Brussels. *La libre esthétique. Exposition des peintres impressionnistes.* 11 works.
1905, November-December	Vienna. Grossherzogliches Museum am Karlsplatz. *Twenty-Fourth Independent Exhibition.* 1 work.
1906, Spring	Berlin, Berliner Secession. *Eleventh Independent Exhibition.* 2 works.
1907, March-April	Vienna, Miethke Gallery. *Paul Gauguin and Others.* 6 sculptures, 4 ceramic works, 21 graphic works, 41 paintings. See L. Hevesi, *Altkunst-Neukunst* (Vienna, 1909).

1907, May	Budapest, Nemzeti Szalon; Javaszi Kiallith *Gauguin, Cézanne and Others*. 65 sculptures, paintings, graphic works.
1907, October-November	Prague, Manès Gallery. *Impressionnistes français*. 3 paintings, 3 pastels.
1907, 14-30 November	Paris, Galerie Bernheim-Jeune. *Fleurs et natures mortes*. 3 works.
1907-8, 16 December-4 January	Paris, Galerie Berheim-Jeune. *Portraits d'hommes*. 2 self-portraits.
1908, March-April	Munich, W. Zimmermann Gallery. *Van Gogh, Gauguin and Others*. 8 works.
1908, 18 April-24 May	Moscow, *The Golden Fleece*. 3 works.
1908-9, 21 December-16 January	Paris, Galerie Druet, 20 rue Royale.
1909, 11 April-9 May	Bremen, Kunsthalle. *Exhibition of Paintings, Drawings and Sculptures from Private Collections*. 2 works.
1909, May-October	Vienna, *Vienna International Exhibition*. 1 work.
1909, 4 August-16 September	Hagen, Museum Volkwang. *Sonderausstellung*. 9 Breton lithographs, engravings for *Germinal*, 10 wood engravings from Pacific period.
1909-10, 27 November-9 January	Berlin, Ausstellungshaus. *Nineteenth Secession, Exhibition of Graphic Arts*. 3 lithographs.
1910, 12 March-17 April	Brussels. *La libre esthétique - l'évolution du paysage*. 5 works.
1910, 20 April-15 May	Florence, Lyceum Club. *First Italian Exhibition of Impressionism*. 1 work, 4 photographs from Tahiti.
1910, 17-28 May	Paris, Galerie Bernheim-Jeune. *Nus*. 2 works.

1910, September	Stockholm, Sveriges Allmänna Konstförening. *Foreign Modern Graphic Arts, from the Thorsten Laurins Collection.* 1 self-portrait.
1910, October-November	Leipzig, Kunstverein. *Exhibition of Eighteenth, Nineteenth, and Twentieth-Century French Art.* 1 work.
1910-11, 8 November-15 January	London, Grafton Galleries. *Manet and the Post-Impressionists.* 46 works, including drawings, pastels, oils.
1910, 19-30 December	Paris, Galerie Bernheim-Jeune. *La faune.* 4 works.
1910	Munich, Thannhauser Gallery. *Die Sammlung Vollard.* Also shown Thannhauser Gallery, Dresden. Exhibition of the Vollard collection.
1911, 26 June 13 July	Paris, Galerie Bernheim-Jeune. *L'eau.* 3 works.
1911, 20 July-5 August	Paris, Galerie Bernheim-Jeune. *La montagne.* 1 work.
1911, October	Cologne. Wallraf-Richartz-Museum. *Contemporary Art in Cologne Private Collections.* 1 work.
1911, November-December	Berlin. 35 Victoriastrasse. *Twenty-Third Secession. Graphic Arts.* Suite of 10 lithographs.
1911, November	London, Stafford Gallery. *Exhibition of Pictures by Paul Cézanne and Paul Gauguin.* 14 works.
1911	Paris, Galerie E. Blot. *Wood Sculptures.*
1912, early	St. Petersburg, Institut français. *Exposition centennale de l'art français.* 19 paintings, 2 drawings. Review: F. Monod, *Gazette des Beaux-Arts* (March 1912):191-98; (April 1912):301-26.
1912, 7 April-end of June	Leipzig, Verein LIA. *Annual Leipzig Exhibition.* 2 wood sculptures.

1912, May	Berlin, *Der Sturm* [third exhibition of graphic arts]. 4 engravings, 1 drawing.
1912, 25 May-30 September	Cologne, Städtische Ausstellungshalle. *Internationale Kunstausstellung des Sonderbund.* [International Exhibition of Art]. 25 works, including oils and watercolors.
1912, June-July	Hagen, Museum Volkwang. *Modern Art: Sculpture, Painting, Engravings.* 7 paintings, 3 engravings.
1912, 18 July-30 September	Frankfurt, Frankfurter Kunstverein. *Nineteenth-Century French Classical Painting.* 6 works.
1912, October	Munich, Hans Goltz Gallery. *Art Nouveau - First Group Exhibition.* 8 works.
1912, 1 October-8 November	Paris, Grand Palais. *Salon d'Automne* [tenth]. 3 works.
1912, 6 October-7 November	Amsterdam, Stedelijk Museum. *Moderne KunstKring* 23 works. Review: *Art Flammand et Hollandais* 18 (1912):163-64.
1912, December	Vienna, Arnold Gallery. *Exhibition of Modern French Works.* 1 work.
1912	Bonn, *Sonderbund Ausstellung.* Foreword by H. von Wedderkop. 75 p.
1912	Düsseldorf *Sonderbund Westdeutscher Kunstfreunde und Künstler.* Included works by Gauguin. Review: H. Von Wedderkop, *Führer Nebst Vorwort* (1912): 42-44.
1913	Frankfurt, Union Artistique.
1913, January	Berlin, Paul Cassirer Gallery. *Collection Reber* (XV Jahrgang, III. Ausstellung). 2 works.
1913, January	Budapest, Ernst Muzeum. *Francia Impressionistàk.* 1 work.
1913-14	Munich, Thannhauser Gallery. *Hangings.*

1913, February	Vienna, Miethke Gallery. *Dr. Oskar Reichel Collection.* 1 work.
1913, 27 February-15 March	New York, Armory of the Sixty-Ninth Regiment. *The Armory Show: International Exhibition of Modern Art.* 13 works. Review: J. Huneker, *New York Times* (11 May 1913):13.
1913, March-April	Vienna, Arnold Gallery. *Collection of Modern French Artists.* 2 works.
1913, 24 March-15 April	Chicago, Chicago Art Institute. *The Armory Show.* 14 sculptures, paintings, watercolors, drawings and engravings.
1913, 28 April-18 May	Boston, Copley Hall. Copley Society of Boston. *The Armory Show.* 14 works (same as Chicago).
1913, May-October	Stuttgart, Königliches Kunstgebäude. *Grosse Kunstausstellung* [Grand Exhibition of Art]. 2 works.
1913, August-September	Munich, Hans Goltz Gallery. *Second General Exhibition.* 1 painting, 1 ceramic.
1913, Autumn	Budapest, Ernst Muzeum. *A XIX Szàdad Nagy Francia Mesterei.* 1 work.
1913-14, 12 October-16 January	London, Dore Galleries. *Post Impressionist and Futurist Exhibition.*
1913-14, December-January	Vienna, Miethke Gallery. *French Masters.* 2 works.
1914	Copenhagen, *Den franske udstilling.* 9 paintings.
1914	Dresden, Ernst Arnold Kunstsalon. *Französische Malerei des 19. Jahrhunderts.*
1914, January	Vienna, Arnold Gallery. *Modern French Masters.* 9 works, including 2 wood sculptures.
1914, 1 February-31 March	Bremen, Kunsthalle. *International Exhibition.* 2 paintings, 2 watercolors.
1914, 12 April-end September	Berlin, Ausstellunghaus Secession. *First Independent Exhibition.* 1 work.

1914, Summer	Munich, Neue Kunst, Hans Goltz Gallery. *Exhibition of Summer, 1914.* 1 ceramic.
1915, February-June	Rome. *Third International Independent Exhibition.* 4 works.
1916, July	Berlin, Der Sturm. *Forty-Third Exhibition--Expressionists, Futurists, and Cubists.* 1 work.
1917, March-April	Stockholm, National Museum. *Fransk-Konst, fran 1800-talet.* 8 works.
1917, October-November	Zurich, Züricher Kuntshaus. *Französische Kunst des XIX. & XX. Jahrhunderts.* 7 works.
1918, 26-27 March	Paris, Galerie Georges Petit. *Catalogue des tableaux modernes et anciens composant la collection Edgar Degas.*
1919	Amsterdam, Frederick Muller. *Van Gogh, Gauguin, Renoir, Collection Mme. Théa Sterheim.*
1921	New York, Metropolitan Museum of Art. *Loan Exhibition of Impressionist and Post-Impressionist Paintings.*
1923	London, Lefevre Galleries. *Gauguin, Van Gogh, Toulouse-Lautrec, Representative Pictures by Renoir.*
1925	Boston, Boston Art Club.
1926, April	Stockholm, Copenhagen, Oslo. *Paul Gauguin, hans arbeten: Skandinavisk i National Museum.*
1927	Berlin, Galerien Thannhauser (at the Berliner Künstlerhaus). *Erst Sonderausstellung in Berlin.*
1927, April-May	Boston, Museum of Fine Arts. *Exhibition of Engravings* (Russel Allen and Fuller Collections).
1928	Berlin, Galerien Thannhauser. Paul Gauguin, Henri Matisse, Claude Monet.

1928	London, British Museum. *French Drawings of the Nineteenth Century*. Review: O. Opresco, *Revue de l'art ancien et moderne* 54:301(Dec. 1928):235-54.
1929, 7 November-7 December	New York, Museum of Modern Art. *First Loan Exhibition: Cézanne, Gauguin, Seurat, Van Gogh* (New York: Condé Nast Press, 1929; reprint, New York: Arno Press, 1972). Foreword by Alfred H. Barr, Jr. Includes biographical notes on the artists. 52 p., 38 pl.
1930	Paris, Salon d'Automne. Review: J. Guenne, *Les Arts plastiques*. Paris, 1931:242-43.
1930	Stockholm. *Matthiessen Collection*. Review: J. de Hoorn, *L'Amour de l'art* 11 (1930):412-20.
1931, May-November	Paris, Palais Permanent des Colonies. *Exposition Coloniale Internationale*.
1931	New York, 56th St. Galleries. Frescoes.
1932, 20 February-20 March	Zurich, Kunsthaus. *Austellung 20, Edvard Munch, Paul Gauguin* 22 p. catalogue.
1932	New York, Durand-Ruel Galleries. *Exhibition of Paintings by Gauguin, Cézanne, and Redon*. Review: H. Furst, *Apollo* 15(1932):65-72.
1934, February-March	Paris, Galerie des Beaux-Arts. *Exhibition Gauguin et ses amis, l'Ecole de Pont-Aven et l'Académie Julian*. Catalogue by Raymond Cogniat, preface by Maurice Denis. 30 p. Review: D. Lord, *Burlington Magazine* 67(1935):84-88.
1936, 1 November-13 December	Toledo, Museum of Art. *Paintings by Cézanne and Gauguin*. 16 p.
1938, 19-31 October	Paris, Galerie Charpentier. *Exposition Georges-Daniel de Monfreid et son ami Paul Gauguin*. Preface by Maurice Denis. 31 p., 14 paintings, 9 sculptures, letters, artifacts.

1938	Amsterdam, Stedelijk Museum. *Hundert jaar fransche kunst*. Included Gauguin works. Review: D. Lord, *Burlington Magazine* 73(Sept. 1938): 131-32.
1938	New York, Keppel Galleries. Prints, woodcuts, paintings.
1938	Paris, Galérie Kaganovitch.
1941	Los Angeles County Art Museum. *From Cézanne to Picasso*. Included several Gauguin paintings.
1945, May	New York, Kleemann Gallery. Paintings, woodcuts. Reviews: *Art Digest* 19(15 May 1945):16; *Art News* 44(15 May 1945):6; *Pictures on Exhibit* 6(May 1945):16.
1948, 8 April-8 May	New York, Wildenstein Gallery. *A Loan Exhibition of Six Masters of Post-Impressionism*. Introduction by Alfred M. Frankfurter. 76 p.
1948, April-May	Reims, Musée Municipal. *De Delacroix à Gauguin*. Review: R. Pernoud, *Arts* (7 May 1948):1.
1949, February	Paris, Galerie Kléber. *Gauguin et ses amis*. Preface and catalogue by Maurice Malingue. Review: F. Stahly, *Werk* 36:4(April 1949): 42-43.
1950, July-September	Quimper, Musée des Beaux-Arts. *Gauguin et le groupe de Pont-Aven*. Introduction by René Huyghe, catalogue by Gilberte Martin-Méry. 71 p., 13 paintings, 3 drawings, 4 prints, 4 sculptures, documents. Review: G. Martin-Méry, Musée de *France* (1950): 189-92.
1951, June	Paris, Galerie André Weil. *Gauguin et ses amis*.
1951	Paris, Galerie Jean Loize. *Les amitiés de peintre Georges-Daniel de Monfreid, de Malliol et de Codet à Segalen, et ses reliques de Gauguin*. Catalogue by Jean Loize.
1952	Paris, Galerie Quatre-Chemins Editart.

1953, August-September	Pont-Aven, Hôtel de Ville. *Commémoration du cinquantenaire de la mort de Paul Gauguin - Exposition d'oeuvres de Paul Gauguin et du Groupe de Pont-Aven.* Introduction by T. Briant.
1954	New York, Wildenstein's. Included works by Gauguin. Review: D. Sutton, *Burlington Magazine* 96(1954):193.
1956, June-July	Copenhagen, Winkel & Magnussen. *Gauguin og hans venner.*
1957	New York, World House. Drawings. Review: *Art News* 58 (June 1959):14.
1958, June-July	Copenhagen, Winkel & Magnussen. *Gauguin og hans venner.*
1958, July-September	Quimper, Musée des Beaux-Arts. *Hommage à Sérusier et aux peintres du groupe de Pont-Aven.*
1958	Brussels, Palais International des Beaux-Arts. *Cinquante ans d'art moderne; Exposition universelle et internationale.*
1960-61	Paris, Musée National d'Art Moderne. *Les Sources du XXe siècle: Les arts en Europe de 1884 à 1914.*
1961, March-April	New York, Finch College Art Gallery. *Second Annual Exhibition of Modern and Old Masters.*
1961, August-September	Pont-Aven, Hôtel de Ville. *Gauguin et ses amis.* Catalogue by Maurice Malingue.
1961	New York, Hirschi and Adler Galleries. *Painters at Pont-Aven.*
1962	Chicago, Main Street Galleries. *Painters at Pont-Aven.*
1963, 4 May-14 July	Hamburg, Kunstverein. *Wegbereiter der modernen Malerei: Cézanne, Gauguin, van Gogh, Seurat.* Text by Hans Platte. 230 p. 33 works.

1963, 19 May	Williamstown, Massachusetts. Sterling and Francine Clark Art Institute. 29 p., 21 prints.
1964, June	Paris, Galerie de l'Elysée. *Exposition de 7 tableaux rares*. 18 p. catalogue. Included Gauguin's *Paysage*.
1965, 14 May-6 September	Bordeaux, Musée des Beaux-Arts. *Masterworks of French Paintings from the Hermitage and Moscow Museums*. Also show at the Louvre, Sept.-21 Dec. Review: K. Champa, *Arts Magazine* 39(Sept. 1965):53-56.
1965	Milan, Galleria del Levante. *Pont-Aven e i Nabis*.
1966, 5 June-September	New York, Solomon R. Guggenheim Museum. *Gauguin and the Decorative Style*. Introduction by Lawrence Alloway, essays by Marilyn Hunt and Rose-Carol Wasthon. Catalogue by Louise Averill. 46 p., 48 works.
1968	New York, Solomon R. Guggenheim Museum. *Neo-Impressionism*. Catalogue by Robert L. Herbert.
1970, May-September	Chicago, Kovler Gallery. *The Graphic Art of Vallotton and the Nabis*. Also shown at Iowa City, University of Iowa Museum of Art, Aug.-Sept.
1970, 8 September-8 November	Munich, Münchner Stadtmuseum. *Malerei nach Fotografie: von der Camera Obscura bis zur Pop Art, eine Dokumentation*.
1970	Hamburg, Museum für Kunst und Gewerbe. *Fächer und Fächerbilder*. Review: H. Spielmann, *Jahr Hamburger Kunstsammlung* 14-15(1970):386.
1970	London, National Gallery. *French School: Early 19th Century, Impressionists, Post Impressionists, etc*. Catalogue by Martha Davies, additions and revisions by Cecil Gould.
1971	Brest, Musée municipal. *Le Temps de Gauguin*.
1971	Toronto, San Francisco, Chicago. *Vuillard*. Text by John Russell. Includes essay "The Influence of Paul Gauguin," by Maurice Denis.

1972	London, Hayward Gallery; Liverpool, Walker Art Gallery. *French Symbolist Painters: Moreau, Puvis de Chavannes, Redon and Their Followers.*
1973	San Diego, Fine Arts Gallery of San Diego. *Dimensions of Polynesia.*
1974, 22 May-29 September	Brooklyn, Brooklyn Museum. *An Exhibition of Paintings, Watercolors, Sculpture and Drawings from the Collection of Mr. and Mrs. Henry Pearlman and Henry and Rose Pearlman Foundation.* Also shown at Utica, New York, Munson-Williams-Proctor Institute, 26 Mar.-31 Aug., 1975; Williamstown, Mass., Sterling and Francine Clark Art Institute, Sept.-15 Dec. 1975. Introduction by John Rewald. 1 woodcut plaque.
1975, 14 January-11 May	New York, Metropolitan Museum of Art. *The Great Wave: The Influence of Japanese Woodcuts on French Prints.* Catalogue by Colta Feller Ives.
1975, 14 May-29 June	Paris, Institut Néerlandais. *Oeuvres écrites de Gauguin et van Gogh.* Also shown at Amsterdam, Rijksmuseum Vincent van Gogh, 8 July-15 Sept. Introduction by Vincent W. van Gogh, catalogue by Sadi de Gorter. 47 p.
1975, 9 July-31 August	Cleveland, Museum of Art. *Japonisme: Japanese Influence on French Art, 1854-1910.* Also shown at New Brunswick, Rutgers University Art Gallery, 4 Oct.-15 Nov.; Baltimore, Walters Art Gallery, 10 Dec.-26 Jan., 1976. Catalogue by Gabriel P. Weisberg, et al.
1975, 24 October-30 November	Toronto, Art Gallery of Ontario. *Puvis de Chavannes and the Modern Tradition.* Catalogue by R. J. Wattenmaker. 38 works by Puvis; 26 other artists including Gauguin.
1976, 6 May-4 June	Paris, Galerie Jaubert. *Georges-Daniel de Monfreid, 1856-1929.* Catalogue by Raymond Cogniat. Paintings by de Monfried. An essay notes his relationship to Paul Gauguin.

1976, May-September	Jerusalem, Israel Museum. *A Tribute to Sam Zacks*. Also shown Tel Aviv, Tel Aviv Museum, Oct. 1976. Catalogue edited by Yona Fischer. Gauguin drawings.
1976-77, 15 October-17 January	Paris, Musée National du Louvre. *Dessins français de l'Art Institut de Chicago de Watteau à Picasso*. Gauguin represented with 47 other artists.
1976-77, 3 December-28 March	Paris, Musée National du Louvre. *Nouvelles acquisitions du Musée d'Orléans*. Introduction by David Ojalvo. 43 works, including some by Gauguin.
1976-77, 17 December-1 March	New York, Museum of Modern Art. *European Master Paintings from Swiss Collections: Post-Impressionism to World War II*. Foreword by William Rubin, catalogue by John Elderfield. Includings paintings by Gauguin.
1977, 28 March-29 May	Paris, Musée National du Louvre. *La Collection Armand Hammer*. Introduction by Emmanuel de Margerie, foreword by John Walker. Early drawings of Gauguin and a sketchbook, 1884-1888.
1977	Paris, Palais de Tokyo. *Le Post-Impressionnisme*.
1977-79	London, Arts Council of Great Britian. *19th and 20th Century Drawings and Prints from the Courtauld Collection*. Also shown at six other locations in Great Britain. Gauguin paintings with works of 24 other artists.
1978, 30 March-1 October	London, British Museum. *From Monet to Toulouse-Lautrec: French Lithographs 1860-1900*. Catalogue by Frances Carey, Anthony Griffiths. Gauguin lithographs.
1978, 2 May-2 June	New York, New York University Grey Art Gallery and Study Center. *Changes in Perspective: 1880-1925*. Introduction by Blanche R. Brown. Essay "The Primitive Celebration: Paul Gauguin," by A. Lee.

1978, 6 June- 18 September	Paris, Grand Palais. *De Renoir à Matisse; 22 chefs d'oeuvre des musées soviétiques et français.* Catalogue edited by Anne Pistel, Michael Hoog; foreword by Héléne Adhemar. Gauguin paintings.
1978, 15 July- 16 October	Quimper, Musée des Beaux-Arts. *L'Ecole de Pont-Aven dans les collections publiques et privées de Bretagne.* Also shown in Rennes and Nantes. Preface by Victor Beyer. Gauguin works.
1978, 19 October- 3 December	Ljubljana, Yugoslavia, Narodna Galerija. *Od Corota do Bonnarda: Francoski Slikarji iz Zbirk Narodnega Muzeja v Beogradu* [From Corot to Bonnard: French Masters in the Collection of the Národni Museum, Belgrade]. Catalogue by Katrina Ambrozic. Summary in French. Gauguin works with 26 other artists.
1978, end of	Pont-Aven. *Le mouvement impressionniste dans l'école de Pont-Aven.* Essays and catalogue by Wladyslawa Jaworska, et al. Gauguin works.
1978	London, Arts Council of Great Britain. *The Mechanised Image: An Historical Perspective on 20th Century Prints.* Also shown at Camden Arts Centre, London. Catalogue by Pat Gilmour. Gauguin prints.
1978	New York, Solomon R. Guggenheim Museum. *Justin K. Thannhauser Collection.* Catalogue by Bibian E. Barnett. 220 p., 86 illus., 70 pl. Included works by Gauguin.
1979	Leningrad, Hermitage. *Francuzskaja Litografia 1890-h Godov* [French Lithography of the 1890s]. Catalogue by Jurij Aleksandrovic Rusakov. Gauguin lithographs.
1979-80, 26 October- 20 January	Houston, Museum of Fine Arts. *The Armand Hammer Collection:Four Centuries of Masterpieces.* Catalogue by Ebria Feinblatt, Charles Millard, Kenneth Donahue, et al. 212 p., 121 pl. Included a sketchbook by Gauguin.
1979-80, 2 November- 6 January	Ann Arbor, University of Michigan Museum of Art. *The Crisis of Impressionism 1878-1882.* Catalogue by Joel Isaacson, et al. Gauguin works.

1979-80, 17 November-16 March	London, Royal Academy of Arts. *Post-Impressionism: Cross Currents in European Painting*. Catalogue by John House. 14 works.
1979-80, 25 November-15 June	Münster, Westfälisches Landesmuseum für Kunst and Kulturgeschichte. *Stilleben in Europa*. Also shown Baden-Baden, Staatliche Kunsthalle, 15 March-15 June. Essay "Stilleben und Avantgarde" by I. Bartsch. 617p.
1980, 26 January-1 March	London, Arts Council of Great Britain. *Post-Impressionist Graphics: Original Prints by French Artists 1880-1903*. Also shown at five other locations in Great Britain. Introduction by Mary Ann Stevens. Gauguin works.
1980, 8 February-14 March	Middleton, Connecticut, Wesleyan University Davison Art Center. *The Prints of Armand Seguin, 1869-1903*. Catalogue by Richard S. Field, et al. 84 p. Reprint of Gauguin's preface to Seguin's 1895 exhibition catalogue appended.
1980, 5 June-21 September	New York, Metropolitan Museum of Art. *Modern Masters: European Paintings from the Museum of Modern Art*. Foreword by Philippe de Montebello. Critical anthology (1950-79) edited by William S. Lieberman. 88 p., 15 pl. Exhibition of 50 master paintings from 1885-1950, including several by Gauguin.
1980	Moscow, Pushkin State Museum of Fine Arts. *French Painting from the Pushkin Museum: 17th to 20th Century*. Catalogue by Irina Kuznetsova and Ergenia Georgievskaya. Included paintings by Gauguin.
1980	Münster, Westfalisches Landesmuseum für Kunst and Kulturgeschichte. *Reliefs: Formprobleme zwischen Malerei und Skulptur in 20. Jahrhundert* [Relief Problems of Form between Painting and Sculpture in the 20th century]. 286 p. Also shown Kunsthaus, Zürich, 1981. Works by Gauguin included.

1980	New York, Metropolitan Museum of Art. *The Painting Print: Monotypes from the Seventeenth Century to the Twentieth Century.* Also shown at the Museum of Fine Arts, Boston. Included prints by Gauguin.
1980	Washington, D.C., National Gallery of Art. *Post-Impressionism: Cross-Currents in European and American Painting, 1980-1906.* Works by Gauguin.
1981, 24 January-22 March	Toronto, Art Gallery of Ontario. *Vincent van Gogh and the Birth of Cloisonism.* Also shown Amsterdam, Rijksmuseum Vincent van Gogh, 9 April-14 June. Catalogue by Bogomila Welsh-Ovcharov. 384 p., 61 illus., 231 pl., 24 col. 25 works.
1981, 7 March-10 May	Worcester, Mass., Art Museum. *The Dial Italics: Arts and Letters in the 1920s; An Anthology of Writings from The Dial magazine, 1920-29.* Edited by Gaye L. Brown. Included works by Gauguin.
1981, 14 May-28 June	Atlanta, High Museum of Art. *Drawings from Georgia Collections, 19th & 20th Centuries.* Also shown at the University of Georgia, Georgia Museum of Art, 12 July-23 Aug. Catalogue by Peter Morrin, Eric Zafran. Gauguin drawings.
1981, 19 May	New York, Christie's Auction of eight masterpieces of Impressionist and Post-Impressionist paintings including Gauguin's *Fruits de Tahiti* (1896).
1981, 27 June-20 September	Florence, Palazzo Pitti. *Arte maestra; da Monet a Picasso. Cento capolavori della Galleria nazionale di Praga.* [Art of the Masters; from Monet to Picasso. One Hundred Masterpieces from the Národni Galerie, Prague]. Text by Achille Bonito Oliva, Jiri Kotalik. Gauguin paintings.
1981, 18 September-13 December	Bielefeld, Kunsthalle. *Henri Matisse, das Goldene Zeitalter* [Henri Matisse, the Golden Age]. Essay, "Matisse and Gauguin," by Douglas Cooper.

1981-82, 7 November-3 January	Toronto, Art Gallery of Ontario. *Gauguin to Moore: Primitivism in Modern Sculpture.* Catalogue by Alan G. Wilkinson. 303 p. Including sculptures and related prints and drawings by Gauguin, along with 21 other artists.
1982, 18 September-5 December	Ghent, Museum voor Schone Kunste. *George Minne de Kunst rond 1900* [George Minne and Art around 1900]. Catalogue by R. Hoozee, M. Tahon-Vanroose, A. Alhadeff, J. Haerens. 268 p. Includes Alhadeff's essay "Minne, Gauguin and Les XX: An Unexplored Encounter."
1982	Canberra, Australian National Gallery. *Paperwork.* Text by Pat Gilmour and Anne Willsford. 81 p. Gauguin's lithographs on yellow paper.
1982-83, 13 October-16 January	Saint-Germain-en-Laye, Musée départemental du Prieuré. *L'éclatement de l'Impressionnisme.* Catalogue by Jeanine Warnod, Marie Amélie Anquetil, et al. 139 p. Gauguin paintings.
1983, 6 March-15 May	New York, Museum of Modern Art. *Prints from Blocks: Gauguin to Now.* Catalogue by Riva Castleman. 84 p. Included Gauguin prints.
1983, 23 April-18 July	Oklahoma City, Oklahoma Museum of Art. *Impressionism/Post-Impressionism: XIX & XX Century Paintings from the Robert Lehman Collection of the Metropolitan Museum of Art.* Introduction by Joan Carpenter, catalogue by George Szabo. 89 p. Included Gauguin paintings, among 29 other artists.
1983, September-15 October	Lugano, Villa La Favorita. *French Paintings from Russia.* 9 paintings. Review: D. Cooper, *Burlington Magazine* 125:966(Sept. 1983):575-76.
1984, 13 January-11 March	Toronto, Art Gallery of Ontario. *The Mystic North: Symbolist Landscape Painting in Northern Europe and North America 1890-1940.* Also shown at Cincinnati Art Museum, 31 March-13 May. Catalogue by Roald Nasgaard, essay on Gauguin's influence. 253 p. Gauguin paintings.

1984, 25 March-20 May	Düsseldorf, Kunstmuseum. *Der Westdeutsche Impuls, 1900-1914: Kunst and Umweltgestaltung im Industriegebiet* [The West German Impulse, 1900-14: Art and the Shaping of the Social Environment in the Industrial Sphere]. Catalogue by Wolfgang Schepers, Gisela Moeller, Stephan von Wiese. 6 vols. Gauguin paintings and sculptures.
1984, 17 June-21 October	Lausanne, Fondation de l'Hermitage. *L'Impressionnisme dans les collections romandes.* Catalogue by Françis Daulte. 200 p. Gauguin paintings.
1984	Ann Arbor, University of Michigan Museum of Art. *The Artistic Revival of the Woodcut in France 1850-1900.* Also shown at Yale University Art Gallery. Catalogue by Jacquelynn Baas, Richard S. Field. Included Gauguin woodcuts.
1984-85, 28 June-22 April	Los Angeles, Los Angeles County Museum of Art. *A Day in the Country: Impressionism and the French Landscape.* Also shown at Chicago Art Institute and Paris, Grand Palais. Catalogue by R. R. Brettell, et al. 375 p. Gauguin paintings.
1984-85, 27 September-15 January	New York, Museum of Modern Art. *'Primitivism' in 20th Century Art: Affinity of the Tribal and the Modern.* Also shown at Detroit Institute of Arts and Dallas Museum of Art. Edited by William Rubin. 2 vols. Essay on Gauguin by Kirk Varnedoe.
1984-85, 12 December-10 February	Copenhagen, Ordrupgaard. *Gauguin og van Gogh i Kobenhavn i 1893* [Gauguin and van Gogh in Copenhagen in 1893]. Catalogue by Merete C. Bodelsen, Kirsten Olesen. 135 p., 87 illus., 44 col. 51 works, including 22 by Gauguin and 17 by van Gogh.
1985, 20 March-19 May	London, Victoria and Albert Museum. *From Manet to Hockney: Modern Artists' Illustrated Books.* Catalogue by Carol Hogben, Rowan Watson. 380 p. Included Gauguin illustrations.

1985, 24 March-23 June	Marcq-en-Baroeul, Fondation Septentrion. *Autour de Gauguin à Pont-Aven 1886-1894.* 36 p. Paintings, drawings, and prints by Gauguin.
1985, 13 July-29 September	Morlaix, Musée de Morlaix. *Maurice Denis et la Bretagne/Maurice Denis à Perros-Guirec.* Also shown at Maison des Traouieros, Perros-Guirec. Catalogue by Geneviève Lacambre, Denise Delouche. 80 p. Essay describes Denis' links with Gauguin.
1985, 7 October-31 December	Saint-Germain-en-Laye, Yvelines, Musée départemental du Prieuré. *Le Chemin de Gauguin: Genèse et Rayonnement.* Texts by Marie-Amélie Anquetil, Michel Hoog, Georges Gomez y Càceres, Robert P. Welsh, Olivier Michel, Yann le Pichon. 236 p. 387 illus., 208 col. 399 works (100 by Gauguin), some by followers. Review: D. Sinz, *Artis* 37:12(1985): 10-13; *Revue du Louvre et des Musées Nationaux de France* 36:1(1986):20.
1985	San Francisco, Fine Arts Museum of San Francisco. *Master Drawings from the Achenbach Foundation for Graphic Arts, the Fine Arts Museum of San Francisco.* Catalogue by Robert Flynn Johnson. Included Gauguin drawings.
1985	Paris, Galeries Nationales du Grand Palais. *L'Impressionnisme et le paysage français.* Works by Gauguin.
1986, 13 March-5 May	New York, Brooklyn Museum. *From Courbet to Cézanne: A New 19th Century Preview of the Musée d'Orsay, Paris.* Also shown at Dallas Museum of Art, 1 June-3 Aug. Catalogue by Michel Laclotte, Guy Cogeval. 224 p. Gauguin paintings.
1986, 27 March-25 May	London, Whitechapel Art Gallery. *In Tandem: The Painter-Sculptor in the Twentieth Century.* Foreword by N. Serota, catalogue by L. Cooke. 144p. Gauguin sculptures, paintings.
1986, 30 March-15 June	Tokyo, Setegaya Art Museum. *Naivety in Art.* Seiji Oshima, et al. Gauguin works.

1986, 7 May- 17 August 1986	Humlebaek, Denmark, Louisiana. *Den globale Dialog: Primitiv og moderne kunst* [The Global Dialogue: Primitive and Modern Art]. Edited by Hans Erik Wallin, Uffe Harder, Hugo Arne Buch. Essay by Mikael Wivel on Gauguin's stay in Copenhagen (Winter, 1884-85). 71 p. Published in an issue of *Louisiana Rey* 26:3(1986). Gauguin paintings.
1986, 31 May- 14 September	Raleigh, North Carolina Museum of Art. *French Paintings from the Chrysler Museum.* Also shown at Museum of Art, Birmingham, Alabama, 6 Nov.-18 Jan. 1987. Introduction by William J. Chiego, catalogue by Jefferson C. Harrison. 139 p. Gauguin paintings.
1986, 19 April-6 July	San Francisco, Fine Arts Museum. *The New Painting: Impressionism 1874-1886.* Also shown at National Gallery of Art, Washington. Catalogue by Charles S. Moffert. 511 p. 5 works.
1986	Paris, Galeries Nationales du Grand Palais. *La sculpture française au XIXe siècle.* Gauguin sculptures.
1986-87, December-February	Naples, Museo di Capodimonte. *Capolavori impressionisti del musei americani* [Impressionist Masterpieces from American Museums]. Also shown at Pinacoteca di Brera, Milan, Mar.-May 1987. Catalogue by Gary Tinterow. 113 p. Gauguin paintings.
1986-89	Amsterdam, Rijksmuseum Vincent van Gogh. *The Prints of the Pont-Aven School: Gauguin and his Circle in Brittany.* Also shown at 10 further venues in the U.S.A., Canada, and London under the auspices of the Smithsonian Institution Traveling Exhibition Service. Foreword by Douglas Druick. Catalogue by Caroline Boyle-Turner and Samuel Josefowitz. 142 p. (see pp. 35-46); 120 illus., 15 col. Included 85 zincographs, etchings, lithographs and woodcuts made between 1888 and 1895 by Gauguin and eight other Pont-Aven artists. Zincograph prints for Café Volpini show and series (1889).

1987, 14 January-8 March	Sunderland, England, Northern Centre for Contemporary Art. *2D/3D: Art and Craft Made and Designed for the Twentieth Century.* Catalogue by Christopher Frayling, et al. 73 p. Essay by Edward Allington comments on the decorative meaning of Gauguin's ceramics.
1987, 15 April-26 July	Boston, Museum of Fine Arts. *Printmaking: The Evolving Image.* Catalogue by Clifford S. Ackley. 39 p. Gauguin prints.
1987, 16 September-8 November	Cleveland, Cleveland Museum of Art. *Creativity in Art and Science.* Catalogue by Edward B. Henning. 143 p. Gauguin paintings.
1987, 2 August-20 September	Essen, Museum Folkwang. *Graphik der Nabis* [Prints by the Nabis]. Catalogue by Hubertus Froning. 48 p. Gauguin prints.
1987, 9 August-15 November	Lugano, Villa Favorita. *Impressionisten und Post-Impressionisten aus Sowjetischen Museen II* [Impressionists and Post-Impressionists from Soviet Museums II]. Catalogue by Albert Kostenevich, Mariha Bessonova, E. Georgievskaya. 143 p. Gauguin paintings.
1987, 19 September-25 October	Bath, Artiste Gallery. *The Self-Portrait: A Modern View.* Also shown at 9 further British venues. Catalogue by Sean Kelly, Edward Lucie-Smith. 152 p. Lucie-Smith describes Gauguin's self-portraits.
1987, 18 November-19 December	Paris, Galerie Daniel Maligne. *Maîtres impressionnistes et modernes.* 72 p. Gauguin paintings.
1987	Cleveland, Cleveland Museum of Art. *Impressionist and Post-Impressionist Masterpieces: The Courtauld Collection.* Also shown at four further U.S. venues. Included Gauguin works.
1987	Washington, D.C., National Gallery of Art. *Master Drawings from the Armand Hammer Collection.* Gauguin works.

1989, 13 January-5 March	Paris, Bibliothèque Nationale. *Gauguin & l'école de Pont-Aven.* Marianne Grivel, Commissioner. 168 p. Review: M. Grivel, *Nouvelles de l'Estampe* 101-102 (1988):35.
1989-90, September-4 February	London, Royal Academy of Arts. *Gauguin and the School of Pont-Aven: Prints and Paintings.* Also shown at the National Gallery of Scotland, 4 Dec. 1989-4 Feb. 1990. Foreword by Douglas Druick. Catalogue by Caroline Boyle-Turner and Samuel Josefowitz. 184 p., 6 paintings, Volpini zincographs (1889), other prints. Reviews: J. Norrie, *Arts Review* 41(6 Oct. 1989):689; C. Hartley, *Burlington Magazine* 131(Nov. 1989):792-93.
1990, 20 May-25 November	New York, Metropolitan Museum of Art. *From Poussin to Matisse: The Russian Taste for French Painting.* Also shown at the Art Institute of Chicago, 8 Sept.-25 Nov. Forewords by Irina Kuznetsova, James Wood, Philippe de Montebello. Essays by Irina Kuznetsova and Albert G. Kostenevich. 188 p., 3 paintings.

Index of Art Works

Includes the titles of art works by Paul Gauguin in all media, as referred to in the entries and annotations.

Actor 938
Agony in the Garden 623, 953
Allées et venues 720, 911
L'Appel 922, 936, 1149, 1150, 1264
Arearea 902, 926, 1116
Te Arii Vahine 796
Te Atua (*The Gods*) 1072
Auti te pape (*The Fresh Water is in Motion*) 1040, 1078
Aux roches noires 584

Banlieue Parisienne 1203
Bathing Girl 905
Be in Love and You Will be Happy 623, 637, 953
La Belle angèle 972, 1180
La Belle cabaretière d'Arles 906
Bonjour, Monsieur Gauguin 1012
Les Bords de la Seine sous la neige (*The Banks of the Seine under the snow*) 949
Te Burao 951, 986
Buste de Madame Emile Schuffenecker 1183

Calvary of the Maiden 900
Carved 'Coco de Mer' 893, 1133
La Chanteuse 1141
Le Cheval blanc (*The White Horse*) 946, 971, 1268
Crucifixion (sculpture) 1083, 1241
Crucifixion (woodcut) 1075

Decorative Landscape 913
Design for a Plate 1011, 1063
D'où venons-nous? Que sommes-nous? Où allons-nous? (Where do we come from? What are we? Where are we going?) 891, 923, 934, 944, 950, 966, 981, 997, 1103, 1136-1138, 1457, 1490
Les Drames de la mer 708, 1050, 1074

Eau mystérieuse 886

Faa Thethe (Pastorale Tahitienne) 997
Te Faruru (To Make Love) 1145
Fans 1114, 1122, 1124
La Femme accroupie 992
La Femme aux figues 1053
Frescoes 1117-1119, 1121, 1123, 1125

La Guerre et la paix 1140

Head of a Tahitian Woman 1028
Hina and te Fatou 1340
Hiva 1031
Hommage à Puvis 99
L'Homme à la hache (Man with an Axe) 743, 920, 941, 993
Human Miseries 584, 688, 916, 1050

I raro te oviri (Under the pandanus) 1189, 1190
Ia Orana Maria (Hail Mary) 100, 743, 914, 942, 943, 962
Idol with a Shell 1083, 1241
Interior with Aline Gauguin 998
Invocation 895

Joseph and Potiphar's Wife 907

Landscape in Brittany 935, 954
Leper (sculpture) 1084
La Lune et la terr; Tahitienne 940

La Madeleine 97
The Magician 976
Magot de la Guadeloupe 1488
Mahana no Atua (Day of the Gods) 892, 952
Manao Tupapau (The Specter Watches over Her) 98, 580, 743, 893, 930, 933, 1133, 1252
Maruru (To be Satisfied) 1068
Maternity 908
Ta Matete (The Market) 894
Menus 1115

Mme la Mort (Madame Death) 94, 95
Mme Roulin portrait 683, 1208

Nave Nave fenua (Delightful land) 1059
Nave Nave mahana (Delighful day) 897
Nevermore 927
Noa Noa 1145
Noix sculptée: fruit des îles 1132

Oà 1031
Oviri (Savage) 1013, 1098, 1102, 1282

Parau na te Varua Ino (Words of the Devil) 899
Paysage de la Martinique 720
Paysage Tahitien 1191
Père Paillard 1094
La Perte du pucelage 925, 985
Petites Bretonnes au bord de la mer 965
Poèmes barbares 999
Portrait d'Atiti mort 924
Portrait de Madame Kohler 904, 1154
Portrait de Mallarmé 967, 1052
Portrait de Suzanne Bambridge 917
Portrait Head 991
Portrait of a Tahitian Woman with Children 1143
Portrait of van Gogh 685
Portrait Vase of Mme. Schuffenecker 1102

Te Ra'au Rahi 936, 1264
Red Dog Landscape 939
Riders on the Shore 973
Roses in a Glass 968
La Route à Osny 970, 1477
Route de Rouen II 1141

Seascape in Brittany 978
Seated Tahitian Figure 979
Self-portrait vase 637
Self-portrait with Halo and Snake 1014
Self-portraits 1000-1018, 1063, 1153, 1249, 1485
She Thinks of Returning 623, 953
Soyez mystérieuses 1090
Soyez symboliste 93, 1488
Still Life with Apples and Grapes 969
Still Life with Flowers and Fruit 1033
Street in Tahiti 919, 983

Tahitian Landscape 995, 1158, 1160, 1161, 1188, 1208
Tahitian series 623, 953
Tahitian Woman (drawing) 1146
Tahitian Women Bathing 932
Tehura 987
Trois Tahitiennes (*Three Tahitians*) 959, 964
Te Tumari no Atua 778, 910, 987, 1280
Two Nudes on a Tahitian Beach 945, 982, 994

L'Univers est crée 1069

Vairaumati tei Oà 1083, 1241
Vase Decorated with Three Breton Girls 1102
Un village Breton 960
Village sous la neige 901
Vintage at Arles--Human Miseries 688, 916, 1257
Vision After the Sermon (*Jacob Wrestling with the Angel*) 520, 641, 887, 890, 896, 909, 990, 1281
Volpini Eve 899

Why are you Sorrowful? 957
Woman in the Waves (*Ondine*) 936, 1090, 1151, 1264
Woman with Fruit 956
Woman with Mango 975

Yellow Christ 893, 903, 909, 912, 931, 947, 1127-1131, 1133, 1230, 1270

Index of Personal Names

References authors, editors, compilers, translators, and other names in the entries and annotations.

Abe, Nobuo 865
Abel, L. 535a
Adam, Paul 102, 103
Adhemar, Hélène 1181
Adlmann, J. von 1132
Adolphe, Helen 887
Agee, James 663, 724
Agostini, Jules 725
Agustoni, Fabrizio 226
Alden, Robert 898
Alexandre, Arsène P. U. 22, 28, 233, 718, 891
Alhadeff, Albert 551
Allen, Robert 1020b
Allen, W. G. Russell 1043
Alley, Ronald 866
Amann, Per 835
Amiet, Cuno 610
Amishai-Maisels, Ziva 65, 684, 899, 1024, 1083, 1223, 1241
Ancey 649
Andersen, Wayne V. 13, 224, 234, 845, 900, 1224, 1242, 1243
Andronikova, Manana Irsklievna 1000
Anger, Isolde 368
Anquetil-Pléssier, Marie Amélie 553
Anquetin, Louis 1266
Ansieau, Joelle 554
Antes, Horst 1337
Antoine, Jules 104-109
Antony de Witt, Antonio 235, 236
Antreasian, Garo Z. 1048

Apollinaire, Guillaume 20
Aquino, Ricardo Bigi de 726
Arguelles, Jose A. 224, 1306
Arnold, Matthias 1025
Arosa, Gustave 692
Arrieta, Rafael Alberto 369
Arrivé, Michel 743
Artur, Gilles 85, 1166
Askeland, Jan 1049
Atkin, Park 769
Aurell, Jorge Benet 1310
Auriant, A. 555
Aurier, G. Albert [Luc le Flaneur] 22, 110-117, 168, 500, 561, 585, 1249
Austin, Florence 770
Austin, Lloyd James 483
Awazu, Norio 237

Baas, Jacquelynn 1035
Babelon, J. 340
Bacoue, Roseline 23
Baderou, Henri 1031
Baderou, Suzanne 1031
Badt, Kurt 843
Baelen, Jean 238
Bailly-Herzberg, Janine 536
Ballin, Mogens 61
Balzac, Honoré de 1249
Bantens, Robert James 484
Bap, Frances 1320a
Bardeau, Jacqueline 239
Barnes, Haydn 255a
Barrucand, Victor 118
Barskaia, Anna G. 888, 1176, 1204
Barth, Wilhelm 556, 1036, 1085
Bartlett, Frederic Clay 1143
Bartlett, Helen Birch 1148
Bataille, Henri 61
Battershaw, Brian 1350
Bauchy, Auguste 48
Baudelaire, Charles Pierre 483, 614, 673, 1225, 1486
Bauer, Henri 119
Baughman, M. L. 1493
Bazarov, Konstantin 1295
Bazin, Germain 901, 1307
Beardsley, Aubrey 1295
Beatty, John Wesley 1308
Beauté, Georges 240

Becker, Beril 241
Beerblock, M. 666b
Beguin, Sylvie 902, 1116
Bell, Mary 1309
Bellamy, Susan 350a
Bellini, Paolo 226
Bender, B. 1408
Benet, Rafael 1310
Benington, Jonathan 557
Bensch, Wolfgang 231a
Berman, P. 956
Bernard, Emile 16, 20, 22, 33, 61, 120, 121, 362, 370, 485, 494, 503, 531, 534, 538, 542, 542, 555, 558, 562, 569, 582, 585, 596, 603, 605, 510, 633, 641, 656, 657, 660, 675, 695, 909, 1017, 1025, 1035, 1090, 1104, 1126, 1244, 1249, 1266, 1267, 1281, 1358
Bernard, Joseph 977
Bernard, Madeleine 660
Bernard-Fort, M. A. 20
Bernhardt, Sarah 1473
Bernheim-Jeune, Josse 718, 1135
Berruer, Pierre 242
Berryer, Anne-Marie 1086
Bertram, Anthony 243
Bessonova, Marina 888, 1176, 1200, 1204
Betz, Gerd 244
Beuys, Joseph 1362
Bevan, R. A. 632
Bevan, R. P. 632
Biad, A. 371
Bidou, Henri 122
Biermann, George 1409
Bijieveld, M. C. A. 678a
Billy, André 1311
Binder, Klaus 1381
Bing, Siegfried 1288, 1304
Birnholz, Alan C. 903
Bjurström, Per 72
Blake, WIlliam 1306
Blanche, Jacques-Emile 486, 559, 1312, 1410
Blanton, Catherine W. 889, 904, 1154
Blavatsky, Helena P. 550, 1240
Bloy, Léon 20
Boccaccio, Giovanni 695, 696
Boccioni, Umberto 1095
Boch, Eugène-Guillaume 696
Bodelsen, Merete Christensen 225, 225a, 245, 372, 373, 681, 844, 845, 879, 880, 905, 1020, 1027, 1080, 1081, 1087, 1088, 1212, 1245

Bois, Jules 648
Bolton, Linda 246, 867
Bompard, Pierre 727
Bonnard, Pierre 493, 578, 586, 636, 945, 996, 1025, 1299
Borel, Pierre 55, 771
Borisov-Musatov, Viktor 1393
Bosman, Anthony 374
Botticelli, Sandro 695, 1000, 1282
Boudaille, Georges 247
Boudot-Lamotte, M. 560
Bouge, L. J. 12, 772, 858
Bouillon, Jean-Paul 1284
Bouret, Jean 375
Bourges, Elémir 20
Bousil, Louis 185
Bowness, Alan 248, 276
Boyle, Caroline Ross 487, 561-563, 1050
Bracquemond, Félix 172, 1284
Bradley, David 663, 724
Brancusi, Constantin 1104, 1340
Braque, Georges 1095, 1325
Brault, Léonce 59, 61
Braun, Barbara 1089, 1246
Braunfels, Wolfgang 1239
Bray, Barbara 1225b
Brennan, Daniel 1462
Brenton, Jane 321a
Bresdin, Rodolphe 539
Brest, R. 377
Breton, André 488, 564
Breton, Jules 584, 1281
Brettell, Richard R. 1202
Briant 73
Brill, Susan 231b, c
Brinkemann, A. E. 565
Le Bronnec, Georges 363, 773, 774, 858
Brooke, Rupert 728, 744
Brooks, V. F. 993
Brooks, Van Wyck 92
Brouillon, Louis (see Jean de Rotonchamp)
Brown, Sara 566, 775
Buckman, E. 283
Bullock, Michael 493a
Bunny, Rupert 1426
Burchard, L. 249
Burger, Fritz 1313
Burgess, Gelett 1411

Burnett, Robert 250
Burroughs, Alan 1412
Buser, Thomas 378
Bussy, Dorothy 511b

Cabanne, Pierre 1314
Cachin, Françoise 251, 252, 682, 830, 1090
Cadorin, Paolo 868
Cahn, Isabelle 253, 254, 379
Camoin, Charles 906
Cannon-Brookes, Peter 1213
Canudo, Ricciotto 1005
Carey 60
Cariel 567
Cariou, André 568
Carley, Lionel 489, 1315
Carlsen, Henning 1503
Carlyle, Thomas 637
Carrière, Eugène 484, 491, 652, 1323
Carries, Jean 1092
Carroll, Jane 231b, c
Cary, Elisabeth Luther 1051
Cassatt, Mary 1299
Castel, Jane 1247
Castets, H. 123
Cate, Philip Denis 1037
Cateforis, D. 907
Cézanne, Paul 20, 297, 483, 502, 531, 531, 532, 545, 580, 585, 617, 643, 667, 690, 697, 709, 814, 839, 879, 1016, 1025, 1031, 1209, 1213, 1219, 1231, 1252, 1260, 1303, 1313, 1347, 1362, 1391, 1401, 1447, 1481, 1484, 1498
Chabot, C. 380
Chadourne 740
Chadwick, Helen Whitney 1082
Chagall, Marc 1270
Chamaillard 615, 647
Champigneulle, Bernard 381
Chaplet, Ernest 646, 1082, 1086, 1092, 1107
Chardourne, Marc 46, 1038
Charensol, Georges 666b
Charles-Bellet, L. 569, 1126
Charlier, Henri 1091
Charmet, Raymond 255
Chasse, Charles 256, 382, 383, 490-493, 571, 572, 776, 1214
Chastel, André 573, 1248
Chater, Arthur G. 283a
Chauval 152

Chazàl, André 281
Cheetham, Mark A. 1249
Cheronnet, L. 777
Cheyron, J. 494
Chirico, Robert 1413
Christoffel, Ulrich 1316
Christophe, Jules 124
Cikovsky, Nicolai 683
Cimabue, Giovanni 1486
Clark, Eliot 908, 1414
Clark, G. 1092
Clavel, Bernard 257
Coatsworth, Elizabeth J. 881
Codet 521
Coellen, Ludwig 1317
Coetzee, S. 909
Cogniat, Raymond 71, 225, 258, 259, 362, 384, 385, 1415
Colleville, Vicomte de 125
Collins, Bradley 684
Collins, R. D. J. 778, 910
Comstock, H. 1161
Constable, W. G. 685
Cooper, Douglas 25, 58, 386, 720, 882, 911, 1152
Coquiot, Gustave 1319
Cork, R. 1416
Corot, Jean-Baptiste Camille 1386, 1391
Cossio del Pomar, Felipe 260-262
Courbet, Gustave 1012, 1391
Courtault, Samuel 1466
Courthion, Pierre 263
Coustet, Robert 539
Cowart, Jack 1208
Cowles, John 1026
Crane, Stephen 1408
Cucchi, Roger 718
Cummings, Nathan 1202

Daddi, Bernardo 1329
Dagnan-Bourveret, Pascal 1281
Daix, Pierre 264
D'Albis, Jean 1093
Dale, Chester 889, 904, 1011, 1063, 1153, 1154
Daleverze, J. 574
Dallet, Jean-Marie 265, 729
Damigella, Anna Maria 266
Damiron, Suzanne 79
Damisch, Hubert 387

Dampt, Jean 1104
D'Angelis, Gaston 267, 288
Danielsson, Bengt 11, 45, 510, 575, 730-734, 779-781, 845, 1504
Danielsson, Marie-Thèrese 731, 734
Dante, Alighieri 695, 696
Danto, A. C. 388, 782
Daragnes, Jean-Gabriel 1039
Darragon, Eric 686
Darses, Simone 227a
Daubler, Theodor 389
Dauchot, Fernand 576, 912
Daudet, Alphonse 686
Daulte, François 1215, 1320
Daulte, M. 1417
Daumier, Honoré 1065, 1095, 1267, 1297, 1448
Daurelle, J. 127
Daval, Jean-Luc 1321
David, Sylvain-Christian 640
Davidson, Marshall B. 783, 1040
Davis, F. 390, 1418
Davis, R. S. 1191
Daws, Gavan 735
Dayot, Armand 128
Debussy, Claude 620
Degas, Edgar 46, 129, 483, 532, 645, 975, 1031, 1095, 1217, 1263, 1285, 1287, 1293, 1295, 1302, 1303, 1384, 1391, 1430, 1476
Delacroix, Eugène 1012, 1267, 1391
Delaherche, Auguste 1092
Delaroche, Achille 130
Dell'Acqua, G. A. 1322
Delius, Frederick 489, 1315
Delouche, Denise 495-499
Delsemme, Paul 500
Delvoy, Robert L. 1225
Demont, Bernard 1250
Denis, Maurice 22, 42, 132, 491, 493, 500, 501, 508, 543, 577, 578, 636, 1035, 1226, 1231, 1251, 1272, 1312
Derain, André 1095, 1104, 1325, 1340, 1484
Desarrois, André 1419
DeStijl 1383
Deverin, Edouard 579
Devoluy, John 391
Diego, Eliseo 1420
Diehl, Gaston 268, 1006
Dietrich, Linnea Stonesifer 13, 580, 1227, 1252, 1253
Dillies 64
Dolent, Jean 133, 1323

Van Dongen 1325
Donnell-Kotrozo, Carol A. 502, 581, 831, 1216
Dorival, Bernard 70, 288, 392, 504, 536, 1254, 1324, 1379
Dorn, R. 25
Dorra, Henri 16, 77, 269, 542, 582-586, 675, 688, 914-916, 1255-1258
Dorsenne, Jean 270, 393
Dow, Arthur Wesley 628
Van Dowski, Lee [Herbert Lewandowski] 272, 273, 394, 587, 869, 1007
Druick, Douglas 864
Dubourg, Jacques 1471
Duca, G. M. Lo 588
Dudensing, G. 635
Dufy, Raoul 1325
Dujardin, Jules 134
Dumont, Henri 274
Dumonthier, Ernest 1175
Dunkel, Gunter 1259
Dunstan, B. 1421
Duret 1296
Durrio, Francisco 644
Duthuit, Georges 1325
Dvorak, Frantisek 1326

Eakins, Thomas 945
Edwards, Hugh 1041
Elgar, Frank 832, 1327
Ellsmoor, Jean
Emmons, James 275b, 833b
Ensor, James 1362
Ernst, Max 1095
Escholier, Raymond 1328
Estienne, Charles 275, 590, 853
Evans, Patrick 518b

Fabrice, Delphi 135
Facy, Maurice 591
Fagus, Félicien 136
Fair, Joseph Brooks 1072
Falguière, Jean Alexandre Joseph 152
Farr, Dennis 1329
Farrell, Eugene 670
Fathke, B. 1330
Fauré, Marguerite 547b
Fayet, Gustave 50, 1156
Fénéon, Félix 139-142, 506, 512, 1278, 1331, 1332
Fernandez, Justino 1333
Fezzi, Elda 231, 737

Field, Richard Sampson 288, 738, 834, 228, 1054-1057
Fierens, Paul 917
Fischel, L. 1423
Fischer, F. W. 1260
Fitton, Mary 278a
Flam, Jack D. 1261
Le Flaneur, Luc (see G. Albert Aurier)
Fletcher, John Gould 276
Florisoone, Michel 592
Focillon, Henri 1334
Fonsmark, Anne-Brigitte 277, 1141
Fontainas, André 19, 21, 22, 143-145, 541, 658
Forain, Jean-Louis 1297
Forges, M. T. de 1425
Forman, Nessa 1058
Forwood, Gillian 1426
Fouchet, Max-Pol 278, 593
Fouquier, Henry 146
Fourcade, Jean-Pierre 85
Francastel, Pierre 1335
Frances, José 1336
Francolin, Claude 279
Fraenkel, Michael 921
Francis, Henry S. 922, 1028, 1059
Frankfurter, A. M. 395, 1136
Franzke, A. 1337
Fraser, Donald Hamilton 890
Freixa, Mireia 1338
Frère, Henri 507
Friedrich, Caspar David 1267
Friesz, Othon 1325
Fry, Edward 502
Fry, Roger E. 891, 923
Fukunaga, Takehiko 280

Gabo, Naum 1383
Gaigneron, A. de 689
Gallego, Julian 396
Galsworthy, John 1466
Gann, Louise Gebhard 1008
Gardner, J. 397
Garnier, Edouard 147
Gattey, Charles Neilson 281
Gauguin, Emil 92, 984
Gauguin, Mette 18, 22, 26, 31, 32, 61, 63, 283, 284, 443, 1503
Gauguin, Paul-René 240
Gauguin, Pedro Maria 282

Gauguin, Pola (Paul Rollon) 283, 284, 310, 401, 432, 1042
Gaunt, W. 411
Gazier, Denise 79
Gedo, John 684
Geffroy, Gustave 61, 150-152, 1339
Geist, Sidney 1340
Genthon, Istvan 509
George, W. 1428, 1429
Gérald, Judith 43, 510, 670
Gerbault, Alain 739
Gerstein, Marc Saul 230, 926, 1114, 1122, 1430
Gide, André 23, 511
Gill, Ian Dickson 927
Gill, Malone 1505
Gilman, Harold 632
Gilmour, P. 232
Ginies, Louis 928
Ginner, Charles 632
Gioseffi, Decio 929
Giotto di Bondone 1297
Girieud, Pierre 871
Giry, Marcel 930
Glynn, E. 1262
Goedeckemeyer, Helmut 1172
Goethe, Johann Wolfgang von 517
Gogh, Jo van 25, 665
Gogh, Laren Vincent W. van 65, 721
Gogh, Theo van 25, 65, 347, 673, 677, 681, 1479
Gogh, Vincent van 20, 25, 26, 28, 33, 62, 65, 297, 298, 347, 362, 483, 502, 514, 520, 531, 532, 540, 542, 580, 585, 596, 617, 633, 643, 663-717, 814, 839, 945, 1012, 1016, 1074, 1209, 1219, 1231, 1252, 1257, 1262, 1266, 1267, 1270, 1272, 1287, 1293, 1295, 1296, 1298, 1302-1304, 1306, 1314, 1330, 1358, 1362, 1408, 1448, 1481, 1484
Goldwater, Robert John 290, 836, 931, 1061, 1129, 1228, 1341, 1432
Goncourt, Edmond de 1296
Gonse 1296
Gonzalès, Eva 483
Goodison, J. W. 880
Goodyear, A. Conger 580, 1252
Gordon, Donald E. 932, 933
Gordon, Irene 541
Gordon, Jan 1342, 1433
Gordon, Ronald 1490
Gore, Frederick Spencer 632, 1465
Gorham, Charles O. 291
Gorman, Stephen 835a

Gorsky, Bernard 739
Grotte, G. 596
Gottheiner, T. 845
Goulinat, J. G. 1156
Goupil 51, 1479
Gourmont, Rédé 1035
Gouzer, Dr. 964
Gowing, Lawrence 934
Goya, Francisco 1065, 1448
Graber, Hans 292, 293
Grabol, Sofie 1503
Graham, Rigby A. 1044
Grautoff, Otto 597
Gravelaine, Frederique de 295, 872, 1210
Gray, Christopher 224
Gray, Frederic Charles 740
Greenacre, Phyllis 1262
Greet, Anne Hyde 1434
Gregg, F. J. 785
Griffin, Jonathan 82
Grimstad, Kirsten 868
Grivel, M. 698, 1062
Groux, Henri de 20
Guérin, Marcel L. 89, 221
Guernin, Joseph 153
Guibal, Jean 413
Guierre, Maurice 1038
Guillard, Georges 1336
Guillemin, Henri 272
Guillot, François 154, 741

Hadley, Suzanne Haney 1229
Hakansson, T. 599
Hale, Charlotte 1211
Hale, Humphrey 330a,b
Halperin, Joan Ungersma 506a, 512
Halsey, Brian Elliot 1230
Hamilton, Florence Wiggin 837
Hamilton, George Heard 1435
Hammacher, A. M. 693
Hammer, Armand 71
Hamon, Renée 742, 787, 788
Hansen, Wilhelm 1175, 1391
Hanson, Elisabeth 295, 667
Hanson, Lawrence 295, 667
Haris, Ludwig 513
Harrison, C. 600

Hartrick, Archibald Standish 514, 1045
Haskell, F. 483
Hauke, César de 1483
Haupt, D. E. 789
Hautecoeur, Louis 296, 935, 1347, 1437
Havard, Henri 155
Havelaar, Just 414
Haweis, Stephen 415
Hayes, Dennis 668
Hayter, Stanley William 1048
Heegaard, Marie 880
Hegel, Georg Wilhelm Friedrich 517
Heim, Roger 1162
Heller, Reinhold 601, 1217, 1263
Heller, Steven 1488
Hennequin, Emile 156
Henning, E. B. 936, 1264
Henry, Marie 511, 1014
Hepp, Alexandre 157
Hepworth, Barbara 1383
Herban, Matthew B. 937, 1231, 1265
Herbert, Robert L. 1345, 1438, 1439
Herrmann, Curt 1440
Hess, Thomas B. 1374
Hess, Walter 1346, 1347
Hewlett, Maurice 56
Hildebrandt, Hans 417
Hill, Audrey Leigh 838
Hillier, Jack 224, 1296
Hilton, Ian 602
Hind, Charles Lewis 939, 1348
Hirayama, Ikuo 289
Hiroshige, Ando 1296
Hirsch, Charles-Henri 158
Hitchings, Sinclair Hamilton 1037
Hobhouse, J. 13, 418
Hodin, J. P. 1349
Hodler, Ferdinand 1313
Hoffman, Edith 1010
Hoffmann, K. 694
Hofmann, Werner 940, 1350
Hofstatter, Hans-Hellmut 603
Hogarth, William 1448
Hohl, Reinhold 941
Hokusai, Katsushika 1296, 1297
Holmes, Charles John 1351
Hoog, Michel 297, 839

Van Hook, Katrina 1011, 1063, 1153
Hoop, Scheffer, D. de 942
Hoppe, Ragnar 851
Hours, Madeleine 790, 873
Huchel 602
Huebner, F. M. 419
Hughes, Robert 420, 852
Hugué, Manolo 644
Hull, E. G. 1001b
Hulse, Michael 359a
Hulsker, J. 697
Humbert, Agnes 515
Huneke, A. 1095
Huneker, James Gibbons 1352, 1441
Hunt, William Holman 1267
Huret, Jules 159
Huyghe, René 39, 69, 80, 288, 298, 299, 791, 1392, 1442
Huysmans, Joris-Karl 15, 20, 23, 160, 1354, 1461

Ibels, Henri-Gabriel 634
Ihle, Elisabeth 283d
Ikeda, Masuo 300
Ikegami, Chuji 516, 1297
Imber, Diana 757b
Imbourg, P. 421
Immerman, Irene (see Leclerc, Andre)
Inaga, S. 1298
Inbopen, Gudrun 517
Ingres, Jean Auguste Dominique 994, 1267, 1486, 1498
Inoue, Yasushi 289
Ives, Colta Feller 1285, 1443
Iwasaki, Yoshikazu 300
Izergina, A. 792

Jacob, Hans 18
Jacobs, Jay 944
Jacobson, Egbert 892
Jacquier, Henri 793
Jaffa, Alisa 247a
Jammes, Paul 23
Jamot, Paul 1444, 1445
Janson, C. 1134
Janson, H. W. 669
Jarry, Alfred 161, 640, 743, 1035
Jaworska, Wladyslawa 518, 604, 605
Jénot, P. 162, 363, 828, 858
Jeudwine, W. R. 1186

Jewell, Edward A. 422
Jirat-Wasiutynski, Vojtech 13, 542, 670, 675, 937, 1012-1014, 1232, 1266
Joachim, Harold 232
Jockle, Clemens 1267
Jodidio, Philip 606
Johnson, Lincoln F. 945
Johnson, Ronald 696, 1357, 1446, 1447
Johnston, Roy 607, 608
Joly-Segalen, Anne 17, 18, 609
Jones, H. 1448
Joyau, Auguste 722
Joyce, David 1320a
Madame Julie (Pont-Aven) 544
Jullian, Philippe 519

Kahn, Gustave 163, 853
Kalophile, Ermite 164, 165
Kandinsky, Wassily 884, 1065, 1249, 1260, 1459, 1465
Kane, William MacGibbon 946, 1019, 1268
Kantor-Gukovskaya, Asya Solomonova 301, 1176, 1204
Kardos, Istvan 1506
Kashiwa, Takeshi 320
Keable, Robert 794, 1064
Kelder, Diane 1358, 1378
Kemp, Roger 1426
Kendall, R. 297
Kerr, John O'Connell 44, 854
Kesler, C. 223
Kessler, Harry 1434
Keynes, Geoffrey 728
Khnopff, Fernand 1217, 1263
Killer, P. 610
Kinjo, Ladislas 1452
Kjellberg, Gerda E. 510
Kjellberg, P. 1096
Klée, Paul 1065
Klein, Barbara 234
Klein, Jerome 1359
Klimt, Gustav 1279
Kloner, Jay Martin 1286
Knapp, James F. 611
Knyphausen, Brita 295b
Kodera, Tsukasa 671
Koestler, Arthur 1360
Kohn, Heinz 1155
Kokoschka, Oskar 1383
Kollwitz, Käthe 1095

Kornfeld, Eberhard W. 232, 1065
Kozloff, M. 1449
Kraemer, J. 283
Kremer, R. 423
Kretschmer 822
Kubin, Alfred 1441
Kunstler, Charles 302, 424-427, 612, 855
Kuspit, Donald B. 613, 614, 684, 1269

Labo, G. 1234
Lacker, D. 947, 1270
Lacombe, Georges 554, 1104
La Farge, Henry 795
La Farge, John 795
Laks, Claudie 1097
Laks, Simon 518b
Landy, Barbara J. 845, 1098, 1233
Lane, Hugh 1466
Langdon, Robert 728, 744
Lange, Eleonare H. 1450
Lange, Holger 1204a
Langer, Alfred Karasek 303
Lari, Giulio 226
Larson, K. 797
Larson, Philip 1451
Lascault, Gilbert 1452
Lass, H. 1066
Lassaigne, Jacques 428, 856
Lassen, Erik 1453
Latorre, Margarita 13
Laukomski, Georges 1454
Laval, Charles 585, 660, 719
Lazar, Bela 304
Leake, Kenneth M. 259b
Lebihan, Olivier 615
Leblond, Marius-Ary 166, 167, 745, 1455
Lebowitz, R. 675
Leclerc, Andre [pseud. for Irene Immerman] 305
Leclercq, Julien 168-171
Lee, Sara 1202
Legrand, Gerard 306
Leinz, Gottlieb 1362
Leithauser, Brad 798
Lemasson, Henri 799
Lenz, Desiderius 487
Lenz, Peter 1267
Leonard, H. Stewart 91, 1206

Lepère, Auguste 1035
Leprohon, Pierre 307
Letheve, Jacques 1363, 1456
Level, André 61
Leveque, J.J. 616
Levi, A. 483
Levieux, Eleanore 13
Lewandowski, Herbert (see Van Dowski, Lee)
Leymarie, Jean 39, 308, 1020
Lhôte, André 18, 1366
Liedholm, Alf-Anton Frederick 1364
Liebermann, Max 1267
Van Liere, E. N. 1271
Lindberg-Hansen, Jacob 1067, 1099
Lipman, Jean 1015
Lissitzky, Eliezer 1065
Lloyd, C. 617
Loiseau, Gustave 534
Loize, Jean 15, 82, 83, 363, 429, 521, 618, 619, 746, 857, 858, 948
Longstreet, Stephen 1021
Loo, Esther van 800
Loon, H. W. van 706
Loppin, Paul 522
Lord, Douglas 33, 250, 283, 949, 1457
Lormel, Louis
Lostalot, Alfred de 172
Loti, Pierre 750
Lövgren, Sven 34, 520
Lubin, Albert 684
Lucas, Christopher 747
Lucie-Smith, Edward 523
Lugne-Poe, Aurelien François 524
Lyons, Lisa 620

MacDonald, J. 951
Macdonald, Violet M. 766
Mack, G. 21
Maeterlinck, Maurice 1225
Mahaut, Henri 71
Maillol, Aristide 507, 521, 619, 620, 1104, 1434
Malczewski, Rafael 996
Malevich, Kasimir 1249
Malingue, Maurice 22, 25, 288, 308-312, 431, 432, 718
Mallarmé, Stéphane 23, 483, 500, 517, 566, 570, 580, 775, 967, 1225, 1277, 1278
Maltese, Corrado 1300
Manceron, Gilles 760

Manet, Edouard 483, 532, 1267, 1285-1288, 1293, 1302, 1303, 1359, 1391, 1401, 1448
Manguin, Henri Charles 1325
Manheim, Ralph 1325
Manson, J. B. 1458
Mantz, Paul 173
Maraini, Antonio 697, 1016
Marc, Franz 932, 933
Marchiori, Giuseppe 313
Marées, Hans von 1259
Marie, Renée 578
Marks-Vandenbroucke, Ursula F. 32, 314, 363, 433, 434, 858
Marois, Pierre 1366
Marquet, Albert 1325
Marensen-Larsen, Britta 1459
Marter, J. M. 1047
Martini, Alberto 315
Marx, M. 39
Masciotta, Michelangelo 874
Masheck, Joseph 518c
Mastai, M. L. D. 1100
Matena, Dick 672
Mathews, Patricia 623, 953
Mathieu, P. L. 654, 1461
Matisse, Henri 508, 569, 651, 1104, 1126, 1219, 1261, 1325, 1330, 1391, 1464, 1466, 1472, 1484
Mattison, D. M. 954
Mauclair, Camille 120, 174, 175, 435, 436, 525, 1367
Maufra, Maxime 39, 562
Maughan, W. Somerset 744, 748, 784, 956, 1186
Mauner, Georges L. 526, 955
Maupassant, Guy de 673
Maurice, René 485, 625
Mauron, Charles 673
Maus, Madeleine-Octave 35, 718
Maus, Octave 35, 176
Mayer, Dolores A. 1069
Mazière, Francis 1507
McGee, C. 1462
McKee, William McCallin 1072
McNair, John 301a
Meier-Graefe, Julius 177, 527, 528
Mellon, Paul 1187
Mellquist, J. 698
Mellon, Paul 1187
Melot, Michel 1487
Menard, Paul 801

Menard, Wilmon B. 802, 803, 956
Merea, Valarie 1503
Merki, Charles 178
Merlhès, Victor 26, 79
Merlin, Angelo 1234
Merrill, Stuart 179
Metken, Gunter 626
Metken, S. 1463
Meyer de Haan, Jacob 511, 547, 576, 1252
Meyer-Riefstahl, Rudolf 437
Michaud, Eric 1272
Michaud, Guy 1368
Mikoyan, Ashkhen 1204
Millais, John Everett 1267
Millet, Jean François 1439
Milner, John 529
Minde 621
Minervino, Florella 737
Minne, Georg 551
Mirbeau, Octave 67, 180-181, 627, 718
Mitchell, H. 273b
Miterwa, K. 699
Mittelstadt, Kuno 316, 1001
Miyakawa, Atsushi 318
Modersohn-Becker, Paula 1279
Modigliani, Amedeo 1095
Moffat, Alexander 700
Moffattt, F. C. 628
Moins, Philippe 335
Molard, Ida 510
Molard, Judith 1503
Molard, William 43, 61, 489, 510
Monay-Vaudover, Daphné 290b, 836b
Mondrian, Piet 1249, 1260, 1262, 1347
Monet, Claude 8, 297, 483, 532, 534, 627, 839, 945, 957, 1209, 1287, 1290, 1293, 1295, 1302, 1335, 1381, 1391
Monfreid, Agnès Huc de 1083, 1241
Monfreid, Georges-Daniel de 17, 18, 21, 50, 61, 184, 185, 352, 398, 438, 521, 537, 574, 588, 594, 618, 619, 629, 813, 859, 964
Mongan, Elizabeth 232
Monkhouse, Cosmo 186
Monnier, G. 1031
Montaigne, Michel 589
Monticelli, Adolphe 113, 673
Moore, Henry 1247
Moran, Thomas 1048
Moreau, Gustave 488, 491

Moret 534
Morice, Charles 18, 22, 47, 81, 82, 87, 88, 136, 187-193, 317, 439, 486, 500, 530, 559, 718, 891, 1106
Morillot 804, 805
Morisot, Berthe 483, 532
Morland, Jacques 630
Mornand, Pierre 531
Morris, William 1434
Morteville, Brigitte 749
Motoe, Kunio 319, 320
Mount, C. 667
Mourey, Gabriel 1193
Mucha, Alphonse 1473
Muehsam, Gerd 1369
Muhlethaler, Bruno 868
Mullaly, Terence 1301
Muller, Joseph-Emile 321, 532, 1370
Mullins, Edwin 1371
Munch, Edvard 489, 584, 814, 1010, 1065, 1217, 1263, 1279, 1315, 1349, 1362, 1444, 1451
Murer 63
Murina, Elena Borisovna 674
Muse, V. 789

Nacenta, Raymond 322
Nakayama, Kimio 865
Nasgaard, Roald 1372
Nash, Steven A. 893, 1133
Natanson, Thadée 194-196, 1373
Near, Pinkney L. 1187
Neff, John Hallmark 1464
Nemeczek, A. 440
Nemes, Marczell de 1193
Nevermann, Hans 806
Newman, Richard 670
Newton, E. 441
Newton, H. Travers 670
Neve, C. 632, 1465
Nicholls, Paul C. 323
Nicholson, Ben 1329
Nietzche, Friedrich 933
Nochlin, Linda 1374
Nocq, Henri 197
Nolde, Emil 1095
Nolet, Dr. 964
Nordenfalk, Carl 702
Nordstom, Gert Z. 1017

Nørregard-Nielsen, Hans Edvard 443
Nourrisier, François 288, 533
Novotny, Fritz 1375
O'Brien, Frederick 18, 807
O'Conor, Roderic 557, 562, 607, 608
Oldfield-Florescu, Sylvia M. 366b
Olédzka, Hanna 329d
Olin, Pierre-M. 198-200
Oliveira, José C. 295d
Olmos, Pedro 324
Olzon, Cösta 283b
Ooka, Makoto 289
Oppler, Ellen Charlotte 1376
Opresco, O. 1032
O'Reilly, Patrick 11, 354, 733, 750, 808-810, 1164, 1165
Ormond, Leonee 1466
Orton, F. 633
Osborn, Max 1199
Oshima, Seiji 1288
Otohiko, Kaja 516
O'Toole, J. H. 634
Overbeck, Johann Friedrich 1267

Pallucchini, Rodolfo 1101
Palmer, Frederick 963
Palue, Pierre 1218
Pankol, Otto 1095
Paris, I. Mark 333a
Passe, Jean 201
Patacky, Denes 1022
Paul, Derek Lionel 637
Le Paul, Charles-Guy 534, 635, 636
Le Paul, Judy 534
Payne, Richard 668
Payro, Julio E. 328, 1377
Pearson, Eleanor 964
Péladan, Joséphin 585, 1235
Pelleau, Paul T. 639
Pennec, Jos 640
Perl, J. 449
Perruchot, Henri 18, 288, 329-332, 450, 451, 751, 752, 811-813, 859
Perucci-Petri U. 641
Peter, Adeline 337
Peters, Robert Louis 332
Petersen, Carl V. 1468
Petit, E. 52
Petrarch 695

Pfister, Kurt 452
Philipsen, Theodor 621, 1141
Phillips, Duncan 1195
Phillips, M. 1070
Picasso, Pablo 484, 644, 940, 945, 1048, 1065, 1095, 1104, 1261, 1357, 1381, 1446, 1447, 1466
Le Pichon, Yann 333, 642
Pickvance, Ronald 26, 225, 866, 1023
Piel, Friedrich 1239
Pielkovo, Ruth 56
Pierre, José 753, 814
Pierre, Michel 334
Pincus-Witten, Robert 1235
Pissarro, Camille 26, 27, 61, 483, 532, 535, 549, 585, 596, 617, 655, 656, 658, 970, 1209, 1296, 1372, 1391, 1475, 1477, 1487
Pissarro, Lucien 535, 658
Pitts, Greg 1102
Planet, Georges 723
Platte, Hans 643, 894, 1378
Plaut, J. S. 966
Pleadwell, Frank Lester 91
Plessier, Ghislaine 644
Pocar, Ervino 348a
Pollock, G. 633
Pollock, Jackson 814
Ponente, Nello 1401
Pool, Phoebe 335
Pope, Arthur 1205
Pope, Karen Kristine Rechnitzer 719, 1469
Porlier 55
Poulain, Gaston 1470
Poussin, Nicolas 1386
Prat, V. 1471
Prather, Marla 336
Preston, Stuart 1379
Prud'hon, Pierre-Paul 907
Puig, René 537, 538
Puvis de Chavannes, Pierre 483, 573, 616, 654, 1425, 1434, 1472
Puy, Jean 1325
Puy, Michel 453, 454, 1380

Raboff, Ernest Lloyd 337
Raffaelli, Jean-François 483
Ramsden, Eric 815
Raphael, Max 1381
Ratcliff, C. 1472
Raynal, Maurice 875

Read, Herbert Edward 338, 455, 1273, 1274, 1382, 1383
Reberschak, S. F. 1473
Redlow, Theodor 1474
Redon, Ari 23
Redon, Odilon 15, 20, 23, 202, 483, 491, 531, 539, 580, 585, 630, 860, 1235, 1252, 1287
Reff, Théodore 645, 1384, 1475, 1476
Régnier, Henri de 1135
Reidemeister, Leopold 1289
Reiff, R. 224
Rembrandt, Harmensz Van Rijn 34, 1000, 1012
René, Jean 339
Renoir, Pierre Auguste 483, 532, 534, 969, 1095, 1209, 1259
Repin, Ilya 1000
Reutersward, Patrik 816
Revault d'Allonnes, Olivier 1226a
Reverseau, Jean-Pierre 1275
Rewald, Alice 540c
Rewald, John 21, 27, 49, 71, 223, 340, 241, 456-458, 535, 540, 541, 970, 1187, 1385, 1477-1479
Rey, Robert 36, 342, 459, 460, 754, 817, 971, 972, 1071, 1103, 1115, 1123, 1386
Reyer, Georges 461
Rheims, Maurice 288, 343
Ribault-Menetière, Jean J. 47, 48, 57
Rich, D. C. 703
Richardson, J. 225
Riedl, Peter Anselm 1173
Riester, R. 1172
Rilke, Rainer Maria 887
Rimbaud, Arthur 759b
Rinuy, P. L. 1104
Rippli-Rónai, József 509
Rivière, Henri 204
Rivière, Jacques 1387
Roberts, Kevin 755
Robinson, Edward G. 1198
Rocha, Augusto da 704
Roddin, G. 1219
Rodin, Auguste 483, 484, 491, 1259, 1340, 1357
Roelandt, Louis 664, 666b
Roger-Marx, Claude 28, 163, 205-208, 288, 344, 705, 1276, 1388, 1480
Roh, Franz 1389
Rohde, Petra-Angelika 756
Roi, V. 1481
Rollins, Louis 974
Romm, A. 1482
Rops, Félicien 688, 916, 1257, 1259

Rookmaker, Hendrik Roelof 1236
Rose, B. 818
Rose, Gilbert 684
Rosenthal, G. 975
Roskill, Mark Wentworth 542, 675, 676, 1033
Ross, Anne 268a
Rossi, Gino 1481
Rostrup, Haavard 31, 363, 462, 1034, 1124, 1390, 1391
Rothschild, Ruth Deborah 1002
Rotonchamp, Jean de [pseud. for Louis Brouillon] 209, 345, 522
Roumy, Valéry 1141
Rousseau, Henri 1362
Rousseau, Theodore 840
Rouvier 36
Rowlands, J. 1483
Roy, Louis 1043, 1072
Rubens, Peter Paul 1000
Rubin, William 1238
Rudel, Jean 1392
Rugière, Paul 819
Ruhmer, Eberhard 886
Rusakova, A. A. 1393, 1393
Russ, Sigrid 1330
Russell, John 346
Russoli, Franco 315
Rutter, F. 1394

Sablonière, Margrit de 347, 463, 677
Safin-Crahay, F. 976, 1178
Sagot, Edmund 82
Sagot-Le Garrec, Berthe 82
Salmon, André 647, 977
Sandstrom, Sven 860
Sanson, M. 731
Sarnoff, Jane 1507
Sartre, Jean-Paul 589
Sar'yan 1000
Saure, Wolfgang 1484
Scalabrin, Nicolétta 1277
Schapiro, Meyer 465
Scheiwiller, Giovanni 235, 349
Schempp, Theodore 706
Scheyer, Ernst 1302
Schiele, Egon 1262, 1279
Schiller, Friedrich von 517
Schlee, N. 1220
Schlegels, Friedrich von 517

Schlemmer, Oscar 1095
Schmalenbach, Werner 1237
Schmidt, Georg 348, 1018
Schmidt-Rottluff, Karl 1095
Schneeberger, Pierre-François 757
Schneider, Bruno F. 350
Schniewind, Carl O. 1147
Schopenhauer, Arthur 1249
Schuffenecker, Emile 22, 28-30, 61, 66, 76, 233, 345, 560, 579, 585, 612, 635, 648, 1183
Schwitters, Kurt 1095
Scotti, Roland 1395
Secker, Hans 980
Sedlak, Jan 351
Segalen, Victor 17, 18, 210, 352, 521, 592, 609, 622, 638, 740, 758-760, 820, 901
Séguin, Armand 7, 68, 211, 562, 1053
Serov, Valentin 1000
Serritslev Petersen, Lise 1278, 1486
Sérusier, Paul 18, 37, 487, 493, 511, 543, 561, 562, 578, 649, 1258
Seton, Marie 1198
Seurat, Georges 483, 520, 532, 542, 564, 573, 580, 633, 636, 643, 651, 658, 675, 1025, 1145, 1209, 1252, 1287, 1293, 1345, 1372, 1431, 1438
Seznec, Jean 483
Shackleton, K. 483
Shapiro, Barbara 1488
Sheon, Aaron 684
Sicurani, Jean 1162
Siemer, L. 821
Siger, Carl 52, 212
Signac, Paul 26, 564, 691, 1025
Sill, L. M. 1489
Simon, M. 1396
Simon, T. F. 1073
Sisley, Alfred 483, 532, 1209, 1391
Sisson, Théodore 213
Sizeranne, Robert de la 1107
Slatkins, W. 1279
Sloan, Thomas L. 981
Slonim, Helen C. 298b
Smith, Bradley 332
Soederstroem, G. 650
Soffici, Ardengo 651, 1397, 1398
Solomon, D. 466
Sommer, Clemens 861
Sotemann, A. L. 707
Soth, Lauren 708, 1074
Souday, Paul 467

Soutreau, Georges 283c
Spanudis, T. 709
Spaulding, John T. 1205
Spink, Reginald 732a
Stadler, Wolfgang 761
Staël, Nicolas de 1471
Stauffer, Christine E. 232
Steadman, David W. 982
Steefel, L. D. 1236
Steermuller, Francis 546
Stefanescu, George 1474
Stefánik, M. R. 1073
Steingraber, Erich 1194
Stein, Meir 1399
Steinberg, Barbara Hope 841
Steineger, Agnes 373
Steingraber, Erich 1194
Steinlen, Théophile Alexandre 1259
Stenning, Henry J. 22
Sterling, Charles 1181
Sternheim, Carl 678
Stevens, Mary Anne 503, 519a
Stevenson, Robert Louis 726, 739, 794, 798
Strauss, M. 1080
Strelka, Joseph 887
Strindberg, August 8, 22, 214, 489, 587, 599, 650, 1503
Strzeminski, Wladyslaw 996
Stuckey, Charles F. 336
Sugana, Gabriele Mandel 227
Sumichrast, F. C. de 342b
Sund, Judy 710
Susumu, S. 1290
Sutherland, Donald 1503
Sutton, Denys 469, 652-654, 985, 1152
Swedenborg, Emanuel 1249
Sydow, Max von 1503
Sykorova, Libuse 1046
Synge, John 611
Szonert, Andrzej 996

Tamarit Crespo, Rafael 762
Tan'o, Yasunori 353
Taralon, Jean 876
Tarbell, Roberta K. 1047
Tardieu, Eugène 41, 215
Tarnowski, Wolfgang 1174
Tavernier, M. L. 354

Tayler, Albert Chevallier 998
Teilhet-Fiske, Jehanne H. 763, 1280
Terrasse, Charles 470
Tharaud, Jean 355
Tharaud, Jerome 355
Theiner, G. 1326
Theis, O. F. 88
Thiis, Jens 471
Thirion, Yvonne 363, 858, 1291, 1304, 1305
Thompson, Richard 655
Thomson, Belinda 356, 656, 1400
Thornton, Alfred 1490
Threfall, Robert 1315
Thyssen-Bornemisza, Baron Heinrich 720
Tillim, Sidney 1221
Tokuda, Y. 822
Tono, Yoshiaki 877
Toru, H. 1290
Toulouse-Lautrec, Henri de 483, 531, 532, 586, 601, 634, 996, 1025, 1065, 1147, 1259, 1296, 1299
Tow, Martin 357
Townsend, W. 732
Traegor, Jörg 1239
Tralbaut, Mark Edo 679, 1108
Trintzius, René 1491
Tristan, Flora 238, 281, 282
Tschann, Gaspard 472
t'Serstevens, A. 740, 823
Tual, R. 546
Tuchman, Maurice 550, 1240
Tugendkhold, I. Akov Aleksandrovich 764
Turner, Joseph Mallord William 1484
Tyler, Parker 545

Ueberwasser, Walter 358
Uhde, Fritz von 1267
Uitert, Evert van 680, 711-713
Utamaro, Kitagawa 1296

Valéry, Paul 483
Valette, Alfred 44
Valette, Marguerite Eymery [Rachilde] 95
Vallery-Radot, Pierre 473
Vallotton, Félix-Edouard 586
Valot, Henriette 313c
Valsecchi, Marco 1492
Vance, Mary Lynn Zink 765, 999

Varenne, Gaston 1077, 1078, 1109, 1110
Varnedoe, Kirk 1238
Vasseur, Pierre 474
Vattier, Suzanne 716
Vauxcelles, Louis 62, 475, 1111, 1112
Veillon, Monique 868
Veit, Philippe 1267
Velàsquez, Diego Rodriguez DeSilva Y. 34, 1000
Velden, Vander 767
Venturi, Lionello 476, 546, 895, 1401
Verdier, Philippe 91, 477, 1113
Verhaeren, Alfred 23
Verkade, Jan 547, 553
Verkade, Willibord 547
Verlaine, Paul 119
Vernon, M. 1493
Vetter, Ewald M. 1239
Viatte, G. 1184
Viel, Philippe 824
Vielliard, Fabien 216
Viirlaid, Helle Kaja 896
Villaret, Bernard 825
Vincent, Madeleine 897, 1185
Visson, Assia R. 658
Vitali, Lamberto 862
Vitry, Paul 1494
Vizzavona-Druet 101
Vlaminck, Maurice de 1325
Voldstedlund, Merete 1503
Vollard, Ambroise 21, 49, 458, 541, 658, 766
Vuillard, Edouard 483, 493, 636, 1025

Wadley, Nicholas 84, 842
Wagner, Richard 1225, 1258, 1277
Waldmann, E. 1169
Walker, John A. 1495
Walker, R. W. 993
Wallis, Anne Armstrong 659
Walter, Elisabeth 660
Walther, Ingo F. 359
Wang, Robert Theodore 548
Ward, Mary Martha 549
Watkins, C. Low 1496
Watson, E. W. 1497
Watson, Forbes 1157
Wauters, A. J. 217
Webb, Geoffrey 994, 1498

Wechsler, Jeffrey 1047
Wedewer, R. 826
Weisberg, Gabriel P. 863, 1281, 1292
Weisberg, Yvonne M. L. 1292
Weitzenhoffer, Frances 541
Welsh, Robert P. 550, 1240, 1402
Welsh-Ovcharov, Bogomila 669
Werefkin, Marianne 1330
Werner, Alfred 1222, 1499
Wernick, R. 1500
Werth, Léon 1403
Whistler, James McNeil 483, 1048, 1290, 1293
White, Barbara Ehrlich 1404
White, Wiebe Alice 222, 878
Whitford, Francis Peter 1293
Wichmann, Siegfried 1294
Wiese, Erich 361, 480
Wildenstein, Daniel 225, 362, 385, 718
Wildenstein, Georges 225, 363, 481, 482, 661, 827-829, 858, 997
Wilenski, Reginald Howard 1405, 1406
Willumsen, Jens Ferdinand 34, 62, 637, 1372
Wilson, T. L. Rodney 767
Wise, Susan 364
Wivel, M. 1282
Wretholm, Eugen 295b
Wright, Willard Huntington 662
Wundt, W. 1448
Wykes-Joyce, Max 998
Wyzewa, Théodor de 218, 219

Yoshikawa, Itsuji 365
Young, M. S. 1501
Young, V. 1502

Zamfirescu, Nina Stanculescu 366
Zauho, Kankokai 877
Zegers, Peter 864
Zelenina, Klavdiia 367
Zervos, Christian 1283, 1407
Zingg, Jean-Pierre 85
Zink, Mary Lynn (see Vance, Mary Lynn Zink)

About the Author

RUSSELL T. CLEMENT is Fine Arts Librarian at the Harold B. Lee Library, Brigham Young University. His previous books include *Who's Who in Oceania, 1980-81* and *Mormons in the Pacific: A Bibliography* (1981). His articles have appeared in the *Journal of American Folklore*, *The Hawaiian Journal of History*, *Library Journal*, and others. He is currently compiling a 15-year index to *Pacific Studies* and an exhibition catalog on Columbus and voyages of discovery.